SENTINEL

THE PATRIOT'S HISTORY READER

Larry Schweikart and **Michael Allen** are the coauthors of *A Patriot's History of the United States* and have each written several books on American history and politics. **Dave Dougherty** is a self-employed businessman and has collaborated with prominent historians on their books, most recently on Schweikart's *What Would the Founders Say?*

Also by Larry Schweikart

Seven Events That Made America America

48 Liberal Lies About American History

Also by Larry Schweikart and Michael Allen

A Patriot's History of the United States

The Patriot's History
Reader

ESSENTIAL DOCUMENTS
FOR EVERY AMERICAN

**Larry Schweikart, Dave Dougherty,
and Michael Allen**

SENTINEL

SENTINEL

Published by the Penguin Group

Penguin Group (USA) Inc., 375 Hudson Street, New York, New York 10014, U.S.A. • Penguin Group (Canada), 90 Eglinton Avenue East, Suite 700, Toronto, Ontario, Canada M4P 2Y3 (a division of Pearson Penguin Canada Inc.) • Penguin Books Ltd, 80 Strand, London WC2R 0RL, England • Penguin Ireland, 25 St Stephen's Green, Dublin 2, Ireland (a division of Penguin Books Ltd) • Penguin Group (Australia), 250 Camberwell Road, Camberwell, Victoria 3124, Australia (a division of Pearson Australia Group Pty Ltd) • Penguin Books India Pvt Ltd, 11 Community Centre, Panchsheel Park, New Delhi – 110 017, India • Penguin Group (NZ), 67 Apollo Drive, Rosedale, Auckland 0632, New Zealand (a division of Pearson New Zealand Ltd) • Penguin Books (South Africa) (Pty) Ltd, 24 Sturdee Avenue, Rosebank, Johannesburg 2196, South Africa

Penguin Books Ltd, Registered Offices:
80 Strand, London WC2R 0RL, England

First published by Sentinel, a member of Penguin Group (USA) Inc. 2011

1   3   5   7   9   10   8   6   4   2

Publisher's Note: While the author has made every effort to provide accurate telephone numbers and Internet addresses at the time of publication, neither the publisher nor the author assumes any responsibility for errors, or for changes that occur after publication. Further, the publisher does not have any control over and does not assume any responsibility for author or third-party Web sites or their content.

LIBRARY OF CONGRESS CATALOGING-IN-PUBLICATION DATA
The patriot's history reader : essential documents for every American /
[compiled by] Larry Schweikart, Dave Dougherty, and Michael Allen.
p.   cm.
Includes index.
Companion to: A patriot's history of the United States.
ISBN 978-1-59523-078-2
1. United States—History—Sources. I. Schweikart, Larry. II. Dougherty,
Dave, 1939– III. Allen, Michael, 1950– IV. Schweikart, Larry.
Patriot's history of the United States
E173.P36 2011
973—dc22   2011011909

Printed in the United States of America
Designed by Daniel Lagin

CONTENTS

Part VI

HUMAN RIGHTS AND DOMESTIC ISSUES   323

Part VII

RISE OF THE NEW WORLD ORDER   383

ACKNOWLEDGMENTS

Ever since *A Patriot's History of the United States* first appeared in 2004, educators, professors, and homeschoolers have asked about supplemental materials, which we attempted to provide with our www.patriotshistoryusa.com Web site. This book arises from the requests for documents to accompany *A Patriot's History* in an educational sense, and therefore the inspiration is truly from our readers.

We would like to thank the staffs of the history departments at the University of Dayton and University of Washington for support; and for our agents, Ed Knappman and Roger Williams, for as always making this exercise a reality. Thanks also to Adrian Zackheim, Brooke Carey, and Amanda Pritzker at Sentinel.

—Larry Schweikart
Dave Dougherty
Michael Allen

INTRODUCTION

Since *A Patriot's History of the United States* was published in 2004, it has become the foremost book on modern American history that defends the United States as a predominantly liberating country, grounded in law, and founded on Judeo-Christian principles. By empowering the so-called common man throughout its period of territorial expansion, and by continuously extending voting and civil rights to previously ineligible groups, the nation not only became the "freest" in human history but arguably the most equal. The unique political philosophy implicit in these actions—giving rise to what is often referred to as "American exceptionalism"—constituted an experiment in democracy that was never attempted before the rise of the United States.

Yet this exceptionalism did not come without struggles, sometimes against foreign oppressors and tyrannies, and sometimes against domestic foes. In its formation the United States carried a potential seed of its own destruction—the institution of slavery. And after multiple compromises papered over this growing abscess, the Civil War forced a denouement. Over time America's population became increasingly diverse, bringing about racial, religious, ethnic, and political tensions, which have at times threatened the very fabric of American society, particularly when resources were scarce. Remarkably, America has survived to the present day under a continuous government, and the inherent flexibility of the Constitution and other founding documents has allowed the American government to preserve the republic while adapting to challenges unknown and unimaginable to its founders.

Our goal in this book is to provide teachers, parents, students, and lay readers with primary source documents that will enhance and illustrate the ideas and principles elaborated in *A Patriot's History of the United States*. It is designed to give the freedom and choices, and while we have debated and discussed our decisions—taking many texts out, putting others in—ultimately it is the individual who must decide which documents bear the most intense analysis. At the same time, we hope this book provides anyone interested in our history a collection of some of the central documents, placed within a context that will aid them in understanding the time, place, and, above all, the philosophical setting of these primary sources.

Perhaps one of the most positive recent trends, brought on partly in response to recent government expansion and the overall liberalization of America, has been a renewed interest among average Americans in the Constitution. That is, for the first time in many cases, ordinary people are acquiring copies of the Constitution and other founding documents to determine what the founders of this nation intended when they established it. That interest has spread to a revival in reading all the colonial- and revolutionary-era documents. This is laudable and much needed, but it should not stop there. Just as government in America has continued to change (and grow), the documents by which presidents, Congress, judges, and bureaucrats have enabled and accelerated that growth demand attention. By examining these documents in their original form, we can understand the founders' vision for our country and at the same time try to figure out how and when our leaders have departed from this vision.

The documents presented here are organized chronologically and highlight the key events and ideas that have shaped the course of American history. Certainly many worthy writings, speeches, laws, or court decisions have been omitted, and some might quibble with a few that we have decided to include. Overall, however, we think the collection of documents presented here not only achieves a certain chronological balance but also reflects the historical changes the nation has undergone. Therefore, while it might have been useful to include the speech in which John F. Kennedy put the United States on a course to reach the moon within a decade, the reality of Kennedy's goal was not seen for many years, and the practical effect of reaching the moon is still widely debated. Similarly, while any number of court cases could have been offered, we have tried to select those that not only changed society at the time but also had lasting implications.

In founding a Protestant Christian nation based on English common law, the American colonists repudiated absolutism and an autocratic form of government. In adopting common law, America asserted the idea that laws are handed from God to the people, and that in making laws elected representatives should look to the customs and traditions of the people, fine-tuning and administering those laws with respect both to tradition and to legal precedent. By itself this concept of law that ultimately resides in the people rather than some supreme lawgiver, whether secular or clerical, was unique. The United States, by adopting this view, stood nearly alone in the world. To function, a system of common law administered by elected officials required a generally virtuous citizenry, and virtue required a moral compass. Morality, in turn, required religious beliefs that recognize a power higher than oneself. In many respects this concept of power residing in the people, and tempered by virtue, is the foundation of American exceptionalism.

From the Mayflower Compact to the Declaration of Independence, Americans dealt with the issue of loyalty to a king and an empire that scarcely acknowledged their existence, much less their equal rights—a much later development. From the Northwest Ordinance to *Brown v. Board of Education*, Americans struggled with the practical application of equality when it came to the rights of citizens. And from George Washington's comments on the military to Barack Obama's speech at Cairo University, the subject of the nation's security in a hostile world has produced important—and often vastly different—views on how the United States should behave. Writers such as Mercy Otis Warren warned that even with the restrictions provided in the Constitution itself, threats to individual liberty would arise from government, whose natural tendency is to grow, and from the public, whose natural tendency is toward apathy.

Until recently, however, most of those who wrote, legislated, rendered judicial decisions, or protested did so on the basis of America's exceptional nature— that this nation acted in ways no other nation would or, at the time, even could, and that we sought changes in the political or social structure precisely because that was "what Americans did." Only in the last twenty years has a serious movement—both in the courts and within the American left as a whole, following the leadership of Europeans functioning under civil law—emerged to attempt to cut the United States down to size, to deny American exceptionalism, and to place the nation as just another member, subject to the laws and, too frequently, whims of foreigners in the "family of nations." While one can bemoan this direction, or praise it, it is this transformation that, in the wider context of American history, we have attempted to trace in this collection of documents. Without appreciating the many small steps epitomized by these documents, which have altered the American political landscape over the years, it is difficult for an individual to understand how the First Amendment's assertion that "Congress shall make no law respecting an establishment of religion, or prohibiting the free exercise thereof" has morphed into a law that prohibits displaying the Ten Commandments in a courthouse. To form a reasoned understanding of where the nation is going and why, the reader must understand where it has come from and the situations it has gone through. This volume attempts to provide the beginnings of that understanding.

—Larry Schweikart
Dave Dougherty
Michael Allen

A NOTE ON SOURCES

Some of the older documents have been edited into modern English, with corrections particularly in punctuation, spelling, and grammar. Selections have been excerpted from longer letters, rulings, speeches, and essays, to focus on the important points in the documents without requiring the reader to wade through long discourses. Although some of the documents exist in multiple versions, no significant controversies exist regarding the content of the materials excerpted here. In most cases, the official or generally accepted version has been used.

The Patriot's History *Reader*

I

THE FORMATION
OF THE NATION

America's founding was unique in that it involved the coalescence of many different ideas and practices that were already in place elsewhere in the world but had never been brought together. Many Europeans enjoyed private property rights (although such concepts were only beginning to be introduced in other parts of the world). Some countries, such as England, had advanced remarkable political systems that acknowledged individual rights and protections from the monarch. Some, like the Dutch, had developed burgeoning quasi-capitalist economies long before Adam Smith outlined his theory of capitalism. Few nations, however, practiced any degree of religious toleration and virtually none had land available for settlement or ownership by the common people.

From the very first successful settlements in the New World, questions of individual rights, the role of religion in government, and the establishment of government, both local and regional, were addressed by the colonists themselves. In part this was an outgrowth of the extreme hardships they endured in their struggle for survival. Taming the land and its resources became a formidable obstacle for the first settlements—Roanoke disappeared; Jamestown barely survived "the starving time"; the Sagadahoc, or Popham, Colony, on the banks of the Kennebec River in Maine, was abandoned within a year; and only slightly more than half of the Plymouth colonists survived to celebrate the first Thanksgiving. From the beginning, hardy souls populated the country and began pushing the boundaries of the United States across the continent, government following in their wake and striving to adapt to the challenging conditions.

During the colonial and revolutionary periods, the dominant philosophy that shaped American political development was that of John Locke. Locke espoused political liberalism stressing property rights, the consent of the governed, limited government, and religious tolerance. According to Locke, man lived in a free "state of nature," entering into a social contract that established government to protect his natural rights. He is generally considered the father of liberalism, based on the aforementioned ideas, but that term has undergone a dramatic change from Locke's time. No doubt he would assess twenty-first-century nanny-state liberalism as having more in common with the absolutism favored by Thomas Hobbes and Louis XIV. Locke's ideas figure prominently in the Declaration of Independence and the Constitution, and one can hear his influence in the words of Samuel Adams, Thomas Paine, and others. But whereas liberalism was restrained by the English monarchy, particularly under the Stuart kings, in America it attained full expression. It could not be subdued while a vast territory immediately to the West was available to harbor and succor dissidents, and limited government was the only reasonable option for the first century after the Revolution.

Two other factors determined the early structure of the United States: Protestant Christianity and common law. By the eighteenth century, American Protestantism espoused latitudinarianism (the tolerance of various religious doctrines and opinions within Christianity), which was not practiced anywhere else in the world. The Constitution prohibited the establishment of a federally sponsored religion, although the individual states could and did endorse or support specific religions or denominations. Nonetheless, persecution for adherence to a religion was abolished legally and fell into disfavor socially, making the United States truly exceptional. Common law, enacted through elected and appointed officials, empowered the people. Government was prohibited from creating or granting rights beyond those given to man by God and God alone. Such concepts were revolutionary during colonial days and are even revolutionary today. One has only to hear some congressman or senator crow about how Congress has created a new "right" to understand how far the federal government has strayed from the intentions of the Founding Fathers.

Common law also allowed the development of a unique concept of citizenship in a world where only subjecthood, either in a political or religious sense, was known. No intermediary was needed between the Protestant Christian and God, and no man was more equal than another. A class of nobility was denied by implication in Jefferson's words in the Declaration of Independence, "that all men are created equal." One man's vote was as good as another's. Although in practice this concept was imperfectly implemented, it was the goal, and at that time only in America did the goal seem attainable. The foundation for exceptionalism was poured, and even when honest disagreements arose, such as those exemplified by Mercy Warren's treatise in opposition to ratifying the Constitution, the ship of state was able to navigate the troubled waters. The reader is urged to compare and contrast the works here in part 1 with those later in this volume to decide for himself how stormy the waters have become or whether the course is being steered appropriately.

CHAPTER 1

The Mayflower Compact, 1620

In 1620 the *Mayflower*, a ship carrying 102 separatist Puritans calling themselves Pilgrims, arrived at Cape Cod. This area was under charter to the Plymouth Council for New England, a competitor to the London-based Virginia Company. The Pilgrims held a patent from the Virginia Company for the establishment of a plantation in Virginia, but here in the North they were squatters and needed a patent from the Plymouth Council to legally settle the area. Due to the ambiguity of their status, some individuals considered themselves exempt from any of the laws, rules, or regulations of the Virginia Company. To address the problem of governmental jurisdiction—and to assure King James I that the Puritans were not seeking to rebel against his authority—a compact was drawn up and signed by the 41 men on board the *Mayflower* as a governing agreement. Some historians point to this compact as the world's first constitution, but it is only an agreement to govern and fails to establish a broad system of governmental functions. Nonetheless, it remained in force until Plymouth was included as part of the Massachusetts Bay Colony in 1691.

Although unique, the compact did not establish the first representative government in North America—that honor fell to the Virginia House of Burgesses, first convened in the preceding year. But unlike the governing documents of Virginia, the compact resulted from the will of the people themselves, not that of a local legislature formed by a royal governor. From the very beginning of New England, the genie of self-government was out of the bottle. In addition, the colony clearly emphasized the importance of their religion in government. Having fled religious persecution in England, they placed their faith in themselves and God, not the king.

The Mayflower Compact

THIS DAY, BEFORE WE CAME TO HARBOR, OBSERVING SOME not well affected to unity and concord, but gave some appearance of faction, it was thought good there should be an association and agreement that we should combine together in one body, and to submit to such government and governors as we should by common consent agree to make and choose, and set our hands on this that follows word for word.

In the name of God, Amen. We whose names are underwritten, the loyal subjects of our dread sovereign lord, King James, by the grace of God, of Great Britain, France, and Ireland, King, defender of the faith, etc., having undertaken, for the glory of God and advancement of the Christian faith and honor of our king and country, a voyage to plant the first colony in the northern parts of Virginia, do by these presents, solemnly and mutually, in the presence of God and one of another, covenant and combine ourselves together into a civil body politic, for our better ordering and preservation and furtherance of the ends aforesaid, and by virtue hereof to exact, constitute, and frame, such just and equal laws, ordinances, acts, constitutions, and offices, from time to time, as shall be thought most meet and convenient for the general good of the colony; unto which we promise all due submission and obedience. In witness whereof we have hereunder subscribed our names at Cape Cod, the 11th of November, in the year of the reign of our sovereign Lord, King James of England, France, and Ireland the eighteenth, and of Scotland the fifty-fourth. Anno Domini 1620.

Sources: The text of the Mayflower Compact is widely available with only a very few minor variations. Some sources give the compact in the spelling, grammar, and punctuation of the time, others use modern English. Nonetheless, there are essentially no variations in meaning or inferences. The primary source used here was William Bradford's, as retrieved on April 20, 2010, from http://www.nationalcenter.org/MayflowerCompact.html and checked against other sources to produce this version. The slightly older version recorded by Edward Winslow in *Mourt's Relation* can be retrieved from http://www.histarch.uiuc.edu/plymouth/mourt1.html.

CHAPTER 2

The Fundamental Orders, 1639

In January of 1639, the Connecticut townships of Windsor, Hartford, and Wethersfield adopted what came to be called the Fundamental Orders. Previously, no government in the history of the world had ever issued a formal document containing the supreme laws for the formation of the government and its powers and limitations, and the orders are generally held to be the world's first constitution. The document included a preamble and a set of laws that remained in effect until 1662, although many of the laws continued to be observed until the colonial charter was abolished in 1818. There are no references to England or English rule, and for all intents and purposes the orders treated the Connecticut Colony as a sovereign state rather than a subservient colony. As with the Mayflower Compact, the orders established the importance of religion, and the presence of the Congregational Church is seen throughout.

The orders were made necessary by a dispute over the ownership of the land on which the towns were founded. The General Court of Massachusetts, which had granted permission for the Congregationalists to settle in the Connecticut Valley and set up their own rules and regulations, created a commission headed by Roger Ludlow to adjudicate the dispute. After seven years of little progress, during which the towns continued to govern themselves, the Fundamental Orders, describing the current governing policies, were written by Ludlow and officially accepted by the colony on January 14. Henceforth the connection to Massachusetts was severed, and Connecticut became fully self-governing, with the orders setting a pattern that would be followed by nearly all the colonies. Congregationalism became the state religion and remained so well into the nineteenth century. There was no separation of church and state here, and although other religions were freely tolerated and there was no persecution, there was also little cultural diversity within the population. This leads us to question whether localities should be allowed to support a specific religion and religious education, while larger governmental units maintain a strict neutrality. In short, in a free society do people have the liberty to establish the faith of the society? If not, is that society free?

The Fundamental Orders earned Connecticut the nickname the Constitution State and based government firmly on the rights of individuals. Some of those rights are enumerated in the orders: governmental powers are limited, and all free men are enfranchised to vote. In many ways, the orders were a harbinger of things to come. A constitution was written by a representative committee, approved by the people, and put into effect under a de facto assumption of local sovereignty. The orders proved enduring: they were incorporated in the royal charter that recognized Connecticut as a colony in 1662, and the individual rights contained in the orders are still present in the state constitution.

The Fundamental Orders

FOR AS MUCH AS IT HATH PLEASED THE ALMIGHTY GOD BY the wise disposition of his divine providence so to order and dispose of things that we the Inhabitants and Residents of Windsor, Hartford, and Wethersfield are now cohabiting and dwelling in and upon the River of Connectecotte and the lands thereunto adjoining; and well knowing where a people are gathered together the word of God requires that to maintain the peace and union of such a people there should be an orderly and decent Government established according to God, to order and dispose of the affairs of the people at all seasons as occasion shall require; do therefore associate and connive ourselves to be as one Public State or Commonwealth; and do, for ourselves and our successors and such as shall be adjoined to us at any time hereafter, enter into Combination and Confederation to gather, to maintain and preserve the liberty and purity of the gospel of our Lord Jesus which we now profess, as also the discipline of the Churches, which according to the truth of the said gospel is now practiced amongst us; as also in our civil affairs to be guided and governed according to such Laws, Rules, Orders and decrees as shall be made, ordered, and decreed, as followeth:

1. It is Ordered, sentenced, and decreed, that there shall be yearly two General Assemblies or Courts, the one the second Thursday in April, the other the second Thursday in September following; the first shall be called the Court of Election, wherein shall be yearly chosen from time to time, so many Magistrates and other public Officers as shall be found requisite: Whereof one to be chosen Governor for the year ensuing and until another be chosen, and no other Magistrate to be chosen for more than one year: provided

always there be six chosen besides the Governor, which being chosen and sworn according to an Oath recorded for that purpose, shall have the power to administer justice according to the Laws here established, and for want thereof, according to the Rule of the Word of God; which choice shall be made by all that are admitted freemen and have taken the Oath of Fidelity, and do cohabit within this Jurisdiction having been admitted Inhabitants by the major part of the Town wherein they live or the major part of such as shall be then present.

2. It is Ordered, sentenced, and decreed, that the election of the aforesaid Magistrates shall be in this manner: every person present and qualified for choice shall bring in (to the person deputed to receive them) one single paper with the name of him written in it whom he desires to have Governor, and he that hath the greatest number of papers shall be Governor for that year. And the rest of the Magistrates or public officers to be chosen in this manner: the Secretary for the time being shall first read the names of all that are to be put to choice and then shall severally nominate them distinctly, and every one that would have the person nominated to be chosen shall bring in one single paper written upon, and he that would not have him chosen shall bring in a blank; and every one that hath more written papers than blanks shall be a Magistrate for that year; which papers shall be received and told by one or more that shall be then chosen by the court and sworn to be faithful therein; but in case there should not be six chosen as aforesaid, besides the Governor, out of those which are nominated, then he or they which have the most written papers shall be a Magistrate or Magistrates for the ensuing year, to make up the aforesaid number.

3. It is Ordered, sentenced, and decreed, that the Secretary shall not nominate any person, nor shall any person be chosen newly into the Magistracy which was not propounded in some General Court before, to be nominated the next election; and to that end it shall be lawful for each of the Towns aforesaid by their deputies to nominate any two whom they conceive fit to be put to election; and the Court may add so many more as they judge requisite.

4. It is Ordered, sentenced, and decreed, that no person be chosen Governor above once in two years, and that the Governor be always a member of some approved Congregation, and formerly of the Magistracy within this Jurisdiction; and that all the Magistrates, Freemen of this Commonwealth; and that no Magistrate or other public officer shall execute any part of his or their office before they are severally sworn, which shall be done in the face of the court if they be present, and in case of absence by some deputed for that purpose.

5. It is Ordered, sentenced, and decreed, that to the aforesaid Court of Election the several Towns shall send their deputies, and when the Elections are

ended they may proceed in any public service as at other Courts. Also the other General Court in September shall be for making of laws, and any other public occasion, which concerns the good of the Commonwealth.

6. It is Ordered, sentenced, and decreed, that the Governor shall, either by himself or by the Secretary, send out summons to the Constables of every Town for the calling of these two standing Courts one month at least before their several times: And also if the Governor and the greatest part of the Magistrates see cause upon any special occasion to call a General Court, they may give order to the Secretary so to do within fourteen days warning: And if urgent necessity so require, upon a shorter notice, giving sufficient grounds for it to the deputies when they meet, or else be questioned for the same; And if the Governor and major part of Magistrates shall either neglect or refuse to call the two General standing Courts or either of them, as also at other times when the occasions of the Commonwealth require, the Freemen thereof, or the major part of them, shall petition to them so to do; if then it be either denied or neglected, the said Freemen, or the major part of them, shall have the power to give order to the Constables of the several Towns to do the same, and so may meet together, and choose to themselves a Moderator, and may proceed to do any act of power which any other General Courts may.

7. It is Ordered, sentenced, and decreed, that after there are warrants given out for any of the said General Courts, the Constable or Constables of each Town, shall forthwith give notice distinctly to the inhabitants of the same, in some public assembly or by going or sending from house to house, that at a place and time by him or them limited and set, they meet and assemble themselves together to elect and choose certain deputies to be at the General Court then following to agitate the affairs of the Commonwealth; which said deputies shall be chosen by all that are admitted Inhabitants in the several Towns and have taken the oath of fidelity; provided that none be chosen a Deputy for any General Court which is not a Freeman of this Commonwealth. The aforesaid deputies shall be chosen in manner following: every person that is present and qualified as before expressed, shall bring the names of such, written in several papers, as they desire to have chosen for that employment, and these three or four, more or less, being the number agreed on to be chosen for that time, that have the greatest number of papers written for them shall be deputies for that Court; whose names shall be endorsed on the back side of the warrant and returned into the Court, with the Constable or Constables' hand unto the same.

8. It is Ordered, sentenced, and decreed, that Windsor, Hartford, and Wethersfield shall have power, each Town, to send four of their Freemen as their deputies to every General Court; and Whatsoever other Town shall be hereafter added to this Jurisdiction, they shall send so many deputies as the

Court shall judge meet, a reasonable proportion to the number of Freemen that are in the said Towns being to be attended therein; which deputies shall have the power of the whole Town to give their votes and allowance to all such laws and orders as may be for the public good, and unto which the said Towns are to be bound.

9. It is Ordered, sentenced, and decreed, that the deputies thus chosen shall have power and liberty to appoint a time and a place of meeting together before any General Court, to advise and consult of all such things as may concern the good of the public, as also to examine their own Elections, whether according to the order, and if they or the greatest part of them find any election to be illegal they may seclude such for present from their meeting, and return the same and their reasons to the Court; and if it be proved true, the Court may fine the party or parties so intruding, and the Town, if they see cause, and give out a warrant to go to a new election in a legal way, either in part or in whole. Also the said deputies shall have power to fine any that shall be disorderly at their meetings, or for not coming in due time or place according to appointment; and they may return the said fines into the Court if it be refused to be paid, and the Treasurer to take notice of it, and to escheat or levy the same as he does other fines.

10. It is Ordered, sentenced, and decreed, that every General Court, except such as through neglect of the Governor and the greatest part of the Magistrates the Freemen themselves do call, shall consist of the Governor, or some one chosen to moderate the Court, and four other Magistrates at least, with the major part of the deputies of the several Towns legally chosen; and in case the Freemen, or major part of them, through neglect or refusal of the Governor and major part of the Magistrates, shall call a Court, it shall consist of the major part of Freemen that are present or their deputies, with a Moderator chosen by them: In which said General Courts shall consist the supreme power of the Commonwealth, and they only shall have power to make laws or repeal them, to grant levies, to admit of Freemen, dispose of lands undisposed of, to several Towns or persons, and also shall have power to call either Court or Magistrate or any other person whatsoever into question for any misdemeanor, and may for just causes displace or deal otherwise according to the nature of the offense; and also may deal in any other matter that concerns the good of this Commonwealth, except the election of Magistrates, which shall be done by the whole body of Freemen. In which Court the Governor or Moderator shall have power to order the Court, to give liberty of speech, and silence unseasonable and disorderly speakings, to put all things to vote, and in case the vote be equal to have the casting voice. But none of these Courts shall be adjourned or dissolved without the consent of the major part of the Court.

11. It is Ordered, sentenced, and decreed, that when any General Court upon the occasions of the Commonwealth have agreed upon any sum, or sums of money to be levied upon the several Towns within this Jurisdiction, that a committee be chosen to set out and appoint what shall be the proportion of every Town to pay of the said levy, provided the committee be made up of an equal number out of each Town.

14th January 1639 the 11 Orders above said are voted.

Source: *The Federal and State Constitutions, Colonial Charters, and Other Organic Laws of the States, Territories, and Colonies Now or Heretofore Forming the United States of America,* ed. Francis Newton Thorpe (Washington, D.C.: Government Printing Office, 1909), 249–51, as available at the Yale Law School, Lillian Goldman Law Library's Avalon Project: Documents in Law, History and Diplomacy. Retrieved April 23, 2010, from http://avalon.law.yale.edu/17th_century/order.asp.

CHAPTER 3

The Rights of the Colonists, Samuel Adams, 1772

Written by Samuel Adams in 1772, this paper asserted that the colonists as men, Christians, and subjects had been ordained by God with certain rights. Adams was appointed to a committee of correspondence by the Boston town meeting early in November, and on the twentieth he presented this paper to be communicated to other towns in Massachusetts and New England. In it he introduces the idea that all men have the right to remain in a state of nature, and that membership in a particular society or state of subjecthood is strictly voluntary. All rights not ceded to a superior power by contract are retained by the individual. In essence, Adams's position on individual rights could be extrapolated into a ringing endorsement, fifteen years in advance, of the Tenth Amendment of the U.S. Constitution, which protects the sovereignty of individual states.

Adams drew heavily on the ideas of the philosopher John Locke (1632–1704), who had proposed new theories of religious toleration and property rights, which he argued were derived from "natural," or God-given, rights that no government could lawfully rescind. Locke maintained that society exists precisely to defend the rights of the individual against the oppressive power of the state.

Although Adams's paper was directed to the issues of the time, particularly England's new obsession with burdensome taxes, the principles of an individual's right to life, liberty, property, and self-defense were timeless and are as applicable today as they were when Adams defined them. In 1772 this lit a fire under the Sons of Liberty and became a giant step toward revolution as the colonists realized they were being denied these basic rights.

The Rights of the Colonists

I. NATURAL RIGHTS OF THE COLONISTS AS MEN

Among the natural rights of the colonists are these: first, a right to life; second, to liberty; third, to property; together with the right to support and defend them in the best manner they can. These are evident branches of, rather than deductions from, the duty of self-preservation, commonly called the first law of nature.

All men have a right to remain in a state of nature as long as they please; and in case of intolerable oppression, civil or religious, to leave the society they belong to, and enter into another.

When men enter into society, it is by voluntary consent; and they have a right to demand and insist upon the performance of such conditions and previous limitations as form an equitable original compact.

Every natural right not expressly given up, or, from the nature of a social compact, necessarily ceded, remains.

All positive and civil laws should conform, as far as possible, to the law of natural reason and equity.

As neither reason requires nor religion permits the contrary, every man living in or out of a state of civil society has a right peaceably and quietly to worship God according to the dictates of his conscience.

"Just and true liberty, equal and impartial liberty," in matters spiritual and temporal, is a thing that all men are clearly entitled to by the eternal and immutable laws of God and nature, as well as by the law of nations and all well-grounded laws, which must have their foundations in the former.

In regard to religion, mutual toleration in the different professions thereof is what all good and candid minds in all ages have ever practiced, and, both by precept and example, inculcated on mankind. And it is now generally agreed among Christians that this spirit of toleration, in the fullest extent consistent with the being of civil society, is the chief characteristical mark of the church. Insomuch that Mr. Locke has asserted and proved, beyond the possibility of contradiction on any solid ground, that such toleration ought to be extended to all whose doctrines are not subversive of society. The only sects which he thinks ought to be, and which by all wise laws are excluded from such toleration, are those who teach doctrines subversive of the civil government under which they live. The Roman Catholics or Papists are excluded by reason of such doctrines as these: that princes excommunicated may be deposed, and those that they call heretics may be destroyed without mercy; besides their recognizing the pope in so absolute a manner, in subversion of government, by introducing, as far as possible into the states under whose protection they enjoy life, liberty, and property, that solecism in politics, *imperium in imperio*, leading directly to the worst anarchy and confusion, civil discord, war, and bloodshed.

The natural liberty of man, by entering into society, is abridged or restrained so far only as is necessary for the great end of society, the best good of the whole.

In the state of nature every man is, under God, judge and sole judge of his own rights and of the injuries done him. By entering into society he agrees to an arbiter or indifferent judge between him and his neighbors; but he no more renounces his original right than by taking a cause out of the ordinary course of law, and leaving the decision to referees or indifferent arbitrators. In the last case, he must pay the referees for time and trouble. He should also be willing to pay his just quota for the support or government, the law, and the constitution; the end of which is to furnish indifferent and impartial judges in all cases that may happen, whether civil, ecclesiastical, marine, or military.

The natural liberty of man is to be free from any superior power on earth, and not to be under the will or legislative authority of man, but only to have the law of nature for his rule.

In the state of nature men may, as the patriarchs did, employ hired servants for the defense of their lives, liberties, and property; and they should pay them reasonable wages. Government was instituted for the purposes of common defense, and those who hold the reins of government have an equitable, natural right to an honorable support from the same principle that "the laborer is worthy of his hire." But then the same community which they serve ought to be the assessors of their pay. Governors have no right to seek and take what they please; by this, instead of being content with the station assigned them, that of honorable servants of the society, they would soon become absolute masters, despots, and tyrants. Hence, as a private man has a right to say what wages he will give in his private affairs, so has a community to determine what they will give and grant of their substance for the administration of public affairs. And in both cases, more are ready to offer their service at the proposed and stipulated price than are able and willing to perform their duty.

In short, it is the greatest absurdity to suppose it in the power of one or any number of men, at the entering into society, to renounce their natural rights, or the means or preserving those rights, when the grand end of civil government, from the very nature of its institution, is for the support, protection, and defense of those very rights; the principal of which, as is before observed, are life, liberty, and property. If men, through fear, fraud, or mistake, should in terms renounce or give up any essential natural right, the eternal law of reason and the grand end of society would absolutely vacate such renunciation. The right to freedom being the gift of God Almighty, it is not in the power on man to alienate this gift and voluntarily become a slave.

II. THE RIGHTS OF THE COLONISTS AS CHRISTIANS

These may be best understood by reading and carefully studying the institutes of the great Lawgiver and Head of the Christian Church, which are to be found clearly written and promulgated in the New Testament.

By the act of the British parliament, commonly called the Toleration Act, every subject in England, except Papists, etc., was restored to, and reestablished in, his natural right to worship God according to the dictates of his own conscience. And, by the charter of this province, it is granted, ordained, and established (that is, declared as an original right) that there shall be liberty of conscience allowed in the worship of God to all Christians, except Papists, inhabiting, or which shall inhabit or be resident within, such province or territory. Magna Charta itself is in substance but a constrained declaration or proclamation and promulgation in the name of the King, Lords, and Commons, of the sense the latter had of their original, inherent, indefeasible natural rights as also those of free citizens equally perdurable with the other. That great author, that great jurist, and even that court writer, Mr. Justice Blackstone, holds that this recognition was justly obtained of King John, sword in hand. And peradventure it must be one day, sword in hand, again rescued and preserved from total destruction and oblivion.

III. THE RIGHTS OF THE COLONISTS AS SUBJECTS

A commonwealth or state is a body politic, or civil society of men, united together to promote their mutual safety and prosperity by means of their union.

The absolute rights of Englishmen and all freemen, in or out of civil society, are principally personal security, personal liberty, and private property.

All persons born in the British American colonies are, by the laws of God and nature and by the common law of England, exclusive of all charters from the Crown, well entitled, and by acts of the British parliament are declared to be entitled, to all the natural, essential, inherent, and inseparable rights, liberties, and privileges of subjects born in Great Britain or within the realm. Among those rights are the following, which no man, or body of men, consistently with their own rights as men and citizens, or members of society, can for themselves give up or take away from others.

First, "the first fundamental positive law of all commonwealths or states is the establishing the legislative power. As the first fundamental natural law, also, which is to govern even the legislative power itself, is the preservation of the society."

Second, the legislative has no right to absolute, arbitrary power over the lives and fortunes of the people; nor can mortals assume a prerogative not only too high for men, but for angels, and therefore reserved for the exercise of the Deity alone.

"The legislative cannot justly assume to itself a power to rule by extempore arbitrary decrees; but it is bound to see that justice is dispensed, and that the rights of the subjects be decided by promulgated, standing, and known laws, and authorized independent judges"; that is, independent, as far as possible, of prince and people. "There should be one rule of justice for rich and poor, for the favorite at court, and the countryman at the plough."

Third, the supreme power cannot justly take from any man any part of his property, without his consent in person or by his representative.

These are some of the first principles of natural law and justice, and the great barriers of all free states and of the British constitution in particular. It is utterly irreconcilable to these principles and to many other fundamental maxims of the common law, common sense, and reason that a British House of Commons should have a right at pleasure to give and grant the property of the colonists. . . .

Now what liberty can there be where property is taken away without consent? . . . Have they [the colonists] all together any more weight or power to return a single member to that House of Commons who have not inadvertently, but deliberately, assumed a power to dispose of their lives, liberties, and properties, than to choose an emperor of China? . . . The inhabitants of this country, in all probability, in a few years will be more numerous than those of Great Britain and Ireland together; yet it is absurdly expected by the promoters of the present measures that these, with their posterity to all generations, should be easy, while their property shall be disposed of by a House of Commons at three thousand miles' distance from them, and who cannot be supposed to have the least care or concern for their real interest; who have not only no natural care for their interest, but must be in effect bribed against it, as every burden they lay on the colonists is so much saved or gained to themselves. Hitherto, many of the colonists have been free from quitrents; but if the breath of a British House of Commons can originate an act for taking away all our money, our lands will go next, or be subject to rack rents from haughty and relentless landlords, who will ride at ease, while we are trodden in the dirt. The colonists have been branded with the odious names of traitors and rebels only for complaining of their grievances. How long such treatment will or ought to be borne is submitted.

Source: Adams's paper, reproduced as document 173 in *Old South Leaflets* (Boston: Directors of the Old South Work, 1906) 7: 417–28. Retrieved April 20, 2010, from http://history.hanover.edu/texts/adamss.html.

CHAPTER 4

Common Sense, Thomas Paine, 1776

Written by Thomas Paine and published in January of 1776, this pamphlet was the most incendiary and effective document in mobilizing American patriots against King George III and Great Britain. A rather long tract, only brief excerpts are presented here, but the ringing tone and effective use of arousing and pejorative terms such as "tyranny" to describe the British monarchy eliminated the argument that King George was a benign ruler who was being misled. Paine took no prisoners, and his rhetoric appealed to raw emotions to arouse the populace.

One of the few deists among the founders—perhaps actually the only one— Paine was an Englishman who had recently arrived in the colonies. Following the American Revolution, Paine returned to Europe, was imprisoned in England, went to France in support of the French Revolution, and very narrowly escaped the guillotine. It's worth noting that Paine clearly states that government must be relatively local to be effective and that the rule of law, coming from God and made by the people, takes precedence over all. These were odd and telling assessments coming from a deist and reinforce the premise that a common-law tradition is necessary to the establishment and long-term survival of a representative democracy.

From *Common Sense*

VOLUMES HAVE BEEN WRITTEN ON THE SUBJECT OF THE struggle between England and America. Men of all ranks have embarked in the controversy, from different motives and with different designs, but all have been intellectual, and the period of debate is over. Arms, as the last resource, must decide the contest; the appeal was the choice of the king, and the continent has accepted the challenge. . . .

The sun never shone on a cause of greater worth. 'Tis not the affair of a city, a county, a province, or a kingdom, but of a continent—of at least one-eighth part of the habitable globe. 'Tis not the concern of a day, a year, or an age; posterity are virtually involved in the contest and will be more or less affected even to the end of time by the proceedings now. Now is the seedtime of continental union, faith, and honor. . . .

I have heard it asserted by some that as America has flourished under her former connection with Great Britain, the same connection is necessary toward her future happiness, and will always have the same effect. Nothing can be more fallacious than this kind of argument. We may as well assert that because a child has thrived upon milk that it is never to have meat, or that the first twenty years of our lives is to become a precedent for the next twenty. . . .

But she had protected us, say some. That she has engrossed us is true, and defended the continent at our expense as well as her own is admitted, and she would have defended Turkey from the same motives, viz., for the sake of trade and dominion.

. . . We have boasted the protection of Great Britain without considering that her motive was *interest* not *attachment*; and that she did not protect us from *our enemies* on *our account* but from *her enemies* on *her own account*.

. . . France and Spain never were, nor perhaps ever will be, our enemies as *Americans* but as our being the *subjects of Great Britain*.

But Britain is the parent country, say some. Then the more shame upon her conduct. Even brutes do not devour their young, nor savages make war upon their families; wherefore, the assertion, if true, turns to her approach. But it happens not to be true, or only partly so, and the phrase "parent" or "mother country" has been jesuitically adopted by the king and his parasites, with a low papistical design of gaining an unfair bias on the credulous weakness of our minds. Europe, and not England, is the parent country of America. This New World had been the asylum for the persecuted lovers of civil and religious liberty from *every part* of Europe. Hither have they fled, not from the tender embraces of the mother but from the cruelty of the monster; and it is so far true of England that the same tyranny which drove the first emigrants from home pursues their descendants still.

. . . Not one-third of the inhabitants, even of this province, are of English descent.* Wherefore, I reprobate the phrase of "parent" or "mother country" applied to England only as being false, selfish, narrow, and ungenerous. . . .

Europe is too thickly planted with kingdoms to be long at peace, and

---

* Paine is discounting Scots, Irish, and Scots-Irish, who, though British, are not English.

whenever a war breaks out between England and any foreign powers, the trade of America goes to ruin *because of her connection with Britain.* . . . Everything that is right or natural pleads for separation. The blood of the slain, the weeping voice of nature cries, 'tis time to part. Even the distance at which the Almighty has placed England and America is a strong and natural proof that the authority of the one over the other was never the design of Heaven. The time, likewise, at which the continent was discovered adds weight to the argument, and the manner in which it was peopled increases the force of it. The Reformation was preceded by the discovery of America: as if the Almighty graciously meant to open a sanctuary to the persecuted in future years, when home should afford neither friendship nor safety. . . .

Though I would carefully avoid giving unnecessary offense, yet I am inclined to believe that all those who espouse the doctrine of reconciliation may be included within the following descriptions: interested men who are not to be trusted, weak men who *cannot* see, prejudiced men who will not see, and a certain set of moderate men who think better of the European world than it deserves; and this last class, by an ill-judged deliberation, will be the cause of more calamities to this continent than all the other three. . . .

. . . Reconciliation is *now* a fallacious dream. Nature has deserted the connection, and art cannot supply her place. For, as Milton wisely expresses, "Never can true reconcilement grow, where wounds of deadly hate have pierced so deep." . . .

. . . There is something very absurd in supposing a continent to be perpetually governed by an island. In no instance has nature made the satellite larger than its primary planet; and as England and America, with respect to each other, reverses the common order of nature, it is evident that they belong to different systems. England to Europe, America to itself. . . .

. . . The powers of governing still remaining in the hands of the king, he will have a negative over the whole legislation of this continent. And as he has shown himself such an inveterate enemy to liberty, and discovered such a thirst for arbitrary power, is he, or is he not, a proper person to say to these colonies, "You shall make no laws but what I please!" And is there any inhabitant of America so ignorant as not to know that according to what is called *present constitution*, this continent can make no laws but what the king gives leave to? And is there any man so unwise not to see that (considering what has happened) he will suffer no law to be made here but such as suit *his* purpose? We may be as effectually enslaved by the want of laws in America as by submitting to laws made for us in England. . . . We are already greater than the king wishes us to be, and will he not hereafter endeavor to make us less? To bring the matter to one point: is the power who is jealous of our prosperity a proper power to govern us? Whoever says no to this question is an *independent*, for independency means no more than whether we shall make our own laws, or, whether the king, the greatest enemy which this continent has or can have, shall tell us, "There shall be no laws but such as I like." . . .

America is only a secondary object in the system of British politics. England consults the good of *this* country no further than it answers her *own* purpose. Wherefore, her own interest leads her to suppress the growth of *ours* in every case which does not promote her advantage, or in the least interferes with it. . . .

. . . The most powerful of all arguments is that nothing but independence, i.e., a continental form of government, can keep the peace of the continent and preserve it inviolate from civil wars. I dread the event of a reconciliation with Britain now, as it is more than probable that it will be followed by a revolt somewhere or other, the consequences of which may be far more fatal than all the malice of Britain.

Thousands are already ruined by British barbarity. (Thousands more will probably suffer the same fate.) Those men have other feelings than us who have nothing suffered. All they *now* possess is liberty: what they before enjoyed is sacrificed to its service; and having nothing more to lose, they disdain submission. . . .

But where, say some, is the king of America? I'll tell you, friend. He reigns above, and does not make havoc of mankind like the royal brute of Britain. Yet, that we may not appear to be defective even in earthly honors, let a day be solemnly set apart for proclaiming the charter; let it be brought forth placed on the divine law, the word of God; let a crown be placed thereon, by which the world may know that so far as we approve of monarchy, that in America *the law is king.* For as in absolute governments the king is law, so in free countries the law ought to be king; and there ought to be no other. But lest any ill use should afterwards arise, let the crown at the conclusion of the ceremony be demolished and scattered among the people whose right it is.

A government of our own is our natural right; and when a man seriously reflects on the precariousness of human affairs, he will become convinced that it is infinitely wiser and safer to form a constitution of our own in a cool deliberate manner, while we have it in our power, than to trust such an interesting event to time and chance. . . .

Ye that tell us of harmony and reconciliation, can ye restore to us the time that is past? Can ye give to prostitution its former innocence? Neither can ye reconcile Britain and America. The last cord now is broken; the people of England are presenting addresses against us. There are injuries which nature cannot forgive; she would cease to be nature if she did. As well can the lover forgive the ravisher of his mistress as the continent forgive the murders of Britain. The Almighty has implanted in us these unextinguishable feelings, for good and wise purposes. They are the guardians of His image in our hearts, and distinguish us from the herd of common animals. The social compact would dissolve and justice be extirpated from the earth, or have only a casual existence, were we callous to the touches of affection. The robber and the murderer would often escape unpunished did not the injuries which our tempers sustain provoke us into justice.

O ye that love mankind! Ye that dare oppose, not only the tyranny but the tyrant, stand forth! Every spot of the Old World is overrun with oppression. Freedom has been haunted round the globe. Asia and Africa have long expelled her. Europe regards her like a stranger, and England has given her warning to depart. O! receive the fugitive, and prepare in time an asylum for mankind.

Source: Although published in pamphlet form in January 1776, this extract is from a later edition: Thomas Paine, *Common Sense* (Philadelphia: W. and T. Bradford, 1791). Multiple versions, with different tracts, appeared in subsequent editions, and the portion presented here appeared under the heading "Thoughts on the Present State of American Affairs." Retrieved June 10, 2010, from http://www.ushistory.org/paine/commonsense/singlehtml.htm.

CHAPTER 5

The Declaration of Independence, 1776

Almost a year after the first shots of the Revolution were fired at Lexington, the Continental Congress took up the issue of declaring independence from Great Britain. The movement rode a tide of patriotism that grew following Parliament's passage of the Prohibitory Act in February, King George's hiring of mercenaries to help put down the rebellion, and widespread enthusiasm over Thomas Paine's *Common Sense*. Confusion reigned throughout the colonies as many "declarations" of independence were made at the local and state level.

Congress moved forward by fits and starts but finally passed a resolution: "Resolved, that these United Colonies are, and of right ought to be, free and independent States, that they are absolved from all allegiance to the British Crown, and that all political connection between them and the State of Great Britain is, and ought to be, totally dissolved." This resolution was passed on July 2, 1776, the true "independence day." Over the next two days, Congress reviewed Jefferson's draft declaration, made a few changes, and deleted a substantial portion that dealt with the slave trade. On July 4, the wording was approved and sent out for publication.

In a very large sense, the Declaration of Independence became the guiding light of the Revolution if not actually a literary representation of the soul of the American patriots. Although some congressmen understood "all men are created equal" to mean "there is no class of nobility," the declaration was soon taken at face value, and the conflict over slavery moved to center stage. Abraham Lincoln would later tie the declaration and the U.S. Constitution together, noting that the Constitution had to be "dedicated to the proposition that all men are created equal." Thus the radical declaration, which severed ties with England, and the Constitution, which ordered the affairs of the United States of America, were in his eyes a single long document separated by eleven years.

Whether or not the declaration is the single most important document in history related to governing human affairs is a question for the reader. Certainly tyranny and freedom are explicitly defined, as are the causes for separation and the contention that America had exhausted every nonviolent alternative. Ultimately, although a government may fail to fully implement and protect the great principles of liberty espoused here, the declaration still challenges the individual to do better and to defend the rights enunciated therein at every opportunity.

The Declaration of Independence

WHEN IN THE COURSE OF HUMAN EVENTS, IT BECOMES NECessary for one people to dissolve the political bands which have connected them with another, and to assume among the powers of the earth, the separate and equal station to which the laws of nature and of nature's God entitle them, a decent respect to the opinions of mankind requires that they should declare the causes which impel them to the separation.

We hold these truths to be self-evident: That all men are created equal; that they are endowed by their Creator with certain unalienable rights; that among these are life, liberty, and the pursuit of happiness. That to secure these rights, governments are instituted among men, deriving their just powers from the consent of the governed. That whenever any form of government becomes destructive to these ends, it is the right of the people to alter or to abolish it, and to institute new government, laying its foundation on such principles and organizing its powers in such form, as to them shall seem most likely to effect their safety and happiness. Prudence, indeed, will dictate that governments long established should not be changed for light and transient causes; and accordingly all experience hath shown that mankind are more disposed to suffer, while evils are sufferable, than to right themselves by abolishing the forms to which they are accustomed. But when a long train of abuses and usurpations, pursuing invariably the same object, evinces a design to reduce them under absolute despotism, it is their right, it is their duty, to throw off such government, and to provide new guards for their future security. Such has been the patient sufferance of these colonies; and such is now the necessity which constrains them to alter their former systems of government. The history of the present King of Great Britain is a history of repeated injuries and usurpations, all having in direct object the establishment of an absolute tyranny over these states. To prove this, let facts be submitted to a candid world.

He has refused his assent to laws, the most wholesome and necessary for the public good.

He has forbidden his governors to pass laws of immediate and pressing importance, unless suspended in their operation till his assent should be obtained; and when so suspended, he has utterly neglected to attend to them.

He has refused to pass other laws for the accommodation of large districts of people, unless those people would relinquish the right of representation in the legislature, a right inestimable to them and formidable to tyrants only.

He has called together legislative bodies at places unusual, uncomfortable, and distant from the depository of their public records, for the sole purpose of fatiguing them into compliance with his measures.

He has dissolved representative houses repeatedly, for opposing with manly firmness his invasions on the rights of the people.

He has refused for a long time, after such dissolutions, to cause others to be elected; whereby the legislative powers, incapable of annihilation, have returned to the people at large for their exercise; the state remaining in the meantime exposed to all the dangers of invasion from without and convulsions within.

He has endeavored to prevent the population of these states; for that purpose obstructing the laws for naturalization of foreigners; refusing to pass others to encourage their migration hither, and raising the conditions of new appropriations of lands.

He has obstructed the administration of justice, by refusing his assent to laws for establishing judiciary powers.

He has made judges dependent on his will alone, for the tenure of their offices, and the amount and payment of their salaries.

He has erected a multitude of new offices, and sent hither swarms of officers to harass our people and eat out their substance.

He has kept among us, in times of peace, standing armies without the consent of our legislature.

He has affected to render the military independent of and superior to civil power.

He has combined with others to subject us to a jurisdiction foreign to our constitution and unacknowledged by our laws, giving his assent to their acts of pretended legislation:

For quartering large bodies of armed troops among us;

For protecting them, by mock trial, from punishment for any murders which they should commit on the inhabitants of these states;

For cutting off our trade with all parts of the world;

For imposing taxes on us without our consent;

For depriving us, in many cases, of the benefits of trial by jury;

For transporting us beyond seas to be tried for pretended offenses;

For abolishing the free system of English laws in a neighboring province, establishing therein an arbitrary government, and enlarging its boundaries so as to render it at once an example and fit instrument for introducing the same absolute rule in these colonies;

For taking away our charters, abolishing our most valuable laws, and altering fundamentally the forms of our governments;

For suspending our own legislatures, and declaring themselves invested with power to legislate for us in all cases whatsoever.

He has abdicated government here, by declaring us out of his protection and waging war against us.

He has plundered our seas, ravaged our coasts, burned our towns, and destroyed the lives of our people.

He is at this time transporting large armies of foreign mercenaries to complete the works of death, desolation, and tyranny already begun with circumstances of cruelty and perfidy scarcely paralleled in the most barbarous ages, and totally unworthy the head of a civilized nation.

He has constrained our fellow citizens taken captive on the high seas to bear arms against their country, to become the executioners of their friends and brethren, or to fall themselves by their hands.

He has excited domestic insurrections among us, and has endeavored to bring on the inhabitants of our frontiers the merciless Indian savages, whose known rule of warfare is undistinguished destruction of all ages, sexes, and conditions.

In every stage of these oppressions we have petitioned for redress in the most humble terms: our repeated petitions have been answered only by repeated injury. A prince, whose character is thus marked by every act which may define a tyrant, is unfit to be the ruler of a free people.

Nor have we been wanting in attention to our British brethren. We have warned them from time to time of attempts by their legislature to extend an unwarrantable jurisdiction over us. We have reminded them of the circumstances of our emigration and settlement here. We have appealed to their native justice and magnanimity, and we have conjured them by the ties of our common kindred to disavow these usurpations, which would inevitably interrupt our connections and correspondence. They too have been deaf to the voice of justice and of consanguinity. We must, therefore, acquiesce in the necessity which denounces our separation, and hold them as we hold the rest of mankind, enemies in war, in peace friends.

We, therefore, the representatives of the United States of America, in General Congress, assembled, appealing to the Supreme Judge of the world for the rectitude of our intentions, do, in the name, and by the authority of the good people of these colonies, solemnly publish and declare, that these united colonies are, and of right ought to be, *free and independent states*; that they are absolved from all allegiance to the British Crown, and that all political connection between them and the state of Great Britain is, and ought to be, totally dissolved; and that, as free and independent states, they have full power to levy war, conclude peace, contract alliances, establish commerce, and to do all other acts and things which independent states may of right do. And for the support of this declaration, with a firm reliance on the protection of Divine Providence, we mutually pledge to each other our lives, our fortunes, and our sacred honor.

Source: The Declaration of Independence is a widely published document; only minor spelling changes were made in the original document on permanent display in Washington, D.C. The text as available at the Yale Law School's Lillian Goldman Law Library's Avalon Project: Documents in Law, History and Diplomacy was retrieved on April 15, 2010, from http://avalon.law.yale.edu/18th_century/declare.asp. An original rough draft as reconstructed by Professor Julian Boyd is contained in *The Papers of Thomas Jefferson*, ed. Julian P. Boyd (Princeton: Princeton University Press, 1950) 1: 243–47, and may be accessed on the Internet at http://www.constitution.org/tj/doi_rough.htm.

CHAPTER 6

The Articles of Confederation and Perpetual Union, 1781

The first national governing document for the newly freed colonies, the Articles of Confederation was written by John Dickinson of Pennsylvania in July of 1777. It underwent a number of revisions before being adopted in November. Its ratification by all the states, which was required before the articles could go into effect, did not take place until 1781. Although frequently maligned by American historians throughout the years as an ineffective national constitution, this document and the government functioning under its articles did have some successes, such as in winning the Revolutionary War and producing both the Land Ordinance of 1785 and the Northwest Ordinance. Its form reflected the experience of the colonial legislatures, and neither the executive branch nor the judiciary was structured sufficiently well to handle the pressing problems that arose after the war ended and the Treaty of Paris was signed. The articles established the government as a confederation, with a president elected by Congress to serve a term of one year and ineligible to serve more than one year out of three. Throughout, it reflects the English Whig view that the legislature was the dominant branch of government and the executive branch was weak and even subservient to the legislature.

Without leadership from an effective executive branch, the new nation's political process rapidly bogged down in spite of the best efforts of the state governments and Congress, but a majority in Congress probably thought the articles needed only to be modified to make the government stronger without sacrificing the principles of confederation. Others, notably James Madison and Alexander Hamilton, recognized that a major overhaul was necessary, and that a federal government was needed if the fledgling country was to survive. Ultimately, the U.S. Constitution replaced the articles in 1788, but not without a fight. The idea of a confederation of sovereign states was cherished by those who saw sectional differences as requiring strong local governments, much like those in Switzerland. However, confederations have proved to be workable only in small countries that do not play major roles in international affairs and can resist or avoid aggressive nations due to special circumstances. The United States harbored potential as a great power with vast resources, making a strong executive branch a necessity. The articles would have perpetuated slavery long past its acceptance internationally, and it is doubtful that making minor changes in the articles would have enabled the United States to survive and become an exceptional nation.

The Articles of Confederation

TO ALL TO WHOM THESE PRESENTS SHALL COME, WE THE undersigned Delegates of the States affixed to our Names send greeting . . .

Articles of Confederation and perpetual Union between the states of New Hampshire, Massachusetts-bay, Rhode Island and Providence Plantations, Connecticut, New York, New Jersey, Pennsylvania, Delaware, Maryland, Virginia, North Carolina, South Carolina, and Georgia.

ARTICLE I

The Style of this Confederacy shall be "The United States of America."

ARTICLE II

Each state retains its sovereignty, freedom, and independence, and every power, jurisdiction, and right, which is not by this Confederation expressly delegated to the United States, in Congress assembled.

ARTICLE III

The said States hereby severally enter into a firm league of friendship with each other, for their common defense, the security of their liberties, and their mutual and general welfare, binding themselves to assist each other, against all force offered to, or attacks made upon them, or any of them, on account of religion, sovereignty, trade, or any other pretense whatever.

ARTICLE IV

The better to secure and perpetuate mutual friendship and intercourse among the people of the different States in this Union, the free inhabitants of each of these States, paupers, vagabonds, and fugitives from justice excepted, shall be entitled to all privileges and immunities of free citizens in the several States; and the people of each State shall have free ingress and regress to and from any other State, and shall enjoy therein all the privileges of trade and commerce, subject to the same duties, impositions, and restrictions as the inhabitants thereof respectively, provided that such restrictions shall not extend so far as to prevent the removal of property imported into any State, to any other State, of which the owner is an inhabitant; provided also that no imposition, duties, or restriction shall be laid by any State, on the property of the United States, or either of them.

If any person guilty of, or charged with, treason, felony, or other high misdemeanor in any State, shall flee from justice, and be found in any of the United States, he shall, upon demand of the Governor or executive power of the State from which he fled, be delivered up and removed to the State having jurisdiction of his offense.

Full faith and credit shall be given in each of these States to the records, acts, and judicial proceedings of the courts and magistrates of every other State.

ARTICLE V

For the most convenient management of the general interests of the United States, delegates shall be annually appointed in such manner as the legislatures of each State shall direct, to meet in Congress on the first Monday in November, in every year, with a power reserved to each State to recall its delegates, or any of them, at any time within the year, and to send others in their stead for the remainder of the year.

No State shall be represented in Congress by less than two, nor more than seven members; and no person shall be capable of being a delegate for more than three years in any term of six years; nor shall any person, being a delegate, be capable of holding any office under the United States, for which he, or another for his benefit, receives any salary, fees, or emolument of any kind.

Each State shall maintain its own delegates in a meeting of the States, and while they act as members of the committee of the States.

In determining questions in the United States in Congress assembled, each State shall have one vote.

Freedom of speech and debate in Congress shall not be impeached or questioned in any court or place out of Congress, and the members of Congress shall be protected in their persons from arrests or imprisonments, during the time of their going to and from, and attendance on Congress, except for treason, felony, or breach of the peace.

ARTICLE VI

No State, without the consent of the United States in Congress assembled, shall send any embassy to, or receive any embassy from, or enter into any conference, agreement, alliance, or treaty with any King, Prince, or State; nor shall any person holding any office of profit or trust under the United States, or any of them, accept any present, emolument, office, or title of any kind whatever from any King, Prince, or foreign State; nor shall the United States in Congress assembled, or any of them, grant any title of nobility.

No two or more States shall enter into any treaty, confederation, or alliance whatever between them, without the consent of the United States in Congress assembled, specifying accurately the purposes for which the same is to be entered into, and how long it shall continue.

No State shall lay any imposts or duties, which may interfere with any stipulations in treaties, entered into by the United States in Congress assembled, with any King, Prince, or State, in pursuance of any treaties already proposed by Congress, to the courts of France and Spain.

No vessel of war shall be kept up in time of peace by any State, except such number only, as shall be deemed necessary by the United States in Congress assembled, for the defense of such State, or its trade; nor shall any body of forces be kept up by any State in time of peace, except such number only, as in the judgment of the United States in Congress assembled, shall be deemed requisite to garrison the forts necessary for the defense of such State; but every State shall always keep up a well-regulated and disciplined militia, sufficiently armed and accoutered, and shall provide and constantly have ready for use, in public stores, a due number of field pieces and tents, and a proper quantity of arms, ammunition, and camp equipage.

No State shall engage in any war without the consent of the United States in Congress assembled, unless such State be actually invaded by enemies, or shall have received certain advice of a resolution being formed by some nation of Indians to invade such State, and the danger is so imminent as not to admit of a delay till the United States in Congress assembled can be consulted; nor shall any State grant commissions to any ships or vessels of war, nor letters of marque or reprisal, except it be after a declaration of war by the United States in Congress assembled, and then only against the Kingdom or State and the subjects thereof, against which war has been so declared, and under such regulations as shall be established by the United States in Congress assembled, unless such State be infested by pirates, in which case vessels of war may be fitted out for that occasion, and kept so long as the danger shall continue, or until the United States in Congress assembled shall determine otherwise.

ARTICLE VII

When land forces are raised by any State for the common defense, all officers of or under the rank of colonel, shall be appointed by the legislature of each State respectively, by whom such forces shall be raised, or in such manner as such State shall direct, and all vacancies shall be filled up by the State which first made the appointment.

ARTICLE VIII

All charges of war, and all other expenses that shall be incurred for the common defense or general welfare, and allowed by the United States in Congress

assembled, shall be defrayed out of a common treasury, which shall be supplied by the several States in proportion to the value of all land within each
State, granted or surveyed for any person, as such land and the buildings and
improvements thereon shall be estimated according to such mode as the United
States in Congress assembled, shall from time to time direct and appoint.

The taxes for paying that proportion shall be laid and levied by the authority and direction of the legislatures of the several States within the time agreed
upon by the United States in Congress assembled.

ARTICLE IX

The United States in Congress assembled, shall have the sole and exclusive
right and power of determining on peace and war, except in the cases mentioned in the sixth article—of sending and receiving ambassadors—entering
into treaties and alliances, provided that no treaty of commerce shall be made
whereby the legislative power of the respective States shall be restrained from
imposing such imposts and duties on foreigners, as their own people are subjected to, or from prohibiting the exportation or importation of any species of
goods or commodities whatsoever—of establishing rules for deciding in all
cases, what captures on land or water shall be legal, and in what manner
prizes taken by land or naval forces in the service of the United States shall
be divided or appropriated—of granting letters of marque and reprisal in times
of peace—appointing courts for the trial of piracies and felonies committed
on the high seas and establishing courts for receiving and determining finally
appeals in all cases of captures, provided that no member of Congress shall
be appointed a judge of any of the said courts.

The United States in Congress assembled shall also be the last resort on
appeal in all disputes and differences now subsisting or that hereafter may
arise between two or more States concerning boundary, jurisdiction, or any
other causes whatever; which authority shall always be exercised in the manner following. Whenever the legislative or executive authority or lawful agent
of any State in controversy with another shall present a petition to Congress
stating the matter in question and praying for a hearing, notice thereof shall
be given by order of Congress to the legislative or executive authority of the
other State in controversy, and a day assigned for the appearance of the parties
by their lawful agents, who shall then be directed to appoint by joint consent,
commissioners or judges to constitute a court for hearing and determining the
matter in question: but if they cannot agree, Congress shall name three persons out of each of the United States, and from the list of such persons each
party shall alternately strike out one, the petitioners beginning, until the number shall be reduced to thirteen; and from that number not less than seven,
nor more than nine names as Congress shall direct, shall in the presence of
Congress be drawn out by lot, and the persons whose names shall be so drawn

or any five of them, shall be commissioners or judges, to hear and finally determine the controversy, so always as a major part of the judges who shall hear the cause shall agree in the determination: and if either party shall neglect to attend at the day appointed, without showing reasons, which Congress shall judge sufficient, or being present shall refuse to strike, the Congress shall proceed to nominate three persons out of each State, and the secretary of Congress shall strike in behalf of such party absent or refusing; and the judgment and sentence of the court to be appointed, in the manner before prescribed, shall be final and conclusive; and if any of the parties shall refuse to submit to the authority of such court, or to appear or defend their claim or cause, the court shall nevertheless proceed to pronounce sentence, or judgment, which shall in like manner be final and decisive, the judgment or sentence and other proceedings being in either case transmitted to Congress, and lodged among the acts of Congress for the security of the parties concerned: provided that every commissioner, before he sits in judgment, shall take an oath to be administered by one of the judges of the supreme or superior court of the State, where the cause shall be tried, "well and truly to hear and determine the matter in question, according to the best of his judgment, without favor, affection or hope of reward": provided also, that no State shall be deprived of territory for the benefit of the United States.

All controversies concerning the private right of soil claimed under different grants of two or more States, whose jurisdictions as they may respect such lands, and the States which passed such grants are adjusted, the said grants or either of them being at the same time claimed to have originated antecedent to such settlement of jurisdiction, shall on the petition of either party to the Congress of the United States, be finally determined as near as may be in the same manner as is before prescribed for deciding disputes respecting territorial jurisdiction between different States.

The United States in Congress assembled shall also have the sole and exclusive right and power of regulating the alloy and value of coin struck by their own authority, or by that of the respective States—fixing the standards of weights and measures throughout the United States—regulating the trade and managing all affairs with the Indians, not members of any of the States, provided that the legislative right of any State within its own limits be not infringed or violated—establishing or regulating post offices from one State to another, throughout all the United States, and exacting such postage on the papers passing through the same as may be requisite to defray the expenses of the said office—appointing all officers of the land forces, in the service of the United States, excepting regimental officers—appointing all the officers of the naval forces, and commissioning all officers whatever in the service of the United States—making rules for the government and regulation of the said land and naval forces, and directing their operations.

The United States in Congress assembled shall have authority to appoint a committee, to sit in the recess of Congress, to be denominated "A Committee of the States," and to consist of one delegate from each State; and to appoint such other committees and civil officers as may be necessary for managing the general affairs of the United States under their direction—to appoint one of their members to preside, provided that no person be allowed to serve in the office of president more than one year in any term of three years; to ascertain the necessary sums of money to be raised for the service of the United States, and to appropriate and apply the same for defraying the public expenses—to borrow money, or emit bills on the credit of the United States, transmitting every half year to the respective States an account of the sums of money so borrowed or emitted—to build and equip a navy—to agree upon the number of land forces, and to make requisitions from each State for its quota, in proportion to the number of white inhabitants in such State; which requisition shall be binding, and thereupon the legislature of each State shall appoint the regimental officers, raise the men and clothes, arm and equip them in a solid-like manner, at the expense of the United States; and the officers and men so clothed, armed, and equipped shall march to the place appointed, and within the time agreed on by the United States in Congress assembled. But if the United States in Congress assembled shall, on consideration of circumstances judge proper that any State should not raise men, or should raise a smaller number of men than the quota thereof, such extra number shall be raised, officered, clothed, armed, and equipped in the same manner as the quota of each State, unless the legislature of such State shall judge that such extra number cannot be safely spread out in the same, in which case they shall raise, officer, clothe, arm, and equip as many of such extra number as they judge can be safely spared. And the officers and men so clothed, armed, and equipped, shall march to the place appointed, and within the time agreed on by the United States in Congress assembled.

The United States in Congress assembled shall never engage in a war, nor grant letters of marque or reprisal in time of peace, nor enter into any treaties or alliances, nor coin money, nor regulate the value thereof, nor ascertain the sums and expenses necessary for the defense and welfare of the United States, or any of them, nor emit bills, nor borrow money on the credit of the United States, nor appropriate money, nor agree upon the number of vessels of war, to be built or purchased, or the number of land or sea forces to be raised, nor appoint a commander in chief of the army or navy, unless nine States assent to the same: nor shall a question on any other point, except for adjourning from day to day be determined, unless by the votes of the majority of the United States in Congress assembled.

The Congress of the United States shall have power to adjourn to any time within the year, and to any place within the United States, so that no period of adjournment be for a longer duration than the space of six months, and shall publish the journal of their proceedings monthly, except such parts thereof relating to treaties, alliances, or military operations, as in their judgment require secrecy; and the yeas and nays of the delegates of each State on any question shall be entered on the journal, when it is desired by any delegates of a State, or any of them, at his or their request shall be furnished with a transcript of the said journal, except such parts as are above excepted, to lay before the legislatures of the several States.

ARTICLE X

The Committee of the States, or any nine of them, shall be authorized to execute, in the recess of Congress, such of the powers of Congress as the United States in Congress assembled, by the consent of the nine States, shall from time to time think expedient to vest them with; provided that no power be delegated to the said Committee, for the exercise of which, by the Articles of Confederation, the voice of nine States in the Congress of the United States assembled be requisite.

ARTICLE XI

Canada acceding to this confederation, and adjoining in the measures of the United States, shall be admitted into, and entitled to all the advantages of this Union; but no other colony shall be admitted into the same, unless such admission be agreed to by nine States.

ARTICLE XII

All bills of credit emitted, monies borrowed, and debts contracted by, or under the authority of Congress, before the assembling of the United States, in pursuance of the present confederation, shall be deemed and considered as a charge against the United States, for payment and satisfaction whereof the said United States, and the public faith are hereby solemnly pledged.

ARTICLE XIII

Every State shall abide by the determination of the United States in Congress assembled, on all questions which by this confederation are submitted to them. And the Articles of this Confederation shall be inviolably observed by every State, and the Union shall be perpetual; nor shall any alteration at any time hereafter be made in any of them; unless such alteration be agreed to in a Congress of the United States, and be afterwards confirmed by the legislatures of every State.

And whereas it hath pleased the Great Governor of the World to incline the hearts of the legislatures we respectively represent in Congress, to approve of, and to authorize us to ratify the said Articles of Confederation and perpetual Union, know ye that we the undersigned delegates, by virtue of the power and authority to us given for that purpose, do by these presents, in the name and in behalf of our respective constituents, fully and entirely ratify and confirm each and every of the said Articles of Confederation and perpetual Union, and all and singular the matters and things therein contained: And we do further solemnly plight and engage the faith of our respective constituents, that they shall abide by the determinations of the United States in Congress assembled, on all questions, which by the said Confederation are submitted to them. And that the Articles thereof shall be inviolably observed by the States we respectively represent, and that the Union shall be perpetual.

In witness whereof we have hereunto set our hands in Congress. Done at Philadelphia in the State of Pennsylvania the ninth day of July in the Year of our Lord One Thousand Seven Hundred and Seventy-Eight, and in the Third Year of the independence of America.

Source: The Federal and State Constitutions, Colonial Charters, and other Organic Laws of the United States, 2nd ed., ed. B. P. Poore (Washington, D.C.: Government Printing Office, 1877), 1: 7–12. As available at the U.S. Constitution Online. Retrieved April 7, 2010, from http://usconstitution.net/articles.html.

CHAPTER 7

On Creating a Peacetime Military Establishment, George Washington, 1783

In February of 1783, King George III issued his Proclamation of Cessation of Hostilities, officially ending the American Revolution. Peace was thought to be simply a matter of time and negotiation. One remaining problem, however, was the existence of a large Continental army, which was somewhat mutinous, unpaid, woefully supplied, and angry with the Continental Congress. Some feared that the army might seize power by force, and a political collapse of the civilian government was a definite possibility. A policy was needed for a peacetime army, if there was to be one.

On April 9, 1783, Alexander Hamilton wrote to George Washington on behalf of his congressional committee requesting the general's views on a permanent army. Washington queried seven of his officers, including Baron von Steuben and Henry Knox, and formulated his reply in a letter dated May 2, 1783. Washington reflected the thinking of his time when it came to suspicions about a standing military. But having seen militias in the field, he was unwilling to be totally dependent on them for the nation's defense. He recommended that militia duty be required of all able-bodied men between eighteen and fifty, and cited Switzerland as an example of a country whose security had been defended by a well-organized militia. Further, Washington declared that every citizen owed his personal service and a portion of his property in defense of his country, a concept very much in disfavor today.

Having served as an officer in the Virginia militia as a young man, the general well knew the militia's strengths and weaknesses. In the colonies each settlement and colony developed its own militia, even adopting conscription to fill units in times of war against Indians. Since militia units were organized locally and generally used arms supplied by the members themselves, they became powerful forces for home rule and independence. Washington saw them as a source of trained men to be taken into an established army in times of war but recognized that discipline was a severe problem that hindered their effectiveness. Provisions were made for the rapid expansion of the militia and regular troops in wartime by maintaining a large officer corps and understrength enlisted establishment. He further provided for the creation of a professional officer corps through training at military academies, for even a "well-trained militia" could not maintain discipline or maneuver effectively without good commanders. Washington stressed defense by maintaining posts in critical locations to maintain communications and favored the location of arsenals inland and away from locations like West Point, where they were subject to attack by maritime powers such as Great Britain.

Yet more than once Washington condemned the prospect of a large standing army. In effect Washington established America's military policy for the next 150 years, and his viewpoint held sway in the United States until the cold war. Although Washington's suggestions appear modest and inexpensive, Congress allowed the Continental army to languish, and within a few years it almost disappeared altogether. As the War of 1812 approached, his plan was dusted off and appropriations made, but the United States went into the war woefully unprepared. Washington had seen the advantages, but also the decided weaknesses, of militias and knew that without a trained military force the United States' security would be at risk. He also knew that in Europe standing armies were tools of oppression, used to keep the masses in their place. Consider whether or not Washington balanced these two concerns.

Sentiments on a Peace Establishment

A PEACE ESTABLISHMENT FOR THE UNITED STATES OF AMERica may in my opinion be classed under four different heads as:

1. A regular and standing force, for garrisoning West Point and such other posts upon our northern, western, and southern frontiers, as shall be deemed necessary to awe the Indians, protect our trade, prevent the encroachment of our neighbors of Canada and the Floridas, and guard us at least from surprises for the security of our magazines.
2. A well-organized militia; upon a plan that will pervade all the states and introduce similarity in their establishment maneuvers, exercise, and arms.
3. Establishing arsenals of all kinds of military stores.
4. Academies, one or more for the instruction of the military art, particularly those branches such as engineering and artillery, which are highly essential, and the knowledge of which is most difficult to obtain. Also manufactories of some kinds of military stores.

Upon each of these, and in the order in which they stand, I shall give my sentiments as concisely as I can, and with that freedom which the Committee has authorized.

Although a large standing army in time of peace hath ever been considered dangerous to the liberties of a country, yet a few troops, under certain circumstances, are not only safe, but indispensably necessary. Fortunately for us our relative situation requires but few. The same circumstances which so effectually retarded, and in the end conspired to defeat the attempts of Britain to subdue us, will now powerfully tend to render us secure. Our distance from the European states in a great degree frees us of apprehension, from their numerous regular forces and the insults and dangers which are to be dreaded from their ambition.

We are too poor to maintain a standing army adequate to our defense, but if our danger from those powers was more imminent and our country more populous and rich, still it could not be done without great oppression of the people. Besides, as soon as we are able to raise funds more than adequate to the discharge of the debts incurred by the Revolution, it may become a question worthy of consideration, whether the surplus should not be applied in preparations for building and equipping a navy, without which, in case of war we could neither protect our commerce, nor yield that assistance to each other, which, on such an extent of seacoast, our mutual safety would require.

Fortifications on the seaboard may be considered in two points of view, first as part of the general defense, and next, as securities to dockyards, and arsenals for ship building, neither of which shall I take into this plan; because the first would be difficult, if not, under our circumstances, impracticable; at any rate amazingly expensive. The other, because it is a matter out of my line, and to which I am by no means competent, as it requires a consideration of many circumstances, to which I have never paid attention. The troops requisite for the post of West Point, magazines, and our northern, western, and southern frontiers, ought to amount to 2,631 officers of all denominations with four regiments of infantry. If this number should be thought large, I would only observe that the British force in Canada is now powerful and by report will be increased, that the frontier is very extensive, that the tribes of Indians within our territory are numerous, soured, and jealous, that communications must be established with the exterior posts, and it may be policy and economy to appear respectable in the eyes of the Indians. In a word, that it is better to reduce our force hereafter, than to have it to increase after some unfortunate disasters may have happened to the garrisons; discouraging to us, and an inducement to the enemy to attempt a repetition of them.

Besides these considerations, we are not to forget that although by the treaty [in respect to the Northwest and Great Lakes], half the waters and the free navigation of the lakes appertain to us, yet in case of a rupture with Great Britain we should in all probability find little benefit from the communications with our upper posts, by the Lakes Erie and Ontario; as it is to be presumed that the naval superiority which they now have on those waters will be maintained. It follows as a consequence, then, that we should open new or improve the present half-explored communications with Detroit and other posts on the lakes, by the waters of the Susquehanna, Potomac, or James Rivers to the Ohio, from whence communications by water may be opened with Lake Erie. This would open several doors for the supply of the garrisons on the lakes, and is absolutely necessary for such others as may be thought advisable to establish upon the Mississippi. . . .

The 2,631 men beforementioned, I would have considered to all intents and purposes as Continental troops; looking to Congress for their orders, their pay, and supplies of every kind.

Not having that particular knowledge of the situation of the southern and western boundaries of the Carolinas and Georgia which is necessary to decide on the posts to be established in that district, the allotment of only one regiment thereto may be judged inadequate; should that be the case, a greater force may be established and a sufficient allowance made them.

A reduction in noncommissioned officers and privates should be made, while the commissioned officers remain the same. The number of men which compose the infantry will be sufficient for my calculation, and the situation of our frontiers renders it convenient to divide them into so many corps as have been mentioned, for the ease and propriety of command. I may also say that in my opinion the number of our commissioned officers has always been disproportionate to the men, and in the detached state in which these regiments must be employed they cannot consistently with the good of service be reduced.

It may also be observed that in case of war and a necessity of assembling their regiments in the field, nothing more will be necessary, than to recruit eighteen men to each company and give the regiment its flank company. Or if we should have occasion to add strength to the garrisons or increase the number of our posts, we may augment nine hundred men including sergeants, without requiring more than the officers of four companies. In short, it will give us a number of officers well skilled in the theory and art of war, who will be ready on any occasion to mix and diffuse their knowledge of discipline to other corps, without that lapse of time, which without such provision, would be necessary to bring entire new corps acquainted with the principles of it.

Besides the four regiments of infantry, one of artillery will be indispensably necessary. The Invalid Corps should also be retained. Motives of humanity, policy, and justice will all combine to prevent their being disbanded.

To this regiment of artillery should be annexed fifty or sixty artificers of the various kinds which will be necessary, who may be distributed in equal numbers into the different companies, and being part of the regiment will be under the direction and command of the commanding officer, to be disposed into different services as circumstances shall require. . . .

The regiment of artillery with the artificers will furnish all the posts in which artillery is placed in proportionate numbers to the strength and importance of them. The residue, with the Corps of Invalids, will furnish guards for the magazines and garrison West Point. The importance of this last mentioned post is so great as justly to have been considered the key of America; it has been so preeminently advantageous to the defense of the United States, and is still so necessary in that view as well as for the preservation of the Union, that the loss of it might be productive of the most ruinous consequences. A naval superiority at sea and on Lake Champlain, connected by a chain of posts on the Hudson River, would effect an entire separation of the states on each side and render it difficult, if not impracticable, for them to cooperate.

Although the total of the troops herein enumerated does not amount to a large number, when we consider their detached situation, not less than two general officers in my opinion will be competent to the duties to be required of them. They will take their instructions from the Secretary at War or person acting at the head of the Military Department, who will also assign them their respective and distinct districts. Each should twice a year visit the posts of his particular district, and notice the condition they are in, inspect the troops, their discipline and police, examine into their wants, and see that strict justice is rendered them and to the public. . . .

The three-years men now in service will furnish the proposed establishment, and from these it is presumed the corps must in the first instance be composed. . . .

When the soldiers for the War have frolicked awhile among their friends, and find they must have recourse to hard labor for a livelihood, I am persuaded numbers of them will reenlist upon almost any terms. Whatever may be adopted with respect to pay, clothing, and emoluments, they should be clearly and unequivocally expressed and promulgated that there may be no deception or mistake. Discontent, desertion, and frequently mutiny, are the natural consequences of these, and it is not more difficult to know how to punish than to prevent these inconveniencies, when it is known that there has been delusion on the part of the recruiting officer, or a breach of compact on the part of the public. . . . A proper difference should be made in pay between the noncommissioned officers (sergeants particularly) and privates, to give them that pride and consequence which is necessary to command. . . .

Soldiers should not be enlisted for less than three years, to commence from the date of their attestations; and the more difference there is in the commencement of their terms of service, the better. This circumstance will be the means of avoiding the danger and inconvenience of entrusting any important posts to raw recruits unacquainted with service. . . .

As a peace establishment may be considered as a change in, if not the commencement of, our military system, it will be the proper time to introduce new and beneficial regulations and to expunge all customs which from experience have been found unproductive of general good. Among the latter I would ask, if promotion by seniority is not one? That it is a good general rule admits of no doubt, but that it should be an invariable one is in my opinion wrong. It cools, if it does not destroy, the incentives to military pride and heroic actions. On the one hand, the sluggard who keeps within the verge of his duty has nothing to fear. On the other hand, the enterprising spirit has nothing to expect. Whereas if promotion was the sure reward of merit, all would contend for rank and the service would be benefited by their struggles for promotion. . . . It would certainly give a spur to emulation, without endangering the rights or just pretensions of the officers.

Before I close my observations under this head of a regular force and the establishment of posts, it is necessary for me to observe that in fixing a post at the north end of Lake Champlain I had three things in view: the absolute command of the entrance into the lake from Canada, a cover to the settlements on the New Hampshire Grants, and the prevention of any illicit intercourse through that channel. But if it is known or should be found that the 45th Degree crosses the lake south of any spot which will command the entrance into it, the primary object fails, and it then becomes a question whether any place beyond Ticonderoga or Crown Point is eligible. . . .

I come next in the order I have prescribed myself, to treat of the arrangements necessary for placing the militia of the continent on a respectable footing for the defense of the empire and in speaking of this great bulwark of our liberties and independence, . . . being convinced at the same time that the only probable means of preventing insult or hostility for any length of time and from being exempted from the consequent calamities of war, is to put the national militia in such a condition as that they may appear truly respectable in the eyes of our friends and formidable to those who would otherwise become our enemies. . . .

. . . Passing by the mercenary armies, which have at one time or another subverted the liberties of almost all the countries they have been raised to defend, we might see, with admiration, the freedom and independence of Switzerland supported for centuries, in the midst of powerful and jealous neighbors, by means of a hardy and well-organized militia. I shall therefore proceed to point out some general outlines of their duty, and conclude this head with a few particular observations on the regulations which I conceive ought to be immediately adopted by the States at the instance and recommendation of Congress.

It may be laid down as a primary position and the basis of our system that every citizen who enjoys the protection of a free government, owes not only a proportion of his property, but even of his personal services to the defense of it, and consequently that the citizens of America (with a few legal and official exceptions) from eighteen to fifty years of age should be borne on the militia rolls, provided with uniform arms, and be so far accustomed to the use of them that the total strength of the country might be called forth at a short notice on any very interesting emergency, and for these purposes they ought to be duly organized into commands of the same formation. . . . They ought to be regularly mustered and trained, and to have their arms and accoutrements inspected at certain appointed times, not less than once or twice in the course of every year. . . . As there are a sufficient proportion of able-bodied young men between the age of eighteen and twenty-five, who from a natural fondness for military parade might easily be enlisted or drafted to form a corps in every State, capable of resisting any sudden impression which might be attempted by a foreign enemy, while the remainder of the national forces would have time to assemble and make preparations for the field. I would wish therefore that . . . a judicious system might be adopted for forming and placing the latter on the best possible establishment. And that while the men of this description shall be viewed as the van and flower of the American forces, ever ready for action and zealous to be employed whenever it may become necessary in the service of their country, they should meet with such exemptions, privileges, or distinctions as might tend to keep alive a true military pride, a nice sense of honor, and a patriotic regard for the public. Such sentiments, indeed, ought to be instilled into our youth with their earliest years, to be cherished and inculcated as frequently and forcibly as possible. . . .

It is likewise much to be wished that it might be made agreeable to officers who have served in the army, to accept commands in the militia; that they might be appointed to them so far as can be done without creating uneasiness and jealousy, and that the principle characters in the community would give a countenance to military improvements, by being present at public reviews and exhibitions, and by bringing into estimation amongst their fellow citizens, those who appear fond of cultivating military knowledge and who excel in the exercise of arms. By giving such a tone to our establishment and by making it universally reputable to bear arms and disgraceful to decline having a share in the performance of military duties; in fine, by keeping up in peace "a well regulated and disciplined militia," we shall take the fairest and best method to preserve, for a long time to come, the happiness, dignity, and independence of our country.

With regard to the third head in contemplation, the "establishment of arsenals of all kinds of military stores," I will only observe that having some time since seen a plan of the Secretary of War which went fully into the discussion of this arrangement, and appeared to be in general perfectly well founded, little more need be said on the subject, especially as I have been given to understand the plan has been lately considerably improved and laid before Congress for their approbation; and indeed there is only one or two points in which I could wish to suggest any alteration.

According to my recollection, five grand magazines are proposed by the Secretary of War, one of which to be fixed at West Point. Now, as West Point is considered, not only by ourselves, but by all who have the least knowledge of the country, as a post of the greatest importance, as it may in time of peace, from its situation on the water, be somewhat obnoxious to surprise or coup de main, and as it would doubtless be a first object with any nation which might commence a war against the United States to seize that post and occupy or destroy the stores, it appears to me that we ought particularly to guard against such an event, so far as may be practicable, and to remove some part of the allurements to enterprise, by establishing the grand arsenals in the interior part of the country, leaving only to West Point an adequate supply for its defense in almost any extremity.

Under the fourth general division of the subject, it was proposed to consider the establishment of military academies and manufactories, as the means of preserving that knowledge and being possessed of those warlike stores which are essential to the support of the sovereignty and independence of the United States.

That an institution calculated to keep alive and diffuse the knowledge of the military art would be highly expedient, and that some kinds of military manufactories and laboratories may and ought to be established, will not admit a doubt. . . . Until a more perfect system of education can be adopted, I would propose that provision should be made at some post or posts where the principal engineers and artillerists shall be stationed, for instructing a certain number of young gentlemen in the theory of the art of war, particularly in all those branches of service which belong to the artillery and engineering departments. Which, from the affinity they bear to each other, and the advantages which I think would result from the measure, I would have blended together, and as this species of knowledge will render them much more accomplished and capable of performing the duties of officers, even in the infantry or any other corps whatsoever, I conceive that appointments to vacancies in the established regiments ought to be made from the candidates who shall have completed their course of military studies and exercises. . . .

Of so great importance is it to preserve the knowledge which has been acquired through the various stages of a long and arduous service, that I cannot conclude without repeating the necessity of the proposed institution, unless we intend to let the science become extinct and to depend entirely upon the foreigners for their friendly aid if ever we should again be involved in hostility. For it must be understood that a corps of able engineers and expert artillerists cannot be raised in a day, nor made such by any exertions, in the same time, which it would take to form an excellent body of infantry from a well-regulated militia.

And as to manufactories and laboratories it is my opinion that if we should not be able to go largely into the business at present, we should nevertheless have a reference to such establishments hereafter, and in the meantime that we ought to have such works carried on, wherever our principal arsenals may be fixed. . . .

Thus have I given my sentiments without reserve on the four different heads into which the subject seemed naturally to divide itself, as amply as my numerous avocations and various duties would permit. Happy shall I be if anything I have suggested may be found of use in forming an establishment which will maintain the lasting peace, happiness, and independence of the United States.

Source: *The Writings of George Washington from the Original Manuscript Sources, 1745–1799*, ed. John C. Fitzpatrick (Washington, D.C.: Government Printing Office, 1938), 26: 374–91.

CHAPTER 8

On Electing a Roman Catholic Bishop, John Carroll, 1785

One of the most important principles that allowed the American colonies to form a united front against Great Britain was that of latitudinarianism, or tolerance for different beliefs and dogmas, among the Christian denominations. This was not limited merely to Protestant churches, and the religious strife so prevalent in Europe was avoided by cooler heads working together for common interests. Latitudinarianism had developed in the American colonies on an ad hoc basis, among people who faced not only hardships and hostile Indians but also unlimited resources and opportunities. Eventually a remarkable change in popular attitudes became evident, and differences in religion were no longer seen as sufficient cause to persecute or kill others. Although most of the states had enshrined Christianity or some Protestant denomination as supported state religions in their constitutions, in general latitudinarianism allowed for churches of various denominations to peaceably exist side by side in the same communities.

Nonetheless, there was a general Protestant fear of Roman Catholicism in America. This was due both to historical reasons embedded in the violence experienced in Europe at the hands of the Inquisition and to the belief that Catholics, because of their submission to Rome, were actually beholden to a foreign power. Many suspected Catholics were at odds with American principles of liberty, and even notables such as John Jay wanted clauses in state constitutions requiring individuals to forswear any allegiance to foreign powers in ecclesiastical as well as secular matters. At the time of the American Revolution there were only two dozen Catholic priests in the thirteen colonies and no Catholic churches. Even in Maryland, which had been founded by George Calvert as a haven for Catholics in the English colonies, Catholics never amounted to more than a small minority. The anti-Catholic hostility was particularly concentrated among Presbyterian Scots-Irish, who had a long history of fighting Catholics in Ireland, and Anglican British.

The Carrolls—John and his brother, Daniel, who signed the Constitution, and cousin Charles, who signed the Declaration of Independence—knew well the hostility of Protestants. They actively confronted these problems as patriots, and Catholics in Maryland readily accepted democratic principles into both their secular and religious lives. Some parishes were highly democratic and under laity control, and even the local election of priests by the laity occurred as Catholics strived mightily to fit in with their neighbors. In 1784 the pope appointed John Carroll as prefect-apostolic of Catholic missions in the United States.

When the Anglican church elected an American bishop in 1783, Carroll thought the timing was good for the acceptance of a Catholic bishop in America. However, he thought this bishop should be elected in America, and not be selected in Rome or through the influence of Catholic notables in other countries. Even more to the point in gaining acceptance and respect in America was his insistence on deleting a sentence in the bishop's oath: "I will to the utmost of my power seek out and oppose schismatics, heretics, and the enemies of our Sovereign Lord and his successors." Such an oath would effectively undo all the goodwill garnered among Protestants through the active participation of the Carrolls and other Catholics in the Revolutionary War.

Accordingly, Carroll wrote the following letter to Rome, asking that Americans be allowed to elect their own bishop. Pope Pius VI approved the American priests' election of Carroll as bishop in 1789 but made his local election a unique event. As Irish Catholics began coming to the United States during the nineteenth century, the pope appointed an Irish Dominican living in Rome as the bishop of New York. In the 1840s Irish Catholic priests flooded in with the Irish immigrants, and latitudinarianism was relegated to the dustbin. The anti-Catholicism that the Carrolls had so successfully mitigated broke out anew and became a potent political force in America until John F. Kennedy was elected president. Since then, and at least partially due to Kennedy's own espousal of latitudinarianism, successful Catholic politicians have become prevalent, particularly in the Democratic Party. By 2000, there were over sixty-five million Roman Catholics in America, and it had become the largest religious denomination in the country.

For many, the election of a Roman Catholic bishop meant they had truly become Americans. Quite contrary to the fears among non-Catholics that the event would mark more dependence on Rome, it allowed American Catholics to feel entirely equal in their religious expression.

Letter of February 27, 1785

THE MOST EMINENT CARDINAL MAY REST ASSURED THAT THE greatest evils would be borne by us rather than renounce the divine authority of the Holy See; that not only we priests who are here, but the Catholic people, seem so firm in the faith that they will never withdraw from obedience to the sovereign pontiff. The Catholic body, however, thinks that some favor should be granted to them by the Holy Father, necessary for their permanent enjoyment of the civil rights which they now enjoy, and to avert the dangers which they fear. From what I have said, and from the framework of public affairs here, Your Eminence must see how objectionable all foreign jurisdiction will be to them. The Catholics therefore desire that no pretext be given to the enemies of our religion to accuse us of depending unnecessarily on a foreign authority; and that some plan may be adopted by which hereafter an ecclesiastical superior may be appointed for this country in such a way as to retain absolutely the spiritual jurisdiction of the Holy See, and at the same time remove all ground of objecting to us, as though we held anything hostile to the national independence. Many of the leading Catholics thought of laying this before His Holiness in a general memorial, especially those who have been either in the Continental Congress or the legislature of Pennsylvania and Maryland, but I induced them to refrain from any such step at least for the present. The Holy Father will perhaps see more clearly what is to be done in this matter if he considers the sixth of the Articles of Perpetual Confederation between the states, which enacts that no one who holds any office under the United States shall be allowed to receive any gift, office, or title of any kind whatsoever from any king, prince, or foreign government, and though this prohibition seems to extend only to those who are appointed to offices in the republic, it will perhaps be wrested by our opponents to apply also to ecclesiastical offices.

We desire, therefore, Most Eminent Cardinal, to provide in every way that the faith in its integrity, due obedience toward the Apostolic See, and perfect union should flourish, and at the same time that whatever can with safety to religion be granted shall be conceded to American Catholics in ecclesiastical government; in this way we hope that the distrust of Protestants now full of suspicion will be diminished, and that thus our affairs can be solidly established.

You have indicated, Most Eminent Cardinal, that it was the intention and design of His Holiness to appoint a vicar apostolic for these states, invested with the Episcopal character and title. While this paternal solicitude for us has filled us with great joy, it also at first inspired some fear; for we knew that heretofore American Protestants never could be induced to allow even a bishop of their own sect, when the attempt was made during the subjection of these provinces to the king of England; hence a fear arose that we would not be permitted to have one. But some months since in a convention of Protestant ministers of the Anglican, or as it is here called, the Episcopal Church, they decreed that as by authority of law they enjoyed the full exercise of their religion, they therefore had the right of appointing for themselves such ministers of holy things as the system and discipline their sect required; namely bishops, priests, and deacons. This decision on their part was not censured by the Congress appointed to frame our laws. As the same liberty in the exercise of religion is granted to us, it necessarily follows that we enjoy the same right in regard to adopting laws for our government.

While the matter stands thus, the Holy Father will decide, and you, Most Eminent Cardinal, will consider whether the time is now opportune for appointing a bishop, what his qualifications should be, and how he should be nominated. On all these points, not as if seeking to obtain my own judgment, but to make this relation more ample, I shall note a few facts.

First, as regards the seasonableness of the step, it may be noted that there will be no excitement in the public mind if a bishop be appointed, as Protestants think of appointing one for themselves. Nay, they even hope to acquire some importance for their sect among the people from the Episcopal dignity. So, too, we trust that we shall not only acquire the same, but that great advantages will follow; inasmuch as this church will then be governed in that manner which Christ our Lord instituted. On the other hand, however, it occurs that as the Most Holy Father has already deigned to provide otherwise for conferring the sacrament of confirmation, there is no actual need for the appointment of a bishop until some candidates are found fitted to receive holy orders; this we hope will be the case in a few years, as you will understand, Most Eminent Cardinal, from a special relation which I purpose writing. When that time comes, we shall perhaps be better able to make a suitable provision for a bishop than from our slender resources we can now do.

In the next place, if it shall seem best to His Holiness to assign a bishop to this country, will it be best to appoint a vicar apostolic or an ordinary with a see of his own? Which will conduce more to the progress of Catholicity; which will contribute most to remove Protestant jealousy of foreign jurisdiction? I know with certainty that this fear will increase if they know that an ecclesiastical superior is so appointed as to be removable from office at the pleasure of the Sacred Congregation de Propaganda Fide, or any other tribunal out of the country, or that he has no power to admit any priest to exercise the sacred function, unless that congregation has approved and sent him to us.

As to the method of nominating a bishop, I will say no more at present than this, that we are imploring God in His wisdom and mercy to guide the judgment of the Holy See, that if it does not seem proper to allow the priests who have labored for so many years in this vineyard of the Lord to propose to the

Holy See the one whom they deem most fit, that some method will be adopted by which a bad feeling may not be excited among the people of this country, Catholic and Protestant.

Source: John Gilmary Shea, *Life and Times of the Most Rev. John Carroll* (New York: Edward O. Jenkins' Sons, 1888), 254–6.

CHAPTER 9

The Northwest Ordinance, 1787

Passed by Congress in 1787, An Ordinance for the Government of the Territory of the United States North West of the River Ohio, commonly called the Northwest Ordinance, was written primarily by Nathan Dane and Rufus King, both representatives to the Second Continental Congress from Massachusetts. In 1784 Virginia had ceded to Congress its claim to lands west of Pennsylvania and north of the Ohio River, and with settlers flooding into the territory, Congress was obligated to take action concerning its government. The result was the Northwest Ordinance, which organized the western lands along the lines laid down by Thomas Jefferson in his *Report of Government for Western Lands* in 1784. The struggling United States thereby announced to the world that it would expand across the Alleghenies, open up the land for settlement, and create new states. Not the least of the ordinance's important features was its provision for the advancement of education in the new lands, the exclusion of slavery north of the Ohio River, and its inclusion of civil liberties. Without the Northwest Ordinance, slavery certainly would have entered Indiana, Illinois, and perhaps before long other northern-tier midwestern states, forever shifting the sectional balance in favor of the South and slavery. Moreover, the experience of American colonists in dealing with England led them to appreciate the necessity for the full political equality of those who moved to new areas.

The ordinance applied to the area of Ohio, Indiana, Illinois, Michigan, and Wisconsin and set the pattern for all other expansion through the creation of territories that could become states after a required population level was reached. Ohio was the first such territory to become a state, in 1803. Although not in the Northwest Territory, Kentucky was separated from Virginia in 1782, with Virginia's consent, and became a state following the principles in the ordinance. The effect of the ordinance was to end squabbling among states over territory and reduce them to permanent parts of the whole even before the Constitution was passed. A de facto recognition of the need for a federal government was present, even if it didn't exist at the time.

An Ordinance for the Government of the Territory of the United States Northwest of the River Ohio

BE IT ORDAINED BY THE UNITED STATES IN CONGRESS ASSEMbled, That the said territory, for the purposes of temporary government, be one district, subject, however, to be divided into two districts, as future circumstances may, in the opinion of Congress, make it expedient. Be it ordained by the authority aforesaid, That the estates, both of resident and nonresident proprietors in the said territory, dying intestate, shall descend to, and be distributed among, their children, and the descendants of a deceased child, in equal parts; the descendants of a deceased child or grandchild to take the share of their deceased parent in equal parts among them: And where there shall be no children or descendants, then in equal parts to the next of kin in equal degree; and among collaterals, the children of a deceased brother or sister of the intestate shall have, in equal parts among them, their deceased parents' share; and there shall in no case be a distinction between kindred of the whole and half blood; saving, in all cases, to the widow of the intestate her third part of the real estate for life, and one-third part of the personal estate; and this law relative to descents and dower, shall remain in full force until altered by the legislature of the district. And until the governor and judges shall adopt laws as hereinafter mentioned, estates in the said territory may be devised or bequeathed by wills in writing, signed and sealed by him or her in whom the estate may be (being of full age), and attested by three witnesses; and real estates may be conveyed by lease and release, or bargain and sale, signed, sealed, and delivered by the person being of full age, in whom the estate may be, and attested by two witnesses, provided such wills be duly proved, and such conveyances be acknowledged, or the execution thereof duly proved, and be recorded within one year after proper magistrates, courts, and registers shall be appointed for that purpose; and personal property may be transferred by delivery; saving, however to the French and Canadian inhabitants, and other settlers of the Kaskaskies, St. Vincent's, and the neighboring villages who have heretofore professed themselves citizens of Virginia, their laws and customs now in force among them, relative to the descent and conveyance, of property.

Be it ordained by the authority aforesaid, That there shall be appointed from time to time by Congress, a governor, whose commission shall continue in force for the term of three years, unless sooner revoked by Congress; he shall reside in the district, and have a freehold estate therein in one thousand acres of land, while in the exercise of his office.

There shall be appointed from time to time by Congress, a secretary, whose commission shall continue in force for four years unless sooner revoked; he shall reside in the district, and have a freehold estate therein in five hundred acres of land, while in the exercise of his office. It shall be his duty to keep and preserve the acts and laws passed by the legislature, and the public records of the district, and the proceedings of the governor in his executive department, and transmit authentic copies of such acts and proceedings, every six months, to the secretary of Congress: There shall also be appointed a court to consist of three judges, any two of whom to form a court, who shall have a common-law jurisdiction, and reside in the district, and have each therein a freehold estate in five hundred acres of land while in the exercise of their offices; and their commissions shall continue in force during good behavior.

The governor and judges, or a majority of them, shall adopt and publish in the district such laws of the original States, criminal and civil, as may be necessary and best suited to the circumstances of the district, and report them to Congress from time to time: which laws shall be in force in the district until the organization of the general assembly therein, unless disapproved of by Congress; but afterwards the legislature shall have authority to alter them as they shall think fit.

The governor, for the time being, shall be commander in chief of the militia, appoint and commission all officers in the same below the rank of general officers; all general officers shall be appointed and commissioned by Congress.

Previous to the organization of the general assembly, the governor shall appoint such magistrates and other civil officers in each county or township, as he shall find necessary for the preservation of the peace and good order in the same: After the general assembly shall be organized, the powers and duties of the magistrates and other civil officers shall be regulated and defined by the said assembly; but all magistrates and other civil officers not herein otherwise directed, shall during the continuance of this temporary government, be appointed by the governor.

For the prevention of crimes and injuries, the laws to be adopted or made shall have force in all parts of the district, and for the execution of process, criminal and civil, the governor shall make proper divisions thereof; and he shall proceed from time to time as circumstances may require, to lay out the parts of the district in which the Indian titles shall have been extinguished, into counties and townships, subject, however, to such alterations as may thereafter be made by the legislature.

So soon as there shall be five thousand free male inhabitants of full age in the district, upon giving proof thereof to the governor, they shall receive authority, with time and place, to elect a representative from their counties or townships to represent them in the general assembly: Provided, That, for every five hundred free male inhabitants, there shall be one representative, and so on progressively with the number of free male inhabitants shall the right of representation increase, until the number of representatives shall amount to twenty-five; after which, the number and proportion of representatives shall be regulated by the legislature: Provided, That no person be eligible or qualified to act as a representative unless he shall have been a citizen of one of the United States three years, and be a resident in the district, or unless he shall have resided in the district three years; and, in either case, shall likewise hold in his own right, in fee simple, two hundred acres of land within the same; Provided, also, That a freehold in fifty acres of land in the district, having been a citizen of one of the States, and being resident in the district, or the like freehold and two years residence in the district, shall be necessary to qualify a man as an elector of a representative.

The representatives thus elected, shall serve for the term of two years; and, in case of the death of a representative, or removal from office, the governor shall issue a writ to the county or township for which he was a member, to elect another in his stead, to serve for the residue of the term.

The general assembly or legislature shall consist of the governor, legislative council, and a house of representatives. The legislative council shall consist of five members, to continue in office five years, unless sooner removed by Congress; any three of whom to be a quorum: and the members of the council shall be nominated and appointed in the following manner, to wit: As soon as representatives shall be elected, the governor shall appoint a time and place for them to meet together; and, when met, they shall nominate ten persons, residents in the district, and each possessed of a freehold in five hundred acres of land, and return their names to Congress; five of whom Congress shall appoint and commission to serve as aforesaid; and, whenever a vacancy shall happen in the council, by death or removal from office, the house of representatives shall nominate two persons, qualified as aforesaid, for each vacancy, and return their names to Congress; one of whom Congress shall appoint and commission for the residue of the term. And every five years, four months at least before the expiration of the time of service of the members of council, the said house shall nominate ten persons, qualified as aforesaid, and return their names to Congress; five of whom Congress shall appoint and commission to serve as members of the council five years, unless sooner removed. And the governor, legislative council, and house of representatives, shall have authority to make laws in all cases, for the good government of the district, not repugnant to the principles and articles in this ordinance established and declared. And all bills, having passed by a majority in the house, and by a majority in the council, shall be referred to the governor for his assent; but no bill, or legislative act whatever, shall be of any force without his assent. The governor shall have power to convene, prorogue, and dissolve the general assembly, when, in his opinion, it shall be expedient.

The governor, judges, legislative council, secretary, and such other officers as Congress shall appoint in the district, shall take an oath or affirmation of fidelity and of office; the governor before the president of congress, and all other officers before the governor. As soon as a legislature shall be formed in the district, the council and house assembled in one room, shall have authority, by joint ballot, to elect a delegate to Congress, who shall have a seat in Congress, with a right of debating but not voting during this temporary government.

And, for extending the fundamental principles of civil and religious liberty, which form the basis whereon these republics, their laws, and constitutions are erected; to fix and establish those principles as the basis of all laws, constitutions, and governments, which forever hereafter shall be formed in the said territory: to provide also for the establishment of States, and permanent government therein, and for their admission to a share in the federal councils on an equal footing with the original States, at as early periods as may be consistent with the general interest: It is hereby ordained and declared by the authority aforesaid, That the following articles shall be considered as articles of compact between the original States and the people and States in the said territory and forever remain unalterable, unless by common consent, to wit:

Art. 1. No person, demeaning himself in a peaceable and orderly manner, shall ever be molested on account of his mode of worship or religious sentiments, in the said territory.

Art. 2. The inhabitants of the said territory shall always be entitled to the benefits of the writ of habeas corpus, and of the trial by jury; of a proportionate representation of the people in the legislature; and of judicial proceedings according to the course of the common law. All persons shall be bailable, unless for capital offenses, where the proof shall be evident or the presumption great. All fines shall be moderate; and no cruel or unusual punishments shall be inflicted. No man shall be deprived of his liberty or property, but by the judgment of his peers or the law of the land; and, should the public exigencies make it necessary, for the common preservation, to take any person's property, or to demand his particular services, full compensation shall be made for the same. And, in the just preservation of rights and property, it is understood and declared, that no law ought ever to be made, or have force in the said territory, that shall, in any manner whatever, interfere with or affect private contracts or engagements, bona fide, and without fraud, previously formed.

Art. 3. Religion, morality, and knowledge, being necessary to good government and the happiness of mankind, schools and the means of education shall forever be encouraged. The utmost good faith shall always be observed towards the Indians; their lands and property shall never be taken from them without their consent; and, in their property, rights, and liberty, they shall never be invaded or disturbed, unless in just and lawful wars authorized by Congress; but laws founded in justice and humanity shall from time to time be made for preventing wrongs being done to them, and for preserving peace and friendship with them.

Art. 4. The said territory, and the States which may be formed therein, shall forever remain a part of this confederacy of the United States of America, subject to the Articles of Confederation, and to such alterations therein as shall be constitutionally made; and to all the acts and ordinances of the United States in Congress assembled, conformable thereto. The inhabitants and settlers in the said territory shall be subject to pay a part of the federal debts contracted or to be contracted, and a proportional part of the expenses of government, to be apportioned on them by Congress according to the same common rule and measure by which apportionments thereof shall be made on the other States; and the taxes for paying their proportion shall be laid and levied by the authority and direction of the legislatures of the district or districts, or new States, as in the original States, within the time agreed upon by the United States in Congress assembled. The legislatures of those districts or new States, shall never interfere with the primary disposal of the soil by the United States in Congress assembled, nor with any regulations Congress may find necessary for securing the title in such soil to the bona fide purchasers. No tax shall be imposed on lands the property of the United States; and in no case shall nonresident proprietors be taxed higher than residents. The navigable waters leading into the Mississippi and St. Lawrence, and the carrying places between the same, shall be common highways and forever free, as well to the inhabitants of the said territory as to the citizens of the United States, and those of any other States that may be admitted into the confederacy, without any tax, impost, or duty therefor.

Art. 5. There shall be formed in the said territory, not less than three nor more than five States; and the boundaries of the States, as soon as Virginia shall alter her act of cession, and consent to the same, shall become fixed and established as follows, to wit: The western State in the said territory, shall be bounded by the Mississippi, the Ohio, and Wabash Rivers; a direct line drawn from the Wabash and Post Vincents, due north, to the territorial line between the United States and Canada; and, by the said territorial line, to the Lake of the Woods and Mississippi. The middle State shall be bounded by the said direct line, the Wabash from Post Vincents to the Ohio, by the Ohio, by a direct line, drawn due north from the mouth of the Great Miami, to the said territorial line, and by the said territorial line. The eastern State shall be bounded by the last mentioned direct line, the Ohio, Pennsylvania, and the said territorial line: Provided, however, and it is further understood and declared, that the boundaries of these three States shall be subject so far to be altered, that, if Congress shall hereafter find it expedient, they shall have authority to form one or two States in that part of the said territory which lies north of an east and west line drawn through the southerly bend or extreme of Lake Michigan. And, whenever any of the said States shall have sixty thousand free inhabitants therein, such State shall be admitted, by its delegates, into the Congress of the United States, on an equal footing with the original States in all respects whatever, and shall be at liberty to form a permanent constitution and State government: Provided, the constitution and government so to be formed shall be republican, and in conformity to the principles contained in these articles; and, so far as it can be consistent with the general interest of the confederacy, such admission shall be allowed at an earlier period, and when there may be a less number of free inhabitants in the State than sixty thousand.

Art. 6. There shall be neither slavery nor involuntary servitude in the said territory, otherwise than in the punishment of crimes whereof the party shall have been duly convicted: Provided, always, That any person escaping into the same, from whom labor or service is lawfully claimed in any one of the original States, such fugitive may be lawfully reclaimed and conveyed to the person claiming his or her labor or service as aforesaid.

Be it ordained by the authority aforesaid, That the resolutions of the 23rd of April, 1784, relative to the subject of this ordinance, be, and the same are hereby repealed and declared null and void.

Source: Archiving Early America, "The Northwest Ordinance, An Ordinance for the Government of the Territory of the United States, Northwest of the River Ohio," supplement to *Columbian Magazine* 1 (1787). Retrieved May 21, 2010, from http://www.earlyamerica.com/earlyamerica/milestones/ordinance/text.html.

CHAPTER 10

The Constitution of the United States, 1787

Prior to the Constitutional Convention, only twelve American states and Switzerland (temporarily) had produced constitutions. As the world's first constitution for a major political entity, the U.S. Constitution set a standard by which
all subsequent constitutions could be measured. That it came to be written in a
nascent state, having won its independence from the world's foremost military
power only a few years earlier, is remarkable and by itself makes the case for
American exceptionalism. Constructed in a convention supposedly convened to
modify the Articles of Confederation, the document came into being as the delegates elected to start from scratch and create a federal form of government with
appropriate powers and form.

The Constitution was far from perfect and embodied ideas that were radical,
untested, and possibly unworkable. A critical element was omitted, a bill of
rights, but this defect was remedied three years later. Various structural defects
were addressed by later amendments, but, discounting the Bill of Rights, the
Constitution has undergone amazingly few changes. That is not to say that
the Constitution has not changed over time—it has, both through constant
extensions of legislative, executive, and judicial powers and judicial interpretations. The "general Welfare of the United States" referred to in the welfare clause
in the preamble and article 1, section 8, has been interpreted to mean the general welfare of the *people* of the United States. The commerce clause in article 1,
section 8, has been interpreted to literally include all commerce in the United
States. The First and Second Amendments have been subjected to many restrictions and reinterpretations, and the Fourteenth Amendment invalidated much of
the Tenth Amendment with respect to state sovereignty and the reserved rights
of the people. The right of eminent domain was not, it has been decided, specifically prohibited by the Fifth Amendment, and the due process clauses in the
Fifth and Fourteenth Amendments have been expanded and subjected to room-
fuls of regulations. Reading the full text as it was originally written allows us to

examine such changes and interpretations and forces us to question the motives of those—namely, power-hungry presidents, legislators, and justices—who would seek to change it. Article 6, for example, allows the president to establish treaties that supersede state laws, and the Supreme Court has consistently held that treaties called "agreements" and "executive agreements" do not have to be ratified by the Senate and can be implemented by majority votes in Congress or by executive orders. In many respects the power of the Supreme Court to alter interpretations of the Constitution to meet contemporary attitudes has nullified the original intent of the greatest liberating document in world history and stripped it of the ability to ensure its own survival.

A major objection to ratifying the Constitution raised in the state conventions was its lack of a bill of rights. Accordingly, the first ten amendments, comprising the Bill of Rights, were ratified as a group in 1791. The Sixteenth Amendment is controversial to the present day and is often assailed as not being fully ratified. The reader interested in the arguments over its questionable ratification is urged to avail himself of studies concerning the issue.

Constitution of the United States of America

WE THE PEOPLE OF THE UNITED STATES, IN ORDER TO FORM a more perfect Union, establish Justice, insure domestic Tranquility, provide for the common defense, promote the general Welfare, and secure the Blessings of Liberty to ourselves and our Posterity, do ordain and establish this Constitution for the United States of America.

ARTICLE I [LEGISLATIVE BRANCH]

Section 1 [Congress]

All legislative Powers herein granted shall be vested in a Congress of the United States, which shall consist of a Senate and House of Representatives.

Section 2 [House of Representatives]

The House of Representatives shall be composed of Members chosen every second Year by the People of the several States, and the Electors in each State shall have the Qualifications requisite for Electors of the most numerous Branch of the State Legislature.

No Person shall be a Representative who shall not have attained to the Age of twenty-five Years, and been seven Years a Citizen of the United States, and who shall not, when elected, be an Inhabitant of that State in which he shall be chosen.

Representatives and direct Taxes shall be apportioned among the several

States which may be included within this Union, according to their respective Numbers, which shall be determined by adding to the whole Number of free Persons, including those bound to Service for a Term of Years, and excluding Indians not taxed, three-fifths of all other Persons. The actual Enumeration shall be made within three Years after the first Meeting of the Congress of the United States, and within every subsequent Term of ten Years, in such Manner as they shall by Law direct. The Number of Representatives shall not exceed one for every thirty Thousand, but each State shall have at Least one Representative; and until such enumeration shall be made, the State of New Hampshire shall be entitled to choose three, Massachusetts eight, Rhode Island and Providence Plantations one, Connecticut five, New York six, New Jersey four, Pennsylvania eight, Delaware one, Maryland six, Virginia ten, North Carolina five, South Carolina five, and Georgia three.

When vacancies happen in the Representation from any State, the Executive Authority thereof shall issue Writs of Election to fill such Vacancies.

The House of Representatives shall choose their Speaker and other Officers; and shall have the sole Power of Impeachment.

Section 3 [Senate]

The Senate of the United States shall be composed of two Senators from each State, chosen by the Legislature thereof, for six Years; and each Senator shall have one Vote.

Immediately after they shall be assembled in Consequence of the first Election, they shall be divided as equally as may be into three Classes. The Seats of the Senators of the first Class shall be vacated at the Expiration of the second Year, of the second Class at the Expiration of the fourth Year, and of the third Class at the Expiration of the sixth Year, so that one-third may be chosen every second Year; and if Vacancies happen by Resignation, or otherwise, during the Recess of the Legislature of any State, the Executive thereof may make temporary Appointments until the next Meeting of the Legislature, which shall then fill such Vacancies.

No Person shall be a Senator who shall not have attained to the Age of thirty Years, and been nine Years a Citizen of the United States, and who shall not, when elected, be an Inhabitant of that State for which he shall be chosen.

The Vice President of the United States shall be President of the Senate, but shall have no Vote, unless they be equally divided.

The Senate shall choose their other Officers, and also a President pro tempore, in the Absence of the Vice President, or when he shall exercise the Office of President of the United States.

The Senate shall have the sole Power to try all Impeachments. When sitting for that Purpose, they shall be on Oath or Affirmation. When the President of the United States is tried, the Chief Justice shall preside: And no

Person shall be convicted without the Concurrence of two-thirds of the Members present.

Judgment in Cases of Impeachment shall not extend further than to removal from Office, and disqualification to hold and enjoy any Office of honor, Trust, or Profit under the United States: but the Party convicted shall nevertheless be liable and subject to Indictment, Trial, Judgment, and Punishment, according to Law.

Section 4 [Elections and Meetings]

The Times, Places, and Manner of holding Elections for Senators and Representatives, shall be prescribed in each State by the Legislature thereof; but the Congress may at any time by Law make or alter such Regulations, except as to the Places of choosing Senators.

The Congress shall assemble at least once in every Year, and such Meeting shall be on the first Monday in December, unless they shall by Law appoint a different Day.

Section 5 [Membership, Rules, Journals, Adjournment]

Each House shall be the Judge of the Elections, Returns, and Qualifications of its own Members, and a Majority of each shall constitute a Quorum to do Business; but a smaller Number may adjourn from day to day, and may be authorized to compel the Attendance of absent Members, in such Manner, and under such Penalties as each House may provide.

Each House may determine the Rules of its Proceedings, punish its Members for disorderly Behavior, and, with the Concurrence of two-thirds, expel a Member.

Each House shall keep a Journal of its Proceedings, and from time to time publish the same, excepting such Parts as may in their Judgment require Secrecy; and the Yeas and Nays of the Members of either House on any question shall, at the Desire of one-fifth of those Present, be entered on the Journal.

Neither House, during the Session of Congress, shall, without the Consent of the other, adjourn for more than three days, nor to any other Place than that in which the two Houses shall be sitting.

Section 6 [Compensation]

The Senators and Representatives shall receive a Compensation for their Services, to be ascertained by Law, and paid out of the Treasury of the United States. They shall in all Cases, except Treason, Felony, and Breach of the Peace, be privileged from Arrest during their Attendance at the Session of their respective Houses, and in going to and returning from the same; and for any Speech or Debate in either House, they shall not be questioned in any other Place.

No Senator or Representative shall, during the Time for which he was elected, be appointed to any civil Office under the Authority of the United States, which shall have been created, or the Emoluments whereof shall have been increased during such time; and no Person holding any Office under the United States, shall be a Member of either House during his Continuance in Office.

Section 7 [Revenue Bills, Legislative Process, Presidential Veto]

All Bills for raising Revenue shall originate in the House of Representatives; but the Senate may propose or concur with Amendments as on other Bills.

Every Bill which shall have passed the House of Representatives and the Senate, shall, before it become a Law, be presented to the President of the United States; If he approve he shall sign it, but if not he shall return it, with his Objections to that House in which it shall have originated, who shall enter the Objections at large on their Journal, and proceed to reconsider it. If after such Reconsideration two-thirds of that House shall agree to pass the Bill, it shall be sent, together with the Objections, to the other House, by which it shall likewise be reconsidered, and if approved by two-thirds of that House, it shall become a Law. But in all such Cases the Votes of both Houses shall be determined by Yeas and Nays, and the Names of the Persons voting for and against the Bill shall be entered on the Journal of each House respectively. If any Bill shall not be returned by the President within ten Days (Sundays excepted) after it shall have been presented to him, the Same shall be a Law, in like Manner as if he had signed it, unless the Congress by their Adjournment prevent its Return, in which Case it shall not be a Law.

Every Order, Resolution, or Vote to which the Concurrence of the Senate and House of Representatives may be necessary (except on a question of Adjournment) shall be presented to the President of the United States; and before the Same shall take Effect, shall be approved by him, or being disapproved by him, shall be repassed by two-thirds of the Senate and House of Representatives, according to the Rules and Limitations prescribed in the Case of a Bill.

Section 8 [Powers]

The Congress shall have Power To lay and collect Taxes, Duties, Imposts, and Excises, to pay the Debts and provide for the common Defense and general Welfare of the United States; but all Duties, Imposts, and Excises shall be uniform throughout the United States;

To borrow Money on the credit of the United States;

To regulate Commerce with foreign Nations, and among the several States, and with the Indian Tribes;

To establish a uniform Rule of Naturalization, and uniform Laws on the subject of Bankruptcies throughout the United States;

To coin Money, regulate the Value thereof, and of foreign Coin, and fix the Standard of Weights and Measures;

To provide for the Punishment of counterfeiting the Securities and current Coin of the United States;

To establish Post Offices and post Roads;

To promote the Progress of Science and useful Arts, by securing for limited Times to Authors and Inventors the exclusive Right to their respective Writings and Discoveries;

To constitute Tribunals inferior to the Supreme Court;

To define and punish Piracies and Felonies committed on the high Seas, and Offenses against the Law of Nations;

To declare War, grant Letters of Marque and Reprisal, and make Rules concerning Captures on Land and Water;

To raise and support Armies, but no Appropriation of Money to that Use shall be for a longer Term than two Years;

To provide and maintain a Navy;

To make Rules for the Government and Regulation of the land and naval Forces;

To provide for calling forth the Militia to execute the Laws of the Union, suppress Insurrections and repel Invasions;

To provide for organizing, arming, and disciplining the Militia, and for governing such Part of them as may be employed in the Service of the United States, reserving to the States respectively, the Appointment of the Officers, and the Authority of training the Militia according to the discipline prescribed by Congress;

To exercise exclusive Legislation in all Cases whatsoever, over such District (not exceeding ten Miles square) as may, by Cession of particular States, and the Acceptance of Congress, become the Seat of the Government of the United States, and to exercise like Authority over all Places purchased by the Consent of the Legislature of the State in which the Same shall be, for the Erection of Forts, Magazines, Arsenals, dock-Yards, and other needful Buildings;—And

To make all Laws which shall be necessary and proper for carrying into Execution the foregoing Powers, and all other Powers vested by this Constitution in the Government of the United States, or in any Department or Officer thereof.

Section 9 [Limitations]

The Migration or Importation of such Persons as any of the States now existing shall think proper to admit, shall not be prohibited by the Congress prior to the Year one thousand eight hundred and eight, but a Tax or Duty may be imposed on such Importation, not exceeding ten dollars for each Person.

The Privilege of the Writ of Habeas Corpus shall not be suspended, unless when in Cases of Rebellion or Invasion the public Safety may require it.

No Bill of Attainder or ex post facto Law shall be passed.

No Capitation, or other direct, Tax shall be laid, unless in Proportion to the Census or Enumeration herein before directed to be taken.

No Tax or Duty shall be laid on Articles exported from any State.

No Preference shall be given by any Regulation of Commerce or Revenue to the Ports of one State over those of another; nor shall Vessels bound to, or from, one State, be obliged to enter, clear, or pay Duties in another.

No Money shall be drawn from the Treasury, but in Consequence of Appropriations made by Law; and a regular Statement and Account of the Receipts and Expenditures of all public Money shall be published from time to time.

No Title of Nobility shall be granted by the United States: And no Person holding any Office of Profit or Trust under them, shall, without the Consent of the Congress, accept of any present, Emolument, Office, or Title, of any kind whatever, from any King, Prince, or foreign State.

Section 10 [States' Powers Prohibited]

No State shall enter into any Treaty, Alliance, or Confederation; grant Letters of Marque and Reprisal; coin Money; emit Bills of Credit; make any Thing but gold and silver Coin a Tender in Payment of Debts; pass any Bill of Attainder, ex post facto Law, or Law impairing the Obligation of Contracts, or grant any Title of Nobility.

No State shall, without the Consent of the Congress, lay any Imposts or Duties on Imports or Exports, except what may be absolutely necessary for executing its inspection Laws; and the net Produce of all Duties and Imposts, laid by any State on Imports or Exports, shall be for the Use of the Treasury of the United States; and all such Laws shall be subject to the Revision and Control of the Congress.

No State shall, without the Consent of Congress, lay any Duty of Tonnage, keep Troops, or Ships of War in time of Peace, enter into any Agreement or Compact with another State, or with a foreign Power, or engage in War, unless actually invaded, or in such imminent Danger as will not admit of delay.

ARTICLE II [EXECUTIVE BRANCH]

Section 1 [President]

The executive Power shall be vested in a President of the United States of America. He shall hold his Office during the Term of four Years, and, together with the Vice President, chosen for the same Term, be elected, as follows:

Each State shall appoint, in such Manner as the Legislature thereof may direct, a Number of Electors, equal to the whole Number of Senators and Representatives to which the State may be entitled in the Congress: but no Senator or Representative, or Person holding an Office of Trust or Profit under the United States, shall be appointed an Elector.

The Electors shall meet in their respective States, and vote by Ballot for two Persons, of whom one at least shall not be an Inhabitant of the same State with themselves. And they shall make a List of all the Persons voted for, and of the Number of Votes for each; which List they shall sign and certify, and transmit sealed to the Seat of the Government of the United States, directed to the President of the Senate. The President of the Senate shall, in the Presence of the Senate and House of Representatives, open all the Certificates, and the Votes shall then be counted. The Person having the greatest Number of Votes shall be the President, if such Number be a Majority of the whole Number of Electors appointed; and if there be more than one who have such Majority, and have an equal Number of Votes, then the House of Representatives shall immediately choose by Ballot one of them for President; and if no Person have a Majority, then from the five highest on the List the said House shall in like Manner choose the President. But in choosing the President, the Votes shall be taken by States, the Representation from each State having one Vote; A Quorum for this Purpose shall consist of a Member or Members from two-thirds of the States, and a Majority of all the States shall be necessary to a Choice. In every Case, after the Choice of the President, the Person having the greatest Number of Votes of the Electors shall be the Vice President. But if there should remain two or more who have equal Votes, the Senate shall choose from them by Ballot the Vice President.

The Congress may determine the Time of choosing the Electors, and the Day on which they shall give their Votes; which Day shall be the same throughout the United States.

No Person except a natural born Citizen, or a Citizen of the United States, at the time of the Adoption of this Constitution, shall be eligible to the Office of President; neither shall any Person be eligible to that Office who shall not have attained to the Age of thirty-five Years, and been fourteen Years a Resident within the United States.

In Case of the Removal of the President from Office, or of his Death, Resignation, or Inability to discharge the Powers and Duties of the said Office, the Same shall devolve on the Vice President, and the Congress may by Law provide for the Case of Removal, Death, Resignation, or Inability, both of the President and Vice President, declaring what Officer shall then act as President, and such Officer shall act accordingly, until the Disability be removed, or a President shall be elected.

The President shall, at stated Times, receive for his Services, a Compensation, which shall neither be increased nor diminished during the Period for which he shall have been elected, and he shall not receive within that Period any other Emolument from the United States, or any of them.

Before he enter on the Execution of his Office, he shall take the following Oath or Affirmation: "I do solemnly swear (or affirm) that I will faithfully execute the Office of President of the United States, and will to the best of my Ability, preserve, protect, and defend the Constitution of the United States."

Section 2 [Presidential Powers]

The President shall be Commander in Chief of the Army and Navy of the United States, and of the Militia of the several States, when called into the actual Service of the United States; he may require the Opinion, in writing, of the principal Officer in each of the executive Departments, upon any Subject relating to the Duties of their respective Offices, and he shall have Power to grant Reprieves and Pardons for Offenses against the United States, except in Cases of Impeachment.

He shall have Power, by and with the Advice and Consent of the Senate, to make Treaties, provided two-thirds of the Senators present concur; and he shall nominate, and by and with the Advice and Consent of the Senate, shall appoint Ambassadors, other public Ministers and Consuls, Judges of the supreme Court, and all other Officers of the United States, whose Appointments are not herein otherwise provided for, and which shall be established by Law: but the Congress may by Law vest the Appointment of such inferior Officers, as they think proper, in the President alone, in the Courts of Law, or in the Heads of Departments. The President shall have Power to fill up all Vacancies that may happen during the Recess of the Senate, by granting Commissions which shall expire at the End of their next Session.

Section 3 [State of the Union, Convening Congress]

He shall from time to time give to the Congress Information of the State of the Union, and recommend to their Consideration such Measures as he shall judge necessary and expedient; he may, on extraordinary Occasions, convene both Houses, or either of them, and in Case of Disagreement between them, with Respect to the Time of Adjournment, he may adjourn them to such Time as he shall think proper; he shall receive Ambassadors and other public Ministers; he shall take Care that the Laws be faithfully executed, and shall Commission all the Officers of the United States.

Section 4 [Removal]

The President, Vice President, and all civil Officers of the United States, shall be removed from Office on Impeachment for, and Conviction of, Treason, Bribery, or other high Crimes and Misdemeanors.

ARTICLE III [JUDICIAL BRANCH]

Section 1 [Judicial Powers]

The judicial Power of the United States shall be vested in one supreme Court, and in such inferior Courts as the Congress may from time to time ordain and establish. The Judges, both of the supreme and inferior Courts, shall hold their Offices during good Behavior, and shall, at stated Times, receive for their Services a Compensation, which shall not be diminished during their Continuance in Office.

Section 2 [Jurisdiction, Trial by Jury]

The judicial Power shall extend to all Cases, in Law and Equity, arising under this Constitution, the Laws of the United States, and Treaties made, or which shall be made, under their Authority; to all Cases affecting Ambassadors, other public Ministers and Consuls; to all Cases of admiralty and maritime Jurisdiction; to Controversies to which the United States shall be a Party; to Controversies between two or more States; between a State and Citizens of another State; between Citizens of different States; between Citizens of the same State claiming Lands under Grants of different States, and between a State, or the Citizens thereof, and foreign States, Citizens, or Subjects.

In all Cases affecting Ambassadors, other public Ministers and Consuls, and those in which a State shall be Party, the supreme Court shall have original Jurisdiction. In all the other Cases before mentioned, the supreme Court shall have appellate Jurisdiction, both as to Law and Fact, with such Exceptions, and under such Regulations as the Congress shall make.

The Trial of all Crimes, except in Cases of Impeachment, shall be by Jury; and such Trial shall be held in the State where the said Crimes shall have been committed; but when not committed within any State, the Trial shall be at such Place or Places as the Congress may by Law have directed.

Section 3 [Treason]

Treason against the United States shall consist only in levying War against them, or in adhering to their Enemies, giving them Aid and Comfort. No Person shall be convicted of Treason unless on the Testimony of two Witnesses to the same overt Act, or on Confession in open Court.

The Congress shall have Power to declare the Punishment of Treason, but no Attainder of Treason shall work Corruption of Blood, or Forfeiture except during the Life of the Person attainted.

ARTICLE IV [STATES]

Section 1 [Each State to Honor All Others]

Full Faith and Credit shall be given in each State to the public Acts, Records, and judicial Proceedings of every other State. And the Congress may by general Laws prescribe the Manner in which such Acts, Records, and Proceedings shall be proved, and the Effect thereof.

Section 2 [Citizenship, Extradition]

The Citizens of each State shall be entitled to all Privileges and Immunities of Citizens in the several States.

A Person charged in any State with Treason, Felony, or other Crime, who shall flee from Justice, and be found in another State, shall on Demand of the executive Authority of the State from which he fled, be delivered up, to be removed to the State having Jurisdiction of the Crime.

No Person held to Service or Labor in one State, under the Laws thereof, escaping into another, shall, in Consequence of any Law or Regulation therein, be discharged from such Service or Labor, but shall be delivered up on Claim of the Party to whom such Service or Labor may be due.

Section 3 [Additional States]

New States may be admitted by the Congress into this Union; but no new State shall be formed or erected within the Jurisdiction of any other State; nor any State be formed by the Junction of two or more States, or Parts of States, without the Consent of the Legislatures of the States concerned as well as of the Congress.

The Congress shall have Power to dispose of and make all needful Rules and Regulations respecting the Territory or other Property belonging to the United States; and nothing in this Constitution shall be so construed as to Prejudice any Claims of the United States, or of any particular State.

Section 4 [Republican Government]

The United States shall guarantee to every State in this Union a Republican Form of Government, and shall protect each of them against Invasion; and on Application of the Legislature, or of the Executive (when the Legislature cannot be convened), against domestic Violence.

ARTICLE V [AMENDMENTS]

The Congress, whenever two-thirds of both Houses shall deem it necessary, shall propose Amendments to this Constitution, or, on the Application of the Legislatures of two-thirds of the several States, shall call a Convention for proposing Amendments, which, in either Case, shall be valid to all Intents and Purposes, as Part of this Constitution, when ratified by the Legislatures of three-fourths of the several States, or by Conventions in three-fourths thereof, as the one or the other Mode of Ratification may be proposed by the Congress; Provided that no Amendment which may be made prior to the Year one thousand eight hundred and eight shall in any Manner affect the first and fourth Clauses in the Ninth Section of the first Article; and that no State, without its Consent, shall be deprived of its equal Suffrage in the Senate.

ARTICLE VI [DEBTS, SUPREMACY, OATHS]

All Debts contracted and Engagements entered into, before the Adoption of this Constitution, shall be as valid against the United States under this Constitution, as under the Confederation.

This Constitution, and the Laws of the United States which shall be made in Pursuance thereof; and all Treaties made, or which shall be made, under the Authority of the United States, shall be the supreme Law of the Land; and the Judges in every State shall be bound thereby, any Thing in the Constitution or Laws of any State to the Contrary notwithstanding.

The Senators and Representatives before mentioned, and the Members of the several State Legislatures, and all executive and judicial Officers, both of the United States and of the several States, shall be bound by Oath or Affirmation, to support this Constitution; but no religious Test shall ever be required as a Qualification to any Office or public Trust under the United States.

ARTICLE VII [RATIFICATION]

The Ratification of the Conventions of nine States, shall be sufficient for the Establishment of this Constitution between the States so ratifying the Same.

Done in Convention by the Unanimous Consent of the States present the Seventeenth Day of September in the Year of our Lord one thousand seven hundred and eighty-seven and of the Independence of the United States of America the Twelfth In witness whereof We have hereunto subscribed our Names,

Go. WASHINGTON—Presidt. and deputy from Virginia

In Convention Monday, September 17th, 1787.

Present

The States of New Hampshire, Massachusetts, Connecticut, Mr. Hamilton from New York, New Jersey, Pennsylvania, Delaware, Maryland, Virginia, North Carolina, South Carolina, and Georgia.

Resolved,

That the preceding Constitution be laid before the United States in Congress assembled, and that it is the Opinion of this Convention, that it should afterwards be submitted to a Convention of Delegates, chosen in each State by the People thereof, under the Recommendation of its Legislature, for their Assent and Ratification; and that each Convention assenting to, and ratifying the Same, should give Notice thereof to the United States in Congress assembled. Resolved, That it is the Opinion of this Convention, that as soon as the Conventions of nine States shall have ratified this Constitution, the United States in Congress assembled should fix a Day on which Electors should be appointed by the States which have ratified the same, and a Day on which the Electors should assemble to vote for the President, and the Time and Place for commencing Proceedings under this Constitution. That after such Publication the Electors should be appointed, and the Senators and Representatives elected: That the Electors should meet on the Day fixed for the Election of the President, and should transmit their Votes certified, signed, sealed, and directed, as the Constitution requires, to the Secretary of the United States in Congress assembled, that the Senators and Representatives should convene at the Time and Place assigned; that the Senators should appoint a President of the Senate, for the sole purpose of receiving, opening, and counting the Votes for President; and, that after he shall be chosen, the Congress, together with the President, should, without Delay, proceed to execute this Constitution.

By the Unanimous Order of the Convention

Go. WASHINGTON—Presidt.

W. JACKSON Secretary.

Bill of Rights

ARTICLE I [NOT RATIFIED]

After the first enumeration required by the first article of the Constitution, there shall be one Representative for every thirty thousand, until the number shall amount to one hundred, after which the proportion shall be so regulated by Congress, that there shall be not less than one hundred Representatives, nor less than one Representative for every forty thousand persons, until the number of Representatives shall amount to two hundred; after which the proportion shall be so regulated by Congress, that there shall not be less than two hundred Representatives, nor more than one Representative for every fifty thousand persons.

ARTICLE II [TWENTY-SEVENTH AMENDMENT, RATIFIED 1992]

No law, varying the compensation for the services of the Senators and Representatives, shall take effect, until an election of Representatives shall have intervened.

ARTICLE III [FIRST AMENDMENT]

Congress shall make no law respecting an establishment of religion, or prohibiting the free exercise thereof; or abridging the freedom of speech, or of the press; or the right of the people peaceably to assemble, and to petition the Government for a redress of grievances.

ARTICLE IV [SECOND AMENDMENT]

A well-regulated Militia, being necessary to the security of a free State, the right of the people to keep and bear Arms, shall not be infringed.

ARTICLE V [THIRD AMENDMENT]

No Soldier shall, in time of peace be quartered in any house, without the consent of the Owner, nor in time of war, but in a manner to be prescribed by law.

ARTICLE VI [FOURTH AMENDMENT]

The right of the people to be secure in their persons, houses, papers, and effects, against unreasonable searches and seizures, shall not be violated, and no Warrants shall issue, but upon probable cause, supported by Oath or affirmation, and particularly describing the place to be searched, and the persons or things to be seized.

ARTICLE VII [FIFTH AMENDMENT]

No person shall be held to answer for a capital, or otherwise infamous crime, unless on a presentment or indictment of a Grand Jury, except in cases arising in the land or naval forces, or in the Militia, when in actual service in time of War or public danger; nor shall any person be subject for the same offense to be twice put in jeopardy of life or limb; nor shall be compelled in any criminal case to be a witness against himself, nor be deprived of life, liberty, or property, without due process of law; nor shall private property be taken for public use, without just compensation.

ARTICLE VIII [SIXTH AMENDMENT]

In all criminal prosecutions, the accused shall enjoy the right to a speedy and public trial, by an impartial jury of the State and district wherein the crime shall have been committed, which district shall have been previously ascertained by law, and to be informed of the nature and cause of the accusation; to be confronted with the witnesses against him; to have compulsory process for obtaining witnesses in his favor, and to have the Assistance of Counsel for his defense.

ARTICLE IX [SEVENTH AMENDMENT]

In Suits at common law, where the value in controversy shall exceed twenty dollars, the right of trial by jury shall be preserved, and no fact tried by a jury, shall be otherwise reexamined in any Court of the United States, than according to the rules of the common law.

ARTICLE X [EIGHTH AMENDMENT]

Excessive bail shall not be required, nor excessive fines imposed, nor cruel and unusual punishments inflicted.

ARTICLE XI [NINTH AMENDMENT]

The enumeration in the Constitution, of certain rights, shall not be construed to deny or disparage others retained by the people.

ARTICLE XII [TENTH AMENDMENT]

The powers not delegated to the United States by the Constitution, nor prohibited by it to the States, are reserved to the States respectively, or to the people.

Additional Amendments to the Constitution

ELEVENTH AMENDMENT [PROPOSED 1794, RATIFIED 1798]

The Judicial power of the United States shall not be construed to extend to any suit in law or equity, commenced or prosecuted against one of the United States by Citizens of another State, or by Citizens or Subjects of any Foreign State.

TWELFTH AMENDMENT [PROPOSED 1803, RATIFIED 1804]

The Electors shall meet in their respective states, and vote by ballot for President and Vice President, one of whom, at least, shall not be an inhabitant of the same state with themselves; they shall name in their ballots the person voted for as President, and in distinct ballots the person voted for as Vice President, and they shall make distinct lists of all persons voted for as President, and of all persons voted for as Vice President, and of the number of votes for each, which lists they shall sign and certify, and transmit sealed to the seat of the government of the United States, directed to the President of the Senate;—The President of the Senate shall, in the presence of the Senate and House of Representatives, open all the certificates and the votes shall then be counted;—The person having the greatest number of votes for President, shall be the President, if such number be a majority of the whole number of Electors appointed; and if no person have such majority, then from the persons having the highest numbers not exceeding three on the list of those voted for as President, the House of Representatives shall choose immediately, by ballot, the President. But in choosing the President, the votes shall be taken by states, the representation from each state having one vote; a quorum for this purpose shall consist of a member or members from two-thirds of the states, and a majority of all the states shall be necessary to a choice. And if the House of Representatives shall not choose a President whenever the right of choice shall devolve upon them, before the fourth day of March next following, then the Vice President shall act as President, as in the case of the death or other con-

stitutional disability of the President.—The person having the greatest number of votes as Vice President, shall be the Vice President, if such number be
a majority of the whole number of Electors appointed, and if no person have
a majority, then from the two highest numbers on the list, the Senate shall
choose the Vice President; a quorum for the purpose shall consist of two-
thirds of the whole number of Senators, and a majority of the whole number
shall be necessary to a choice. But no person constitutionally ineligible to the
office of President shall be eligible to that of Vice President of the United
States.

THIRTEENTH AMENDMENT [PROPOSED 1865, RATIFIED 1865]

Section 1

Neither slavery nor involuntary servitude, except as a punishment for crime
whereof the party shall have been duly convicted, shall exist within the United States, or any place subject to their jurisdiction.

Section 2

Congress shall have power to enforce this article by appropriate legislation.

FOURTEENTH AMENDMENT [PROPOSED 1866, RATIFIED 1868*]

Section 1

All persons born or naturalized in the United States, and subject to the jurisdiction thereof, are citizens of the United States and of the State wherein they
reside. No State shall make or enforce any law which shall abridge the privileges or immunities of citizens of the United States; nor shall any State deprive
any person of life, liberty, or property, without due process of law; nor deny to
any person within its jurisdiction the equal protection of the laws.

Section 2

Representatives shall be apportioned among the several States according to
their respective numbers, counting the whole number of persons in each
State, excluding Indians not taxed. But when the right to vote at any election
for the choice of electors for President and Vice President of the United States,
Representatives in Congress, the Executive and Judicial officers of a State, or
the members of the Legislature thereof, is denied to any of the male inhabitants of such State, being twenty-one years of age, and citizens of the United
States, or in any way abridged, except for participation in rebellion, or other
crime, the basis of representation therein shall be reduced in the proportion
which the number of such male citizens shall bear to the whole number of
male citizens twenty-one years of age in such State.

---

* See Fourteenth Amendment Law Library for the argument that it was not ratified.

Section 3

No person shall be a Senator or Representative in Congress, or elector of President and Vice President, or hold any office, civil or military, under the United States, or under any State, who, having previously taken an oath, as a member of Congress, or as an officer of the United States, or as a member of any State legislature, or as an executive or judicial officer of any State, to support the Constitution of the United States, shall have engaged in insurrection or rebellion against the same, or given aid or comfort to the enemies thereof. But Congress may by a vote of two-thirds of each House, remove such disability.

Section 4

The validity of the public debt of the United States, authorized by law, including debts incurred for payment of pensions and bounties for services in suppressing insurrection or rebellion, shall not be questioned. But neither the United States nor any State shall assume or pay any debt or obligation incurred in aid of insurrection or rebellion against the United States, or any claim for the loss or emancipation of any slave; but all such debts, obligations, and claims shall be held illegal and void.

Section 5

The Congress shall have power to enforce, by appropriate legislation, the provisions of this article.

FIFTEENTH AMENDMENT [PROPOSED 1869, RATIFIED 1870]

Section 1

The right of citizens of the United States to vote shall not be denied or abridged by the United States or by any State on account of race, color, or previous condition of servitude.

Section 2

The Congress shall have power to enforce this article by appropriate legislation.

SIXTEENTH AMENDMENT [PROPOSED 1909, RATIFIED 1913]

The Congress shall have power to lay and collect taxes on incomes, from whatever source derived, without apportionment among the several States, and without regard to any census or enumeration.

SEVENTEENTH AMENDMENT [PROPOSED 1912, RATIFIED 1913]

The Senate of the United States shall be composed of two Senators from each State, elected by the people thereof, for six years; and each Senator shall have one vote. The electors in each State shall have the qualifications requisite for electors of the most numerous branch of the State legislatures. When vacancies happen in the representation of any State in the Senate, the executive authority of such State shall issue writs of election to fill such vacancies: Provided, That the legislature of any State may empower the executive thereof to make temporary appointments until the people fill the vacancies by election as the legislature may direct. This amendment shall not be so construed as to affect the election or term of any Senator chosen before it becomes valid as part of the Constitution.

EIGHTEENTH AMENDMENT [PROPOSED 1917, RATIFIED 1919, REPEALED 1933]

Section 1

After one year from the ratification of this article the manufacture, sale, or transportation of intoxicating liquors within, the importation thereof into, or the exportation thereof from the United States and all territory subject to the jurisdiction thereof for beverage purposes is hereby prohibited.

Section 2

The Congress and the several States shall have concurrent power to enforce this article by appropriate legislation.

Section 3

This article shall be inoperative unless it shall have been ratified as an amendment to the Constitution by the legislatures of the several States, as provided in the Constitution, within seven years from the date of the submission hereof to the States by the Congress.

NINETEENTH AMENDMENT [PROPOSED 1919, RATIFIED 1920]

The right of citizens of the United States to vote shall not be denied or abridged by the United States or by any State on account of sex. Congress shall have power to enforce this article by appropriate legislation.

TWENTIETH AMENDMENT [PROPOSED 1932, RATIFIED 1933]

Section 1

The terms of the President and Vice President shall end at noon on the 20th day of January, and the terms of Senators and Representatives at noon on the 3rd day of January, of the years in which such terms would have ended if this article had not been ratified; and the terms of their successors shall then begin.

Section 2

The Congress shall assemble at least once in every year, and such meeting shall begin at noon on the 3rd day of January, unless they shall by law appoint a different day.

Section 3

If, at the time fixed for the beginning of the term of the President, the President elect shall have died, the Vice President elect shall become President. If a President shall not have been chosen before the time fixed for the beginning of his term, or if the President elect shall have failed to qualify, then the Vice President elect shall act as President until a President shall have qualified; and the Congress may by law provide for the case wherein neither a President elect nor a Vice President elect shall have qualified, declaring who shall then act as President, or the manner in which one who is to act shall be selected, and such person shall act accordingly until a President or Vice President shall have qualified.

Section 4

The Congress may by law provide for the case of the death of any of the persons from whom the House of Representatives may choose a President whenever the right of choice shall have devolved upon them, and for the case of the death of any of the persons from whom the Senate may choose a Vice President whenever the right of choice shall have devolved upon them.

Section 5

Sections 1 and 2 shall take effect on the 15th day of October following the ratification of this article.

Section 6

This article shall be inoperative unless it shall have been ratified as an amendment to the Constitution by the legislatures of three-fourths of the several States within seven years from the date of its submission.

TWENTY-FIRST AMENDMENT [PROPOSED 1933, RATIFIED 1933]

Section 1

The eighteenth article of amendment to the Constitution of the United States is hereby repealed.

Section 2

The transportation or importation into any State, Territory, or possession of the United States for delivery or use therein of intoxicating liquors, in violation of the laws thereof, is hereby prohibited.

Section 3

This article shall be inoperative unless it shall have been ratified as an amendment to the Constitution by conventions in the several States, as provided in the Constitution, within seven years from the date of the submission hereof to the States by the Congress.

TWENTY-SECOND AMENDMENT
[PROPOSED 1947, RATIFIED 1951]

Section 1

No person shall be elected to the office of the President more than twice, and no person who has held the office of President, or acted as President, for more than two years of a term to which some other person was elected President shall be elected to the office of the President more than once. But this Article shall not apply to any person holding the office of President when this Article was proposed by the Congress, and shall not prevent any person who may be holding the office of President, or acting as President, during the term within which this Article becomes operative from holding the office of President or acting as President during the remainder of such term.

Section 2

This article shall be inoperative unless it shall have been ratified as an amendment to the Constitution by the legislatures of three-fourths of the several States within seven years from the date of its submission to the States by the Congress.

TWENTY-THIRD AMENDMENT
[PROPOSED 1960, RATIFIED 1961]

Section 1

The District constituting the seat of Government of the United States shall appoint in such manner as the Congress may direct: A number of electors of President and Vice President equal to the whole number of Senators and Representatives in Congress to which the District would be entitled if it were a State, but in no event more than the least populous State; they shall be in addition to those appointed by the States, but they shall be considered, for the purposes of the election of President and Vice President, to be electors appointed by a State; and they shall meet in the District and perform such duties as provided by the twelfth article of amendment.

Section 2

The Congress shall have power to enforce this article by appropriate legislation.

TWENTY-FOURTH AMENDMENT
[PROPOSED 1962, RATIFIED 1964]

Section 1

The right of citizens of the United States to vote in any primary or other election for President or Vice President, for electors for President or Vice President, or for Senator or Representative in Congress, shall not be denied or abridged by the United States or any State by reason of failure to pay any poll tax or other tax.

Section 2

The Congress shall have power to enforce this article by appropriate legislation.

TWENTY-FIFTH AMENDMENT
[PROPOSED 1965, RATIFIED 1967]

Section 1

In case of the removal of the President from office or of his death or resignation, the Vice President shall become President.

Section 2

Whenever there is a vacancy in the office of the Vice President, the President shall nominate a Vice President who shall take office upon confirmation by a majority vote of both Houses of Congress.

Section 3

Whenever the President transmits to the President pro tempore of the Senate and the Speaker of the House of Representatives his written declaration that he is unable to discharge the powers and duties of his office, and until he transmits to them a written declaration to the contrary, such powers and duties shall be discharged by the Vice President as Acting President.

Section 4

Whenever the Vice President and a majority of either the principal officers of the executive departments or of such other body as Congress may by law provide, transmit to the President pro tempore of the Senate and the Speaker of the House of Representatives their written declaration that the President is unable to discharge the powers and duties of his office, the Vice President shall immediately assume the powers and duties of the office as Acting President.

Thereafter, when the President transmits to the President pro tempore of the Senate and the Speaker of the House of Representatives his written declaration that no inability exists, he shall resume the powers and duties of his office unless the Vice President and a majority of either the principal officers of the executive department or of such other body as Congress may by law provide, transmit within four days to the President pro tempore of the Senate and the Speaker of the House of Representatives their written declaration that the President is unable to discharge the powers and duties of his office. Thereupon Congress shall decide the issue, assembling within forty-eight hours for that purpose if not in session. If the Congress, within twenty-one days after receipt of the latter written declaration, or, if Congress is not in session, within twenty-one days after Congress is required to assemble, determines by two-thirds vote of both Houses that the President is unable to discharge the powers and duties of his office, the Vice President shall continue to discharge the same as Acting President; otherwise, the President shall resume the powers and duties of his office.

TWENTY-SIXTH AMENDMENT
[PROPOSED 1971, RATIFIED 1971]

Section 1

The right of citizens of the United States, who are eighteen years of age or older, to vote shall not be denied or abridged by the United States or by any State on account of age.

Section 2

The Congress shall have power to enforce this article by appropriate legislation.

TWENTY-SEVENTH AMENDMENT
[PROPOSED 1789, RATIFIED 1992]

No law, varying the compensation for the services of the Senators and Representatives, shall take effect, until an election of Representatives shall have intervened.

Source: Constitution Society, "Constitution for the United States of America." Retrieved May 14, 2010, from http://www.constitution.org/constit_.htm.

CHAPTER 11

Observations on the New Constitution, Mercy Otis Warren, 1788

Written anonymously by Mercy Otis Warren in Boston in 1788, *Observations on the New Constitution, and on the Federal and State Conventions*, credited on its title page to the pen of "a Columbian patriot," was for a number of years attributed to Elbridge Gerry, a Massachusetts Democrat-Republican who had refused to sign the Constitution because it did not contain a bill of rights. Mercy, the sister of James Otis, an early patriot who wrote "The Rights of the British Colonies Asserted and Proved" and openly opposed Parliament's power in the colonies, was entirely self-educated but became arguably the foremost female patriot and writer, respected during her lifetime by many of the most important men in the United States. Before the Revolution, she published a number of plays in which her characters thinly disguised treatments of various royal officials, and she unabashedly fomented rebellion for the cause of independence. During the Revolution, Warren recorded its history and later, in 1805, published a three-volume work, *History of the Rise, Progress, and Termination of the American Revolution*. Mercy Warren was later supplanted by Abigail Adams as the "first lady" of the Revolution, but Warren clearly possesses the better claim.

Frustrated with the restrictions placed upon her due to her sex, she saw the American Revolution as an opportunity to achieve genuine equality among individuals through the philosophy of respecting the God-given rights of all individuals, as embodied in the Declaration of Independence. Warren became increasingly radicalized throughout her life and opposed the establishment of a strong central government, which she equated with the establishment of tyranny. She joined like-minded individuals in opposing the ratification of the Constitution and published her *Observations* as a counterpoint to the Federalist essays being produced by Alexander Hamilton, James Madison, and John Jay. Corresponding regularly with many of the famous founders, she nevertheless generally failed to move them with her arguments.

In her pamphlet opposing the ratification of the Constitution, Warren demonstrated her ability to apply logical analysis to politics, providing an excellent example of anti-Federalist writing. The Constitution as submitted for ratification contained no bill of rights—a defect Warren found inexcusable and reason enough, by itself, to deny ratification. She was as concerned about the process of creating the Constitution as she was about the product. She did not believe Madison, Hamilton, or Jay when they soft-pedaled fears about the potential growth of government, or about Congress being able to determine its own pay, or about the concentration of power at the national level. She warned of the problems a big government threatened to create, and proved prescient in warning that many threats posed by the Constitution would ultimately affect individuals. Warren also realized that an apathetic citizenry could pose a similar danger.

From *Observations on the New Constitution, and on the Federal and State Conventions*

MANKIND MAY AMUSE THEMSELVES WITH THEORETIC SYStems of liberty, and trace its social and moral effects on sciences, virtue, industry, and every improvement of which the human mind is capable; but we can only discern its true value by the practical and wretched effects of slavery . . . and the Southern [states] . . . are languishing in hopeless poverty; and when asked, what is become of the flower of their crop, and the rich produce of their farms—they may answer. . . . [i]n the more literal language of truth, the exigencies of government require that the collectors of the revenue should transmit it to the Federal City.

Animated with the firmest zeal for the interest of this country, the peace and union of the American States, and the freedom and happiness of a people who have made the most costly sacrifices in the cause of liberty, who have braved the power of Britain, weathered the convulsions of war, and waded through the blood of friends and foes to establish their independence and to support the freedom of the human mind; I cannot silently witness this degradation without calling on them, before they are compelled to blush at their own servitude, and to turn back their languid eyes on their lost liberties. . . . And when patriotism is discountenanced and public virtue becomes the ridicule of the sycophant—when every man of liberality, firmness, and penetration who cannot lick the hand stretched out to oppress, is deemed an enemy to the State—then is the gulf of despotism set open, and the grades to slavery, though rapid, are scarce perceptible—then genius drags heavily its iron chain—science is neglected, and real merit flies to the shades for security from reproach—the mind becomes enervated, and the national character sinks to a kind of apathy with only energy sufficient to curse the breast that gave it milk. . . . Self-defense is a primary law of nature, which no subsequent law of society can abolish; this primeval principle, the immediate gift of the Creator, obliges every one to remonstrate against the strides of ambition, and a wanton lust of domination, and to resist the first approaches of tyranny, which at this day threaten to sweep away the rights for which the brave Sons of America have fought with an heroism scarcely paralleled even in ancient republics. . . . On these shores freedom has planted her standard, dipped in the purple tide that flowed from the veins of her martyred heroes; and here every uncorrupted American yet hopes to see it supported by the vigor, the justice, the wisdom, and unanimity of the people, in spite of the deep-laid plots, the secret intrigues, or the bold effrontery of those interested and avaricious adventurers for place, who intoxicated with the ideas of distinction and preferment have prostrated every worthy principle beneath the shrine of ambition. Yet these are the men who tell us republicanism is dwindled into theory—that we are incapable of enjoying our liberties—and that we must have a master. . . . But the revolutions in principle which time produces among mankind, frequently exhibits the most mortifying instances of human weakness; and this alone can account for the extraordinary appearance of a few names, once distinguished in the honorable walks of patriotism, but now found in the list of the Massachusetts assent to the ratification of a Constitution, which, by the undefined meaning of some parts, and the ambiguities of expression in others, is dangerously adapted to the purposes of an immediate aristocratic tyranny. . . .

All writers on government agree, and the feelings of the human mind witness the truth of these political axioms, that man is born free and possessed of certain unalienable rights—that government is instituted for the protection, safety, and happiness of the people, and not for the profit, honor, or private interest of any man, family, or class of men—that the origin of all power is in the people, and that they have an incontestable right to check the creatures of their own creation, vested with certain powers to guard the life, liberty, and property of the community. And if certain selected bodies of men, deputed on these principles, determine contrary to the wishes and expectations of their constituents, the people have an undoubted right to reject their decisions, to call for a revision of their conduct, to depute others in their room, or if they think proper, to demand further time for deliberation on matters of the greatest moment: it therefore is an unwarrantable stretch of authority or influence, if any methods are taken to preclude this peaceful and reasonable mode of enquiry and decision. . . .

[1.] . . . When society has thus deputed a certain number of their equals to take care of their personal rights, and the interest of the whole community, it must be considered that responsibility is the great responsibility. Man is not immediately corrupted, but power without limitation, or amenability, may endanger the brightest virtue—whereas frequent return to the bar of their Constituents is the strongest check against the corruptions to which men are liable, either from the intrigues of others of more subtle genius, or the propensities of their own hearts,—and the gentlemen who have so warmly advocated in the late Convention of the Massachusetts, the change from annual to biennial elections; may have been in the same predicament . . . but it is unnecessary to dwell long on this article, as the best political writers have supported the principles of annual elections with a precision, that cannot be confuted, though they may be darkened, by the sophistical arguments that have been thrown out with design, to undermine all the barriers of freedom.

2. There is no security in the proffered system, either for the rights of conscience or the liberty of the Press: Despotism usually while it is gaining ground, will suffer men to think, say, or write what they please; but when once established, if it is thought necessary to serve the purposes of arbitrary power, the most unjust restrictions may take place in the first instance, and an imprimatur on the Press in the next may silence the complaints, and forbid the most decent remonstrances of an injured and oppressed people.

3. There are no well-defined limits of the Judiciary Powers; they seem to be left as a boundless ocean, that has broken over the chart of the Supreme Lawgiver, "thus far shalt thou go and no further," and as they cannot be comprehended by the clearest capacity, or the most sagacious mind, it would be an Herculean labor to attempt to describe the dangers with which they are replete.

4. The Executive and the Legislative are so dangerously blended as to give just cause of alarm, and everything relative thereto, is couched in such ambiguous terms, in such vague and indefinite expression, as is a sufficient ground without any objection, for the reprobation of a system, that the authors dare not hazard to a clear investigation.

5. The abolition of trial by jury in civil causes—this mode of trial the learned Judge Blackstone observes, "has been coeval with the first rudiments of civil government, that property, liberty, and life depend on maintaining in its legal force the constitutional trial by jury." He bids his readers pause, and with Sir Matthew Hale observes how admirably this mode is adapted to the investigation of truth beyond any other the world can produce. . . .

6. Though it has been said by Mr. Wilson and many others, that a Standing Army is necessary for the dignity and safety of America, yet freedom revolts at the idea, when the Divan, or the Despot, may draw out his dragoons to suppress the murmurs of a few, who may yet cherish those sublime principles

which call forth the exertions, and lead to the best improvements of the human mind. . . . By the edicts of an authority vested in the sovereign power by the proposed constitution, the militia of the country, the bulwark of defense, and the security of national liberty if no longer under the control of civil authority; but at the rescript of the Monarch or the aristocracy, . . . they may be sent into foreign countries for the fulfillment of treaties, stipulated by the President and two-thirds of the Senate.

7. Notwithstanding the delusory promise to guarantee a Republican form of government to every State in the Union, if the most discerning eye could discover any meaning at all in the engagement, there are no resources left for the support of internal government or the liquidation of the debts of the State. Every source of revenue is in the monopoly of Congress, and if the several legislatures in their enfeebled state, should against their own feelings be necessitated to attempt a dry tax for the payment of their debts and the support of internal police, even this may be required for the purposes of the general government.

8. As the new Congress is empowered to determine their own salaries, the requisitions for this purpose may not be very moderate, and the drain for public moneys will probably rise past all calculation. . . .

9. There is no provision for a rotation, nor anything to prevent the perpetuity of office in the same hands for life—which by a little well-timed bribery, will probably be done, to the exclusion of men of the best abilities from their share in the offices of government. By this neglect we lose the advantages of that check to the overbearing insolence of office, which by rendering him ineligible at certain periods, keeps the mind of man in equilibrium, and teaches him the feelings of the governed, and better qualifies him to govern in his turn.

10. The inhabitants of the United States, are liable to be dragged from the vicinity of their own country, or state, to answer the litigious or unjust suit of an adversary, on the most distant borders of the Continent: in short the appellate jurisdiction of the Supreme Federal Court, includes an unwarrantable stretch of power over the liberty, life, and property of the subject, through the wide Continent of America.

11. One Representative to thirty thousand inhabitants is a very inadequate representation; and every man who is not lost to all sense of freedom to his country, must reprobate the idea of Congress altering by law, or on any pretence whatever, interfering with any regulations for time, places, and manner of choosing our own Representatives.

12. If the sovereignty of America is designed to be elective, the circumscribing the votes to only ten electors in this State, and the same proportion in all the others, is nearly tantamount to the exclusion of the voice of the people in the

choice of their first magistrate. It is vesting the choice solely in an aristocratic junta, who may easily combine in each State to place at the head of
the Union the most convenient instrument for despotic sway.

13. A Senate chosen for six years will, in most instances, be an appointment for
life, as the influence of such a body over the minds of the people will be
coequal to the extensive powers with which they are vested, and they will
not only forget, but be forgotten by their constituents—a branch of the
Supreme Legislature thus set beyond all responsibility is totally repugnant
to every principle of a free government.

14. There is no provision by a bill of rights to guard against the dangerous
encroachments of power in too many instances to be named: but I cannot
pass over in silence the insecurity in which we are left with regard to warrants unsupported by evidence, . . . to subject ourselves to the insolence of
any petty revenue officer to enter our houses, search, insult, and seize at
pleasure. The rights of individuals ought to be the primary object of all government, and cannot be too securely guarded by the most explicit declarations in their favor.

15. The difficulty, if not impracticability, of exercising the equal and equitable
powers of government by a single legislature over an extent of territory that
reaches from the Mississippi to the Western lakes, and from them to the
Atlantic Ocean, is an insuperable objection to the adoption of the new
system.

16. It is an undisputed fact that not one legislature in the United States had
the most distant idea when they first appointed members for a convention, entirely commercial, or when they afterwards authorized them to consider on some amendments of the Federal union, that they would without
any warrant from their constituents, presume on so bold and daring a stride,
as ultimately to destroy the state governments, and offer a consolidated
system.

17. The first appearance of the article which declares the ratification of nine
states sufficient for the establishment of the new system, wears the face of
dissension, is a subversion of the union of Confederated States, and tends to
the introduction of anarchy and civil convulsions, and may be a means of
involving the whole country in blood.

18. The mode in which this constitution is recommended to the people to judge
without either the advice of Congress or the legislatures of the several states
is very reprehensible—it is an attempt to force it upon them before it could
be thoroughly understood, and may leave us in that situation, that in the first
moments of slavery in the minds of the people agitated by the remembrance
of their lost liberties, will be like the sea in a tempest, that sweeps down
every mound of security.

It is needless to enumerate other instances, in which the proposed constitution appears contradictory to the first principles which ought to govern mankind; and it is equally so to enquire into the motives that induced to so bold a step as the annihilation of the independence and sovereignty of the thirteen distinct states. . . .

We were then told by him [the Governor], in all the soft language of insinuation, that no form of government, of human construction can be perfect; that we had nothing to fear; that we had no reason to complain; that we had only to acquiesce in their illegal claims, and to submit to the requisition of Parliament, and doubtless the lenient hand of government would redress all grievances, and remove the oppressions of the people. Yet we soon saw armies of mercenaries encamped on our plains, our commerce ruined, our harbors blockaded, and our cities burnt. It may be replied that this was in consequence of an obstinate defense of our privileges; this may be true; but let the best informed historian produce an instance when bodies of men were entrusted with power, and the proper checks relinquished, if they were ever found destitute of ingenuity sufficient to furnish pretences to abuse it. . . .

It is presumed the great body of the people unite in sentiment with the writer of these observations, who most devoutly prays that public credit may rear her declining head, and remunerative justice pervade the land; nor is there a doubt if a free government is continued, that time and industry will enable both the public and private debtor to liquidate their arrearages in the most equitable manner. They wish to see the Confederated States bound together by the most indissoluble union, but without renouncing their separate sovereignties and independence, and becoming tributaries to a consolidated fabric of aristocratic tyranny. . . . "The great art of governing is to lay aside all prejudices and attachments to particular opinions, classes or individual characters to consult the spirit of the people; to give way to it; and in so doing, to give it a turn capable of inspiring those sentiments, which may induce them to relish a change, which an alteration of circumstances may hereafter make necessary." . . .

. . . But if after all, on a dispassionate and fair discussion, the people generally give their voices for a voluntary dereliction of their privileges, let every individual who chooses the active scenes of life strive to support the peace and unanimity of his country, though every other blessing may expire—And while the statesman is plodding for power, and the courtier practicing the arts of dissimulation without check—while the rapacious are growing rich by oppression, and fortune throwing her gifts into the lap of fools, let the sublimer characters, the philosophic lovers of freedom who have wept over her exit, retire to the calm shades of contemplation, there they may look down with pity on the inconsistency of human nature, the revolutions of states; the rise of kingdoms, and the fall of empires.

Source: Mercy Otis Warren's *Observations on the New Constitution, and on the Federal and State Conventions* was originally published as a pamphlet in Boston in 1788 and later reprinted in Brooklyn in 1887.

II

GROWING PAINS IN
THE NEW NATION

Although America had won its independence and established a constitution, the question of whether it could actually put its ideals into practice remained to be answered. One of the first indicators of how the nation would be governed came from George Washington's first inaugural address, which revealed that, if nothing else, the system would function well when men of character operated the levers of government. An early test to the structure came with the *Marbury v. Madison* case, in which the U.S. Supreme Court assumed for itself the power of judicial review, a power not expressly granted in the Constitution. Over the forty-year period from 1789 to 1829, the shape, size, and scope of government power were routinely tested; terms and concepts in the Constitution became better defined, often to the surprise of one branch of government or the other; and the challenge of interposition or nullification by the states arose on more than one occasion.

The federal government grew constantly, and four other stresses were apparent during this time: the issue of slavery and its extension into new territories and states; the meddling by England in American affairs and even a serious attempt to acquire territorial concessions from the infant nation; sectionalism that pitted the agrarian West against the developing Northeast, the South against the North, and New England against everyone; and managing the growth and expansion of the country, which reached its continental (or lower forty-eight) limits with the Gadsden Purchase in 1853.

The nation overcame three of these four stresses with moderate difficulty, but the issue of slavery festered and grew ever larger. Shortsighted attempts at solutions simply made matters worse and hardened attitudes. Britain's answer— paying compensation to slave owners for the loss of their property—became infeasible as slavery grew to enormous proportions in some parts of the South even though the importation of slaves from other countries was forbidden in 1808. Indeed, slave property was the single most valuable commodity in America in the antebellum period. In a very real sense, the United States did well during this period on all issues except the one that was most important. The country, its people, and its government were truly exceptional but had failed to deal with slavery in a timely fashion. In the following period, the country would have to make up for this shortcoming with the blood of its people.

CHAPTER 12

George Washington's First
Inaugural Address, 1789

George Washington took his oath of office as the nation's first president on April 30, 1789, in New York City, on the balcony of the Senate Chamber at Federal Hall on Wall Street. He had been unanimously elected president by the first electoral college, in which each elector cast two votes. John Adams was elected vice president, with the second-highest number of votes. Robert R. Livingston, the chancellor of New York, administered the oath of office. Following the swearing-in ceremony, Washington gave the following address to a joint session of Congress inside the Senate Chamber.

This address is the gold standard by which all subsequent inaugural addresses have been judged, and three features stand out: a trust in, and reliance on, God; the lack of any specific program or agenda other than to fulfill the duties of the office, whatever they might be, to the best of his ability; and a promise to take no pay other than a reimbursement of expenses. An air of remarkable humility also emerges. The effect generated was one of extreme nobility, something that many subsequent presidents never attained in practice, particularly in modern times. Although it is popular for modern candidates to disavow any ambition to be president, Washington actually ran away from the job as best he could. He literally had to be talked into taking the position after he had already been elected. He could have made almost any demand in exchange for his services, but did not. The reader should note the similarities and differences between Washington's address and those by more modern presidents. Washington's humility is as sincere as it is apparent, and his reasons for serving—for eight years— in an office he truly did not desire set the standard by which all subsequent presidents should be measured.

First Inaugural Address

FELLOW-CITIZENS OF THE SENATE AND OF THE HOUSE OF Representatives:

Among the vicissitudes incident to life no event could have filled me with greater anxieties than that of which the notification was transmitted by your order, and received on the 14th day of the present month. On the one hand, I was summoned by my country, whose voice I can never hear but with venera-tion and love, from a retreat which I had chosen with the fondest predilection, and, in my flattering hopes, with an immutable decision, as the asylum of my declining years—a retreat which was rendered every day more necessary as well as more dear to me by the addition of habit to inclination, and of frequent interruptions in my health to the gradual waste committed on it by time.

On the other hand, the magnitude and difficulty of the trust to which the voice of my country called me, being sufficient to awaken in the wisest and most experienced of her citizens a distrustful scrutiny into his qualifications, could not but overwhelm with despondence one who (inheriting inferior endow-ments from nature and unpracticed in the duties of civil administration) ought to be peculiarly conscious of his own deficiencies. In this conflict of emotions all I dare aver is that it has been my faithful study to collect my duty from a just appreciation of every circumstance by which it might be affected. . . .

Such being the impressions under which I have, in obedience to the public summons, repaired to the present station, it would be peculiarly improper to omit in this first official act my fervent supplications to that Almighty Being who rules over the universe, who presides in the councils of nations, and whose providential aids can supply every human defect, that His benediction may consecrate to the liberties and happiness of the people of the United States a Government instituted by themselves for these essential purposes, and may enable every instrument employed in its administration to execute with success the functions allotted to his charge. In tendering this homage to the Great Author of every public and private good, I assure myself that it expresses your sentiments not less than my own, nor those of my fellow-citizens at large less than either. No people can be bound to acknowledge and adore the Invisible Hand which conducts the affairs of men more than those of the United States. Every step by which they have advanced to the character of an independent nation seems to have been distinguished by some token of providential agency; and in the important revolution just accomplished in the system of their united government the tranquil deliberations and voluntary consent of so many distinct communities from which the event has resulted cannot be compared with the means by which most governments have been established without some return of pious gratitude, along with an humble anticipation of the future blessings which the past seem to presage. These reflections, arising out of the present crisis, have forced themselves too strongly on my mind to be suppressed. You will join with me, I trust, in thinking that there are none under the influence of which the proceedings of a new and free government can more auspiciously commence.

By the article establishing the executive department it is made the duty of the President "to recommend to your consideration such measures as he shall judge necessary and expedient." The circumstances under which I now meet you will acquit me from entering into that subject further than to refer to the great constitutional charter under which you are assembled, and which, in defining your powers, designates the objects to which your attention is to be given. It will be more consistent with those circumstances, and far more congenial with the feelings which actuate me, to substitute, in place of a recommendation of particular measures, the tribute that is due to the talents, the rectitude, and the patriotism which adorn the characters selected to devise and adopt them. In these honorable qualifications I behold the surest pledges that as on one side no local prejudices or attachments, no separate views nor party animosities, will misdirect the comprehensive and equal eye which ought to watch over this great assemblage of communities and interests, so, on another, that the foundation of our national policy will be laid in the pure and immutable principles of private morality, and the preeminence of free government be exemplified by all the attributes which can win the affections of its citizens and command the respect of the world. I dwell on this prospect with every satisfaction which an ardent love for my country can inspire, since there is no truth more thoroughly established than that there exists in the economy and course of nature an indissoluble union between virtue and happiness; between duty and advantage; between the genuine maxims of an honest and magnanimous policy and the solid rewards of public prosperity and felicity; since we ought to be no less persuaded that the propitious smiles of Heaven can never be expected on a nation that disregards the eternal rules of order and right which Heaven itself has ordained; and since the preservation of the sacred fire of liberty and the destiny of the republican model of government are justly considered, perhaps, as *deeply*, as *finally*, staked on the experiment entrusted to the hands of the American people.

Besides the ordinary objects submitted to your care, it will remain with your judgment to decide how far an exercise of the occasional power delegated by the fifth article of the Constitution is rendered expedient at the present juncture by the nature of objections which have been urged against the system, or by the degree of inquietude which has given birth to them.

Instead of undertaking particular recommendations on this subject, in which I could be guided by no lights derived from official opportunities, I shall again give way to my entire confidence in your discernment and pursuit of the public good; for I assure myself that whilst you carefully avoid every alteration which might endanger the benefits of an united and effective government, or which ought to await the future lessons of experience, a reverence for the characteristic rights of freemen and a regard for the public harmony will sufficiently influence your deliberations on the question how far the former can be impregnably fortified or the latter be safely and advantageously promoted.

To the foregoing observations I have one to add, which will be most properly addressed to the House of Representatives. It concerns myself, and will therefore be as brief as possible. When I was first honored with a call into the service of my country, then on the eve of an arduous struggle for its liberties, the light in which I contemplated my duty required that I should renounce every pecuniary compensation. From this resolution I have in no instance departed; and being still under the impressions which produced it, I must decline as inapplicable to myself any share in the personal emoluments which may be indispensably included in a permanent provision for the executive department, and must accordingly pray that the pecuniary estimates for the station in which I am placed may during my continuance in it be limited to such actual expenditures as the public good may be thought to require.

Having thus imparted to you my sentiments as they have been awakened by the occasion which brings us together, I shall take my present leave; but not without resorting once more to the benign Parent of the Human Race in humble supplication that, since He has been pleased to favor the American people with opportunities for deliberating in perfect tranquility, and dispositions for deciding with unparalleled unanimity on a form of government for the security of their union and the advancement of their happiness, so His divine blessing may be equally conspicuous in the enlarged views, the temperate consultations, and the wise measures on which the success of this Government must depend.

Source: *A Compilation of the Messages and Papers of the Presidents 1789–1899,* ed. James D. Richardson (Washington, D.C.: Government Printing Office, 1909), 1: 51–4. Retrieved May 1, 2010, from http://onlinebooks.library.upenn.edu/webbin/gutbook/lookup?num=11314.

CHAPTER 13

Marbury v. Madison, 1803

The case of *William Marbury v. James Madison, Secretary of State of the United States*, 5 U.S. 137 (1803), argued before the Supreme Court in 1802 and decided in February 1803, established the precedent that the Supreme Court could subject acts by Congress to judicial review and, as appropriate, declare them unconstitutional and unenforceable. The importance of this principle can hardly be overstated—never before in the history of mankind had a sovereign government empowered a judiciary to overturn a legislative act. This was American exceptionalism at its best.

The case under consideration arose when the outgoing president, John Adams, appointed William Marbury to a district judgeship in one of his "midnight" appointments, and the incoming president, Thomas Jefferson, instructed his secretary of state, James Madison, to withhold the delivery of Marbury's commission. Marbury therefore sued Madison in the Supreme Court, under the Judiciary Act of 1789, for a writ of mandamus to compel Secretary Madison to deliver his commission. The chief justice, John Marshall, delivered the opinion of the Court, thoroughly addressing all the issues in the case. He found Marbury's case compelling, but also that the portion of the Judiciary Act that allowed Marbury to seek a writ of mandamus directly from the Supreme Court was unconstitutional. Therefore the Court could not issue the writ. The problem was that the Court had been granted original jurisdiction in only a few specific situations, and Marbury's was not one of them. Given the specifics of the Constitution, Marshall held that Congress could not ignore the Constitution and grant powers not contained therein.

The importance of judicial review became the central legal concept to arise from *Marbury v. Madison*. The principle of judicial review originated with Edward Coke in England in 1610, and although discarded in English jurisprudence, the idea took root in various American colonies. Judicial review was applied in conflicts between state statutes and state constitutions, but even so it was not explicitly mentioned in the Constitution. Even in the wake of *Marbury v. Madison*, it was not widely cited in American judicial rulings before the 1850s. Nevertheless, the case enshrined judicial review in American jurisprudence and reflected the mood at the time, which considered the judiciary the weakest of the government's branches.

Chief Justice Marshall's decision both recognized limits on the power of the Court with respect to jurisdiction and vastly increased it, by setting up the Court as an arbitrator on the constitutionality of laws in the United States. Marshall accomplished this, in essence, by declaring that an unconstitutional law could not be enforced through the courts. As a result, any such law became moot.

The founders built few safeguards against modern "judicial activism" into the Constitution, having little experience of—and thus little concern for—activist courts. Virtually no court in England could override decisions of the king or Parliament. Nor, lacking a formal written constitution, did any Englishman have a document to which he could appeal. Without such a precedent handed down from English legal tradition, did Marshall overstep his constitutional bounds? Alternatively, if there was no judicial review, what would prevent Congress from enacting unconstitutional laws?

Marbury v. Madison

MR. CHIEF JUSTICE MARSHALL DELIVERED THE OPINION OF the Court.

At the last term, on the affidavits then read and filed with the clerk, a rule was granted in this case, requiring the secretary of state to show cause why a mandamus should not issue, directing him to deliver to William Marbury his commission as a justice of the peace for the county of Washington, in the District of Columbia.

No cause has been shown, and the present motion is for a mandamus. The peculiar delicacy of this case, the novelty of some of its circumstances, and the real difficulty attending the points which occur in it, require a complete exposition of the principles on which the opinion to be given by the Court is founded. These principles have been, on the side of the applicant, very ably argued at the bar. In rendering the opinion of the Court, there will be some departure in form, though not in substance, from the points stated in that argument.

In the order in which the Court has viewed this subject, the following questions have been considered and decided.

1. Has the applicant a right to the commission he demands?
2. If he has a right, and that right has been violated, do the laws of his country afford him a remedy?
3. If they do afford him a remedy, is it a mandamus issuing from this court?

The first object of inquiry is: Has the applicant a right to the commission he demands?

His right originates in an act of Congress passed in February 1801, concerning the District of Columbia. After dividing the District into two counties, the eleventh section of this law enacts, "that there shall be appointed in and for each of the said counties, such number of discrete persons to be justices of the peace as the President of the United States shall, from time to time, think expedient, to continue in office for five years."

It appears from the affidavits, that in compliance with this law, a commission for William Marbury as a justice of peace for the county of Washington was signed by John Adams, then president of the United States; after which the seal of the United States was affixed to it; but the commission has never reached the person for whom it was made out. In order to determine whether he is entitled to this commission, it becomes necessary to inquire whether he has been appointed to the office. For if he has been appointed, the law continues him in office for five years, and he is entitled to the possession of those evidences of office, which, being completed, became his property. The second section of the second article of the Constitution declares, "the president shall nominate, and, by and with the advice and consent of the senate, shall appoint ambassadors, other public ministers and consuls, and all other officers of the United States, whose appointments are not otherwise provided for." The third section declares, that "he shall commission all the officers of the United States." . . .

The commission being signed, the subsequent duty of the secretary of state is prescribed by law, and not to be guided by the will of the president. He is to affix the seal of the United States to the commission, and is to record it. . . .

It is therefore decidedly the opinion of the Court, that when a commission has been signed by the president, the appointment is made; and that the commission is complete when the seal of the United States has been affixed to it by the secretary of state.

Where an officer is removable at the will of the executive, the circumstance which completes his appointment is of no concern; because the act is at any time revocable; and the commission may be arrested, if still in the office. But when the officer is not removable at the will of the executive, the appointment is not revocable and cannot be annulled. It has conferred legal rights which cannot be resumed.

The discretion of the executive is to be exercised until the appointment has been made. But having once made the appointment, his power over the office is terminated in all cases, where by law the officer is not removable by him. The right to the office is then in the person appointed, and he has the absolute, unconditional power of accepting or rejecting it.

Mr. Marbury, then, since his commission was signed by the president and sealed by the secretary of state, was appointed; and as the law creating the office gave the officer a right to hold for five years independent of the executive, the appointment was not revocable; but vested in the officer legal rights which are protected by the laws of his country.

To withhold the commission, therefore, is an act deemed by the Court not warranted by law, but violative of a vested legal right.

This brings us to the second inquiry; which is: If he has a right, and that right has been violated, do the laws of his country afford him a remedy?

The very essence of civil liberty certainly consists in the right of every individual to claim the protection of the laws, whenever he receives an injury. . . .

The government of the United States has been emphatically termed a government of laws, and not of men. It will certainly cease to deserve this high appellation, if the laws furnish no remedy for the violation of a vested legal right . . .

. . . Is it to be contended that where the law in precise terms directs the performance of an act in which an individual is interested, the law is incapable of securing obedience to its mandate? Is it on account of the character of the person against whom the complaint is made? Is it to be contended that the heads of departments are not amenable to the laws of their country?

Whatever the practice on particular occasions may be, the theory of this principle will certainly never be maintained. No act of the legislature confers so extraordinary a privilege, nor can it derive countenance from the doctrines of the common law. . . .

The power of nominating to the Senate, and the power of appointing the person nominated, are political powers, to be exercised by the president according to his own discretion. When he has made an appointment, he has exercised his whole power, and his discretion has been completely applied to the case. If, by law, the officer be removable at the will of the president, then a new appointment may be immediately made, and the rights of the officer are terminated. But as a fact which has existed cannot be made never to have existed, the appointment cannot be annihilated; and consequently if the officer is by law not removable at the will of the president, the rights he has acquired are protected by the law, and are not resumable by the president. They cannot be extinguished by executive authority, and he has the privilege of asserting them in like manner as if they had been derived from any other source.

The question whether a right has vested or not, is, in its nature, judicial, and must be tried by the judicial authority. If, for example, Mr. Marbury had taken the oaths of a magistrate, and proceeded to act as one; in consequence of which a suit had been instituted against him, in which his defense had depended on his being a magistrate; the validity of his appointment must have been determined by judicial authority.

So, if he conceives that by virtue of his appointment he has a legal right either to the commission which has been made out for him or to a copy of that commission, it is equally a question examinable in a court, and the decision of the Court upon it must depend on the opinion entertained of his appointment. That question has been discussed, and the opinion is, that the latest point of time which can be taken as that at which the appointment was complete, and evidenced, was when, after the signature of the president, the seal of the United States was affixed to the commission.

It is then the opinion of the Court:

1. That by signing the commission of Mr. Marbury, the president of the United States appointed him a justice of peace for the county of Washington in the District of Columbia; and that the seal of the United States, affixed thereto by the secretary of state, is conclusive testimony of the verity of the signature, and of the completion of the appointment; and that the appointment conferred on him a legal right to the office for the space of five years.
2. That, having this legal title to the office, he has a consequent right to the commission; a refusal to deliver which is a plain violation of that right, for which the laws of his country afford him a remedy.

It remains to be inquired whether

3. He is entitled to the remedy for which he applies. This depends on:
   1. The nature of the writ applied for, and
   2. The power of this Court.

1. The nature of the writ.

Blackstone, in the third volume of his *Commentaries*, page 110, defines a mandamus to be: "a command issuing in the king's name from the court of king's bench, and directed to any person, corporation, or inferior court of judicature within the king's dominions, requiring them to do some particular thing therein specified which appertains to their office and duty, and which the court of king's bench has previously determined, or at least supposes, to be consonant to right and justice."

Lord Mansfield, in 3 Burrows, 1266, in the case of *The King v. Baker et al.*

states with much precision and explicitness the cases in which this writ may be used. "Whenever," says that very able judge, "there is a right to execute an office, perform a service, or exercise a franchise (more especially if it be in a matter of public concern or attended with profit), and a person is kept out of possession, or dispossessed of such right, and has no other specific legal remedy, this court ought to assist by mandamus, upon reasons of justice, as the writ expresses, and upon reasons of public policy, to preserve peace, order and good government." In the same case he says, "'this writ ought to be used upon all occasions where the law has established no specific remedy, and where in justice and good government there ought to be one." . . .

This writ, if awarded, would be directed to an officer of government, and its mandate to him would be, to use the words of Blackstone, "to do a particular thing therein specified, which appertains to his office and duty, and which the court has previously determined or at least supposes to be consonant to right and justice." Or, in the words of Lord Mansfield, the applicant, in this case, has a right to execute an office of public concern, and is kept out of possession of that right.

These circumstances certainly concur in this case.

Still, to render the mandamus a proper remedy, the officer to whom it is to be directed, must be one to whom, on legal principles, such writ may be directed; and the person applying for it must be without any other specific and legal remedy.

. . . The intimate political relation, subsisting between the president of the United States and the heads of departments, necessarily renders any legal investigation of the acts of one of those high officers peculiarly irksome, as well as delicate; and excites some hesitation with respect to the propriety of entering into such investigation. Impressions are often received without much reflection or examination; and it is not wonderful that in such a case as this, the assertion, by an individual, of his legal claims in a court of justice, to which claims it is the duty of that court to attend, should at first view be considered by some, as an attempt to intrude into the cabinet, and to intermeddle with the prerogatives of the executive.

It is scarcely necessary for the Court to disclaim all pretensions to such a jurisdiction. An extravagance, so absurd and excessive, could not have been entertained for a moment. The province of the Court is, solely, to decide on the rights of individuals, not to inquire how the executive, or executive officers, perform duties in which they have discretion. Questions, in their nature political, or which are, by the Constitution and laws, submitted to the executive, can never be made in this court.

But . . . what is there in the exalted station of the officer, which shall bar a citizen from asserting, in a court of justice, his legal rights, or shall forbid a court to listen to the claim or to issue a mandamus directing the performance of a duty not depending on executive discretion, but on particular acts of congress and the general principles of law?

If one of the heads of departments commits any illegal act, under color of his office, by which an individual sustains an injury, it cannot be pretended that his office alone exempts him from being sued in the ordinary mode of proceeding, and being compelled to obey the judgment of the law. How then can his office exempt him from this particular mode of deciding on the legality of his conduct, if the case be such a case as would, were any other individual the party complained of, authorize the process?

It is not by the office of the person to whom the writ is directed, but the nature of the thing to be done, that the propriety or impropriety of issuing a mandamus is to be determined. Where the head of a department acts in a case in which executive discretion is to be exercised; in which he is the mere organ of executive will; it is again repeated, that any application to a court to control, in any respect, his conduct, would be rejected without hesitation.

But where he is directed by law to do a certain act affecting the absolute rights of individuals, in the performance of which he is not placed under the particular direction of the president, and the performance of which the president cannot lawfully forbid, and therefore is never presumed to have forbidden—as for example, to record a commission, or a patent for land, which has received all the legal solemnities; or to give a copy of such record—in such cases, it is not perceived on what ground the courts of the country are further excused from the duty of giving judgment, that right to be done to an injured individual, than if the same services were to be performed by a person not the head of a department. . . .

This, then, is a plain case of a mandamus, either to deliver the commission, or a copy of it from the record; and it only remains to be inquired, whether it can issue from this court.

The act to establish the judicial courts of the United States authorizes the Supreme Court "to issue writs of mandamus, in cases warranted by the principles and usages of law, to any courts appointed, or persons holding office, under the authority of the United States."

The secretary of state, being a person, holding an office under the authority of the United States, is precisely within the letter of the description; and if this court is not authorized to issue a writ of mandamus to such an officer, it must be because the law is unconstitutional, and therefore absolutely incapable of conferring the authority, and assigning the duties which its words purport to confer and assign.

The Constitution vests the whole judicial power of the United States in one Supreme Court, and such inferior courts as Congress shall, from time to time, ordain and establish. This power is expressly extended to all cases arising under the laws of the United States; and consequently, in some form, may be exercised over the present case; because the right claimed is given by a law of the United States.

In the distribution of this power it is declared that "the Supreme Court shall have original jurisdiction in all cases affecting ambassadors, other public ministers and consuls, and those in which a state shall be a party. In all other cases, the Supreme Court shall have appellate jurisdiction." . . .

When an instrument organizing fundamentally a judicial system, divides it into one supreme, and so many inferior courts as the legislature may ordain and establish; then enumerates its powers, and proceeds so far to distribute them, as to define the jurisdiction of the Supreme Court by declaring the cases in which it shall take original jurisdiction, and that in others it shall take appellate jurisdiction, the plain import of the words seems to be, that in one class of cases its jurisdiction is original, and not appellate; in the other it is appellate, and not original. . . .

To enable this court then to issue a mandamus, it must be shown to be an exercise of appellate jurisdiction, or to be necessary to enable them to exercise appellate jurisdiction.

It has been stated at the bar that the appellate jurisdiction may be exercised in a variety of forms, and that if it be the will of the legislature that a mandamus should be used for that purpose, that will must be obeyed. This is true; yet the jurisdiction must be appellate, not original. It is the essential criterion of appellate jurisdiction, that it revises and corrects the proceedings in a cause already instituted, and does not create that case. Although, therefore, a mandamus may be directed to courts, yet to issue such a writ to an officer for the delivery of a paper, is in effect the same as to sustain an original action for that paper, and therefore seems not to belong to appellate, but to original jurisdiction.

The authority, therefore, given to the Supreme Court, by the act establishing the judicial courts of the United States, to issue writs of mandamus to public officers, appears not to be warranted by the Constitution; and it becomes necessary to inquire whether a jurisdiction, so conferred, can be exercised.

The question, whether an act, repugnant to the Constitution, can become the law of the land, is a question deeply interesting to the United States; but, happily, not of an intricacy proportioned to its interest. It seems only necessary to recognize certain principles, supposed to have been long and well established, to decide it.

That the people have an original right to establish, for their future government, such principles as, in their opinion, shall most conduce to their own happiness, is the basis on which the whole American fabric has been erected. The exercise of this original right is a very great exertion; nor can it nor ought it to be frequently repeated. The principles, therefore, so established are deemed fundamental. And as the authority, from which they proceed, is supreme, and can seldom act, they are designed to be permanent. This original and supreme will organizes the government, and assigns to different departments their respective powers. It may either stop here; or establish certain limits not to be transcended by those departments.

The government of the United States is of the latter description. . . .

. . . The Constitution is either a superior, paramount law, unchangeable by ordinary means, or it is on a level with ordinary legislative acts, and like other acts, is alterable when the legislature shall please to alter it.

If the former part of the alternative be true, then a legislative act contrary to the Constitution is not law: if the latter part be true, then written constitutions are absurd attempts, on the part of the people, to limit a power in its own nature illimitable.

Certainly all those who have framed written constitutions contemplate them as forming the fundamental and paramount law of the nation, and consequently the theory of every such government must be that an act of the legislature repugnant to the constitution is void.

This theory is essentially attached to a written constitution, and is consequently to be considered by this court as one of the fundamental principles of our society. It is not therefore to be lost sight of in the further consideration of this subject.

If an act of the legislature repugnant to the Constitution is void, does it, notwithstanding its invalidity, bind the courts and oblige them to give it effect? Or, in other words, though it be not law, does it constitute a rule as operative as if it was a law? This would be to overthrow in fact what was established in theory; and would seem, at first view, an absurdity too gross to be insisted on. It shall, however, receive a more attentive consideration.

It is emphatically the province and duty of the judicial department to say what the law is. Those who apply the rule to particular cases must, of necessity, expound and interpret that rule. If two laws conflict with each other, the courts must decide on the operation of each.

So, if a law be in opposition to the Constitution, if both the law and the Constitution apply to a particular case, so that the Court must either decide that case conformably to the law, disregarding the Constitution, or conformably to the Constitution, disregarding the law, the Court must determine which of these conflicting rules governs the case. This is of the very essence of judicial duty. . . .

Those, then, who controvert the principle that the Constitution is to be considered, in court, as a paramount law, are reduced to the necessity of maintaining that courts must close their eyes on the Constitution, and see only the law.

This doctrine would subvert the very foundation of all written constitutions. It would declare that an act, which, according to the principles and theory of our government, is entirely void, is yet, in practice, completely obligatory. It would declare that if the legislature shall do what is expressly forbidden, such act, notwithstanding the express prohibition, is in reality effectual. It would be giving to the legislature a practical and real omnipotence with the same breath which professes to restrict their powers within narrow limits. It is prescribing limits, and declaring that those limits may be passed at pleasure. . . .

It is declared that "no tax or duty shall be laid on articles exported from any state." Suppose a duty on the export of cotton, of tobacco, or of flour, and a suit instituted to recover it. Ought judgment to be rendered in such a case? . . .

The Constitution declares that "no bill of attainder or ex post facto law shall be passed."

If, however, such a bill should be passed and a person should be prosecuted under it, must the court condemn to death those victims whom the Constitution endeavors to preserve? . . .

From these and many other selections which might be made, it is apparent that the framers of the Constitution contemplated that instrument as a rule for the government of courts, as well as of the legislature.

Why otherwise does it direct the judges to take an oath to support it? This oath certainly applies, in an especial manner, to their conduct in their official character. How immoral to impose it on them, if they were to be used as the instruments, and the knowing instruments, for violating what they swear to support!

The oath of office, too, imposed by the legislature, is completely demonstrative of the legislative opinion on this subject. It is in these words: "I do solemnly swear that I will administer justice without respect to persons, and do equal right to the poor and to the rich; and that I will faithfully and impartially discharge all the duties incumbent on me as according to the best of my abilities and understanding, agreeably to the Constitution and laws of the United States."

Why does a judge swear to discharge his duties agreeably to the constitution of the United States, if that constitution forms no rule for his government? . . .

Thus, the particular phraseology of the Constitution of the United States confirms and strengthens the principle, supposed to be essential to all written constitutions, that a law repugnant to the Constitution is void, and that courts, as well as other departments, are bound by that instrument.

The rule must be discharged.

Source: *Reports of Cases Argued and Adjudged in the Supreme Court of the United States*, ed. William Cranch (Washington, D.C.: Government Printing Office, 1804), 1: 137ff. As available from Cornell University Law School, Legal Information Institute. Retrieved May 4, 2010, from http://www.law.cornell.edu/supct/html/historics/USSC_CR_0005_0137_ZO.html.

CHAPTER 14

James Madison's Address for a Declaration of War, 1812

In June of 1812, James Madison addressed Congress over concerns regarding a series of belligerent acts by Great Britain against the United States that he believed warranted a military response and a declaration of war. Britain had continued its policy of "impressment," in which British naval officers boarded American merchant ships, deemed American citizens either "deserters" from the Royal Navy or British subjects by denying naturalization, and forced them into service aboard British men-of-war. American ships were routinely boarded, illegally and with impunity. But the United States was woefully unprepared for a conflict, either on land or at sea. By committing the nation to a war with a leading European military power—which possessed the world's finest navy—Madison risked the nation's very existence. The war hawks, namely those Congressmen who sought war, hoped to expand America's borders, perhaps bringing Canada into the United States. Yet Madison mentioned nothing of this expansionism in his speech.

To a large degree, Madison's address epitomized the War of 1812, which was poorly conceived, misdirected, and nearly catastrophic. The British strategy was to separate New England from the rest of the United States and lay claim to New England, New York, and Michigan, and then, after seizing New Orleans, to claim all land west of the Mississippi. The first objective, to be accomplished through a victory in 1814 following the strategy employed by General Burgoyne in 1777, was denied them at the Battle of Plattsburgh by the commander of the American naval forces, Thomas McDonough; the second, after Edward Pakenham's defeat at New Orleans. It may be difficult today to understand the extent of Britain's arrogance in 1814 as the world's greatest superpower. Even after the Plattsburgh defeat and British commander George Prévost's retreat back to Canada, many Britons were in favor of sending Wellington (who volunteered to go) to America with an army of fifty thousand Napoleonic War veterans. Given that the United States was still depending on militia and its navy was bottled up in port, it is most likely that a long war would have ensued. As Englishman William Corbett said, "We must completely subjugate the Americans. . . . A great kingdom, the mistress of the sea, and Dictatress of Europe, on the one side; and the last of the republics on the other. The world is now going to see whether a republic, without a stand-ing army, [will] be able to contend single-handed against a kingdom with a thou-sand ships of war, and [an] army of two hundred thousand men. May the end be favorable to this country [England] and mankind in general."* Meanwhile, New England threatened to secede in opposition to the war, American efforts against Canada came to naught, the American navy was driven from the high seas, Washington was seized and burned, and only the defense of Baltimore together with McDonough's victory at Plattsburgh narrowly convinced the British peace negotiators to conclude a treaty that merely restored the prewar status between the two countries.

As with any war speech, Madison's rationale for sending American troops into combat should be examined with an eye toward possible alternatives, weigh-ing the risk against possible undesirable outcomes and, above all, the legitimacy and constitutionality of the request.

Speech to Congress, June 1, 1812

I COMMUNICATE TO CONGRESS CERTAIN DOCUMENTS, BEING a continuation of those heretofore laid before them on the subject of our affairs with Great Britain.

Without going back beyond the renewal in 1803 of the war in which Great Britain is engaged, and omitting unrepaired wrongs of inferior magnitude, the conduct of her Government presents a series of acts hostile to the United States as an independent and neutral nation.

British cruisers have been in the continued practice of violating the Amer-ican flag on the great highway of nations, and of seizing and carrying off per-sons sailing under it, not in the exercise of a belligerent right founded on the law of nations against an enemy, but of a municipal prerogative over British subjects. British jurisdiction is thus extended to neutral vessels in a situation where no laws can operate but the law of nations and the laws of the country to which the vessels belong, and a self-redress is assumed which, if British subjects were wrongfully detained and alone concerned, is that substitution of force for a resort to the responsible sovereign which falls within the defini-tion of war. Could the seizure of British subjects in such cases be regarded as within the exercise of a belligerent right, the acknowledged laws of war, which

---

* David G. Fitz-Enz, *The Final Invasion* (Lincoln: University of Nebraska Press, 2009), 178.

forbid an article of captured property to be adjudged without a regular investigation before a competent tribunal, would imperiously demand the fairest trial where the sacred rights of persons were at issue. In place of such a trial these rights are subjected to the will of every petty commander.

The practice, hence, is so far from affecting British subjects alone that, under the pretext of searching for these, thousands of American citizens, under the safeguard of public law and of their national flag, have been torn from their country and from everything dear to them; have been dragged on board ships of war of a foreign nation and exposed, under the severities of their discipline, to be exiled to the most distant and deadly climes, to risk their lives in the battles of their oppressors, and to be the melancholy instruments of taking away those of their own brethren.

Against this crying enormity, which Great Britain would be so prompt to avenge if committed against herself, the United States have in vain exhausted remonstrances and expostulations, and that no proof might be wanting of their conciliatory dispositions, and no pretext left for a continuance of the practice, the British Government was formally assured of the readiness of the United States to enter into arrangements such as could not be rejected if the recovery of British subjects were the real and the sole object. The communication passed without effect.

British cruisers have been in the practice also of violating the rights and the peace of our coasts. They hover over and harass our entering and departing commerce. To the most insulting pretensions they have added the most lawless proceedings in our very harbors, and have wantonly spilt American blood within the sanctuary of our territorial jurisdiction. The principles and rules enforced by that nation, when a neutral nation, against armed vessels of belligerents hovering near her coasts and disturbing her commerce, are well known. When called on, nevertheless, by the United States to punish the greater offenses committed by her own vessels, her Government has bestowed on their commanders additional marks of honor and confidence.

Under pretended blockades, without the presence of an adequate force and sometimes without the practicability of applying one, our commerce has been plundered in every sea, the great staples of our country have been cut off from their legitimate markets, and a destructive blow aimed at our agricultural and maritime interests. . . . And to render the outrage the more signal these mock blockades have been reiterated and enforced in the face of official communications from the British Government declaring as the true definition of a legal blockade "that particular ports must be actually invested and previous warning given to vessels bound to them not to enter."

Not content with these occasional expedients for laying waste our neutral trade, the cabinet of Britain resorted at length to the sweeping system of blockades, under the name of orders in council, which has been molded and managed as might best suit its political views, its commercial jealousies, or the avidity of British cruisers.

To our remonstrances against the complicated and transcendent injustice of this innovation the first reply was that the orders were reluctantly adopted by Great Britain as a necessary retaliation on decrees of her enemy proclaiming a general blockade of the British Isles at a time when the naval force of that enemy dared not issue from his own ports. She was reminded without effect that her own prior blockades, unsupported by an adequate naval force actually applied and continued, were a bar to this plea; that executed edicts against millions of our property could not be retaliation on edicts confessedly impossible to be executed; that retaliation, to be just, should fall on the party setting the guilty example, not on an innocent party which was not even chargeable with an acquiescence in it.

When deprived of this flimsy veil for a prohibition of our trade with her enemy by the repeal of his prohibition of our trade with Great Britain, her cabinet, instead of a corresponding repeal or a practical discontinuance of its orders, formally avowed a determination to persist in them against the United States until the markets of her enemy should be laid open to British products, thus asserting an obligation on a neutral power to require one belligerent to encourage by its internal regulations the trade of another belligerent, contradicting her own practice toward all nations, in peace as well as in war, and betraying the insincerity of those professions which inculcated a belief that, having resorted to her orders with regret, she was anxious to find an occasion for putting an end to them.

Abandoning still more all respect for the neutral rights of the United States and for its own consistency, the British Government now demands as prerequisites to a repeal of its orders as they relate to the United States that a formality should be observed in the repeal of the French decrees nowise necessary to their termination nor exemplified by British usage, and that the French repeal, besides including that portion of the decrees which operates within a territorial jurisdiction, as well as that which operates on the high seas, against the commerce of the United States should not be a single and special repeal in relation to the United States, but should be extended to whatever other neutral nations unconnected with them may be affected by those decrees. And as an additional insult, they are called on for a formal disavowal of conditions and pretensions advanced by the French Government for which the United States are so far from having made themselves responsible that, in official explanations which have been published to the world, and in a correspondence of the American minister at London with the British minister for foreign affairs such a responsibility was explicitly and emphatically disclaimed.

It has become, indeed, sufficiently certain that the commerce of the United States is to be sacrificed, not as interfering with the belligerent rights of Great Britain; not as supplying the wants of her enemies, which she herself supplies; but as interfering with the monopoly which she covets for her own commerce and navigation. She carries on a war against the lawful commerce of a friend that she may the better carry on commerce with an enemy—a commerce polluted by the forgeries and perjuries which are for the most part the only passports by which it can succeed.

Anxious to make every experiment short of the last resort of injured nations, the United States have withheld from Great Britain, under successive modifications, the benefits of a free intercourse with their market, the loss of which could not but outweigh the profits accruing from her restrictions of our commerce with other nations. . . . To these appeals her Government has been equally inflexible, as if willing to make sacrifices of every sort rather than yield to the claims of justice or renounce the errors of a false pride. Nay, so far were the attempts carried to overcome the attachment of the British cabinet to its unjust edicts that it received every encouragement within the competency of the executive branch of our Government to expect that a repeal of them would be followed by a war between the United States and France, unless the French edicts should also be repealed. Even this communication, although silencing forever the plea of a disposition in the United States to acquiesce in those edicts originally the sole plea for them, received no attention.

If no other proof existed of a predetermination of the British Government against a repeal of its orders, it might be found in the correspondence of the minister plenipotentiary of the United States at London and the British secretary for foreign affairs in 1810, on the question whether the blockade of May 1806 was considered as in force or as not in force. It had been ascertained that the French Government, which urged this blockade as the ground of its Berlin decree, was willing in the event of its removal to repeal that decree, which, being followed by alternate repeals of the other offensive edicts, might abolish the whole system on both sides. This inviting opportunity for accomplishing an object so important to the United States, and professed so often to be the desire of both the belligerents, was made known to the British Government. As that Government admits that an actual application of an adequate force is necessary to the existence of a legal blockade, and it was notorious that if such a force had ever been applied its long discontinuance had annulled the blockade in question, there could be no sufficient objection on the part of Great Britain to a formal revocation of it, and no imaginable objection to a declaration of the fact that the blockade did not exist. The declaration would have been consistent with her avowed principles of blockade, and would have enabled the United States to demand from France the pledged repeal of her decrees, either with success, in which case the way would have been opened for a general repeal of the belligerent edicts, or without success, in which case the United States would have been justified in turning their measures exclusively against France. The British Government would, however, neither rescind the blockade nor declare its nonexistence, nor permit its nonexistence to be inferred and affirmed by the American plenipotentiary. On the contrary, by representing the blockade to be comprehended in the orders in council, the United States were compelled so to regard it in their subsequent proceedings.

There was a period when a favorable change in the policy of the British cabinet was justly considered as established. The minister plenipotentiary of His Britannic Majesty here proposed an adjustment of the differences more immediately endangering the harmony of the two countries. The proposition was accepted with the promptitude and cordiality corresponding with the invariable professions of this Government. A foundation appeared to be laid for a sincere and lasting reconciliation. The prospect, however, quickly vanished. The whole proceeding was disavowed by the British Government without any explanations which could at that time repress the belief that the disavowal proceeded from a spirit of hostility to the commercial rights and prosperity of the United States; and it has since come into proof that at the very moment when the public minister was holding the language of friendship and inspiring confidence in the sincerity of the negotiation with which he was charged a secret agent of his Government was employed in intrigues having for their object a subversion of our Government and a dismemberment of our happy union.

In reviewing the conduct of Great Britain toward the United States our attention is necessarily drawn to the warfare just renewed by the savages on one of our extensive frontiers—a warfare which is known to spare neither age nor sex and to be distinguished by features peculiarly shocking to humanity. It is difficult to account for the activity and combinations which have for some time been developing themselves among tribes in constant intercourse with British traders and garrisons without connecting their hostility with that influence and without recollecting the authenticated examples of such interpositions heretofore furnished by the officers and agents of that Government.

Such is the spectacle of injuries and indignities which have been heaped on our country, and such the crisis which its unexampled forbearance and conciliatory efforts have not been able to avert. It might at least have been expected that an enlightened nation, if less urged by moral obligations or invited by friendly dispositions on the part of the United States, would have found in its true interest alone a sufficient motive to respect their rights and their tranquility on the high seas; that an enlarged policy would have favored that free and general circulation of commerce in which the British nation is at all times interested, and which in times of war is the best alleviation of its calamities to herself as well as to other belligerents; and more especially that the British cabinet would not, for the sake of a precarious and surreptitious intercourse with hostile markets, have persevered in a course of measures which necessarily put at hazard the invaluable market of a great and growing country, disposed to cultivate the mutual advantages of an active commerce.

Other counsels have prevailed. Our moderation and conciliation have had no other effect than to encourage perseverance and to enlarge pretensions. We behold our seafaring citizens still the daily victims of lawless violence, committed on the great common and highway of nations, even within sight of the country which owes them protection. We behold our vessels, freighted with the products of our soil and industry, or returning with the honest proceeds of them, wrested from their lawful destinations, confiscated by prize courts no longer the organs of public law but the instruments of arbitrary edicts, and their unfortunate crews dispersed and lost, or forced or inveigled in British ports into British fleets, whilst arguments are employed in support of these aggressions which have no foundation but in a principle equally supporting a claim to regulate our external commerce in all cases whatsoever.

We behold, in fine, on the side of Great Britain a state of war against the United States, and on the side of the United States a state of peace toward Great Britain.

Whether the United States shall continue passive under these progressive usurpations and these accumulating wrongs, or, opposing force to force in defense of their national rights, shall commit a just cause into the hands of the Almighty Disposer of Events, avoiding all connections which might entangle it in the contest or views of other powers, and preserving a constant readiness to concur in an honorable reestablishment of peace and friendship, is a solemn question which the Constitution wisely confides to the legislative department of the Government. In recommending it to their early deliberations I am happy in the assurance that the decision will be worthy the enlightened and patriotic councils of a virtuous, a free, and a powerful nation. . . .

Source: *A Compilation of the Messages and Papers of the Presidents 1789–1899*, ed. James D. Richardson (Washington, D.C.: Government Printing Office, 1909), 1: 499–505. As available at Project Gutenberg. Retrieved May 5, 2010, from http://www .gutenberg.org/dirs/1/0/8/9/10895/10895.txt.

CHAPTER 15

Missouri Enabling Act, 1820

The Missouri Enabling Act, the legislative act produced by the compromise crafted in Congress by Henry Clay to keep the number of free and slave states in the United States equal, went into effect on March 6, 1820. The year before, Alabama had been admitted into the union, bringing the slave and free states into parity at eleven each, and now Maine and Missouri were to be admitted, Maine as a free state, Missouri as a slave state. Maine was admitted in March 1820, but another year of rancorous debate would ensue before Missouri was accepted as a state. This act permitted slavery in Missouri but extended a line west from Missouri's southern border above which slavery would not be allowed except in the state of Missouri itself.

Thomas Jefferson said the Missouri Compromise—as it came to be called— awakened him like "a fire bell in the night" because he realized that the problem of slavery was coming to dominate the national discourse. Northern population growth had already given free states control of the House of Representatives, and Delaware, Maryland, and Kentucky were slave states with substantial antislavery populations. The Missouri Compromise only delayed a solution rather than providing a permanent one. Next to come was the question of slavery in, and the timing of statehood for, Arkansas, Michigan, Texas, Florida, Iowa, and Wisconsin, and eventually everything fell apart with California, Minnesota, Oregon, and Kansas—all free territories—seeking admission as states.

Everyone knew that parity between slave and free states could not be maintained forever, but the only other approach attempted was Martin Van Buren's, which involved the creation of a national party that would ignore the issue of slavery and reward its supporters with party and government jobs. Within forty years, however, the folly of Van Buren's system was exposed when the presidency fell into the hands of a northerner, Abraham Lincoln, who had vowed to keep slavery out of the territories. In effect, the short-term patches made the eventual long-term solution, when it came, all the more violent and disruptive.

An Act to Authorize the People of the Missouri Territory to Form a Constitution and State Government, and for the Admission of Such State into the Union on an Equal Footing with the Original States, and to Prohibit Slavery in Certain Territories

BE IT ENACTED BY THE SENATE AND HOUSE OF REPRESENTA-
tives of the United States of America, in Congress assembled, That the inhabitants of that portion of the Missouri territory included within the boundaries herein after designated, be, and they are hereby, authorized to form for themselves a constitution and state government, and to assume such name as they shall deem proper; and the said state, when formed, shall be admitted into the Union, upon an equal footing with the original states, in all respects whatsoever.

Section 2. And be it further enacted, that the said state shall consist of all the territory included within the following boundaries, to wit: Beginning in the middle of the Mississippi River, on the parallel of thirty-six degrees of north latitude; thence west, along that parallel of latitude, to the St. Francois River; thence up, and following the course of that river, in the middle of the main channel thereof, to the parallel of latitude of thirty-six degrees and thirty minutes; thence west, along the same, to a point where the said parallel is intersected by a meridian line passing through the middle of the mouth of the Kansas River, where the same empties into the Missouri River, thence, from the point aforesaid north, along the said meridian line, to the intersection of the parallel of latitude which passes through the rapids of the river Des Moines, making the said line to correspond with the Indian boundary line; thence east, from the point of intersection last aforesaid, along the said parallel of latitude, to the middle of the channel of the main fork of the said river Des Moines; thence down and along the middle of the main channel of the said river Des Moines, to the mouth of the same, where it empties into the Mississippi River; thence, due east, to the middle of the main channel of the Mississippi River; thence down, and following the course of the Mississippi River, in the middle of the main channel thereof, to the place of beginning: Provided, the said state shall ratify the boundaries aforesaid. And provided also, that the said state shall have concurrent jurisdiction on the river Mississippi, and every other river bordering on the said state so far as the said rivers shall form a common boundary to the said state; and any other state or states, now or hereafter to be formed and bounded by the same, such rivers to be common to both; and that the river Mississippi, and the navigable rivers and waters leading into the same, shall be common highways, and forever free, as well to the inhabitants of the said state as to other citizens of the United States, without any tax, duty, impost, or toll, therefore, imposed by the said state.

Section 3. And be it further enacted, that all free white male citizens of the United States, who shall have arrived at the age of twenty-one years, and have resided in said territory three months previous to the day of election, and all other persons qualified to vote for representatives to the general assembly of the said territory, shall be qualified to be elected and they are hereby qualified and authorized to vote, and choose representatives to form a convention, who shall be apportioned amongst the several counties. . . .

Section 4. And be it further enacted, that the members of the convention thus duly elected, shall be, and they are hereby authorized to meet at the seat of government of said territory on the second Monday of the month of June next; and the said convention, when so assembled, shall have power and authority to adjourn to any other place in the said territory, which to them shall seem best for the convenient transaction of their business; and which convention, when so met, shall first determine by a majority of the whole number elected, whether it be, or be not, expedient at that time to form a constitution and state government for the people within the said territory, as included within the boundaries above designated; and if it be deemed expedient, the convention shall be, and hereby is, authorized to form a constitution and state government; or, if it be deemed more expedient, the said convention shall provide by ordinance for electing representatives to form a constitution or frame of government; which said representatives shall be chosen in such manner, and in such proportion as they shall designate; and shall meet at such time and place as shall be prescribed by the said ordinance; and shall then form for the people of said territory, within the boundaries aforesaid, a constitution and state government: Provided, That the same, whenever formed, shall be republican, and not repugnant to the constitution of the United States; and that the legislature of said state shall never interfere with the primary disposal of the soil by the United States, nor with any regulations Congress may find necessary for securing the title in such soil to the bona fide purchasers; and that no tax shall be imposed on lands the property of the United States; and in no case shall nonresident proprietors be taxed higher than residents.

Section 5. And be it further enacted, that until the next general census shall be taken, the said state shall be entitled to one representative in the House of Representatives of the United States.

Section 6. And be it further enacted, that the following propositions be, and the same are hereby, offered to the convention of the said territory of Missouri, when formed, for their free acceptance or rejection, which, if accepted by the convention, shall be obligatory upon the United States:

First. That section numbered sixteen in every township, and when such section has been sold, or otherwise disposed of, other lands equivalent thereto, and as contiguous as may be, shall be granted to the state for the use of the inhabitants of such township, for the use of schools.

Second. That all salt springs, not exceeding twelve in number, with six sections of land adjoining to each, shall be granted to the said state for the use of said state, the same to be selected by the legislature of the said state, on or before the first day of January, in the year one thousand eight hundred and twenty-five; and the same, when so selected, to be used under such terms, conditions, and regulations, as the legislature of said state shall direct: Provided, That no salt spring, the right whereof now is, or hereafter shall be, confirmed or adjudged to any individual or individuals, shall, by this section, be granted to the said state: And provided also, That the legislature shall never sell or lease the same, at anyone time, for a longer period than ten years, without the consent of Congress.

Third. That five percent of the net proceeds of the sale of lands lying within the said territory or state, and which shall be sold by Congress, from and after the first day of January next, after deducting all expenses incident to the same, shall be reserved for making public roads and canals, of which three-fifths shall be applied to those objects within the state, under the direction of the legislature thereof; and the other two-fifths in defraying, under the direction of Congress, the expenses to be incurred in making of a road or roads, canal or canals, leading to the said state.

Fourth. That four entire sections of land be, and the same are hereby, granted to the said state, for the purpose of fixing their seat of government thereon; which said sections shall, under the direction of the legislature of said state, be located, as near as may be, in one body, at any time, in such townships and ranges as the legislature aforesaid may select, on any of the public lands of the United States: Provided, That such locations shall be made prior to the public sale of the lands of the United States surrounding such location.

Fifth. That thirty-six sections, or one entire township, which shall be designated by the president of the United States, together with the other lands heretofore reserved for that purpose, shall be reserved for the use of a seminary of learning, and vested in the legislature of said state, to be appropriated solely to the use of such seminary by the said legislature: Provided, That the five foregoing propositions herein offered, are on the condition that the convention of the said state shall provide, by an ordinance, irrevocable without the consent or the United States, that every and each tract of land sold by the United States, from and after the first day of January next, shall remain exempt from any tax laid by order or under the authority of the state, whether for state, county, or township, or any other purpose whatever, for the term of five years from and after the day of sale; and further, that the bounty lands granted, or hereafter to be granted, for military services during the late war, shall, while they continue to be held by the patentees, or their heirs, remain exempt as aforesaid from taxation for the term of three year; from and after the date of the patents respectively.

Section 7. And be it further enacted, that in case a constitution and state government shall be formed for the people of the said territory of Missouri, the said convention or representatives, as soon thereafter as may be, shall cause a true and attested copy of such constitution or frame of state government, as shall be formed or provided, to be transmitted to Congress.

Section 8. And be it further enacted, that in all that territory ceded by France to the United States, under the name of Louisiana, which lies north of thirty-six degrees and thirty minutes north latitude, not included within the limits of the state, contemplated by this act, slavery and involuntary servitude, otherwise than in the punishment of crimes, whereof the parties shall have been duly convicted, shall be, and is hereby, forever prohibited: Provided always, That any person escaping into the same, from whom labor or service is lawfully claimed, in any state or territory of the United States, such fugitive may be lawfully reclaimed and conveyed to the person claiming his or her labor or service as aforesaid.

Source: The Public Statutes at Large of the United States of America from the Organization of the Government in 1789 to March 3, 1856, ed. Richard Peters (Boston: Little Brown, 1856), 3: 545–8. As available at the National Archives and Records Administration's Ourdocuments.gov. Retrieved April 30, 2010, from http://www.ourdocuments.gov/doc.php?doc=22&page=transcript.

CHAPTER 16

The Monroe Doctrine, 1823

The Monroe Doctrine, as it is known today, was established during President James Monroe's seventh annual message to Congress on December 2, 1823. The speech originally included remarks indicating American interest in various European events, including the activities of the Holy Alliance, which subsequently became the Concert of Europe, but Monroe's secretary of state, John Quincy Adams, argued persuasively against them. The Spanish empire in the Western Hemisphere was breaking up into independent nations, and their weak governments and economies could tempt various European powers into seeking new colonial empires. Great Britain sought to protect its trade relationships, and the British foreign minister suggested that the United States and Britain issue a joint "hands-off" statement. Monroe rejected the British initiative but was forced into action when Russia laid claim to the Northwest and attempted to control trade in that area. Accordingly, a clear message was delivered that the United States would tolerate no European interference in Western Hemisphere affairs, and America would take no part in European matters. Excluded from this policy were European colonies already established in the Americas, such as England's Canada and Spain's Cuba, that were not in revolt against their mother countries, and the doctrine, as a foreign policy, worked surprisingly well until 1917, when President Woodrow Wilson took the United States into the First World War. The key element, however, that made the doctrine effective for the first seventy-years was its support by Great Britain and the Royal Navy—the primary world power in the Atlantic Ocean.

The reader should reflect on the European powers' penchant toward imperialism during the nineteenth century and what might have developed in the Western Hemisphere had no such doctrine been in place. Have things become better since the United States abandoned its policy of not becoming involved in Europe's wars and political structures? Why was the doctrine not enforced against Cuba during the period when a European country, the USSR, supported the hostile state?

From the President's Annual Message to Congress, 1823

AT THE PROPOSAL OF THE RUSSIAN IMPERIAL GOVERNMENT, made through the minister of the emperor residing here, a full power and instructions have been transmitted to the minister of the United States at St. Petersburg to arrange, by amicable negotiation, the respective rights and interests of the two nations on the northwest coast of this continent. A similar proposal has been made by His Imperial Majesty to the government of Great Britain, which has likewise been acceded to. The government of the United States has been desirous, by this friendly proceeding, of manifesting the great value which they have invariably attached to the friendship of the emperor, and their solicitude to cultivate the best understanding with his government. In the discussions to which this interest has given rise, and in the arrangements by which they may terminate the occasion has been judged proper for asserting, as a principle in which the rights and interests of the United States are involved, that the American continents, by the free and independent condition which they have assumed and maintain, are henceforth not to be considered as subjects for future colonization by any European powers. . . .

It was stated at the commencement of the last session that a great effort was then making in Spain and Portugal, to improve the condition of the people of those countries, and that it appeared to be conducted with extraordinary moderation. It need scarcely be remarked, that the result has been, so far, very different from what was then anticipated. Of events in that quarter of the globe, with which we have so much intercourse, and from which we derive our origin, we have always been anxious and interested spectators. The citizens of the United States cherish sentiments the most friendly, in favor of the liberty and happiness of their fellow men on that side of the Atlantic. In the wars of the European powers, in matters relating to themselves, we have never taken any part, nor does it comport with our policy to do so. It is only when our rights are invaded, or seriously menaced, that we resent injuries, or make preparation for our defense. With the movements in this hemisphere, we are, of necessity, more immediately connected, and by causes which must be obvious to all enlightened and impartial observers. The political system of the allied powers is essentially different, in this respect, from that of America. This difference proceeds from that which exists in their respective governments. And to the defense of our own, which has been achieved by the loss of so much blood and treasure, and matured by the wisdom of their most enlightened citizens, and under which we have enjoyed unexampled felicity, this whole nation is devoted. We owe it, therefore, to candor, and to the amicable relations existing between the United States and those powers, to declare, that we should consider any attempt on their part to extend their system to any portion of this hemisphere, as dangerous to our peace and safety. With the existing colonies or dependencies of any European power we have not interfered, and shall not interfere. But with the governments who have declared their independence, and maintained it, and whose independence we have, on great consideration, and on just principles, acknowledged, we could not view any interposition for the purpose of oppressing them, or controlling, in any other manner, their destiny, by any European power in any other light than as the manifestation of an unfriendly disposition towards the United States. In the war between those new governments and Spain we declared our neutrality at the time of their recognition, and to this we have adhered, and shall continue to adhere, provided no change shall occur, which, in the judgment of the competent authorities of this government, shall make a corresponding change, on the part of the United States, indispensable to their security.

The late events in Spain and Portugal show that Europe is still unsettled. Of this important fact, no stronger proof can be adduced than that the allied powers should have thought it proper, on any principle satisfactory to them-selves, to have interposed, by force, in the internal concerns of Spain. . . . Our policy, in regard to Europe, which was adopted at an early stage of the wars which have so long agitated that quarter of the globe, nevertheless remains the same, which is, not to interfere in the internal concerns of any of its powers; to consider the government de facto as the legitimate government for us; to cultivate friendly relations with it, and to preserve those relations by a frank, firm, and manly policy; meeting, in all instances, the just claims of every power; submitting to injuries from none. But, in regard to these continents, circumstances are eminently and conspicuously different. It is impossible that the allied powers should extend their political system to any portion of either continent, without endangering our peace and happiness: nor can anyone believe that our southern brethren, if left to themselves, would adopt it of their own accord. It is equally impossible, therefore, that we should behold such interposition, in any form, with indifference. If we look to the comparative strength and resources of Spain and those new governments, and their dis-tance from each other, it must be obvious that she can never subdue them. It is still the true policy of the United States to leave the parties to themselves, in the hope that other powers will pursue the same course.

Source: *A Compilation of the Messages and Papers of the Presidents 1789–1899*, ed. James D. Richardson (Washington, D.C.: Government Printing Office, 1909), II: 207–20. As available at the Independence Hall Association's UShistory.org. Retrieved May 5, 2010, from http://www.ushistory.org/documents/monroe.htm.

CHAPTER 17

Address on States' Rights and Nullification, John C. Calhoun, 1832

The Nullification Crisis, in which the power of states to nullify federal laws was questioned, pitted against each other two stubborn Scots-Irish pioneers of similar background, Andrew Jackson and John C. Calhoun, president and vice president of the United States. Jackson grew up in the Waxhaws, North Carolina, lost his mother and two brothers during the Revolutionary War, and was orphaned at fourteen. Calhoun lived in Abbeville, South Carolina, lost an uncle to loyalists during the Revolutionary War, his grandmother to the Cherokees, and was orphaned at thirteen. The issue at hand was Jackson's Tariff of 1832, which Calhoun and South Carolina saw as transferring wealth to northern states by keeping prices high for northern finished goods while leaving raw cotton unprotected. Calhoun championed states' rights and held the position that unconstitutional federal laws could be nullified by states as a means of defending their rights, the Constitution, and the people against an out-of-control federal government. For this position, he drew upon the concept of interposition—in which a state could interpose its laws between the federal government and the citizens—developed by James Madison and Thomas Jefferson in the Kentucky and Virginia Resolutions (1798–9). Jackson was sympathetic to South Carolina's position but tended to see the situation as a threat to the union. At a Jefferson Day dinner, Jackson toasted, "Our Federal Union—it must be preserved." Calhoun countered, "To the Union—next to our liberty, the most dear."

Calhoun gave the following address to accompany the passage of South Carolina's Ordinance of Nullification on November 24, 1832. Much of the address had been written four years earlier for his tract *South Carolina Exposition and Protest* but had undergone careful revision. In December Calhoun resigned as vice president to represent his state in the fight, and returned to the Senate. Henry Clay brokered a compromise and the situation was defused, but the principles were resurrected again when South Carolina seceded from the Union in 1860. The arguments presented by South Carolina were never subjected to adjudication and still attract adherents today. States were endowed by the Constitution with certain reserved powers according to the Tenth Amendment, but Jackson—like so many presidents since—seemed willing to ignore the constitutional sovereignty of states in favor of more federal power. Historian William W. Freehling has called the crisis a "prelude to the Civil War,"* but even today it leads one to question whether states have any rights at all if the federal government is always free to usurp them.

From an Address to the Convention of the People of South Carolina, November 1832

WE, THEN, HOLD IT AS UNQUESTIONABLE, THAT, ON THE SEParation from the Crown of Great Britain, the people of the several colonies became free and independent States, possessed of the full right of self-government; and that no power can be rightfully exercised over them, but by the consent and authority of their respective States, expressed or implied. We also hold it as totally unquestionable, that the Constitution of the United States is a compact between the people of the several States, constituting free, independent, and sovereign communities; that the Government it created was formed and appointed to execute, according to the provisions of the instrument, the powers therein granted, as the joint agent of the several States; that all its acts, transcending these powers, are simply and of themselves, null and void, and that in case of such infractions, it is the right of the States, in their sovereign capacity, each acting for itself and its citizens, in like manner as they adopted the Constitution, to judge thereof in the last resort, and to adopt such measures—not inconsistent with the compact—as may be deemed fit, to arrest the execution of the act within their respective limits. Such we hold to be the right of the States, in reference to an unconstitutional act of the Government; nor do we deem their duty to exercise it on proper occasions, less certain and imperative, than the right itself is clear.

We hold it to be a very imperfect conception of the obligation, which each State contracted in ratifying the Constitution, and thereby becoming a member of the Union, to suppose that it would be fully and faithfully discharged, simply by abstaining, on its part, from exercising the powers delegated to the Government of the Union, or by sustaining it in the due execution of those powers. These are, undoubtedly, important federal duties, but there is another not less important, to resist the Government, should it, under color of exer-

---

* William H. Freehling. *Prelude to Civil War: The Nullification Controversy in South Carolina, 1816–1836.* (Oxford: Oxford University Press, 1992.)

cising the delegated, encroach on the reserved powers. The duty of the States is no less clear in the one case than in the other; and the obligation as binding in the one as in the other; and in like manner the solemn obligation of an oath, imposed by the States through the Constitution, on all public functionaries, federal and State, to support that instrument, comprehends the one as well as the other duty; as well that of maintaining the Government in the due exercise of its powers, as that of resisting it when it transcends them.

But the obligation of a State to resist the encroachments of the Government on the reserved powers, is not limited simply to the discharge of its federal duties. We hold that it embraces another, if possible, more sacred— that of protecting its citizens, derived from their original sovereign character, viewed in their separate relations. There are none of the duties of a State of higher obligation. It is, indeed, the primitive duty, preceding all others, and in its nature paramount to them all; and so essential to the existence of a State, that she cannot neglect or abandon it, without forfeiting all just claims to the allegiance of her citizens, and with it, her sovereignty itself. In entering into the Union, the States by no means exempted themselves from the obligation of this, the first and most sacred of their duties; nor, indeed, can they without sinking into subordinate and dependent corporations. It is true, that in ratifying the Constitution, they placed a large and important portion of the rights of their citizens, under the joint protection of all the States, with a view to their more effectual security; but it is not less so, that they reserved, at the same time, a portion still larger, and not less important, under their own immediate guardianship; and in relation to which, the original obligation, to protect the rights of their citizens, from whatever quarter assailed, remained unchanged and unimpaired.

Nor is it less true, that the General Government, created in order to preserve the rights placed under the joint protection of the States, and which, when restricted to its proper sphere, is calculated to afford them the most perfect security, may become, when not so restricted, the most dangerous enemy to the rights of their citizens, including those reserved under the immediate guardianship of the States respectively, as well as those under their joint protection; and thus, the original and inherent obligation of the States to protect their citizens, is united with that which they have contracted to support the Constitution; thereby rendering it the most sacred of all their duties to watch over and resist the encroachments of the Government; and on the faithful performance of which, we solemnly believe the duration of the Constitution and the liberty and happiness of the country depend.

But, while we hold the rights and duties of the States to be such as we have stated, we are deeply impressed with the conviction, that it is due to the relation existing between them, as members of a common Union, and the respect which they ought ever to entertain towards the Government ordained to carry into effect the important objects for which the Constitution was formed, that the occasion to justify a State in interposing its authority, ought to be one of necessity; where all other peaceful remedies have been unsuccessfully tried; and where the only alternative is, interposition on one side, or oppression of its citizens, and imminent danger to the Constitution and liberty of the country on the other; and such we hold to be the present.

That the prohibitory, or protective system, which, as has been stated, is embraced in the acts which we have declared to be unconstitutional, and therefore null and void, is, in fact, unconstitutional, unequal, and oppressive in its operation on this, and the other staple and exporting States, and danger- ous to the Constitution and liberty of the country, and that (all other peaceful remedies having been tried without success) an occasion has occurred, where it becomes the right and duty of the State to interpose its authority to arrest the evil within its limits, we hold to be certain; and it is under this deep and solemn conviction, that we have acted. . . .

When we reflect on the principle on which the system rests, and from which the government claims the power to control the labor and capital of the country, and the bitter fruits it has already produced, the decay and impover- ishment of an entire section of the country, and the wide spread of discord and corruption, we cannot doubt that there is involved in the issue not only the prosperity of this and the other staple and exporting states, but also the Con- stitution and liberty of the country. In rearing up the system it was not pre- tended, nor is it now, that there is in the Constitution any positive grant of power to protect manufactures; nor can it be denied that frequent attempts were made in the Convention to obtain the power, and that they all failed. And yet, without any grant and notwithstanding the failure to obtain one, it has become one of the leading powers of the government, influencing more exten- sively its movements and affecting more deeply and permanently the relative interests and condition of the states and the probable fate of the government itself than any or all of the enumerated powers united.

From whatever source its advocates may derive this power, whether from the right "to lay and collect taxes, duties, imposts, and excises," or from that "to regulate commerce," it plainly rests on the broad assumption that the power to impose duties may be applied, not only to effect the original objects—to raise revenue, or regulate commerce—but also to protect manufactures; and this, not as an incidental but as a substantive and independent power, without reference to revenue or commerce; and in this character it has been used in building up the present system.

That such a power, resting on such a principle, is unauthorized by the Constitution; that it has become an instrument in the hands of the great dominant interests of the country, to oppress the weaker; that it must ulti- mately concentrate the whole power of the community in the general government and abolish the sovereignty of the states; and that discord, corruption, and, eventually, despotism must follow if the system be not resisted, we hold to be certain. Already we see the commencement of this disastrous train of consequences—the oppression of the weaker; the assumption by government of the right to determine, finally and conclusively, the extent of its own powers; the denial and denunciation of the right of the states to judge of their reserved powers and to defend them against the encroachments of the government, followed by discord, corruption, and the steady advance of despotic power.

That something is wrong, all admit; and that the assumption by government of a power so extensive and dangerous . . . is the true cause of the existing disorder and the only adequate one that can be assigned, we cannot entertain a doubt. To this unequal and excessive fiscal action of the government may be immediately and clearly traced the growing discontent and alienation on the part of the oppressed portion of the community and the greedy pursuit of office; and with it, the increasing spirit of servility, subserviency, and the corruption on the other, which all must see and acknowledge, and which every lover of the country and its institutions must deplore. Nor is it less clear that this dangerous assumption, by which the reserved powers of the states have been transferred to the general government, is rapidly concentrating, by a necessary operation, the whole power of the government in the hands of the executive. We must be blind to the lessons of reason and experience not to see that the more a government interferes with the labor and wealth of a community, the more it exacts from one portion and bestows on another, just in the same proportion must the power of that department, which is vested with its patronage, be increased. It ought not, then, to be a subject of surprise that, with this vast increase of the power and revenues of the federal government and its unequal fiscal action, both in the collection and distribution of the latter, the power of the executive, on whose will be the disposition of the patronage of the government mainly depends, and on which, in turn, depends that powerful, active, and mercenary corps of expectants, created by the morbid moneyed action of the government, should be, of late, so greatly and dangerously increased. It is indeed not difficult to see that the present state of things, if continued, must end, and that speedily, in raising this department of the government into a irresponsible and despotic power, with the capacity of perpetuating itself through its own influence; first, virtually appointing its successor, or, by controlling the presidential election, through the patronage of the government; and finally, as the virtue and patriotism of the people decay, by the introduction and open establishment of the hereditary principle. . . .

. . . In taking the stand which she has, the State has been solely influenced by a conscientious sense of duty to her citizens and to the Constitution without the slightest feeling of hostility towards the interests of any section of the country, or the remotest view to revolution, or wish to terminate her connection with the Union; to which she is now, as she ever has been, devotedly attached. Her object is not to destroy, but to restore and preserve. And, in asserting her right to defend her reserved powers, she disclaims all pretension to control or interfere with the action of the government within its proper sphere, or to assume any powers that she has delegated to the government or conceded to the confederated states. She simply claims the right of exercising the powers which, in adopting the Constitution, she reserved to herself; and among them, the most important and essential of all, the right to judge, in the last resort, of the extent of her reserved powers, a right never delegated not surrendered, nor, indeed, could be, while the State retains her sovereignty. That it has not been, we appeal with confidence to the Constitution itself, which contains not a single grant that, on a fair construction, can be held to comprehend the power . . . . [I]t is not the State that interposes to arrest an unconstitutional act, but the government that passed it, which resists the authority of the Union. The government has not the right to add a particle to its powers; and to assume, on its part, the exercise of a power not granted, is plainly to oppose the confederated authority of the states, to which the right of granting powers exclusively belongs; and, in so doing, the Union itself, which they represent. On the contrary, a state, as a member of the body in which the authority of the Union resides, in arresting an unconstitutional act of government, within its limits, so far from opposing, in reality supports the Union, and that in the only effectual mode in which it can be done in such cases. To divest the states of this right would be, in effect, to give to the government that authority over the Constitution which belongs to them exclusively; and which can only be preserved to them, by leaving to each state—as the Constitution has done—to watch over and defend its reserved powers against the encroachments of the Government, and in performing which, it acts, at the same time, as a faithful and vigilant sentinel over the confederate powers of the states. . . .

. . . We hold that our country has arrived at the very point of difficulty and danger contemplated by the framers of the Constitution in providing for a General Convention of the states of the Union; and that, of course, the question now remaining to be tested is whether there be sufficient moral elevation, patriotism, and intelligence in the country to adjust, through the interposition of this highest of tribunals, whose right none can question, the conflicts which now threaten the very existence of our institutions, and liberty itself, and which, as experience has proved, there is no other body belonging to the system having sufficient weight of authority to terminate.

Such, at least, is our conviction; and we have acted accordingly. It now rests with the other states to determine whether a General Convention shall be called or not. And on that determination hangs, we solemnly believe, the future fate of the country. If it should be in favor of a call, we may, with almost perfect certainty, entertain the prospect of a speedy and happy termination of all our difficulties, followed by peace, prosperity, and lengthened political existence. But if not, we shall, by rejecting the remedy provided by the wisdom of our ancestors, prove that we deserve the fate which, in that event, will, in all probability, await the country.

Sources: *Reports and Public Letters of John C. Calhoun*, ed. Richard Kenner Crallé (New York: D. Appleton and Company, 1888), VI: 193–209; and *John C. Calhoun: Selected Writings and Speeches*, ed. H. Lee Cheek Jr. (Washington, D.C.: Regnery Publishing, 2003), 399–410.

CHAPTER 18

Veto of the Bank of the United States, Andrew Jackson, 1832

In many respects President Jackson's "poor versus rich" veto of the bill to issue a charter to the Second Bank of the United States defined his presidency. Neither the House nor the Senate was able to override the veto, and with Jackson winning reelection to another term in the fall, the Bank of the United States was dead in all but name. In many ways this was a populist victory over wealthy interests, but the bank made its reappearance in 1913 as the Federal Reserve bank, again a private corporation but one functioning without oversight either by Congress or the executive branch as was exercised on the Bank of the United States. Interestingly enough, a Democratic president, Jackson, killed the bank in 1832; and a Democratic president, Woodrow Wilson, with a straight party-line vote in Congress, created the Federal Reserve.

Although power politics aimed at the bank's president, Nicholas Biddle, played a part in Jackson's opposition, there was also fear that foreign interests might soon control the bank and use it for hostile purposes. In fact, little evidence ever surfaced that foreign interests sought to control or influence either of the two national banks (the charter of First Bank of the United States expired in 1811). For a century, historians blamed the demise of the bank for the credit expansion of 1833–6 and subsequent panic in 1837. But in the late 1960s, research by Peter Temin laid that view to rest by showing that somewhat natural causes—the production of silver followed by its sudden halt—sparked both the inflation and the panic. Jackson may have acted without cause, but his veto had little economic effect. Jackson's criticisms of the bank seem to resemble modern concerns over the secrecy and power of the Federal Reserve System. Yet his arguments were not entirely honest: his attempt to deprive the Whigs of a major source of patronage and remove potential political enemies counted for as much as his arguments against a national bank. Nonetheless, the United States proceeded to become the world's greatest economic power without a central bank, and Jackson would undoubtedly consider that as vindication of his position. Central banking systems make favored bankers extremely wealthy and powerful, yet it was Jackson's party—supposedly populist—that eventually reinstalled one in the United States.

President's Veto Message Regarding the Bank of the United States, July 10, 1832

THE BILL "TO MODIFY AND CONTINUE" THE ACT ENTITLED "AN act to incorporate the subscribers to the Bank of the United States" was presented to me on the 4th July instant. Having considered it with that solemn regard to the principles of the Constitution which the day was calculated to inspire, and come to the conclusion that it ought not to become a law, I herewith return it to the Senate, in which it originated, with my objections. . . .

The present corporate body, denominated the president, directors, and company of the Bank of the United States, will have existed at the time this act is intended to take effect twenty years. It enjoys an exclusive privilege of banking under the authority of the General Government, a monopoly of its favor and support, and, as a necessary consequence, almost a monopoly of the foreign and domestic exchange. The powers, privileges, and favors bestowed upon it in the original charter, by increasing the value of the stock far above its par value, operated as a gratuity of many millions to the stockholders.

An apology may be found for the failure to guard against this result in the consideration that the effect of the original act of incorporation could not be certainly foreseen at the time of its passage. The act before me proposes another gratuity to the holders of the same stock, and in many cases to the same men, of at least seven millions more. This donation finds no apology in any uncertainty as to the effect of the act. . . .

Every monopoly and all exclusive privileges are granted at the expense of the public, which ought to receive a fair equivalent. The many millions which this act proposes to bestow on the stockholders of the existing bank must come directly or indirectly out of the earnings of the American people. . . .

. . . If we must have such a corporation, why should not the Government sell out the whole stock and thus secure to the people the full market value of the privileges granted? Why should not Congress create and sell twenty-eight millions of stock, incorporating the purchasers with all the powers and privileges secured in this act and putting the premium upon the sales into the Treasury?

But this act does not permit competition in the purchase of this monopoly. It seems to be predicated on the erroneous idea that the present stockholders have a prescriptive right not only to the favor but to the bounty of Government. It appears that more than a fourth part of the stock is held by foreigners and the residue is held by a few hundred of our own citizens, chiefly of the richest class. For their benefit does this act exclude the whole American people from competition in the purchase of this monopoly and dispose of it for many millions less than it is worth. . . .

. . . I cannot perceive the justice or policy of this course. . . .

The modifications of the existing charter proposed by this act are not such, in my view, as make it consistent with the rights of the States or the liberties of the people. . . . All the objectionable principles of the existing corporation, and most of its odious features, are retained without alleviation.

The fourth section . . . secures to the State banks a legal privilege in the Bank of the United States which is withheld from all private citizens. If a State bank in Philadelphia owe the Bank of the United States and have notes issued by the St. Louis branch, it can pay the debt with those notes, but if a merchant, mechanic, or other private citizen be in like circumstances he cannot by law pay his debt with those notes, but must sell them at a discount or send them to St. Louis to be cashed. This boon conceded to the State banks, though not unjust in itself, is most odious because it does not measure out equal justice to the high and the low, the rich and the poor. To the extent of its practical effect it is a bond of union among the banking establishments of the nation, erecting them into an interest separate from that of the people, and its necessary tendency is to unite the Bank of the United States and the State banks in any measure which may be thought conducive to their common interest.

The ninth section of the act recognizes principles of worse tendency than any provision of the present charter. . . .

. . . When by a tax on resident stockholders the stock of this bank is made worth 10 or 15 percent more to foreigners than to residents, most of it will inevitably leave the country.

Thus will this provision in its practical effect deprive the eastern as well as the southern and western States of the means of raising revenue from the extension of business and great profits of this institution. It will make the American people debtors to aliens in nearly the whole amount due to this bank, and send across the Atlantic from two to five millions of specie every year to pay the bank dividends. . . .

Is there no danger to our liberty and independence in a bank that in its nature has so little to bind it to our country? The president of the bank has told us that most of the State banks exist by its forbearance. Should its influence become concentrated, as it may under the operation of such an act as this, in the hands of a self-elected directory whose interests are identified with those of the foreign stockholders, will there not be cause to tremble for the purity of our elections in peace and for the independence of our country in war? . . .

. . . Of the course which would be pursued by a bank almost wholly owned by the subjects of a foreign power, and managed by those whose interests, if not affections, would run in the same direction there can be no doubt. All its operations within would be in aid of the hostile fleets and armies without. Controlling our currency, receiving our public moneys, and holding thousands of our citizens in dependence, it would be more formidable and dangerous than the naval and military power of the enemy.

If we must have a bank with private stockholders, every consideration of sound policy and every impulse of American feeling admonishes that it should be *purely American*. . . .

The original act of incorporation, section 2I, enacts "that no other bank shall be established by any future law of the United States during the continuance of the corporation hereby created, for which the faith of the United States is hereby pledged: Provided, Congress may renew existing charters for banks within the District of Columbia not increasing the capital thereof, and may also establish any other bank or banks in said District with capitals not exceeding in the whole $6,000,000 if they shall deem it expedient." This provision is continued in force by the act before me fifteen years from the ad of March 1836.

If Congress possessed the power to establish one bank, they had power to establish more than one if in their opinion two or more banks had been "necessary" to facilitate the execution of the powers delegated to them in the Constitution. If they possessed the power to establish a second bank, it was a power derived from the Constitution to be exercised from time to time, and at any time when the interests of the country or the emergencies of the Government might make it expedient. It was possessed by one Congress as well as another, and by all Congresses alike, and alike at every session. But the Congress of 1816 have taken it away from their successors for twenty years, and the Congress of 1832 proposes to abolish it for fifteen years more. . . . They may *properly* use the discretion vested in them, but they may not limit the discretion of their successors. This restriction on themselves and grant of a monopoly to the bank is therefore unconstitutional.

In another point of view this provision is a palpable attempt to amend the Constitution by an act of legislation. The Constitution declares that "the Congress shall have power to exercise exclusive legislation in all cases whatsoever" over the District of Columbia. Its constitutional power, therefore, to establish banks in the District of Columbia and increase their capital at will is unlimited and uncontrollable by any other power than that which gave authority to the Constitution. Yet this act declares that Congress shall not increase the capital of existing banks, nor create other banks with capitals exceeding in the whole $6,000,000. The Constitution declares that Congress shall have power to exercise exclusive legislation over this District "in all cases whatsoever," and this act declares they shall not. Which is the supreme law of the land? This provision cannot be "necessary" or "proper" or constitutional unless the absurdity be admitted that whenever it be "necessary and proper" in the opinion of Congress they have a right to barter away one portion of the powers vested in them by the Constitution as a means of executing the rest.

On two subjects only does the Constitution recognize in Congress the power to grant exclusive privileges or monopolies. It declares that "Congress shall have power to promote the progress of science and useful arts by securing for limited times to authors and inventors the exclusive right to their respective writings and discoveries." Out of this express delegation of power have grown our laws of patents and copyrights. As the Constitution expressly delegates to Congress the power to grant exclusive privileges in these cases as the means of executing the substantive power "to promote the progress of science and useful arts," it is consistent with the fair rules of construction to conclude that such a power was not intended to be granted as a means of accomplishing any other end. On every other subject which comes within the scope of congressional power there is an ever-living discretion in the use of proper means, which cannot be restricted or abolished without an amendment of the Constitution. Every act of Congress, therefore, which attempts by grants of monopolies or sale of exclusive privileges for a limited time, or a time without limit, to restrict or extinguish its own discretion in the choice of means to execute its delegated powers is equivalent to a legislative amendment of the Constitution, and palpably unconstitutional. . . .

The Government of the United States has no constitutional power to purchase lands within the States except "for the erection of forts, magazines, arsenals, dockyards, and other needful buildings," and even for these objects only "by the consent of the legislature of the State in which the same shall be." By making themselves stockholders in the bank and granting to the corporation the power to purchase lands for other purposes they assume a power not granted in the Constitution and grant to others what they do not themselves possess. It is not necessary to the receiving, safekeeping, or transmission of the funds of the Government that the bank should possess this power, and it is not proper that Congress should thus enlarge the powers delegated to them in the Constitution.

The old Bank of the United States possessed a capital of only $11,000,000, which was found fully sufficient to enable it with dispatch and safety to perform all the functions required of it by the Government. The capital of the present bank is $35,000,000—at least twenty-four more than experience has proved to be necessary to enable a bank to perform its public functions. The public debt which existed during the period of the old bank and on the establishment of the new has been nearly paid off, and our revenue will soon be reduced. This increase of capital is therefore not for public but for private purposes.

. . . The principle laid down by the Supreme Court concedes that Congress cannot establish a bank for purposes of private speculation and gain, but only as a means of executing the delegated powers of the General Government. . . .

It is maintained by some that the bank is a means of executing the constitutional power "to coin money and regulate the value thereof." Congress have established a mint to coin money and passed laws to regulate the value thereof. The money so coined, with its value so regulated, and such foreign coins as Congress may adopt are the only currency known to the Constitution. But if they have other power to regulate the currency, it was conferred to be exercised by themselves, and not to be transferred to a corporation. If the bank be established for that purpose, with a charter unalterable without its consent, Congress have parted with their power for a term of years, during which the Constitution is a dead letter. It is neither necessary nor proper to transfer its legislative power to such a bank, and therefore unconstitutional. . . .

Upon the formation of the Constitution the States guarded their taxing power with peculiar jealousy. They surrendered it only as it regards imports and exports. In relation to every other object within their jurisdiction, whether persons, property, business, or professions, it was secured in as ample a manner as it was before possessed. All persons, though United States officers, are liable to a poll tax by the States within which they reside. The lands of the United States are liable to the usual land tax, except in the new States, from whom agreements that they will not tax unsold lands are exacted when they are admitted into the Union. Horses, wagons, any beasts or vehicles, tools, or property belonging to private citizens, though employed in the service of the United States, are subject to State taxation. Every private business, whether carried on by an officer of the General Government or not, whether it be mixed with public concerns or not, even if it be carried on by the Government of the United States itself, separately or in partnership, falls within the scope of the taxing power of the State. Nothing comes more fully within it than banks and the business of banking, by whomsoever instituted and carried on. Over this whole subject matter it is just as absolute, unlimited, and uncontrollable as if the Constitution had never been adopted, because in the formation of that instrument it was reserved without qualification.

The principle is conceded that the States cannot rightfully tax the operations of the General Government. They cannot tax the money of the Government deposited in the State banks, nor the agency of those banks in remitting it; but will any man maintain that their mere selection to perform this public service for the General Government would exempt the State banks and their ordinary business from State taxation? Had the United States, instead of establishing a bank at Philadelphia, employed a private banker to keep and transmit their funds, would it have deprived Pennsylvania of the right to tax his bank and his usual banking operations? It will not be pretended. Upon what principal, then, are the banking establishments of the Bank of the United States and their usual banking operations to be exempted from taxation? It is not their public agency or the deposits of the Government which the States claim a right to tax, but their banks and their banking powers, instituted and exercised within State jurisdiction for their private emolument—those powers and privileges for which they pay a bonus, and which the States tax in their own banks. . . .

It cannot be necessary to the character of the bank as a fiscal agent of the Government that its private business should be exempted from that taxation to which all the State banks are liable, nor can I conceive it "proper" that the substantive and most essential powers reserved by the States shall be thus attacked and annihilated as a means of executing the powers delegated to the General Government. It may be safely assumed that none of those sages who had an agency in forming or adopting our Constitution ever imagined that any portion of the taxing power of the States not prohibited to them nor delegated to Congress was to be swept away and annihilated as a means of executing certain powers delegated to Congress.

If our power over means is so absolute that the Supreme Court will not call in question the constitutionality of an act of Congress the subject of which "is not prohibited, and is really calculated to effect any of the objects intrusted to the Government," although, as in the case before me, it takes away powers expressly granted to Congress and rights scrupulously reserved to the States, it becomes us to proceed in our legislation with the utmost caution. Though not directly, our own powers and the rights of the States may be indirectly legislated away in the use of means to execute substantive powers. We may not enact that Congress shall not have the power of exclusive legislation over the District of Columbia, but we may pledge the faith of the United States that as a means of executing other powers it shall not be exercised for twenty years or forever. We may not pass an act prohibiting the States to tax the banking business carried on within their limits, but we may, as a means of executing our powers over other objects, place that business in the hands of our agents and then declare it exempt from State taxation in their hands. Thus may our own powers and the rights of the States, which we cannot directly curtail or invade, be frittered away and extinguished in the use of means employed by us to execute other powers. . . .

Under such circumstances the bank comes forward and asks a renewal of its charter for a term of fifteen years upon conditions which not only operate as a gratuity to the stockholders of many millions of dollars, but will sanction any abuses and legalize any encroachments.

Suspicions are entertained and charges are made of gross abuse and violation of its charter. An investigation unwillingly conceded and so restricted in time as necessarily to make it incomplete and unsatisfactory discloses enough to excite suspicion and alarm. In the practices of the principal bank partially unveiled, in the absence of important witnesses, and in numerous charges confidently made and as yet wholly uninvestigated there was enough to induce a majority of the committee of investigation—a committee which was selected from the most able and honorable members of the House of Representatives—to recommend a suspension of further action upon the bill and a prosecution of the inquiry. As the charter had yet four years to run, and as a renewal now was not necessary to the successful prosecution of its business, it was to have been expected that the bank itself, conscious of its purity and proud of its character, would have withdrawn its application for the present, and demanded the severest scrutiny into all its transactions. In their declining to do so there seems to be an additional reason why the functionaries of the Government should proceed with less haste and more caution in the renewal of their monopoly.

The bank is professedly established as an agent of the executive branch of the Government, and its constitutionality is maintained on that ground. Neither upon the propriety of present action nor upon the provisions of this act was the executive consulted. It has had no opportunity to say that it neither needs nor wants an agent clothed with such powers and favored by such exemptions. There is nothing in its legitimate functions which makes it necessary or proper. Whatever interest or influence, whether public or private, has given birth to this act, it cannot be found either in the wishes or necessities of the executive department, by which present action is deemed premature, and the powers conferred upon its agent not only unnecessary, but dangerous to the Government and country.

It is to be regretted that the rich and powerful too often bend the acts of government to their selfish purposes. Distinctions in society will always exist under every just government. Equality of talents, of education, or of wealth cannot be produced by human institutions. In the full enjoyment of the gifts of Heaven and the fruits of superior industry, economy, and virtue, every man is equally entitled to protection by law; but when the laws undertake to add to these natural and just advantages artificial distinctions, to grant titles, gratuities, and exclusive privileges, to make the rich richer and the potent more powerful, the humble members of society—the farmers, mechanics, and laborers—who have neither the time nor the means of securing like favors to themselves, have a right to complain of the injustice of their Government. There are no necessary evils in government. Its evils exist only in its abuses. If it would confine itself to equal protection, and, as Heaven does its rains, shower its favors alike on the high and the low, the rich and the poor, it would be an unqualified blessing. In the act before me there seems to be a wide and unnecessary departure from these just principles. . . .

Experience should teach us wisdom. Most of the difficulties our Government now encounters and most of the dangers which impend over our Union have sprung from an abandonment of the legitimate objects of Government by our national legislation, and the adoption of such principles as are embodied in this act. Many of our rich men have not been content with equal protection and equal benefits, but have besought us to make them richer by act of Congress. . . . It is time to pause in our career to review our principles, and if possible revive that devoted patriotism and spirit of compromise which distinguished the sages of the Revolution and the fathers of our Union. . . .

I have now done my duty to my country. If sustained by my fellow citizens, I shall be grateful and happy; if not, I shall find in the motives which impel me ample grounds for contentment and peace. In the difficulties which surround us and the dangers which threaten our institutions there is cause for neither dismay nor alarm. For relief and deliverance let us firmly rely on that kind Providence which I am sure watches with peculiar care over the destinies of our Republic, and on the intelligence and wisdom of our countrymen. Through His abundant goodness and heir patriotic devotion our liberty and Union will be preserved.

Source: *A Compilation of the Messages and Papers of the Presidents* (New York: Bureau of National Literature, Inc., 1897). As available at the Yale Law School, Lillian Goldman Law Library's Avalon Project: Documents in Law, History and Diplomacy. Retrieved on May 4, 2010, from http://avalon.law.yale.edu/19th_century/ajveto01.asp.

III

SLAVERY, CIVIL RIGHTS, AND THE CIVIL WAR

After decades of continuous but unresolved debate over slavery, the crisis finally came to a head. Under pressure from the North and fearing the consequences of an ever-greater loss of political power, the Deep South looked to states' rights and, particularly, the assumed right to secede from the Union to protect both the institution of slavery in general and its valued property in slaves. For nonslaveholders the issue centered around their rights—no one from the North was going to tell them what they could or couldn't do—but also rested in the desire of even the lowliest whites to have a class of people to look down upon. The election of Lincoln confirmed the South's inability to control the presidency—perhaps forever—and even before he took office the South fell back on itself to form a new national government. The complexity of the issues became apparent when the four states of the upper South—Virginia, North Carolina, Tennessee, and Arkansas—did not secede until Lincoln called for troops to defend the Union, and the slaveholding border states—Delaware, Maryland, Kentucky, and Missouri—did not secede at all. In addition, West Virginia broke away from Virginia and was admitted as a free state, and Union sentiment ran strong in the Appalachians all the way to northern Alabama.

If the soul of America was embodied in the Declaration of Independence, this was the era of its most thoroughly tested soul-searching. Women began to assert themselves and agitate for full rights as citizens and increased roles in business, education, and public affairs, but the primary test that remained was slavery and the status of Negroes, both free and slave. Nowhere is the struggle for the essence of America more evident than in the documents contained in the following section.

In many respects, the Caucasians of European extraction and Negroes of African extraction came from separate galaxies, and forming a common society to allow both races to function together effectively in a representative democracy certainly seemed inconceivable to the vast majority of Americans at the time.

It had never occurred previously on such a scale in any country in the world, once again thrusting the United States into a pathfinder role emphasizing its exceptionalism. Negroes made up only 10 percent of the U.S. population in 1860, and previous solutions to handling readily identified and dissimilar minorities in other countries had involved either extermination or expulsion or a combination of both. Yet America ultimately found in this crisis the opportunity to recognize a new humanity in itself, and Negroes were assimilated into the general population. It would take generations, but America eventually chose to follow its conscience, not its pocketbook.

The conflict over slavery ultimately brought out the best in Americans, even those who fought for the Confederacy. The majority of Southerners fought for their regional, local, and individual rights and their families, friends, and comrades—loyalties that are certainly not to be denigrated. Henceforth the term "American" as defined by American citizens and foreign observers would come to mean someone who lived the American way of life—in essence embodying the idea of what makes an American. This person still followed common law and believed in American exceptionalism but also believed that American culture and institutions could and should be exported throughout the world.

CHAPTER 19

Seneca Falls Declaration of Sentiments, 1848

The Seneca Falls Convention, considered the birthplace of the women's suffrage movement, originated at a tea honoring a visit by Lucretia Mott to New York and attended by Elizabeth Cady Stanton, Mary Ann McClintock, and several others. All the women were Quakers, except Stanton, which was significant given the comparative sexual equality among Quakers and the sect's long history of opposition to slavery. Energized by Mott, a highly skilled speaker, the women decided to hold a convention of equality-minded women, to discuss options and potential actions, in Seneca Falls, New York, Stanton's hometown. They advertised the meeting to discuss women's rights in the *Seneca County Courier* and met in the Wesleyan Methodist Chapel on July 19–20, 1848. About three hundred people attended, among them forty men including Frederick Douglass, the noted African American abolitionist. The Declaration of Sentiments Stanton drafted was modeled after the Declaration of Independence, listing grievances (the perpetrating "he" in this case man, rather than King George III) and twelve resolutions that established women's equality to men.

All the resolutions were voted on and passed unanimously except the ninth, which called upon the women of the country to secure the right to vote. Many of the women present felt this step went too far and would jeopardize the attainment of the other goals. However, Stanton and Douglass argued persistently for the resolution, and it finally passed with a slight majority. Sixty-eight women and thirty-two men signed the declaration, although many withdrew their names under the subsequent withering barrage of criticism and ridicule in the press and, more importantly, from their friends, associates, and political leaders. The declaration demanded all the rights that feminists subsequently claimed until the twentieth century, when issues concerning contraception, abortion, service in the military, and gender-neutral parenting were raised. In spite of generally derisive newspaper coverage, women's rights movements began developing around the country, with the declaration as their primary guiding document. From that point forward, it was only a matter of time before the Nineteenth Amendment was passed, finally granting women the right to vote.

The tenor of the declaration is a condemnation of the limits men had placed on women, namely by denying them political and civil rights. The reader should note that the declaration did not specifically ask the government to do anything. On the contrary, it appealed to the people, men and women, to do what was right according to God's law. This was much different from the demands of the feminists of the 1960s and 1970s, who not only sought government action but in some ways envisioned women's roles without men, not alongside them.

Seneca Falls Declaration of Sentiments and Resolutions

WHEN, IN THE COURSE OF HUMAN EVENTS, IT BECOMES NEC-essary for one portion of the family of man to assume among the people of the earth a position different from that which they have hitherto occupied, but one to which the laws of nature and of nature's God entitle them, a decent respect to the opinions of mankind requires that they should declare the causes that impel them to such a course.

We hold these truths to be self-evident: that all men and women are created equal; that they are endowed by their Creator with certain inalienable rights; that among these are life, liberty, and the pursuit of happiness; that to secure these rights governments are instituted, deriving their just powers from the consent of the governed. Whenever any form of government becomes destructive of these ends, it is the right of those who suffer from it to refuse allegiance to it, and to insist upon the institution of a new government, laying its foundation on such principles, and organizing its powers in such form, as to them shall seem most likely to effect their safety and happiness. Prudence, indeed, will dictate that governments long established should not be changed for light and transient causes; and accordingly all experience hath shown that mankind are more disposed to suffer, while evils are sufferable, than to right themselves by abolishing the forms to which they were accustomed. But when a long train of abuses and usurpations, pursuing invariably the same object, evinces a design to reduce them under absolute despotism, it is their duty to throw off such government, and to provide new guards for their future security.

Such has been the patient sufferance of the women under this government, and such is now the necessity which constrains them to demand the equal station to which they are entitled.

The history of mankind is a history of repeated injuries and usurpations on the part of man toward woman, having in direct object the establishment of an absolute tyranny over her. To prove this, let facts be submitted to a candid world.

He has never permitted her to exercise her inalienable right to the elective franchise.

He has compelled her to submit to laws, in the formation of which she had no voice.

He has withheld from her rights which are given to the most ignorant and degraded men—both natives and foreigners.

Having deprived her of this first right of a citizen, the elective franchise, thereby leaving her without representation in the halls of legislation, he has oppressed her on all sides.

He has made her, if married, in the eye of the law, civilly dead.

He has taken from her all right in property, even to the wages she earns.

He has made her, morally, an irresponsible being, as she can commit many crimes with impunity, provided they be done in the presence of her husband. In the covenant of marriage, she is compelled to promise obedience to her husband, he becoming, to all intents and purposes, her master—the law giving him power to deprive her of her liberty, and to administer chastisement.

He has so framed the laws of divorce, as to what shall be the proper causes, and in case of separation, to whom the guardianship of the children shall be given, as to be wholly regardless of the happiness of women—the law, in all cases, going upon a false supposition of the supremacy of man, and giving all power into his hands.

After depriving her of all rights as a married woman, if single, and the owner of property, he has taxed her to support a government which recognizes her only when her property can be made profitable to it.

He has monopolized nearly all the profitable employments, and from those she is permitted to follow, she receives but a scanty remuneration. He closes against her all the avenues to wealth and distinction which he considers most honorable to himself. As a teacher of theology, medicine, or law, she is not known.

He has denied her the facilities for obtaining a thorough education, all colleges being closed against her.

He allows her in Church, as well as State, but a subordinate position, claiming Apostolic authority for her exclusion from the ministry, and, with some exceptions, from any public participation in the affairs of the Church.

He has created a false public sentiment by giving to the world a different code of morals for men and women, by which moral delinquencies which exclude women from society, are not only tolerated, but deemed of little account in man.

He has usurped the prerogative of Jehovah himself, claiming it as his right to assign for her a sphere of action, when that belongs to her conscience and to her God.

He has endeavored, in every way that he could, to destroy her confidence in her own powers, to lessen her self-respect, and to make her willing to lead a dependent and abject life.

Now, in view of this entire disfranchisement of one-half the people of this country, their social and religious degradation, in view of the unjust laws above mentioned, and because women do feel themselves aggrieved, oppressed, and fraudulently deprived of their most sacred rights, we insist that they have immediate admission to all the rights and privileges which belong to them as citizens of the United States.

In entering upon the great work before us, we anticipate no small amount of misconception, misrepresentation, and ridicule; but we shall use every instrumentality within our power to effect our object. We shall employ agents, circulate tracts, petition the State and National legislatures, and endeavor to enlist the pulpit and the press in our behalf. We hope this Convention will be followed by a series of Conventions embracing every part of the country.

RESOLUTIONS

Whereas, the great precept of nature is conceded to be that "man shall pursue his own true and substantial happiness," Blackstone in his *Commentaries* remarks that this law of Nature, being coeval with mankind and dictated by God himself, is, of course, superior in obligation to any other. It is binding over all the globe, in all countries and at all times; no human laws are of any validity if contrary to this, and such of them as are valid derive all their force, and all their validity, and all their authority, mediately and immediately, from this original; therefore,

Resolved, That such laws as conflict, in any way, with the true and substantial happiness of woman, are contrary to the great precept of nature and of no validity, for this is "superior in obligation to any other."

Resolved, That all laws which prevent woman from occupying such a station in society as her conscience shall dictate, or which place her in a position inferior to that of man, are contrary to the great precept of nature and therefore of no force or authority.

Resolved, That woman is man's equal, was intended to be so by the Creator, and the highest good of the race demands that she should be recognized as such.

Resolved, That the women of this country ought to be enlightened in regard to the laws under which they live, that they may no longer publish their degradation by declaring themselves satisfied with their present position, nor their ignorance, by asserting that they have all the rights they want.

Resolved, That inasmuch as man, while claiming for himself intellectual superiority, does accord to women moral superiority, it is preeminently his duty to encourage her to speak and teach, as she has an opportunity, in all religious assemblies.

Resolved, That the same amount of virtue, delicacy, and refinement of behavior that is required of woman in the social state should also be required of man, and the same transgressions should be visited with equal severity on both man and woman.

Resolved, That the objection of indelicacy and impropriety, which is so often brought against woman when she addresses a public audience, comes with a very ill grace from those who encourage, by their attendance, her appearance on the stage, in the concert, or in feats of the circus.

Resolved, That woman has too long rested satisfied in the circumscribed limits which corrupt customs and a perverted application of the Scriptures have marked out for her, and that it is time she should move in the enlarged sphere which her great Creator has assigned her.

Resolved, That it is the duty of the women of this country to secure to themselves their sacred right to the elective franchise.

Resolved, That the equality of human rights results necessarily from the fact of the identity of the race in capabilities and responsibilities.

Resolved, That the speedy success of our cause depends upon the zealous and untiring efforts of both men and women for the overthrow of the monopoly of the pulpit, and for the securing to women an equal participation with men in the various trades, professions, and commerce.

Resolved, therefore, That, being invested by the Creator with the same capabilities and the same consciousness of responsibility for their exercise, it is demonstrably the right and duty of women, equally with man, to promote every righteous cause by every righteous means; and especially in regard to the great subjects of morals and religion, it is self-evidently her right to participate with her brother in teaching them, both in private and in public, by writing and by speaking, by any instrumentalities proper to be used, and in any assemblies proper to be held; and this being a self-evident truth growing out of the divinely implanted principles of human nature, any custom or authority adverse to it, whether modern or wearing the hoary sanction of antiquity, is to be regarded as a self-evident falsehood, and at war with mankind.

Source: *History of Woman Suffrage*, ed. Elizabeth Cady Stanton, Susan B. Anthony, and Matilda Joslyn Gage (New York: Fowler & Wells, 1881), 1: 70–73.

CHAPTER 20

Scott v. Sandford, 1857

The Dred Scott case was argued in the Supreme Court of the United States in the December term of 1856. Scott was a slave born in Virginia who was later sold to an army officer in Missouri. He traveled with his owner to live in Illinois and Minnesota before returning to Missouri. After his owner died, Scott sued to be declared free since he had resided for many years in Illinois, a free state, and Minnesota, at the time a free territory. He was even allowed to marry while in Minnesota, an indication that he possessed a right to enter into a legal contract, something slaves were forbidden to do.

After winding its way through Missouri state courts (which simultaneously ruled that as a slave Scott could not sue, yet could appeal), and the federal system, the case reached the U.S. Supreme Court, where Scott lost. Although the opinion of the chief justice, in this case Roger B. Taney, is generally held as the ruling for the majority, all seven concurring justices wrote opinions, as well as the two dissenting justices. Taney held that no slave or descendent of a slave could be a citizen of the United States, so Scott possessed no right to sue in federal court. The Court also upheld the principle that slavery was a state issue, and that Congress possessed no authority to prohibit slavery in the territories. On those grounds, both the Missouri Compromise (1820) and the Compromise of 1850 were unconstitutional. Moreover, "the people" (referring to the current doctrine of popular sovereignty) could not prohibit slavery either. *Only* a state—one that had slavery as a default position already in place in its constitution—could amend its state constitution to prohibit slavery. The Court effectively turned back the clock, as ex-slaves had held full voting rights in several northern states since before the Constitution was written.

Ramifications were widespread, from greatly invigorating the Republican Party to helping cause the financial panic of 1857. Abraham Lincoln, running in the 1858 Illinois senate race against Stephen Douglas, forced Douglas to repudiate the decision, thereby costing him the South and the presidency in 1860.* The case's greatest impact was in hastening the Civil War, as it seemed to impose Southern doctrine on Northern states. The South may have won in court, but the next decision was to be decided on the battlefield. The reader should examine Taney's overreaching in his opinion—now generally considered the worst Supreme Court decision in history—and how such actions, taken from a position of power, frequently bring about a result opposite to the one desired. Is it possible that Lincoln would have lost to Douglas in 1860 if Dred Scott had been freed by the Court and ex-slaves declared acceptable as U.S. citizens? The reader should speculate on the course the United States might have taken had Lincoln not been elected and when the end of slavery would have come and through what mechanism. Would America's exceptionalism have become a joke? Would the United States have survived? Was there any chance of peaceably resolving the slavery issue? What does the Court's unwillingness to consider previous decisions that had tended toward abolitionism and racial equality say about "judicial activism"?

Dred Scott, Plaintiff in Error, v. John F. A. Sandford

CHIEF JUSTICE TANEY DELIVERED THE OPINION OF THE COURT [on March 6, 1857]. . . .

The question is simply this: Can a Negro, whose ancestors were imported into this country, and sold as slaves, become a member of the political community formed and brought into existence by the Constitution of the United States, and as such become entitled to all the rights, and privileges, and immunities, guarantied by that instrument to the citizen? One of which rights is the privilege of suing in a court of the United States in the cases specified in the Constitution.

It will be observed, that the plea applies to that class of persons only whose ancestors were Negroes of the African race, and imported into this country, and sold and held as slaves. The only matter in issue before the court, therefore, is, whether the descendants of such slaves, when they shall be emancipated, or who are born of parents who had become free before their birth, are citizens of a State, in the sense in which the word "citizen" is used in the Constitution of the United States. And this being the only matter in dispute on the pleadings, the court must be understood as speaking in this opinion of that class only, that is, of those persons who are the descendants of Africans who were imported into this country, and sold as slaves. . . .

---

* William W. Freehling, *The Road to Disunion* (New York: Oxford University Press, 2007), 2:272.

In discussing this question, we must not confound the rights of citizenship which a State may confer within its own limits, and the rights of citizenship as a member of the Union. It does not by any means follow, because he has all the rights and privileges of a citizen of a State, that he must be a citizen of the United States. He may have all of the rights and privileges of the citizen of a State, and yet not be entitled to the rights and privileges of a citizen in any other State. . . .

It is true, every person, and every class and description of persons, who were at the time of the adoption of the Constitution recognized as citizens in the several States, became also citizens of this new political body; but none other; it was formed by them, and for them and their posterity, but for no one else. And the personal rights and privileges guaranteed to citizens of this new sovereignty were intended to embrace those only who were then members of the several State communities, or who should afterwards by birthright or otherwise become members, according to the provisions of the Constitution and the principles on which it was founded. It was the union of those who were at that time members of distinct and separate political communities into one political family, whose power, for certain specified purposes, was to extend over the whole territory of the United States. And it gave to each citizen rights and privileges outside of his State which he did not before possess, and placed him in every other State upon a perfect equality with its own citizens as to rights of person and rights of property; it made him a citizen of the United States.

It becomes necessary, therefore, to determine who were citizens of the several States when the Constitution was adopted. And in order to do this, we must recur to the Governments and institutions of the thirteen colonies, when they separated from Great Britain and formed new sovereignties, and took their places in the family of independent nations. We must inquire who, at that time, were recognized as the people or citizens of a State, whose rights and liberties had been outraged by the English Government; and who declared their independence, and assumed the powers of Government to defend their rights by force of arms.

In the opinion of the court, the legislation and histories of the times, and the language used in the Declaration of Independence, show, that neither the class of persons who had been imported as slaves, nor their descendants, whether they had become free or not, were then acknowledged as a part of the people, nor intended to be included in the general words used in that memorable instrument.

It is difficult at this day to realize the state of public opinion in relation to that unfortunate race, which prevailed in the civilized and enlightened portions of the world at the time of the Declaration of Independence, and when the Constitution of the United States was framed and adopted. But the public history of every European nation displays it in a manner too plain to be mistaken.

They had for more than a century before been regarded as beings of an inferior order, and altogether unfit to associate with the white race, either in social or political relations; and so far inferior, that they had no rights which the white man was bound to respect; and that the Negro might justly and lawfully be reduced to slavery for his benefit. He was bought and sold, and treated as an ordinary article of merchandise and traffic, whenever a profit could be made by it. This opinion was at that time fixed and universal in the civilized portion of the white race. It was regarded as an axiom in morals as well as in politics, which no one thought of disputing, or supposed to be open to dispute; and men in every grade and position in society daily and habitually acted upon it in their private pursuits, as well as in matters of public concern, without doubting for a moment the correctness of this opinion. . . .

The language of the Declaration of Independence is equally conclusive. It begins by declaring that, "When in the course of human events it becomes necessary for one people to dissolve the political bands which have connected them with another, and to assume among the powers of the earth the separate and equal station to which the laws of nature and nature's God entitle them, a decent respect for the opinions of mankind requires that they should declare the causes which impel them to the separation."

It then proceeds to say: "We hold these truths to be self-evident: that all men are created equal; that they are endowed by their Creator with certain unalienable rights; that among them is life, liberty, and the pursuit of happiness; that to secure these rights, Governments are instituted, deriving their just powers from the consent of the governed."

The general words above quoted would seem to embrace the whole human family, and if they were used in a similar instrument at this day would be so understood. But it is too clear for dispute, that the enslaved African race were not intended to be included, and formed no part of the people who framed and adopted this declaration; for if the language, as understood in that day, would embrace them, the conduct of the distinguished men who framed the Declaration of Independence would have been utterly and flagrantly inconsistent with the principles they asserted; and instead of the sympathy of mankind, to which they so confidently appealed, they would have deserved and received universal rebuke and reprobation.

Yet the men who framed this declaration were great men—high in literary acquirements—high in their sense of honor, and incapable of asserting principles inconsistent with those on which they were acting. They perfectly understood the meaning of the language they used, and how it would be understood by others; and they knew that it would not in any part of the civilized world be supposed to embrace the Negro race, which, by common consent, had been excluded from civilized Governments and the family of nations, and doomed to slavery. They spoke and acted according to the then established doctrines and principles, and in the ordinary language of the day, and no one misunderstood them. The unhappy black race were separated from the white by indelible marks, and laws long before established, and were never thought of or spoken of except as property, and when the claims of the owner or the profit of the trader were supposed to need protection.

This state of public opinion had undergone no change when the Constitution was adopted, as is equally evident from its provisions and language.

The brief preamble sets forth by whom it was formed, for what purposes, and for whose benefit and protection. It declares that it is formed by the people of the United States; that is to say, by those who were members of the different political communities in the several States; and its great object is declared to be to secure the blessings of liberty to themselves and their posterity. It speaks in general terms of the people of the United States, and of citizens of the several States, when it is providing for the exercise of the powers granted or the privileges secured to the citizen. It does not define what description of persons are intended to be included under these terms, or who shall be regarded as a citizen and one of the people. It uses them as terms so well understood, that no further description or definition was necessary.

But there are two clauses in the Constitution which point directly and specifically to the Negro race as a separate class of persons, and show clearly that they were not regarded as a portion of the people or citizens of the Government then formed.

One of these clauses reserves to each of the thirteen States the right to import slaves until the year 1808, if it thinks proper. And the importation which it thus sanctions was unquestionably of persons of the race of which we are speaking, as the traffic in slaves in the United States had always been confined to them. And by the other provision the States pledge themselves to each other to maintain the right of property of the master, by delivering up to him any slave who may have escaped from his service, and be found within their respective territories. By the first above-mentioned clause, therefore, the right to purchase and hold this property is directly sanctioned and authorized for twenty years by the people who framed the Constitution. And by the second, they pledge themselves to maintain and uphold the right of the master in the manner specified, as long as the Government they then formed should endure. And these two provisions show, conclusively, that neither the description of persons therein referred to, nor their descendants, were embraced in any of the other provisions of the Constitution; for certainly these two clauses were not intended to confer on them or their posterity the blessings of liberty, or any of the personal rights so carefully provided for the citizen. . . .

Undoubtedly, a person may be a citizen, that is, a member of the community who form the sovereignty, although he exercises no share of the political power, and is incapacitated from holding particular offices. Women and

minors, who form a part of the political family, cannot vote; and when a property qualification is required to vote or hold a particular office, those who have
not the necessary qualification cannot vote or hold the office, yet they are
citizens.

So, too, a person may be entitled to vote by the law of the State, who is not
a citizen even of the State itself. And in some of the States of the Union foreigners not naturalized are allowed to vote. And the State may give the right
to free Negroes and mulattoes, but that does not make them citizens of the
State, and still less of the United States. And the provision in the Constitution
giving privileges and immunities in other States, does not apply to them.

Neither does it apply to a person who, being the citizen of a State, migrates
to another State. For then he becomes subject to the laws of the State in which
he lives, and he is no longer a citizen of the State from which he removed. And
the State in which he resides may then, unquestionably, determine his status
or condition, and place him among the class of persons who are not recognized
as citizens, but belong to an inferior and subject race; and may deny him the
privileges and immunities enjoyed by its citizens.

But so far as mere rights of person are concerned, the provision in question
is confined to citizens of a State who are temporarily in another State, without
taking up their residence there. It gives them no political rights in the State,
as to voting or holding office, or in any other respect. For the citizen of one
State has no right to participate in the government of another. But if he ranks
as a citizen in the State to which he belongs, within the meaning of the Constitution of the United States, then, whenever he goes into another State, the
Constitution clothes him, as to the rights of person, with all the privileges and
immunities which belong to citizens of the State. And if persons of the African
race are citizens of a State, and of the United States, they would be entitled
to all of these privileges and immunities in every State, and the State could
not restrict them; for they would hold these privileges and immunities under
the paramount authority of the Federal Government, and its courts would he
bound to maintain and enforce them, the constitution and laws of the State
to the contrary notwithstanding. And if the States could limit or restrict them,
or place the party in an inferior grade, this clause of the Constitution would
be unmeaning, and could have no operation, and would give no rights to the
citizen when in another State. He would have none but what the State itself
chose to allow him. This is evidently not the construction or meaning of the
clause in question. It guarantees rights to the citizen, and the State cannot
withhold them. And these rights are of a character, and would lead to consequences which make it absolutely certain that the African race were not
included under the name of citizens of a State, and were not in the contemplation of the framers of the Constitution when these privileges and immunities
were provided for the protection of the citizen in other States. . . .

No one, we presume, supposes that any change in public opinion or feeling, in relation to this unfortunate race, in the civilized nations of Europe, or in this country, should induce the court to give to the words of the Constitution a more liberal construction in their favor than they were intended to bear when the instrument was framed and adopted. Such an argument would be altogether inadmissible in any tribunal called on to interpret it. If any of its provisions are deemed unjust, there is a mode prescribed in the instrument itself by which it may be amended; but while it remains unaltered, it must be construed now as it was understood at the time of its adoption

It is not only the same in words, but the same in meaning, and delegates the same power to the Government, and reserves and secures the same rights and privileges to the citizen; and as long as it continues to exist in its present form, it speaks not only in the same words, but with the same meaning and intent with which it spoke when it came from the hands of its framers, and was voted on and adopted by the people of the United States. Any other rule of construction would abrogate the judicial character of this court, and make it the mere reflex of the popular opinion or passion of the day. This court was not created by the Constitution for such purposes. Higher and graver trusts have been confided to it, and it must not falter in the path of duty.

What the construction was at that time, we think can hardly admit of doubt. We have the language of the Declaration of Independence and of the Articles of Confederation, in addition to the plain words of the Constitution itself; we have the legislation of the different States, before, about the time, and since, the Constitution was adopted; we have the legislation of Congress from the time of its adoption to a recent period; and we have the constant and uniform action of the executive department, all concurring together, and leading to the same result. And if anything in relation to the construction of the Constitution can be regarded as settled, it is that which we now give to the word "citizen" and the word "people."

And upon a full and careful consideration of the subject, the court is of opinion, that, upon the facts stated in the plea in abatement, Dred Scott was not a citizen of Missouri within the meaning of the Constitution of the United States, and not entitled as such to sue in its courts; and, consequently, that the Circuit Court had no jurisdiction of the case, and that the judgment on the plea in abatement is erroneous. . . .

The case before us still more strongly imposes upon this court the duty of examining whether the court below has not committed an error, in taking jurisdiction and giving a judgment for costs in favor of the defendant; for, in *Capron v. Van Noorden*, the judgment was reversed, because it did not appear that the parties were citizens of different States. They might or might not be. But in this case it does appear that the plaintiff was born a slave; and if the facts upon which he relies have not made him free, then it appears affirmatively on the record that he is not a citizen, and consequently his suit against Sandford was not a suit between citizens of different States, and the court had no authority to pass any judgment between the parties. The suit ought in this view of it, to have been dismissed by the Circuit Court, and its judgment in favor of Sandford is erroneous, and must be reversed.

It is true that the result either way, by dismissal or by a judgment for the defendant, makes very little, if any, difference in a pecuniary or personal point of view to either party. But the fact that the result would be very nearly the same to the parties in either form of judgment, would not justify this court in sanctioning an error in the judgment which is patent on the record, and which, if sanctioned, might be drawn into precedent, and lead to serious mischief and injustice in some future suit.

We proceed, therefore, to inquire whether the facts relied on by the plaintiff entitled him to his freedom. . . .

In considering this part of the controversy, two questions arise: (1) Was he, together with his family, free in Missouri by reason of the stay in the territory of the United States hereinbefore mentioned? And (2) If they were not, is Scott himself free by reason of his removal to Rock Island, in the State of Illinois, as stated in the above admissions?

We proceed to examine the first question.

The act of Congress, upon which the plaintiff relies, declares that slavery and involuntary servitude, except as a punishment for crime, shall be forever prohibited in all that part of the territory ceded by France, under the name of Louisiana, which lies north of thirty-six degrees thirty minutes north latitude, and not included within the limits of Missouri. And the difficulty which meets us at the threshold of this part of the inquiry is, whether Congress was authorized to pass this law under any of the powers granted to it by the Constitution; for if the authority is not given by that instrument, it is the duty of this court to declare it void and inoperative, and incapable of conferring freedom upon anyone who is held as a slave under the laws of any one of the States.

The counsel for the plaintiff has laid much stress upon that article in the Constitution which confers on Congress the power "to dispose of and make all needful rules and regulations respecting the territory or other property belonging to the United States;" but, in the judgment of the court, that provision has no bearing on the present controversy, and the power there given, whatever it may be, is confined, and was intended to be confined, to the territory which at that time belonged to, or was claimed by, the United States, and was within their boundaries as settled by the treaty with Great Britain, and can have no influence upon a territory afterwards acquired from a foreign Government. It was a special provision for a known and particular territory, and to meet a present emergency, and nothing more. . . .

This brings us to examine by what provision of the Constitution the present Federal Government, under its delegated and restricted powers, is authorized to acquire territory outside of the original limits of the United States, and what powers it may exercise therein over the person or property of a citizen of the United States, while it remains a Territory, and until it shall be admitted as one of the States of the Union.

There is certainly no power given by the Constitution to the Federal Government to establish or maintain colonies bordering on the United States or at a distance, to be ruled and governed at its own pleasure; nor to enlarge its territorial limits in any way, except by the admission of new States. That power is plainly given; and if a new State is admitted, it needs no further legislation by Congress, because the Constitution itself defines the relative rights and powers, and duties of the States, and the citizens of the State, and the Federal Government. But no power is given to acquire a Territory to be held and governed permanently in that character.

And indeed the power exercised by Congress to acquire territory and establish a Government there, according to its own unlimited discretion, was viewed with great jealousy by the leading statesmen of the day. And in the Federalist No. 38, written by Mr. Madison, he speaks of the acquisition of the Northwestern Territory by the confederated States, by the cession from Virginia, and the establishment of a Government there, as an exercise of power not warranted by the Articles of Confederation, and dangerous to the liberties of the people. And he urges the adoption of the Constitution as a security and safeguard against such an exercise of power.

We do not mean, however, to question the power of Congress in this reject. The power to expand the territory of the United States by the admission of new States is plainly given; and in the construction of this power by all the departments of the Government, it has been held to authorize the acquisition of territory, not fit for admission at the time, but to be admitted as soon as its population and situation would entitle it to admission. It is acquired to become a State, and not to be held as a colony and governed by Congress with absolute authority; and as the propriety of admitting a new State is committed to the sound discretion of Congress, the power to acquire territory for that purpose, to be held by the United States until it is in a suitable condition to become a State upon an equal footing with the other States, must rest upon the same discretion. It is a question for the political department of the Government, and not the judicial; and whatever the political department of the Government shall recognize as within the limits of the United States, the judicial department is also bound to recognize, and to administer in it the laws of the United States, so far as they apply, and to maintain in the Territory the authority and rights of the Government, and also the personal rights and rights of property of individual citizens, as secured by the Constitution. All we mean to say on this point is, that, as there is no express regulation in the Constitution defining the power which the General Government may exercise over the person or property of a citizen in a Territory thus acquired, the court must necessarily look to the provisions and principles of the Constitution, and its distribution of powers, for the rules and principles by which its decision must be governed.

Taking this rule to guide us, it may be safely assumed that citizens of the United States who migrate to a Territory belonging to the people of the United States, cannot be ruled as mere colonists, dependent upon the will of the General Government, and to be governed by any laws it may think proper to impose. The principle upon which our Governments rest, and upon which alone they continue to exist, is the union of States, sovereign and independent within their own limits in their internal and domestic concerns, and bound together as one people by a General Government, possessing certain enumerated and restricted powers, delegated to it by the people of the several States, and exercising supreme authority within the scope of the powers granted to it, throughout the dominion of the United States. A power, therefore, in the General Government to obtain and hold colonies and dependent territories, over which they might legislate without restriction, would be inconsistent with its own existence in its present form. Whatever it acquires, it acquires for the benefit of the people of the several States who created it. It is their trustee acting for them, and charged with the duty of promoting the interests of the whole people of the Union in the exercise of the powers specifically granted. . . .

But the power of Congress over the person or property of a citizen can never be a mere discretionary power under our Constitution and form of Government. The powers of the Government and the rights and privileges of the citizen are regulated and plainly defined by the Constitution itself. And when the Territory becomes a part of the United States, the Federal Government enters into possession in the character impressed upon it by those who created it. It enters upon it with its powers over the citizen strictly defined, and limited by the Constitution, from which it derives its own existence, and by virtue of which alone it continues to exist and act as a Government and sovereignty. It has no power of any kind beyond it; and it cannot, when it enters a Territory of the United States, put off its character, and assume discretionary or despotic powers which the Constitution has denied to it. It cannot create for itself a new character separated from the citizens of the United States, and the duties it owes them under the provisions of the Constitution. The Territory being a part of the United States, the Government and the citizen both enter it under the authority of the Constitution, with their respective rights defined and marked out; and the Federal Government can exercise no power over his person or property, beyond what that instrument confers, nor lawfully deny any right which it has reserved.

A reference to a few of the provisions of the Constitution will illustrate this proposition.

For example, no one, we presume, will contend that Congress can make any law in a Territory respecting the establishment of religion, or the free exercise thereof, or abridging the freedom of speech or of the press, or the right of the people of the Territory peaceably to assemble, and to petition the Government for the redress of grievances.

Nor can Congress deny to the people the right to keep and bear arms, nor the right to trial by jury, nor compel anyone to be a witness against himself in a criminal proceeding.

These powers, and others, in relation to rights of person, which it is not necessary here to enumerate, are, in express and positive terms, denied to the General Government; and the rights of private property have been guarded with equal care. Thus the rights of property are united with the rights of person, and placed on the same ground by the Fifth Amendment to the Constitution, which provides that no person shall be deprived of life, liberty, and property, without due process of law. And an act of Congress which deprives a citizen of the United States of his liberty or property, merely because he came himself or brought his property into a particular Territory of the United States, and who had committed no offense against the laws, could hardly be dignified with the name of due process of law.

So, too, it will hardly be contended that Congress could by law quarter a soldier in a house in a Territory without the consent of the owner, in time of peace; nor in time of war, but in a manner prescribed by law. Nor could they by law forfeit the property of a citizen in a Territory who was convicted of treason, for a longer period than the life of the person convicted; nor take private property for public use without just compensation.

The powers over person and property of which we speak are not only not granted to Congress, but are in express terms denied, and they are forbidden to exercise them. And this prohibition is not confined to the States, but the words are general, and extend to the whole territory over which the Constitution gives it power to legislate, including those portions of it remaining under Territorial Government, as well as that covered by States. It is a total absence of power everywhere within the dominion of the United States, and places the citizens of a Territory, so far as these rights are concerned, on the same footing with citizens of the States, and guards them as firmly and plainly against any inroads which the General Government might attempt, under the plea of implied or incidental powers. And if Congress itself cannot do this—if it is beyond the powers conferred on the Federal Government—it will be admitted, we presume, that it could not authorize a Territorial Government to exercise them. It could confer no power on any local Government, established by its authority, to violate the provisions of the Constitution.

It seems, however, to be supposed that there is a difference between property in a slave and other property, and that different rules may be applied to it in expounding the Constitution of the United States. And the laws and usages of nations, and the writings of eminent jurists upon the relation of master and slave, and their mutual rights and duties, and the powers which Governments may exercise over it, have been dwelt upon in the argument.

But in considering the question before us, it must be borne in mind that there is no law of nations standing between the people of the United States and their Government, and interfering with their relation to each other. The powers of the Government, and the rights of the citizen under it, are positive and practical regulations plainly written down. The people of the United States have delegated to it certain enumerated powers, and forbidden it to exercise others. It has no power over the person or property of a citizen but what the citizens of the United States have granted. And no laws or usages of other nations, or reasoning of statesmen or jurists upon the relations of master and slave, can enlarge the powers of the Government, or take from the citizens the rights they have reserved. And if the Constitution recognizes the right of property of the master in a slave, and makes no distinction between that description of property and other property owned by a citizen, no tribunal, acting under the authority of the United States, whether it be legislative, executive, or judicial, has a right to draw such a distinction, or deny to it the benefit of the provisions and guarantees which have been provided for the protection of private property against the encroachments of the Government.

Now, as we have already said in an earlier part of this opinion, upon a different point, the right of property in a slave is distinctly and expressly affirmed in the Constitution. The right to traffic in it, like an ordinary article of merchandise and property, was guaranteed to the citizens of the United States in every State that might desire it, for twenty years. And the Government in express terms is pledged to protect it in all future time, if the slave escapes from his owner. This is done in plain words—too plain to be misunderstood. And no word can be found in the Constitution which gives Congress a greater power over slave property, or which entitles property of that kind to less protection than property of any other description. The only power conferred is the power coupled with the duty of guarding and protecting the owner in his rights.

Upon these considerations, it is the opinion of the court that the act of Congress which prohibited a citizen from holding and owning property of this kind in the Territory of the United States north of the line therein mentioned, is not warranted by the Constitution, and is therefore void; and that neither Dred Scott himself, nor any of his family, were made free by being carried into this territory, even if they had been carried there by the owner, with the intention of becoming a permanent resident.

We have so far examined the case, as it stands under the Constitution of the United States, and the powers thereby delegated to the Federal Government.

But there is another point in the case which depends on State power and State law. And it is contended on the part of the plaintiff, that he is made free by being taken to Rock Island, in the State of Illinois, independently of his residence in the Territory of the United States; and being so made free, he was not again reduced to a state of slavery by being brought back to Missouri.

Our notice of this part of the case will be very brief; for the principle on which it depends was decided in this court, upon much consideration, in the case of *Strader et al. v. Graham*. . . . In that case, the slaves had been taken from Kentucky to Ohio, with the consent of the owner, and afterwards brought back to Kentucky. And this court held that their status or condition, as free or slave, depended upon the laws of Kentucky, when they were brought back into that State, and not of Ohio; and that this court had no jurisdiction to revise the judgment of a State court upon its own laws. This was the point directly before the court, and the decision that this court had not jurisdiction turned upon it, as will be seen by the report of the case.

So in this case. As Scott was a slave when taken into the State of Illinois by his owner, and was there held as such, and brought back in that character, his status, as free or slave, depended on the laws of Missouri, and not of Illinois.

It has, however, been urged in the argument, that by the laws of Missouri he was free on his return, and that this case, therefore, cannot be governed by the case of *Strader et al. v. Graham,* where it appeared, by the laws of Kentucky, that the plaintiffs continued to be slaves on their return from Ohio. But whatever doubts or opinions may, at one time, have been entertained upon this subject, we are satisfied, upon a careful examination of all the cases decided in the State courts of Missouri referred to, that it is now firmly settled by the decisions of the highest court in the State, that Scott and his family upon their return were not free, but were, by the laws of Missouri, the property of the defendant; and that the Circuit Court of the United States had no jurisdiction, when, by the laws of the State, the plaintiff was a slave, and not a citizen.

Source: *Reports of Cases Argued and Adjudged in the Supreme Court of the United States,* ed. Benjamin C. Howard (Washington, D.C.: Government Printing Office, 1857), 19: 393ff. Retrieved May 5, 2010, from http://supreme.justia.com/us/60/393/case .html.

CHAPTER 21

On *Dred Scott*, Frederick Douglass, 1857

Frederick Douglass, the prominent Negro abolitionist who had gained fame through his writing and speaking abilities, delivered the following speech at the anniversary celebration of the American Abolition Society in New York, on May 14, 1857, two months after the Dred Scott decision was handed down. Frederick Douglass was born a slave in Talbot County, Maryland, escaped to the North in 1838, and became legally free in 1846 when supporters in London purchased him from his former owner and issued him manumission papers. Having learned to read and write at an early age from the wife of his owner, Douglass became a featured speaker at abolitionist rallies in the North beginning in 1841. He wrote the story of his life, *Narrative of the Life of Frederick Douglass, an American Slave*, in 1845, and the book was so successful that it made him into a major public figure.*

As the leading Negro figure in the United States, it was natural that his opinion on the Dred Scott decision carried enormous weight throughout the North. This speech was made to an enraged group of abolitionists who hung on Douglass's every word. Although Douglass made many incendiary speeches, some filled with hate for the perfidious white man, to this group he spoke with passion but also with logic and optimism. It was a statesmanlike performance and possibly one of the best abolitionist speeches of the period. As he predicted, the Dred Scott decision was the beginning of the end for slavery—within ten years it would be abolished. Douglass gave a face to the evil of slavery and provided an articulate voice that reached many communities throughout the North and around which people could rally. At the time when Stephen Douglas was calling for restraint and compromise and Lincoln was qualifying his antislavery remarks, Frederick Douglass was taking no prisoners. The reader is urged to

---

* *Frederick Douglass: Selected Speeches and Writings*, ed. Philip S. Foner (Chicago: Lawrence Hill Books, 1999), xiii.

consider Douglass in respect to slavery and compare him to Martin Luther King Jr. and the civil rights movement in the 1960s. In what ways were they alike and in what ways were they different? Without these men would the antislavery and civil rights movements have been different or less effective?

Address on May 14, 1857

WHILE FOUR MILLIONS OF OUR FELLOW COUNTRYMEN ARE IN chains; while men, women, and children are bought and sold on the auction block with horses, sheep, and swine; while the remorseless slave whip draws the warm blood of our common humanity—it is meet that we assemble as we have done today, and lift up our hearts and voices in earnest denunciation of the vile and shocking abomination. It is not for us to be governed by our hopes or our fears in this great work; yet it is natural on occasions like this, to survey the position of the great struggle which is going on between slavery and freedom, and to dwell upon such signs of encouragement as may have been lately developed, and the state of feeling these signs or events have occasioned in us and among the people generally. It is a fitting time to take an observation to ascertain where we are, and what our prospects are.

To many, the prospects of the struggle against slavery seem far from cheering. Eminent men, North and South, in Church and State, tell us that the omens are all against us. Emancipation, they tell us, is a wild, delusive idea; the price of human flesh was never higher than now; slavery was never more closely entwined about the hearts and affections of the southern people than now; that whatever of conscientious scruple, religious conviction, or public policy, which opposed the system of slavery forty or fifty years ago, has subsided; and that slavery never reposed upon a firmer basis than now.

Completing this picture of the happy and prosperous condition of this system of wickedness, they tell us that this state of things is to be set to our account. Abolition agitation has done it all. How deep is the misfortune of my poor, bleeding people, if this be so! How lost their condition, if even the efforts of their friends but sink them deeper in ruin!

Without assenting to this strong representation of the increasing strength and stability of slavery, without denouncing what of untruth pervades it, I own myself not insensible to the many difficulties and discouragements, that beset us on every hand. They fling their broad and gloomy shadows across the pathway of every thoughtful colored man in this country. For one, I see them clearly, and feel them sadly. With an earnest, aching heart, I have long looked for the realization of the hope of my people. Standing, as it were, barefoot, and treading upon the sharp and flinty rocks of the present, and looking out upon the boundless sea of the future, I have sought, in my humble way, to penetrate the intervening mists and clouds, and, perchance, to descry, in the dim and shadowy distance, the white flag of freedom, the precise speck of time at which the cruel bondage of my people should end, and the long entombed millions rise from the foul grave of slavery and death. But of that time I can know nothing, and you can know nothing. All is uncertain at that point. One thing, however, is certain: slaveholders are in earnest, and mean to cling to their slaves as long as they can, and to the bitter end. They show no sign of a wish to quit their iron grasp upon the sable throats of their victims. Their motto is, "a firmer hold and a tighter grip" for every new effort that is made to break their cruel power. The case is one of life or death with them, and they will give up only when they must do that or do worse.

In one view the slaveholders have a decided advantage over all opposition. It is well to notice this advantage—the advantage of complete organization. They are organized; and yet were not at the pains of creating their organizations. The State governments, where the system of slavery exists, are complete slavery organizations. The church organizations in those States are equally at the service of slavery; while the Federal Government, with its army and navy, from the chief magistracy in Washington, to the Supreme Court, and thence to the chief marshalship at New York, is pledged to support, defend, and propagate the crying curse of human bondage. The pen, the purse, and the sword are united against the simple truth, preached by humble men in obscure places.

This is one view. It is, thank God, only one view; there is another, and a brighter view. David, you know, looked small and insignificant when going to meet Goliath, but looked larger when he had slain his foe. The Malakoff was, to the eye of the world, impregnable, till the hour it fell before the shot and shell of the allied army. Thus hath it ever been. Oppression, organized as ours is, will appear invincible up to the very hour of its fall. Sir, let us look at the other side, and see if there are not some things to cheer our heart and nerve us up anew in the good work of emancipation.

Take this fact—for it is a fact—the antislavery movement has, from first to last, suffered no abatement. It has gone forth in all directions, and is now felt in the remotest extremities of the republic.

It started small, and was without capital either in men or money. The odds were all against it. It literally had nothing to lose, and everything to gain. There was ignorance to be enlightened, error to be combated, conscience to be awakened, prejudice to be overcome, apathy to be aroused, the right of speech to be secured, mob violence to be subdued, and a deep, radical change to be inwrought in the mind and heart of the whole nation. This great work, under God, has gone on, and gone on gloriously.

Amid all changes, fluctuations, assaults, and adversities of every kind, it has remained firm in its purpose, steady in its aim, onward and upward, defying all opposition, and never losing a single battle. Our strength is in the growth of antislavery conviction, and this has never halted.

There is a significant vitality about this abolition movement. It has taken a deeper, broader, and more lasting hold upon the national heart than ordinary reform movements. Other subjects of much interest come and go, expand and contract, blaze and vanish, but the huge question of American slavery, comprehending, as it does, not merely the weal or the woe of four millions, and their countless posterity, but the weal or the woe of this entire nation, must increase in magnitude and in majesty with every hour of its history. From a cloud not bigger than a man's hand, it has overspread the heavens. It has risen from a grain not bigger than a mustard seed. Yet see the fowls of the air, how they crowd its branches.

Politicians who cursed it, now defend it; ministers, once dumb, now speak in its praise; and presses, which once flamed with hot denunciations against it, now surround the sacred cause as by a wall of living fire. Politicians go with it as a pillar of cloud by day, and the press as a pillar of fire by night. With these ancient tokens of success, I, for one, will not despair of our cause.

Those who have undertaken to suppress and crush out this agitation for liberty and humanity, have been most woefully disappointed. Many who have engaged to put it down, have found themselves put down. The agitation has pursued them in all their meanderings, broken in upon their seclusion, and, at the very moment of fancied security, it has settled down upon them like a mantle of unquenchable fire. Clay, Calhoun, and Webster each tried his hand at suppressing the agitation; and they went to their graves disappointed and defeated.

Loud and exultingly have we been told that the slavery question is settled, and settled forever. You remember it was settled thirty-seven years ago, when Missouri was admitted into the Union with a slaveholding constitution, and slavery prohibited in all territory north of thirty-six degrees of north latitude. Just fifteen years afterwards, it was settled again by voting down the right of petition, and gagging down free discussion in Congress. Ten years after this it was settled again by the annexation of Texas, and with it the war with Mexico. In 1850 it was again settled. This was called a final settlement. By it slavery was virtually declared to be the equal of liberty, and should come into the Union on the same terms. By it the right and the power to hunt down men, women, and children, in every part of this country, was conceded to our southern brethren, in order to keep them in the Union. Four years after this settlement, the whole question was once more settled, and settled by a settlement which unsettled all the former settlements.

The fact is, the more the question has been settled, the more it has needed settling. The space between the different settlements has been strikingly on the decrease. The first stood longer than any of its successors; the second, ten years; the third, five years; the fourth stood four years; and the fifth has stood the brief space of two years.

This last settlement must be called the Taney settlement. We are now told, in tones of lofty exultation, that the day is lost—all lost—and that we might as well give up the struggle. The highest authority has spoken. The voice of the Supreme Court has gone out over the troubled waves of the national conscience, saying peace, be still.

This infamous decision of the slaveholding wing of the Supreme Court maintains that slaves are within the contemplation of the Constitution of the United States, property; that slaves are property in the same sense that horses, sheep, and swine are property; that the old doctrine that slavery is a creature of local law is false; that the right of the slaveholder to his slave does not depend upon the local law, but is secured wherever the Constitution of the United States extends; that Congress has no right to prohibit slavery anywhere; that slavery may go in safety anywhere under the Star-Spangled Banner; that colored persons of African descent have no rights that white men are bound to respect; that colored men of African descent are not and cannot be citizens of the United States.

You will readily ask me how I am affected by this devilish decision—this judicial incarnation of wolfishness? My answer is, and no thanks to the slaveholding wing of the Supreme Court, my hopes were never brighter than now. I have no fear that the national conscience will be put to sleep by such an open, glaring, and scandalous tissue of lies as that decision is, and has been, over and over, shown to be.

The Supreme Court of the United States is not the only power in this world. It is very great, but the Supreme Court of the Almighty is greater. Judge Taney can do many things, but he cannot perform impossibilities. He cannot bale out the ocean, annihilate the firm old earth, or pluck the silvery star of liberty from our northern sky. He may decide, and decide again; but he cannot reverse the decision of the Most High. He cannot change the essential nature of things—making evil good, and good evil.

Happily for the whole human family, their rights have been defined, declared, and decided in a court higher than the Supreme Court. "There is a law," says Brougham, "above all the enactments of human codes, and by that law, unchangeable and eternal, man cannot hold property in man."

Your fathers have said that man's right to liberty is self-evident. There is no need of argument to make it clear. The voices of nature, of conscience, of reason, and of revelation, proclaim it as the right of all rights, the foundation of all trust, and of all responsibility. Man was born with it. It was his before he comprehended it. The deed conveying it to him is written in the center of his soul, and is recorded in Heaven. The sun in the sky is not more palpable to the sight than man's right to liberty is to the moral vision. To decide against this right in the person of Dred Scott, or the humblest and most whip-scarred bondman in the land, is to decide against God. It is an open rebellion against God's government. It is an attempt to undo what God has done, to blot out the broad distinction instituted by the All Wise between men and things, and to change the image and superscription of the ever-living God into a speechless piece of merchandise.

Such a decision cannot stand. God will be true though every man be a liar. We can appeal from this hell-black judgment of the Supreme Court, to the court of common sense and common humanity. We can appeal from man to God. If there is no justice on earth, there is yet justice in Heaven. You may close your Supreme Court against the black man's cry for justice, but you cannot, thank God, close against him the ear of a sympathizing world, nor shut up the court of Heaven. All that is merciful and just, on earth and in Heaven, will execrate and despise this edict of Taney.

If it were at all likely that the people of these free States would tamely submit to this demoniacal judgment, I might feel gloomy and sad over it, and possibly it might be necessary for my people to look for a home in some other country. But as the case stands, we have nothing to fear.

In one point of view, we, the abolitionists and colored people, should meet this decision, unlooked for and monstrous as it appears, in a cheerful spirit. This very attempt to blot out forever the hopes of an enslaved people may be one necessary link in the chain of events preparatory to the downfall and complete overthrow of the whole slave system.

The whole history of the antislavery movement is studded with proof that all measures devised and executed with a view to ally and diminish the antislavery agitation, have only served to increase, intensify, and embolden that agitation. This wisdom of the crafty has been confounded, and the counsels of the ungodly brought to naught. It was so with the Fugitive Slave Bill. It was so with the Kansas-Nebraska Bill; and it will be so with this last and most shocking of all pro-slavery devices, this Taney decision.

When great transactions are involved, where the fate of millions is concerned, where a long enslaved and suffering people are to be delivered, I am superstitious enough to believe that the finger of the Almighty may be seen bringing good out of evil, and making the wrath of man redound to his honor, hastening the triumph of righteousness.

The American people have been called upon, in a most striking manner, to abolish and put away forever the system of slavery. The subject has been pressed upon their attention in all earnestness and sincerity. The cries of the slave have gone forth to the world, and up to the throne of God. This decision, in my view, is a means of keeping the nation awake on the subject. It is another proof that God does not mean that we shall go to sleep, and forget that we are a slaveholding nation.

Step by step we have seen the slave power advancing; poisoning, corrupting, and perverting the institutions of the country; growing more and more haughty, imperious, and exacting. The white man's liberty has been marked out for the same grave with the black man's.

The ballot box is desecrated, God's law set at naught, armed legislators stalk the halls of Congress, freedom of speech is beaten down in the Senate. The rivers and highways are infested by border ruffians, and white men are made to feel the iron heel of slavery. This ought to arouse us to kill off the hateful thing. They are solemn warnings to which the white people, as well as the black people, should take heed.

If these shall fail, judgment, more fierce or terrible, may come. The lightning, whirlwind, and earthquake may come. Jefferson said that he trembled for his country when he reflected that God is just, and his justice cannot sleep forever. The time may come when even the crushed worm may turn under the tyrant's feet. Goaded by cruelty, stung by a burning sense of wrong, in an awful moment of depression and desperation, the bondman and bondwoman at the south may rush to one wild and deadly struggle for freedom. Already slaveholders go to bed with bowie knives, and apprehend death at their dinners. Those who enslave, rob, and torment their cooks, may well expect to find death in their dinner pots.

The world is full of violence and fraud, and it would be strange if the slave, the constant victim of both fraud and violence, should escape the contagion. He, too, may learn to fight the devil with fire, and for one, I am in no frame of mind to pray that this may be long deferred.

Two remarkable occurrences have followed the presidential election; one was the unaccountable sickness traced to the National Hotel at Washington, and the other was the discovery of a plan among the slaves, in different localities, to slay their oppressors. Twenty or thirty of the suspected were put to death. Some were shot, some hanged, some burned, and some died under the lash. One brave man owned himself well acquainted with the conspiracy, but said he would rather die than disclose the facts. He received seven hundred and fifty lashes, and his noble spirit went away to the God who gave it. The name of this hero has been by the meanness of tyrants suppressed. Such a man redeems his race. He is worthy to be mentioned with the Hofers and Tells, the noblest heroes of history. These insurrectionary movements have been put down, but they may break out at any time, under the guidance of higher intelligence, and with a more invincible spirit.

The fire thus kindled, may be revived again;
The flames are extinguished, but the embers remain;
One terrible blast may produce an ignition,
Which shall wrap the whole South in wild conflagration.
The pathway of tyrants lies over volcanoes
The very air they breathe is heavy with sorrows;
Agonizing heart-throbs convulse them while sleeping,
And the wind whispers Death as over them sweeping.

By all the laws of nature, civilization, and of progress, slavery is a doomed system. Not all the skill of politicians, North and South, not all the sophistries of judges, not all the fulminations of a corrupt press, not all the hypocritical prayers, or the hypocritical refusals to pray of a hollow-hearted priesthood, not all the devices of sin and Satan, can save the vile thing from extermination.

Already a gleam of hope breaks upon us from the southwest. One southern city has grieved and astonished the whole South by a preference for freedom. The wedge has entered. Dred Scott, of Missouri, goes into slavery, but St. Louis declares for freedom. The judgment of Taney is not the judgment of St. Louis. It may be said that this demonstration in St. Louis is not to be taken as an evidence of sympathy with the slave; that it is purely a white man's victory. I admit it. Yet I am glad that white men, bad as they generally are, should gain a victory over slavery. I am willing to accept a judgment against slavery, whether supported by white or black reasons—though I would much rather have it supported by both. He that is not against us, is on our part.

Come what will, I hold it to be morally certain that, sooner or later, by fair means or foul means, in quiet or in tumult, in peace or in blood, in judgment or in mercy, slavery is doomed to cease out of this otherwise goodly land, and liberty is destined to become the settled law of this republic. I base my sense of the certain overthrow of slavery, in part, upon the nature of the American government, the Constitution, the tendencies of the age, and the character of the American people; and this, notwithstanding the important decision of Judge Taney.

I know of no soil better adapted to the growth of reform than American soil. I know of no country where the conditions for affecting great changes in the settled order of things, for the development of right ideas of liberty and humanity, are more favorable than here in these United States.

The very groundwork of this government is a good repository of Christian civilization. The Constitution, as well as the Declaration of Independence, and the sentiments of the founders of the republic, give us a platform broad enough, and strong enough, to support the most comprehensive plans for the freedom and elevation of all the people of this country, without regard to color, class, or clime.

There is nothing in the present aspect of the antislavery question which should drive us into the extravagance and nonsense of advocating a dissolution of the American Union as a means of overthrowing slavery, or freeing the North from the malign influence of slavery upon the morals of the northern people. While the press is at liberty, and speech is free, and the ballot box is open to the people of the sixteen free States; while the slaveholders are but four hundred thousand in number, and we are fourteen millions; while the mental and moral power of the nation is with us; while we are really the strong and they are the weak, it would look worse than cowardly to retreat from the Union.

If the people of the North have not the power to cope with these four hundred thousand slaveholders inside the Union, I see not how they could get out of the Union. The strength necessary to move the Union must ever be less than is required to break it up. If we have got to conquer the slave power to get out of the Union, I for one would much rather conquer, and stay in the Union. The latter, it strikes me, is the far more rational mode of action.

I make these remarks in no servile spirit, nor in any superstitious reverence for a mere human arrangement. If I felt the Union to be a curse, I should not be far behind the very chiefest of the disunion abolitionists in denouncing it. But the evil to be met and abolished is not in the Union. The power arrayed against us is not a parchment.

It is not in changing the dead form of the Union, that slavery is to be abolished in this country. We have to do not with the dead, but the living; not with the past, but the living present.

Those who seek slavery in the Union, and who are everlastingly dealing blows upon the Union, in the belief that they are killing slavery, are most woefully mistaken. They are fighting a dead form instead of a living and powerful reality. It is clearly not because of the peculiar character of our Constitution that we have slavery, but the wicked pride, love of power, and selfish perverseness of the American people. Slavery lives in this country not because of any paper Constitution, but in the moral blindness of the American people, who persuade themselves that they are safe, though the rights of others may be struck down.

Besides, I think it would be difficult to hit upon any plan less likely to abolish slavery than the dissolution of the Union. The most devoted advocates of slavery, those who make the interests of slavery their constant study, seek a dissolution of the Union as their final plan for preserving slavery from abolition, and their ground is well taken. Slavery lives and flourishes best in the absence of civilization; a dissolution of the Union would shut up the system in its own congenial barbarism. The dissolution of the Union would not give the North one single additional advantage over slavery to the people of the North, but would manifestly take from them many which they now certainly possess.

Within the Union we have a firm basis of antislavery operation. National welfare, national prosperity, national reputation and honor, and national scrutiny; common rights, common duties, and common country, are so many bridges over which we can march to the destruction of slavery. To fling away these advantages because James Buchanan is president or Judge Taney gives a lying decision in favor of slavery, does not enter into my notion of common sense. Mr. Garrison and his friends have been telling us that, while in the Union, we are responsible for slavery; and in so telling us, he and they have told us the truth. But in telling us that we shall cease to be responsible for slavery by dissolving the Union, he and they have not told us the truth.

There now, clearly, is no freedom from responsibility for slavery, but in the abolition of slavery. We have gone too far in this business now to sum up our whole duty in the cant phrase of "no Union with slaveholders."

To desert the family hearth may place the recreant husband out of the sight of his hungry children, but it cannot free him from responsibility. Though he should roll the waters of three oceans between him and them, he could not roll from his soul the burden of his responsibility to them; and, as with the private family, so in this instance with the national family. To leave the slave in his chains, in the hands of cruel masters who are too strong for him, is not to free ourselves from responsibility. Again: If I were on board of a pirate ship, with a company of men and women whose lives and liberties I had put in jeopardy, I would not clear my soul of their blood by jumping in the long boat, and singing out, "No union with pirates." My business would be to remain on board, and while I never would perform a single act of piracy again, I should exhaust every means given me by my position, to save the lives and liberties of those against whom I had committed piracy. In like manner, I hold it is our duty to remain inside this Union, and use all the power to restore to enslaved millions their precious and God-given rights. The more we have done by our voice and our votes, in times past, to rivet their galling fetters, the more clearly and solemnly comes the sense of duty to remain, to undo what we have done. Where, I ask, could the slave look for release from slavery if the Union were dissolved? I have an abiding conviction founded upon long and careful study of the certain effects of slavery upon the moral sense of slaveholding communities, that if the slaves are ever delivered from bondage, the power will emanate from the free States. All hope that the slaveholders will be self-moved to this great act of justice, is groundless and delusive. Now, as of old, the Redeemer must come from above, not from beneath. To dissolve the Union would be to withdraw the emancipating power from the field.

But I am told this is the argument of expediency. I admit it, and am prepared to show that what is expedient in this instance is right. "Do justice, though the heavens fall." Yes, that is a good motto, but I deny that it would be doing justice to the slave to dissolve the Union and leave the slave in his chains to get out by the clemency of his master, or the strength of his arms. Justice to the slave is to break his chains, and going out of the Union is to leave him in his chains, and without any probable chance of getting out of them.

But I come now to the great question as to the constitutionality of slavery. The recent slaveholding decision, as well as the teachings of antislavery men, make this a fit time to discuss the constitutional pretensions of slavery.

The people of the North are a law-abiding people. They love order and respect the means to that end. This sentiment has sometimes led them to the folly and wickedness of trampling upon the very life of law, to uphold its dead form. This was so in the execution of that thrice-accursed Fugitive Slave Bill. Burns and Simms were sent back to the hell of slavery after they had looked upon Bunker Hill, and heard liberty thunder in Faneuil Hall. The people permitted this outrage in obedience to the popular sentiment of reverence for law. While men thus respect law, it becomes a serious matter so to interpret the law as to make it operate against liberty. I have a quarrel with those who fling the Supreme Law of this land between the slave and freedom. It is a serious matter to fling the weight of the Constitution against the cause of human liberty, and those who do it, take upon them a heavy responsibility. Nothing but absolute necessity, shall, or ought to drive me to such a concession to slavery.

When I admit that slavery is constitutional, I must see slavery recognized in the Constitution. I must see that it is there plainly stated that one man of a certain description has a right of property in the body and soul of another man of a certain description. There must be no room for a doubt. In a matter so important as the loss of liberty, everything must be proved beyond all reasonable doubt.

The well-known rules of legal interpretation bear me out in this stubborn refusal to see slavery where slavery is not, and only to see slavery where it is.

The Supreme Court has, in its day, done something better than make slaveholding decisions. It has laid down rules of interpretation which are in harmony with the true idea and object of law and liberty.

It has told us that the intention of legal instruments must prevail; and that this must be collected from its words. It has told us that language must be construed strictly in favor of liberty and justice.

It has told us where rights are infringed, where fundamental principles are overthrown, where the general system of the law is departed from, the legislative intention must be expressed with irresistible clearness, to induce a court of justice to suppose a design to effect such objects.

These rules are as old as law. They rise out of the very elements of law. It is to protect human rights, and promote human welfare. Law is in its nature opposed to wrong, and must everywhere be presumed to be in favor of the right. The pound of flesh, but not one drop of blood, is a sound rule of legal interpretation.

Besides there is another rule of law, as well, of common sense, which requires us to look to the ends for which a law is made, and to construe its details in harmony with the ends sought.

Now let us approach the Constitution from the standpoint thus indicated, and instead of finding in it a warrant for the stupendous system of robbery, comprehended in the term "slavery," we shall find it strongly against that system.

"We, the people of the United States, in order to form a more perfect Union, establish justice, insure domestic tranquility, provide for the common defense, promote the general welfare, and secure the blessings of liberty to ourselves and our posterity, do ordain and establish this constitution for the United States of America."

Such are the objects announced by the instrument itself, and they are in harmony with the Declaration of Independence, and the principles of human well-being. Six objects are here declared: "Union," "defense," "welfare," "tranquility," and "justice," and "liberty."

Neither in the preamble nor in the body of the Constitution is there a single mention of the term "slave" or "slaveholder," "slave master" or "slave state," neither is there any reference to the color, or the physical peculiarities, of any part of the people of the United States. Neither is there anything in the Constitution standing alone, which would imply the existence of slavery in this country.

"We, the people": not we, the white people; not we, the citizens, or the legal voters; not we, the privileged class, and excluding all other classes but we, the people; not we, the horses and cattle, but we the people—the men and women, the human inhabitants of the United States, do ordain and establish this Constitution, etc.

I ask, then, any man to read the Constitution, and tell me where, if he can, in what particular that instrument affords the slightest sanction of slavery?

Where will he find a guarantee for slavery? Will he find it in the declaration that no person shall be deprived of life, liberty, or property, without due process of law? Will he find it in the declaration that the Constitution was established to secure the blessing of liberty? Will he find it in the right of the people to be secure in their persons and papers, and houses, and effects? Will he find it in the clause prohibiting the enactment by any State of a bill of attainder?

These all strike at the root of slavery, and any one of them, but faithfully carried out, would put an end to slavery in every State in the American Union. Take, for example, the prohibition of a bill of attainder. That is a law entailing on the child the misfortunes of the parent. This principle would destroy slavery in every State of the Union.

The law of slavery is a law of attainder. The child is property because its parent was property, and suffers as a slave because its parent suffered as a slave.

Thus the very essence of the whole slave code is in open violation of a fundamental provision of the Constitution, and is in open and flagrant violation of all the objects set forth in the Constitution. . . .

How is the constitutionality of slavery made out, or attempted to be made out? First, by discrediting and casting away as worthless the most beneficent rules of legal interpretation; by disregarding the plain and commonsense reading of the instrument itself; by showing that the Constitution does not mean what it says, and says what it does not mean, by assuming that the written Constitution is to be interpreted in the light of a secret and unwritten understanding of its framers, which understanding is declared to be in favor of slavery. It is in this mean, contemptible, underhand method that the Constitution is pressed into the service of slavery.

They do not point us to the Constitution itself, for the reason that there is nothing sufficiently explicit for their purpose; but they delight in supposed intentions—intentions nowhere expressed in the Constitution, and everywhere contradicted in the Constitution. . . .

The argument here is, that the Constitution comes down to us from a slaveholding period and a slaveholding people; and that, therefore, we are bound to suppose that the Constitution recognizes colored persons of African descent, the victims of slavery at that time, as debarred forever from all participation in the benefit of the Constitution and the Declaration of Independence, although the plain reading of both includes them in their beneficent range.

As a man, an American, a citizen, a colored man of both Anglo-Saxon and African descent, I denounce this representation as a most scandalous and devilish perversion of the Constitution, and a brazen misstatement of the facts of history.

But I will not content myself with mere denunciation; I invite attention to the facts.

It is a fact, a great historic fact, that at the time of the adoption of the Constitution, the leading religious denominations in this land were antislavery, and were laboring for the emancipation of the colored people of African descent.

The church of a country is often a better index of the state of opinion and feeling than is even the government itself.

The Methodists, Baptists, Presbyterians, and the denomination of Friends, were actively opposing slavery, denouncing the system of bondage, with language as burning and sweeping as we employ at this day.

Take the Methodists. In 1780, that denomination said: "The Conference acknowledges that slavery is contrary to the laws of God, man, and nature, and hurtful to society—contrary to the dictates of conscience and true religion, and doing to others that we would not do unto us." In 1784, the same church declared, "that those who buy, sell, or give slaves away, except for the purpose to free them, shall be expelled immediately." In 1785, it spoke even more stringently on the subject. It then said: "We hold in the deepest abhorrence the practice of slavery, and shall not cease to seek its destruction by all wise and proper means.". . .

Let us now see how slavery was regarded by the Presbyterian Church at that early date.

In 1794, the general assembly of that body pronounced the following judgment in respect to slavery, slaveholders, and slaveholding: "1st Timothy, 1st chapter, loth verse: The law was made for man-stealers. 'This crime among the Jews exposed the perpetrators of it to capital punishment.' Exodus, XXI, 15. And the apostle here classes them with sinners of the first rank. The word he uses in its original import, comprehends all who are concerned in bringing any of the human race into slavery, or in retaining them in it. Stealers of men are all those who bring off slaves or freemen, and keep, sell, or buy them. 'To steal a freeman,' says Grotius, 'Is the highest kind of theft.' In other instances, we only steal human property, but when we steal or retain men in slavery, we seize those who, in common with ourselves, are constituted, by the original grant, lords of the earth."

I might quote, at length, from the sayings of the Baptist Church and the sayings of eminent divines at this early period, showing that Judge Taney has grossly falsified history, but will not detain you with these quotations. The testimony of the church, and the testimony of the founders of this republic, from the declaration downward, prove Judge Taney false; as false to history as he is to law.

Washington and Jefferson, and Adams, and Jay, and Franklin, and Rush, and Hamilton, and a host of others, held no such degrading views on the subject of slavery as are imputed by Judge Taney to the fathers of the republic. All, at that time, looked for the gradual but certain abolition of slavery, and shaped the Constitution with a view to this grand result.

George Washington can never be claimed as a fanatic, or as the representative of fanatics. The slaveholders impudently use his name for the base purpose of giving respectability to slavery. Yet, in a letter to Robert Morris, Washington uses this language—language which, at this day, would make him a terror of the slaveholders, and the natural representative of the Republican Party. "There is not a man living, who wishes more sincerely than I do, to see some plan adopted for the abolition of slavery; but there is only one proper and effectual mode by which it can be accomplished, and that is by Legislative authority; and this, as far as my suffrage will go, shall not be wanting."

Washington only spoke the sentiment of his times. There were, at that time, abolition societies in the slave States—abolition societies in Virginia, in North Carolina, in Maryland, in Pennsylvania, and in Georgia—all slaveholding States. Slavery was so weak, and liberty so strong, that free speech could attack the monster to its teeth. Men were not mobbed and driven out of the presence of slavery, merely because they condemned the slave system. The system was then on its knees imploring to be spared, until it could get itself decently out of the world.

In the light of these facts, the Constitution was framed, and framed in conformity to it.

It may, however, be asked, if the Constitution were so framed that the rights of all the people were naturally protected by it, how happens it that a large part of the people have been held in slavery ever since its adoption? Have the people mistaken the requirements of their own Constitution?

The answer is ready. The Constitution is one thing, its administration is another, and, in this instance, a very different and opposite thing. I am here to vindicate the law, not the administration of the law. It is the written Constitution, not the unwritten Constitution, that is now before us. If, in the whole range of the Constitution, you can find no warrant for slavery, then we may properly claim it for liberty.

Good and wholesome laws are often found dead on the statute book. We may condemn the practice under them and against them, but never the law itself. To condemn the good law with the wicked practice, is to weaken, not to strengthen our testimony.

It is no evidence that the Bible is a bad book, because those who profess to believe the Bible are bad. The slaveholders of the South, and many of their wicked allies at the North, claim the Bible for slavery; shall we, therefore, fling the Bible away as a pro-slavery book? It would be as reasonable to do so as it would be to fling away the Constitution.

We are not the only people who have illustrated the truth, that a people may have excellent law, and detestable practices. Our Savior denounces the Jews, because they made void the law by their traditions. We have been guilty of the same sin.

The American people have made void our Constitution by just such traditions as Judge Taney and Mr. Garrison have been giving to the world of late, as the true light in which to view the Constitution of the United States. I shall follow neither. It is not what Moses allowed for the hardness of heart, but what God requires, ought to be the rule.

It may be said that it is quite true that the Constitution was designed to secure the blessings of liberty and justice to the people who made it, and to the posterity of the people who made it, but was never designed to do any such thing for the colored people of African descent.

This is Judge Taney's argument, and it is Mr. Garrison's argument, but it is not the argument of the Constitution. The Constitution imposes no such mean and satanic limitations upon its own beneficent operation. And, if the Constitution makes none, I beg to know what right has anybody, outside of the Constitution, for the special accommodation of slaveholding villainy, to impose such a construction upon the Constitution?

The Constitution knows all the human inhabitants of this country as "the people." It makes, as I have said before, no discrimination in favor of, or against, any class of the people, but is fitted to protect and preserve the rights of all, without reference to color, size, or any physical peculiarities. Besides, it has been shown by William Goodell and others, that in eleven out of the old thirteen States, colored men were legal voters at the time of the adoption of the Constitution.

In conclusion, let me say, all I ask of the American people is, that they live up to the Constitution, adopt its principles, imbibe its spirit, and enforce its provisions.

When this is done, the wounds of my bleeding people will be healed, the chain will no longer rust on their ankles, their backs will no longer be torn by the bloody lash, and liberty, the glorious birthright of our common humanity, will become the inheritance of all the inhabitants of this highly favored country.

Source: Central Library of Rochester and Monroe County, Historic Monographs Collection, digitized monograph: *Two Speeches by Frederick Douglass; One on West India Emancipation, Delivered at Canandaigua. Aug. 4th, and the Other on the Dred Scott Decision, Delivered in New York on the Occasion of the Anniversary of the American Abolition Society, May, 1857* (Rochester, NY: O. P. Dewey, American Office, 1857), 27–46.

CHAPTER 22

The Georgia Debate on Secession, 1860

With the election of Abraham Lincoln to the presidency in November of 1860, secessionist movements began in all the Southern states. Although there was no "typical" legislative action, in Georgia a committee of the legislature arranged for a debate to take place over the proper course for Georgia between "separatists" and "cooperationists," their terms for secessionists and unionists. The speakers were Thomas R. R. Cobb, Robert Toombs, and Henry Benning, for the separatists, and Alexander Stephens and Benjamin Hill, for the cooperationists. Toombs and Stephens were the primary antagonists, both leading statesmen and very close friends. Toombs was a gifted orator who probably would have become president of the Confederacy had he not fallen victim to backroom dealings by Thomas R. R. Cobb and had to settle for being the Confederacy's first secretary of state and a brigadier general. Stephens became the Confederacy's vice president. Their stature added to the importance of their speeches.

Other states approached secession with caution, as in Arkansas, where the legislature initially voted to remain in the Union. South Carolina, on the other hand, took the lead in voting to secede. The seven states of the Deep South, from South Carolina to Texas, voted to secede during the winter before Lincoln took office, and the upper South, including Virginia, North Carolina, Tennessee, and Arkansas, followed after Lincoln called for troops to defend the Union. The arguments across the South echoed the Georgia debate, and some states— Tennessee, Arkansas, and Virginia—furnished troops to the Union in surprising numbers. The South had lost the population battle and with it control of Congress. Would any argument have prevailed on the Georgians to remain in the Union? Was there really any alternative to secession given that the South wanted to maintain slavery? And would a confederation have been ultimately viable in the long run?

For Secession, Robert Toombs

I VERY MUCH REGRET, IN APPEARING BEFORE YOU AT YOUR request, to address you on the present state of the country and the prospect before us, that I can bring you no good tidings. The stern, steady march of events has brought us in conflict with our nonslaveholding confederates upon the fundamental principles of our compact of Union. We have not sought this conflict; we have sought too long to avoid it; our forbearance has been construed into weakness, our magnanimity into fear, until the vindication of our manhood, as well as the defense of our rights, is required at our hands. The door of conciliation and compromise is finally closed by our adversaries, and it remains only to us to meet the conflict with the dignity and firmness of men worthy of freedom.

We need no declaration of independence. Above eighty-four years ago, our fathers won that by the sword from Great Britain, and above seventy years ago, Georgia, with twelve other confederates, as free, sovereign, and independent states, having perfect governments already in existence, for purposes clearly defined, erected a common agent for the attainment of these purposes by the exercise of those powers, and called this agent the United States of America.

The basis, the cornerstone of this government, was the perfect equality of the free, sovereign, and independent states which made it. They were unequal in population, wealth, and territorial extent; they had great diversities of interests, pursuits, institutions, and laws; but they had common interests, mainly exterior, which they proposed to protect by this common agent—a constitutional united government—without in any degree subjecting their inequalities and diversities to federal control or action. . . .

The instant the government was organized, at the very first Congress, the Northern states evinced a general desire and purpose to use it for their own benefit and to pervert its powers for sectional advantage; and they have steadily pursued that policy to this day. They demanded a monopoly of the business of shipbuilding, and got a prohibition against the sale of foreign ships to citizens of the United States, which exists to this day. They demanded a monopoly of the coasting trade, in order to get higher freights than they could get in open competition with the carriers of the world. And now, today, if a foreign vessel in Savannah offers to take your rice, cotton, grain, or lumber to New York, or any other American port, for nothing, your laws prohibit it, in order that Northern shipowners may get enhanced prices for doing your carrying. . . .

Thus stands the account between the North and the South. Under its ordinary and most favorable action, bounties and protection to every interest and every pursuit in the North, to the extent of at least $50 million per annum, besides the expenditure of at least $60 million out of every $70 million of the public expenditure among them, thus making the Treasury a perpetual fertilizing stream to them and their industry, and a suction pump to drain away our substance and parch up our lands.

With these vast advantages, ordinary and extraordinary, one would have supposed the North would have been content, and would have at least respected the security and tranquility of such obedient and profitable brethren; but such is not human nature. They despised the patient victims of their avarice, and they very soon began a war upon our political rights and social institutions, marked by every act of perfidy and treachery which could add a darker hue to such a warfare. In 1820, the Northern party (and I mean by that term now and whenever else it is used, or its equivalent, in these remarks, the antislavery or abolition party of the North) endeavored to exclude the state of Missouri from admission into the Union, because she chose to protect African slavery in the new state. . . .

This act of exclusion violated the express provisions of the treaty of 1802, to which the national faith was pledged; violated the well-settled policy of the government, at least from Adams's administration to that day; and has, since slavery was adjudicated by the Supreme Court of the United States, violated the Constitution itself. . . .

The South at all times demanded nothing but equality in the common territories, equal enjoyment of them with their property to that extended to Northern citizens and their property—nothing more. . . . In 1790 we had less than eight hundred thousand slaves. Under our mild and humane administration of the system, they have increased above four million. . . . Before the end of this century, at precisely the same rate of increase, the Africans among us in a subordinate condition will amount to eleven million persons. What shall be done with them? We must expand or perish. . . . We demand the equal right with the North to go into the common territories with all of our property, slaves included, and to be there protected in its peaceable enjoyment by the federal government, until such territories may come into the Union as equal states—then we admit them with or without slavery, as the people themselves may decide for themselves. . . .

By the laws of nations, founded on natural justice, no nation, nor the subjects or citizens of any nation, have the right to disturb the peace or security of any other nation or people, much less to conspire, excite insurrection, discontent, or the commission of crimes among them, and all these are held to be good causes of war. For twenty years this party has, by abolition societies, by publications made by them, by the public press, through the pulpit and their own legislative halls, and every effort—by reproaches, by abuse, by vilification, by slander—to disturb our society, our tranquility, to excite discontent between the different classes of our people, and to excite our slaves to insurrection. No nation in the world would submit to such conduct from any other nation. I will not willingly do so from this abolition party. . . .

The executive power, the last bulwark of the Constitution to defend us against these enemies of the Constitution, has been swept away, and we now stand without a shield, with bare bosoms presented to our enemies, and we demand at your hands the sword for our defense, and if you will not give it to us, we will take it—take it by the divine right of self-defense, which governments neither give nor can take away.

Therefore, redress for past and present wrongs demands resistance to the rule of Lincoln and his abolition horde over us; he comes at their head to shield and protect them in the perpetration of these outrages upon us, and, what is more, he comes at their head to aid them in consummating their avowed purposes by the power of the federal government. Their main purpose, as indicated by all their acts of hostility to slavery, is its final and total abolition. His party declares it; their acts prove it. He has declared it; I accept his declaration. The battle of the irrepressible conflict has hitherto been fought on his side alone. We demand service in this war. Surely no one will deny that the election of Lincoln is the endorsement of the policy of those who elected him, and an endorsement of his own opinions. . . .

Hitherto, they have carried on this warfare by state action, by individual action, by appropriation, by the incendiary's torch and the poisoned bowl. They were compelled to adopt this method because the federal executive and the federal judiciary were against them. They will have possession of the federal executive with its vast power, patronage, prestige of legality, its army, its navy, and its revenue on the 4th of March next. Hitherto, it has been on the side of the Constitution and the right; after the 4th of March it will be in the hands of your enemy. Will you let him have it?

Then strike while it is yet today. Withdraw your sons from the army, from the navy, and every department of the federal public service. Keep your own taxes in your own coffers—buy arms with them and throw the bloody spear into this den of incendiaries and assassins, and let God defend the right. . . .

But we are told that secession would destroy the fairest fabric of liberty the world ever saw, and that we are the most prosperous people in the world under it. . . . The arguments I now hear in favor of this Northern connection are identical in substance and almost in the same words as those which were used in 1775 and 1776 to sustain the British connection. . . . The very men who use these arguments admit that this Constitution, this compact is violated, broken, and trampled under foot by the abolition party. Shall we surrender the jewels because their robbers and incendiaries have broken the casket? Is this the way to preserve liberty? I would lief surrender it back to the British Crown as to the abolitionists. I will defend it from both. Our purpose is to defend those liberties. What baser fate could befall us or this great experiment of free government than to have written upon its tomb: "Fell by the hands of abolitionists and the cowardice of its natural defenders." If we quail now, this will be its epitaph.

We are said to be a happy and prosperous people. We have been, because we have hitherto maintained our ancient rights and liberties—we will be until we surrender them. They are in danger: come, freemen, to the rescue. If we are prosperous, it is due to God, ourselves, and the wisdom of our state government. . . . I have already vainly asked for the law of the federal government that promotes our prosperity. I have shown you many that retard that prosperity—many that drain our coffers for the benefit of our bitterest foes. I say bitterest foes—show me the nation in the world that hates, despises, vilifies, or plunders us like our abolition "brethren" in the North. There is none.

I can go to England or France, or any other country in Europe with my slave without molestation or violating any law. I can go anywhere except in my own country, whilom called "the glorious Union"; here alone am I stigmatized as a felon; here alone am I an outlaw; here alone am I under the ban of the empire; here alone I have neither security nor tranquility; here alone are organized governments ready to protect the incendiary, the assassin who burns my dwelling or takes my life or those of my wife and children; here alone are hired emissaries paid by brethren to glide through the domestic circle and intrigue insurrection with all of its nameless horrors.

My countrymen, "If you have nature in you, bear it not." Withdraw yourselves from such a confederacy; it is your right to do so—your duty to do so. I know not why the abolitionists should object to it, unless they want to torture and plunder you. If they resist this great sovereign right, make another war of independence, for that then will be the question; fight its battles over again— reconquer liberty and independence. As for me, I will take any place in the great conflict for rights which you may assign. I will take none in the federal government during Mr. Lincoln's administration.

If you desire a senator after the 4th of March, you must elect one in my place. I have served you in the state and national councils for nearly a quarter of a century without once losing your confidence. I am yet ready for the public service when honor and duty call. I will serve you anywhere where it will not degrade and dishonor my country. Make my name infamous forever, if you will, but save Georgia. I have pointed out your wrongs, your danger, your duty. You have claimed nothing but that rights be respected and that justice be done. Emblazon it on your banner—fight for it, win it, or perish in the effort.

Against Secession, Alexander H. Stephens

I APPEAR BEFORE YOU TONIGHT AT THE REQUEST OF MEM-bers of the legislature and others to speak of matters of the deepest interest that can possibly concern us all of an earthly character. There is nothing— no question or subject connected with this life—that concerns a free people so intimately as that of the government under which they live. We are now, indeed, surrounded by evils. Never since I entered upon the public stage has the country been so environed with difficulties and dangers that threatened the public peace and the very existence of society as now. I do not now appear before you at my own instance. It is not to gratify desire of my own that I am here. Had I consulted my own ease and pleasure I should not be before you; but, believing that it is the duty of every good citizen to give his counsels and views whenever the country is in danger, as to the best policy to be pursued, I am here. For these reasons, and these only, do I bespeak a calm, patient, and attentive hearing. . . .

The first question that presents itself is—Shall the people of the South secede from the Union in consequence of the election of Mr. Lincoln to the presidency of the United States? My countrymen, I tell you frankly, candidly, and earnestly that I do not think that they ought. In my judgment, the election of no man, constitutionally chosen to that high office, is sufficient cause for any state to separate from the Union. It ought to stand by and aid still in maintaining the Constitution of the country. To make a point of resistance to the government, to withdraw from it because a man has been constitutionally elected, puts us in the wrong. We are pledged to maintain the Constitution. Many of us have sworn to support it. Can we, therefore, for the mere election of a man to the presidency, and that, too, in accordance with the prescribed forms of the Constitution, make a point of resistance to the government with-out becoming the breakers of that sacred instrument ourselves, withdraw our-selves from it? Would we not be in the wrong?

Whatever fate is to befall this country, let it never be laid to the charge of the people of the South, and especially to the people of Georgia, that we were untrue to our national engagements. Let the fault and the wrong rest upon others. If all our hopes are to be blasted, if the republic is to go down, let us be found to the last moment standing on the deck, with the Constitution of the United States waving over our heads. Let the fanatics of the North break the Constitution, if such is their fell purpose. Let the responsibility be upon them. I shall speak presently more of their acts; but let not the South, let us not be the ones to commit the aggression. We went to the election with the people. The result was different from what we wished; but the election has been constitutionally held. Were we to make a point of resistance to the government and go out of the Union on that account, the record would be made up hereafter against us. . . .

My countrymen, I am not of those who believe this Union has been a curse up to this time. True men, men of integrity, entertain different views from me on this subject. I do not question their right to do so; I would not impugn their motives in so doing. Nor will I undertake to say that this government of our fathers is perfect. There is nothing perfect in this world of a human origin. Nothing connected with human nature, from man himself to any of his works. You may select the wisest and best men for your judges, and yet how many defects are there in the administration of justice? You may select the wisest and best men for your legislators, and yet how many defects are apparent in your laws? And it is so in our government. . . .

I come now to the main question put to me, and on which my counsel has been asked. That is, what the present legislature should do in view of the dangers that threaten us, and the wrongs that have been done us by several of our confederate states in the Union, by the acts of their legislatures nullifying the Fugitive Slave Law, and in direct disregard of their constitutional obligations. What I shall say will not be in the spirit of dictation. It will be simply my own judgment for what it is worth. It proceeds from a strong conviction that according to it our rights, interests, and honor—our present safety and future security—can be maintained without yet looking to the last resort, the ultima ratio regum. That should not be looked to until all else fails. That may come. On this point I am hopeful but not sanguine. But let us use every patriotic effort to prevent it while there is ground for hope.

If any view that I may present, in your judgment, be inconsistent with the best interest of Georgia, I ask you as patriots not to regard it. After hearing me and others whom you have advised with, act in the premises according to your own conviction of duty as patriots. I speak now particularly to the members of the legislature present. There are, as I have said, great dangers ahead. Great dangers may come from the election I have spoken of. If the policy of Mr. Lincoln and his Republican associates shall be carried out, or attempted to be carried out, no man in Georgia will be more willing or ready than myself to defend our rights, interest, and honor at every hazard, and to the last extremity.

What is this policy? It is, in the first place, to exclude us by an act of Congress from the territories with our slave property. He is for using the power of the general government against the extension of our institutions. Our position at this point is and ought to be, at all hazards, for perfect equality between all the states, and the citizens of all the states, in the territories, under the

Constitution of the United States. If Congress should exercise its power against this, then I am for standing where Georgia planted herself in 1850. These were plain propositions which were then laid down in her celebrated platform as sufficient for the disruption of the Union if the occasion should ever come; on these Georgia has declared that she will go out of the Union; and for these she would be justified by the nations of the earth in so doing. . . .

Northern states . . . have violated their plighted faith; what ought we to do in view of this? That is the question. What is to be done? By the law of nations you would have a right to demand the carrying out of this article of agreement [the Fugitive Slave Law], and I do not see that it should be otherwise with respect to the states of the Union. And in case it is not done, we would, by these principles, have the right to commit acts of reprisal on those faithless governments, and seize upon their property, or that of their citizens wherever found. The states of this Union stand upon the same footing with foreign nations in this respect. But by the law of nations we are equally bound, before proceeding to violent measures, to set forth our grievances before the offending government; to give them an opportunity to redress the wrong. Has our state yet done this? I think not. . . .

Let us, therefore, not act hastily in this matter. Let your committee on the state of the republic make out a bill of grievances; let it be sent by the governor to those faithless states, and if reason and argument shall be tried in vain—all shall fail to induce them to return to their constitutional obligations—I would be for retaliatory measures, such as the governor has suggested to you. This mode of resistance in the Union is our power. It might be effectual, and, if in the last resort, we would be justified in the eyes of nations, not only in separating from them but by using force. . . .

I view of all these questions of difficulty, let a convention of the people of Georgia be called, to which they may be all referred. Let the sovereignty of the people speak. . . .

Should Georgia determine to go out of the Union, I speak for one, though my views might not agree with them, whatever the result might be, I shall bow to the will of her people. Their cause is my cause, and their destiny is my destiny; and I trust this will be the ultimate course of all. The greatest curse that can befall a free people is civil war. . . .

I am for exhausting all that patriotism can demand before taking the last step. I would invite, therefore, South Carolina to a conference. I would ask the same of all the other Southern states, so that if the evil has got beyond our control, which God, in His mercy, grant may not be the case, let us not be divided among ourselves—but, if possible, secure the united cooperation of all the Southern states; and then, in the face of the civilized world, we may justify our action; and, with the wrong all on the other side, we can appeal to the God of battles to aid us in our cause. . . .

If all this fails, we shall at least have the satisfaction of knowing that we have done our duty and all that patriotism could require.

Sources: Documents 67 (Toombs) and 147½ (Stephens) in *The Rebellion Record: A Diary of American Events*, ed. Frank Moore (New York: G. P. Putnam and Henry Holt, 1864), 1: 362–8 and 219–28.

CHAPTER 23

Abraham Lincoln's First Inaugural Address, 1861

Lincoln began writing his inaugural address while still in Springfield, Illinois, and he repeatedly changed his draft in the two months before his inauguration. He toned down the address in an attempt to be as conciliatory as possible to the Democrats and the South, although he recognized that it would be extremely difficult, if not impossible, to coax the seven states that had already seceded back into the Union without force. There were three other groups of states, however, that he was attempting to influence: in the upper South, North Carolina, Virginia, Tennessee, and Arkansas, which were waiting to see what he would do about the states in secession, and what policies he would institute, before deciding to remain in the Union or secede; the border states of Delaware, Maryland, Kentucky, and Missouri, which he wished to hold in the Union at all costs; and last, but not least, he needed to whip up enthusiasm in the North to support his administration and fight the civil war that looked to be unavoidable.

The atmosphere in Washington was grim and tense that March when he made the address, as rumors of assassination plots and Southern aggression circulated on every street corner. The speech has been widely held by historians to be the most important inaugural address made by an American president to that time, and it generally accomplished its purpose. The Deep South saw it as a declaration of war, the upper South and border states heard possibilities for additional compromises, and the North considered it an olive branch held out to the South. However, South Carolina's firing on Fort Sumter on April 12, 1861, followed by Lincoln's April 15 call for troops, effectively ended all attempts at a peaceful solution. The reader should carefully read Lincoln's position regarding enforcement of any law not yet repealed, even if the enforcer does not approve of the law. Would he agree with twenty-first-century federal discretion in enforcement? Given that seven states had already seceded, did he choose the best possible approach to the three factions: the South, his partisans in the North, and the wavering Democrats who held the balance of power? Why did he give the South assurances concerning slavery? Given your experience with modern presidents, would any in the last thirty years have adopted this tone toward what were, in fact, states engaged in treason and rebellion?

Inaugural Address, March 4, 1861

FELLOW-CITIZENS OF THE UNITED STATES:

In compliance with a custom as old as the government itself, I appear before you to address you briefly and to take in your presence the oath prescribed by the Constitution of the United States to be taken by the president before he enters on the execution of this office.

I do not consider it necessary at present for me to discuss those matters of administration about which there is no special anxiety or excitement. Apprehension seems to exist among the people of the southern states that by the accession of a Republican administration their property and their peace and personal security are to be endangered. There has never been any reasonable cause for such apprehension. Indeed, the most ample evidence to the contrary has all the while existed and been open to their inspection. It is found in nearly all the published speeches of him who now addresses you. I do but quote from one of those speeches when I declare that:

"I have no purpose, directly or indirectly, to interfere with the institution of slavery in the States where it exists. I believe I have no lawful right to do so, and I have no inclination to do so."

Those who nominated and elected me did so with full knowledge that I had made this and many similar declarations and had never recanted them; and more than this, they placed in the platform for my acceptance, and as a law to themselves and to me, the clear and emphatic resolution which I now read:

"Resolved, that the maintenance inviolate of the rights of the states, and especially the right of each state to order and control its own domestic institutions according to its own judgment exclusively, is essential to that balance of power on which the perfection and endurance of our political fabric depend; and we denounce the lawless invasion by armed force of the soil of any state or territory, no matter what pretext, as among the gravest of crimes."

I now reiterate these sentiments, and in doing so I only press upon the public attention the most conclusive evidence of which the case is susceptible, that the property, peace, and security of no section are to be in any wise endangered by the now incoming administration. I add, too, that all the protection which, consistently with the Constitution and the laws, can be given will be cheerfully given to all the states when lawfully demanded, for whatever cause—as cheerfully to one section as to another.

There is much controversy about the delivering up of fugitives from service or labor. The clause I now read is as plainly written in the Constitution as any other of its provisions:

"No person held to service or labor in one State, under the laws thereof, escaping into another, shall in consequence of any law or regulation therein be discharged from such service or labor, but shall be delivered up on claim of the party to whom such service or labor may be due."

It is scarcely questioned that this provision was intended by those who made it for the reclaiming of what we call fugitive slaves; and the intention of the lawgiver is the law. All members of Congress swear their support to the whole Constitution—to this provision as much as to any other. To the proposition, then, that slaves whose cases come within the terms of this clause "shall be delivered up" their oaths are unanimous. Now, if they would make the effort in good temper, could they not with nearly equal unanimity frame and pass a law by means of which to keep good that unanimous oath?

There is some difference of opinion whether this clause should be enforced by national or by state authority, but surely that difference is not a very material one. If the slave is to be surrendered, it can be of but little consequence to him or to others by which authority it is done. And should anyone in any case be content that his oath shall go unkept on a merely unsubstantial controversy as to how it shall be kept?

Again: in any law upon this subject ought not all the safeguards of liberty known in civilized and humane jurisprudence be introduced, so that a free-man be not in any case surrendered as a slave? And might it not be well at the same time to provide by law for the enforcement of that clause in the Constitution which guarantees that "the citizens of each State shall be entitled to all privileges and immunities of citizens in the several States"?

I take the official oath today with no mental reservations and with no purpose to construe the Constitution or laws by any hypercritical rules; and while I do not choose now to specify particular acts of Congress as proper to be enforced, I do suggest that it will be much safer for all, both in official and private stations, to conform to and abide by all those acts which stand unrepealed than to violate any of them, trusting to find impunity in having them held to be unconstitutional.

It is seventy-two years since the first inauguration of a president under our national Constitution. During that period fifteen different and greatly distinguished citizens have in succession administered the executive branch of the government. They have conducted it through many perils, and generally with great success. Yet, with all this scope of precedent, I now enter upon the same task for the brief constitutional term of four years under great and peculiar difficulty. A disruption of the federal Union, heretofore only menaced, is now formidably attempted.

I hold that in contemplation of universal law and of the Constitution the union of these states is perpetual. Perpetuity is implied, if not expressed, in the fundamental law of all national governments. It is safe to assert that no government proper ever had a provision in its organic law for its own termination. Continue to execute all the express provisions of our national Constitution, and the Union will endure forever, it being impossible to destroy it except by some action not provided for in the instrument itself.

Again: if the United States be not a government proper, but an association of states in the nature of contract merely, can it, as a contract, be peaceably unmade by less than all the parties who made it? One party to a contract may violate it—break it, so to speak—but does it not require all to lawfully rescind it?

Descending from these general principles, we find the proposition that in legal contemplation the Union is perpetual confirmed by the history of the Union itself. The Union is much older than the Constitution. It was formed, in fact, by the Articles of Association in 1774. It was matured and continued by the Declaration of Independence in 1776. It was further matured, and the faith of all the then thirteen states expressly plighted and engaged that it should be perpetual, by the Articles of Confederation in 1778. And finally, in 1787, one of the declared objects for ordaining and establishing the Constitution was "to form a more perfect Union."

But if destruction of the Union by one or by a part only of the states be lawfully possible, the Union is less perfect than before the Constitution, having lost the vital element of perpetuity.

It follows from these views that no state upon its own mere motion can lawfully get out of the Union; that resolves and ordinances to that effect are legally void, and that acts of violence within any state or states against the authority of the United States are insurrectionary or revolutionary, according to circumstances.

I therefore consider that in view of the Constitution and the laws the Union is unbroken, and to the extent of my ability, I shall take care, as the Constitution itself expressly enjoins upon me, that the laws of the Union be faithfully executed in all the states. Doing this I deem to be only a simple duty on my part, and I shall perform it so far as practicable unless my rightful masters, the American people, shall withhold the requisite means or in some authoritative manner direct the contrary. I trust this will not be regarded as a menace, but only as the declared purpose of the Union that it will constitutionally defend and maintain itself.

In doing this there needs to be no bloodshed or violence, and there shall be none unless it be forced upon the national authority. The power confided to me will be used to hold, occupy, and possess the property and places belonging to the government and to collect the duties and imposts; but beyond what may be necessary for these objects, there will be no invasion, no using of force against or among the people anywhere. Where hostility to the United States in any interior locality shall be so great and universal as to prevent competent resident citizens from holding the federal offices, there will be no attempt to force obnoxious strangers among the people for that object. While the strict legal right may exist in the government to enforce the exercise of these offices, the attempt to do so would be so irritating and so nearly impracticable withal that I deem it better to forego for the time the uses of such offices. The mails, unless repelled, will continue to be furnished in all parts of the Union. So far as possible the people everywhere shall have that sense of perfect security which is most favorable to calm thought and reflection. The course here indicated will be followed unless current events and experience shall show a modification or change to be proper, and in every case and exigency my best discretion will be exercised, according to circumstances actually existing and with a view and a hope of a peaceful solution of the national troubles and the restoration of fraternal sympathies and affections.

That there are persons in one section or another who seek to destroy the Union at all events and are glad of any pretext to do it I will neither affirm nor deny; but if there be such, I need address no word to them. To those, however, who really love the Union may I not speak?

Before entering upon so grave a matter as the destruction of our national fabric, with all its benefits, its memories, and its hopes, would it not be wise to ascertain precisely why we do it? Will you hazard so desperate a step while there is any possibility that any portion of the ills you fly from have no real existence? Will you, while the certain ills you fly to are greater than all the real ones you fly from, will you risk the commission of so fearful a mistake?

All profess to be content in the Union if all constitutional rights can be maintained. Is it true, then, that any right plainly written in the Constitution has been denied? I think not. Happily, the human mind is so constituted that no party can reach to the audacity of doing this. Think, if you can, of a single instance in which a plainly written provision of the Constitution has ever been denied. If by the mere force of numbers a majority should deprive a minority of any clearly written constitutional right, it might in a moral point of view justify revolution; certainly would if such right were a vital one. But such is not our case. All the vital rights of minorities and of individuals are so plainly assured to them by affirmations and negations, guarantees and prohibitions, in the Constitution that controversies never arise concerning them. But no organic law can ever be framed with a provision specifically applicable to every question which may occur in practical administration. No foresight can anticipate nor any document of reasonable length contain express provisions for all possible questions. Shall fugitives from labor be surrendered by national or by state authority? The Constitution does not expressly say. May Congress prohibit slavery in the territories? The Constitution does not expressly say. Must Congress protect slavery in the territories? The Constitution does not expressly say.

From questions of this class spring all our constitutional controversies, and we divide upon them into majorities and minorities. If the minority will not acquiesce, the majority must, or the government must cease. There is no other alternative, for continuing the government is acquiescence on one side or the other. If a minority in such case will secede rather than acquiesce, they make a precedent which in turn will divide and ruin them, for a minority of their own will secede from them whenever a majority refuses to be controlled by such minority. For instance, why may not any portion of a new confederacy a year or two hence arbitrarily secede again, precisely as portions of the present Union now claim to secede from it? All who cherish disunion sentiments are now being educated to the exact temper of doing this.

Is there such perfect identity of interests among the states to compose a new union as to produce harmony only and prevent renewed secession?

Plainly the central idea of secession is the essence of anarchy. A majority held in restraint by constitutional checks and limitations, and always changing easily with deliberate changes of popular opinions and sentiments, is the only true sovereign of a free people. Whoever rejects it does of necessity fly to anarchy or to despotism. Unanimity is impossible. The rule of a minority, as a permanent arrangement, is wholly inadmissible; so that, rejecting the majority principle, anarchy or despotism in some form is all that is left.

I do not forget the position assumed by some that constitutional questions are to be decided by the Supreme Court, nor do I deny that such decisions must be binding in any case upon the parties to a suit as to the object of that suit, while they are also entitled to very high respect and consideration in all parallel cases by all other departments of the government. And while it is obviously possible that such decision may be erroneous in any given case, still the evil effect following it, being limited to that particular case, with the chance that it may be overruled and never become a precedent for other cases, can better be borne than could the evils of a different practice. At the same time, the candid citizen must confess that if the policy of the government upon vital questions affecting the whole people is to be irrevocably fixed by decisions of the Supreme Court, the instant they are made in ordinary litigation between parties in personal actions the people will have ceased to be their own rulers, having to that extent practically resigned their government into the hands of that eminent tribunal. Nor is there in this view any assault upon the court or the judges. It is a duty from which they may not shrink to decide cases properly brought before them, and it is no fault of theirs if others seek to turn their decisions to political purposes.

One section of our country believes slavery is right and ought to be extended, while the other believes it is wrong and ought not to be extended. This is the only substantial dispute. The fugitive-slave clause of the Constitution and the law for the suppression of the foreign slave trade are each as well enforced, perhaps, as any law can ever be in a community where the moral sense of the people imperfectly supports the law itself. . . . This, I think, cannot be perfectly cured, and it would be worse in both cases after the separation of the sections than before. The foreign slave trade, now imperfectly suppressed, would be ultimately revived without restriction in one section, while fugitive slaves, now only partially surrendered, would not be surrendered at all by the other.

Physically speaking, we cannot separate. We cannot remove our respective sections from each other nor build an impassable wall between them. A husband and wife may be divorced and go out of the presence and beyond the reach of each other, but the different parts of our country cannot do this. They cannot but remain face to face, and intercourse, either amicable or hostile, must continue between them. Is it possible, then, to make that intercourse more advantageous or more satisfactory after separation than before? Can aliens make treaties easier than friends can make laws? Can treaties be more faithfully enforced between aliens than laws can among friends? Suppose you go to war, you cannot fight always; and when, after much loss on both sides and no gain on either, you cease fighting, the identical old questions, as to terms of intercourse, are again upon you.

This country, with its institutions, belongs to the people who inhabit it. Whenever they shall grow weary of the existing government, they can exercise their constitutional right of amending it or their revolutionary right to dismember or overthrow it. I cannot be ignorant of the fact that many worthy and patriotic citizens are desirous of having the national Constitution amended. While I make no recommendation of amendments, I fully recognize the rightful authority of the people over the whole subject, to be exercised in either of the modes prescribed in the instrument itself; and I should, under existing circumstances, favor rather than oppose a fair opportunity being afforded the people to act upon it. . . . I understand a proposed amendment to the Constitution—which amendment, however, I have not seen—has passed Congress, to the effect that the federal government shall never interfere with the domestic institutions of the states, including that of persons held to service. To avoid misconstruction of what I have said, I depart from my purpose not to speak of particular amendments so far as to say that, holding such a provision to now be implied constitutional law, I have no objection to its being made express and irrevocable.

The chief magistrate derives all his authority from the people, and they have referred none upon him to fix terms for the separation of the states. The people themselves can do this if also they choose, but the executive as such has nothing to do with it. His duty is to administer the present government as it came to his hands and to transmit it unimpaired by him to his successor.

Why should there not be a patient confidence in the ultimate justice of the people? Is there any better or equal hope in the world? In our present differences, is either party without faith of being in the right? If the Almighty Ruler of Nations, with His eternal truth and justice, be on your side of the North, or on yours of the South, that truth and that justice will surely prevail by the judgment of this great tribunal of the American people.

By the frame of the government under which we live this same people have wisely given their public servants but little power for mischief, and have with equal wisdom provided for the return of that little to their own hands at very short intervals. While the people retain their virtue and vigilance no administration by any extreme of wickedness or folly can very seriously injure the government in the short space of four years.

My countrymen, one and all, think calmly and well upon this whole subject. Nothing valuable can be lost by taking time. If there be an object to hurry any of you in hot haste to a step which you would never take deliberately, that object will be frustrated by taking time; but no good object can be frustrated by it. Such of you as are now dissatisfied still have the old Constitution unimpaired, and, on the sensitive point, the laws of your own framing under it; while the new administration will have no immediate power, if it would, to change either. If it were admitted that you who are dissatisfied hold the right side in the dispute, there still is no single good reason for precipitate action. Intelligence, patriotism, Christianity, and a firm reliance on Him who has never yet forsaken this favored land are still competent to adjust in the best way all our present difficulty.

In your hands, my dissatisfied fellow-countrymen, and not in mine, is the momentous issue of civil war. The government will not assail you. You can have no conflict without being yourselves the aggressors. You have no oath registered in heaven to destroy the government, while I shall have the most solemn one to "preserve, protect, and defend it."

I am loath to close. We are not enemies, but friends. We must not be enemies. Though passion may have strained it must not break our bonds of affection. The mystic chords of memory, stretching from every battlefield and patriot grave to every living heart and hearthstone all over this broad land, will yet swell the chorus of the Union, when again touched, as surely they will be, by the better angels of our nature.

Source: Document 64 in *The Rebellion Record*, ed. Frank Moore (New York: G. P. Putnam and Henry Holt, 1864), 1: 36–9.

CHAPTER 24

The Emancipation Proclamation, Abraham Lincoln, 1863

Although popular conception sees the Emancipation Proclamation as one of the great historical documents in American history, it was a controversial political edict in the Lincoln administration, and the timing of its release was hotly debated. Although the war in the West was going well in 1862, it was not until the North experienced its first victory in the eastern theater at Antietam in September that Lincoln felt sufficiently optimistic to issue the Preliminary Emancipation Proclamation, to go into effect on January 1 of the following year. Lincoln had earlier struck down proclamations by military commanders that freed slaves in their jurisdictions, notably those by Generals Fremont and Hunter, but had freed the slaves in Washington, D.C., on April 16, 1862, when he signed the Compensated Emancipation Act.

The Emancipation Proclamation applied only to the states in rebellion, and made exceptions of some areas already under Union control, and so had the practical effect of freeing slaves only in certain areas not mentioned in the act that were occupied by the Union army. Notably, the border states were not mentioned, and emancipation in those states would wait until their legislatures acted or the Thirteenth Amendment took effect on December 6, 1865. The primary impact was to make British and French recognition of the Confederacy more difficult, while raising Northern morale and embittering the South by occupying the moral high ground. In the following months, particularly in the West, slaves were freed under the proclamation as Union forces advanced, which enabled recruitment of ex-slaves into the Union army and forestalled any substantial Southern recruitment of slaves into their forces. The timing of the proclamation was critical. Although slave rebellions during the war were nonexistent, Lincoln overlooked slavery in the border states to keep their support and thought a military victory in a major battle was required to secure his position before issuing such a radical proclamation.

By the President of the United States of America: A Proclamation

WHEREAS, ON THE TWENTY-SECOND DAY OF SEPTEMBER, IN the year of our Lord one thousand eight hundred and sixty-two, a proclamation was issued by the president of the United States, containing, among other things, the following, to wit:

That on the first day of January, in the year of our Lord one thousand eight hundred and sixty-three, all persons held as slaves within any state or designated part of a state, the people whereof shall then be in rebellion against the United States, shall be then, thenceforward, and forever free; and the executive government of the United States, including the military and naval authority thereof, will recognize and maintain the freedom of such persons, and will do no act or acts to repress such persons, or any of them, in any efforts they may make for their actual freedom.

That the executive will, on the first day of January aforesaid, by proclamation, designate the states and parts of states, if any, in which the people thereof, respectively, shall then be in rebellion against the United States; and the fact that any state, or the people thereof, shall on that day be, in good faith, represented in the Congress of the United States by members chosen thereto at elections wherein a majority of the qualified voters of such state shall have participated, shall, in the absence of strong countervailing testimony, be deemed conclusive evidence that such state, and the people thereof, are not then in rebellion against the United States.

Now, therefore I, Abraham Lincoln, president of the United States, by virtue of the power in me vested as commander-in-chief, of the army and navy of the United States in time of actual armed rebellion against the authority and government of the United States, and as a fit and necessary war measure for suppressing said rebellion, do, on this first day of January, in the year of our Lord one thousand eight hundred and sixty-three, and in accordance with my purpose so to do publicly proclaimed for the full period of one hundred days, from the day first above mentioned, order and designate as the states and parts of states wherein the people thereof respectively, are this day in rebellion against the United States, the following, to wit:

Arkansas, Texas, Louisiana (except the parishes of St. Bernard, Plaquemines, Jefferson, St. John, St. Charles, St. James Ascension, Assumption, Terrebonne, Lafourche, St. Mary, St. Martin, and Orleans, including the City of New Orleans), Mississippi, Alabama, Florida, Georgia, South Carolina, North Carolina, and Virginia, (except the forty-eight counties designated as West Virginia, and also the counties of Berkley, Accomac, Northampton, Elizabeth

City, York, Princess Ann, and Norfolk, including the cities of Norfolk and Portsmouth), and which excepted parts, are for the present, left precisely as if this proclamation were not issued.

And by virtue of the power, and for the purpose aforesaid, I do order and declare that all persons held as slaves within said designated states, and parts of states, are, and henceforward shall be free; and that the executive government of the United States, including the military and naval authorities thereof, will recognize and maintain the freedom of said persons.

And I hereby enjoin upon the people so declared to be free to abstain from all violence, unless in necessary self-defense; and I recommend to them that, in all cases when allowed, they labor faithfully for reasonable wages.

And I further declare and make known, that such persons of suitable condition, will be received into the armed service of the United States to garrison forts, positions, stations, and other places, and to man vessels of all sorts in said service.

And upon this act, sincerely believed to be an act of justice, warranted by the Constitution, upon military necessity, I invoke the considerate judgment of mankind, and the gracious favor of Almighty God.

In witness whereof, I have hereunto set my hand and caused the seal of the United States to be affixed.

Done at the city of Washington, this first day of January, in the year of our Lord one thousand eight hundred and sixty-three, and of the independence of the United States of America the eighty-seventh.

By the President: Abraham Lincoln

Wiliam H. Seward, Secretary of State.

Source: National Archives and Records Administration. Retrieved May 24, 2010, from http://www.archives.gov/exhibits/featured_documents/emancipation_proclamation/ transcript.html.

IV

THE PROGRESSIVE ERA, RADICALS, JIM CROW, AND WORLD WAR I

Following the Civil War, the country struggled to heal. In some areas, particularly Missouri, Arkansas, and Tennessee, local animosities died hard and guerrilla activities continued until the early 1870s. The jim crow laws in the South arrested to a large degree blacks' progress in joining the body politic following Reconstruction, and the Democratic Party in the South became increasingly conservative and even reactionary. The Supreme Court ruling in *Plessy v. Ferguson* validated segregation, but black leaders such as Booker T. Washington remained undaunted. Northerners who felt they had solved the slavery problem turned their attention to another oppressed group: the Indians. They saw American Indians as "noble savages," with many redeeming features, while settlers in the West viewed the Indians from a very different perspective.

An entirely new political movement appeared, progressivism. The Progressives sought government power to weed out corruption in politics, hammer corporate greed, and redistribute wealth. Under the Progressives, the penal system refocused itself on rehabilitation instead of punishment, and the federal government became increasingly large and powerful. Progressivism often ignored disparities between the races, seeking instead to address differences between classes. Consequently, some of the worst racial injustices in history occurred while some of the most eloquent rhetoric on civil rights was being uttered.

As the century entered its last decades, industrialization in the North required factory workers in large numbers, and this demand was met through immigrants arriving largely from oppressed working classes in central and eastern Europe. These immigrants possessed no understanding of common law, and many recognized no difference between the president of the United States and an autocratic European monarch. Radicalization of recent immigrants spread rapidly, and communism and socialism made their appearance as part and parcel of progressivism. Two presidents were assassinated, industrial leaders such as Henry Clay Frick were shot, labor strikes and riots took place, and the head of the Socialist Party, Eugene V. Debs, heralded a new age of progressive socialism.

Academic elites followed European university structures and espoused "academic freedom," whereby faculty and administrations recognized no accountability to the people, students, or the benefactors of their institutions. The populism of William Jennings Bryan accelerated the progressivism of Theodore Roosevelt, William Howard Taft, and Woodrow Wilson. Roosevelt embraced a rather unique form of American progressivism based on American exceptionalism, and Taft continued Roosevelt's policies, while Wilson looked to Europe for guidance and took a decidedly academic approach to governing. Ultimately, the triumvirate of Progressive presidents signed into law massive assaults on big business, implemented both the Federal Reserve System and the Sixteenth Amendment instituting income tax, and introduced Prohibition.

In 1913, under Wilson, the Federal Reserve, based on demands from the thousands of small "unit banks" across the nation, was designed by European banker Paul Warburg and five others at Jekyll Island in Georgia to provide the United States with a private central banking facility. America bankrolled Britain and France in World War I, and after numerous attacks on American shipping and civilians, Wilson took a very reluctant American nation into the conflict in 1917, calling for a Progressive agenda of making "the world safe for democracy." Although his naive approach to treaties and world government was ridiculed at Versailles, Wilson continued the adventurism he had begun in Mexico during its revolution and sent troops to Russia to fight the Bolshevik army in 1918. The era ended with America firmly on the world stage for better or worse, addressing European problems with European and international solutions. Exceptionalism had entered a new phase that would be unrecognizable to the Founding Fathers.

CHAPTER 25

Present Aspects of the Indian Problem, Carl Schurz, 1881

S enator Carl Schurz was secretary of the interior under President Rutherford B. Hayes and was known for his enlightened treatment of the American Indians. He addressed many problems through the Bureau of Indian Affairs but ultimately came to feel that the Indians faced a simple choice: extinction or civilization. In a very large sense, this was a new dilemma for a conquering nation: prior to the late nineteenth century conquering peoples simply amalgamated or exterminated subject tribes or peoples who failed to maintain their independence through some system of dependence and tribute. In the United States, tribute flowed to the conquered people as reparations for their losses—a political concept entirely new in the history of man. Mexico, for example, was paid for the territory it lost in its war with the United States.

Schurz wished eventually to eliminate the Bureau of Indian Affairs, not only by educating and civilizing the Indians, but by placing them on land, fully titled for each family, and eliminating the remaining unassigned reservation land through sale. In any case the nomadic, hunter-gatherer way of life would end, and as Indians adopted the "white man's way" they could achieve American citizenship. (One reformer, Merrill Gates, proudly announced the intention to get the Indian "out of the blanket and into trousers."[*]) The present-day map, however, shows extensive Indian reservations, and the Bureau of Indian Affairs is alive and well, doling out millions of dollars to Indians for their maintenance and managing over fifty-five million acres of land. Indians have remained in a dependent state for well over a hundred years, and critics allege that government handouts created a permanent state of welfare dependency.

---

[*] Edmund Jefferson Danzinger Jr. "United States Indian Policy During the Late Nineteenth Century: Change and Continuity." http://www.rbhayes.org/hayes/content/files/Hayes_Historical_Journal/usindianpolicyhhj.htm.

Present Aspects of the Indian Problem

THAT THE HISTORY OF OUR INDIAN RELATIONS PRESENTS, IN great part, a record of broken treaties, of unjust wars, and of cruel spoliation, is a fact too well known to require proof or to suffer denial. But it is only just to the government of the United States to say that its treaties with Indian tribes were, as a rule, made in good faith, and that most of our Indian wars were brought on by circumstances for which the government itself could not fairly be held responsible. Of the treaties, those were the most important by which the government guaranteed to Indian tribes certain tracts of land as reservations to be held and occupied by them forever under the protection of the United States, in the place of other lands ceded by the Indians. There is no reason to doubt that in most, if not all, of such cases, those who conducted Indian affairs on the part of the government, not anticipating the rapid advance of settlement, sincerely believed in the possibility of maintaining those reservations intact for the Indians, and that, in this respect, while their intentions were honest, their foresight was at fault. There are men still living who spent their younger days near the borders of "Indian country" in Ohio and Indiana, and it is a well-known fact that, when the Indian Territory was established west of the Mississippi, it was generally thought that the settlements of white men would never crowd into that region, at least not for many generations. Thus were such reservations guaranteed by the Government with the honest belief that the Indians would be secure in their possession, which, as subsequent events proved, was a gross error of judgment.

It is also a fact that most of the Indian wars grew, not from any desire of the government to disturb the Indians in the territorial possessions guaranteed to them, but from the restless and unscrupulous greed of frontiersmen who pushed their settlements and ventures into the Indian country, provoked conflicts with the Indians, and then called for the protection of the government against the resisting and retaliating Indians, thus involving it in the hostilities which they themselves had begun. It is true that in some instances Indian wars were precipitated by acts of rashness and violence on the part of military men without orders from the government, while the popular impression that Indian outbreaks were generally caused by the villainy of government agents, who defrauded and starved the Indians, is substantially unfounded. Such frauds and robberies have no doubt been frequently committed. It has also happened that Indian tribes were exposed to great suffering and actual starvation in consequence of the neglect of Congress to provide the funds necessary to fulfill treaty stipulations. But things of this kind resulted but seldom in actual hostilities. To such wrongs the Indians usually submitted with a more enduring patience than they receive credit for, although in some instances, it must be admitted, outrages were committed by Indians without provocation, which resulted in trouble on a large scale.

In mentioning these facts, it is not my purpose to hold the government entirely guiltless of the wrongs inflicted upon the Indians. It has, undoubtedly, sometimes lacked in vigor when Indian tribes needed protection. It has, in many cases, yielded too readily to the pressure of those who wanted to possess themselves of Indian lands. Still less would I justify some high-handed proceedings on the part of the government in moving peaceable Indian tribes from place to place without their consent, trying to rectify old blunders by new acts of injustice. But I desire to point out that by far the larger part of our Indian troubles have sprung from the greedy encroachments of white men upon Indian lands, and that, hostilities being brought about in this manner, in which the Indians uniformly succumbed, old treaties and arrangements were overthrown to be supplanted by new ones of a similar character which eventually led to the same results. In the light of events, the policy of assigning to the Indian tribes large tracts of land as permanent reservations, within the limits of which they might continue to roam at pleasure, with the expectation that they would never be disturbed thereon, appears as a grand mistake, a natural, perhaps even an unavoidable mistake in times gone by, but a mistake for all that, for that policy failed to take into account the inevitable pressure of rapidly and irresistibly advancing settlement and enterprise. While duly admitting and confessing the injustice done, we must understand the real nature of the difficulty if we mean to solve it.

No intelligent man will today for a moment entertain the belief that there is still a nook or corner of this country that has the least agricultural or mineral value in it, beyond the reach of progressive civilization. . . . The settler and miner are beginning, or at least threatening, to invade every Indian reservation that offers any attraction, and it is a well-known fact that the frontiersman almost always looks upon Indian lands as the most valuable in the neighborhood, simply because the Indian occupies them and the white man is excluded from them. . . . The fact that wild Indians—and here it is proper to say that when in this discussion Indians are spoken of as "wild," and their habits of life as "savage," these terms are not used in their extreme sense, but as simply meaning "uncivilized," there being of course among them, in that respect, a difference of degrees—hold immense tracts of country which, possessed by them, are of no advantage to anybody, while, as is said, thousands upon thousands of white people stand ready to cultivate them and to make them contribute to the national wealth, is always apt to make an impression upon minds not accustomed to nice discrimination. . . . What is to become of the Indians?

In trying to solve this question, we have to keep in view the facts here recited. However we may deplore the injustice which these facts have brought, and are still bringing, upon the red men, yet with these facts we have to deal. . . . It is true that the Indian reservations now existing cover a great many millions of acres, containing very valuable tracts of agricultural, grazing, and mineral land; that the area now cultivated, or that can possibly be cultivated by the Indians, is comparatively very small; that by far the larger portion is lying waste. Is it not, in view of the history of more than two centuries, useless to speculate in our minds how these many millions of acres can be preserved in their present state for the Indians to roam upon—how the greedy push of settlement and enterprise might be permanently checked for the protection of the red man's present possessions, as hunting grounds upon which, moreover, there is now but very little left to hunt? . . . It will be easy for the rough and reckless frontiersmen to pick quarrels with the Indians. The speculators, who have their eyes upon every opportunity for gain, will urge them on. The watchfulness of the government will, in the long run, be unavailing to prevent collisions. . . . The conflict once brought on, the white man and the red man will stand against one another, and, in spite of all its good intentions and its sense of justice, the forces of the government will find themselves engaged on the side of the white man. The Indians will be hunted down at whatever cost. It will simply be a repetition of the old story, and that old story will be eventually repeated whenever there is a large and valuable Indian reservation surrounded by white settlements. Unjust, disgraceful, as this may be, it is not only probable, but almost inevitable. . . .

What does, under such circumstances, wise and humane statesmanship demand? Not that we should close our eyes to existing facts; but that, keeping those facts clearly in view, we should discover among the possibilities that which is most just and best for the Indians. I am profoundly convinced that a stubborn maintenance of the system of large Indian reservations must eventually result in the destruction of the red men, however faithfully the government may endeavor to protect their rights. . . . What we can and should do is, in general terms, to fit the Indians, as much as possible, for the habits and occupations of civilized life, by work and education; to individualize them in the possession and appreciation of property, by allotting to them lands in severalty, giving them a fee-simple title individually to the parcels of land they cultivate, inalienable for a certain period, and to obtain their consent to a disposition of that part of their lands which they cannot use, for a fair compensation, in such a manner that they no longer stand in the way of the development of the country as an obstacle, but form part of it and are benefited by it.

The circumstances surrounding them place before the Indians this stern alternative: extermination or civilization. The thought of exterminating a race, once the only occupant of the soil upon which so many millions of our own people have grown prosperous and happy, must be revolting to every American who is not devoid of all sentiments of justice and humanity. To civilize them, which was once only a benevolent fancy, has now become an absolute necessity, if we mean to save them.

Can Indians be civilized? This question is answered in the negative only by those who do not want to civilize them. My experience in the management of Indian affairs, which enabled me to witness the progress made even among the wildest tribes, confirms me in the belief that it is not only possible but easy to introduce civilized habits and occupations among Indians, if only the proper means are employed. . . . That care and guidance is necessarily the task of the government which, as to the Indians at least, must exercise paternal functions until they are sufficiently advanced to take care of themselves.

In this respect, some sincere philanthropists seem inclined to run into a serious error in insisting that first of all things it is necessary to give to the Indian the rights and privileges of American citizenship, to treat him in all respects as a citizen, and to relieve him of all restraints to which other Americans citizens are not subject. I do not intend to go here into a disquisition on the legal status of the Indian, on which elaborate treatises have been written, and learned judicial decisions rendered, without raising it above dispute. The end to be reached is unquestionably the gradual absorption of the Indians in the great body of American citizenship. When that is accomplished, then, and only then, the legal status of the Indian will be clearly and finally fixed. . . . But full citizenship must be regarded as the terminal, not as the initial, point of their development. The first necessity, therefore, is not at once to give it to them, but to fit them for it. And to this end, nothing is more indispensable than the protecting and guiding care of the government during the dangerous period of transition from savage to civilized life. . . .

To fit the Indians for their ultimate absorption in the great body of American citizenship, three things are suggested by common sense as well as philanthropy:

1. That they be taught to work by making work profitable and attractive to them.
2. That they be educated, especially the youth of both sexes.
3. That they be individualized in the possession of property by settlement in severalty with a fee-simple title, after which the lands they do not use may be disposed of for general settlement and enterprise without danger and with profit to the Indians.

This may seem a large program, strangely in contrast with the old wild life of the Indians, but they are now more disposed than ever before to accept it. Even those of them who have so far been in a great measure living upon the chase, are becoming aware that the game is fast disappearing, and will no longer be sufficient to furnish them a sustenance. In a few years the buffalo will be exterminated, and smaller game is gradually growing scarce except in the more inaccessible mountain regions. The necessity of procuring food in some other way is thus before their eyes. . . .

To this end it seems indispensable that agricultural work be their principal occupation. But we need not be troubled by any misgivings on this head. The reports of early explorers show that most of our Indian tribes, without having passed through the pastoral state, did cultivate the soil in a rough way and on a small scale when first seen by white men, and that subsequently they continued that pursuit to a greater or less extent, even while they were driven from place to place. The promotion of agricultural work among them will therefore only be a revival and development of an old practice. The progress they now make shows how naturally they take to it. And if the government, as it should, continues to furnish them with domestic animals, cattle raising in a small way may become, not their principal business, but a proper and valuable addition to their agricultural work. . . . Many Indians who, but a few years ago, did nothing but hunt and fight, are now engaged in building houses for their families, and, with some instruction and aid on the part of the government, they are doing reasonably well. Here and there an Indian is found who shows striking ability as a trader. All these things are capable of large and rapid development, if pushed forward and guided with wisdom and energy. . . . The significant point is that, recognizing the change in their situation, Indian men now almost generally accept work as a necessity, while formerly all the drudgery was done by their women. The civilized tribes in the Indian Territory and elsewhere have already proved their capacity for advancement in a greater measure.

One of the most important agencies in the civilizing process is, of course, education in schools. The first step was the establishment on the reservations of day schools for Indian children. The efforts made by the government in that direction may not always have been efficiently conducted; but it is also certain that, in the nature of things, the result of that system could not be satisfactory. . . .

The Indian, in order to be civilized, must not only learn how to read and write but how to live. On most of the Indian reservations he lives only among his own kind, excepting the teachers and the few white agency people. He may feel the necessity of changing his mode of life ever so strongly; he may hear of civilization ever so much; but as long as he has not with his own eyes seen civilization at work, it will remain to him only a vague, shadowy idea—a new-fangled, outlandish contrivance, the objects of which cannot be clearly appreciated by him in detail. . . . If the Indian is to become civilized, the most efficient method will be to permit him to see and watch civilization at work in its own atmosphere. In order to learn to live like the white man, he should see and observe how the white man lives in his own surroundings, what he is doing, and what he is doing it for. . . . Such considerations led the government, under the last administration, largely to increase the number of Indian pupils at the Normal School at Hampton, Va., and to establish an institution for the education of Indian children at Carlisle, in Pennsylvania, where the young Indians would no longer be under the influence of the Indian camp or village, but in immediate contact with the towns, farms, and factories of civilized people, living and working in the atmosphere of civilization. . . .

The results gained at these institutions are very striking. The native squalor of the Indian boys and girls rapidly gives way to neat appearance. A new intelligence, lighting up their faces, transforms their expression. Many of them show an astonishing eagerness to learn, quickness of perception, pride of accomplishment, and love for their teachers. . . .

When the Indian pupils have received a sufficient course of schooling, they are sent back to their tribes, to make themselves practically useful there, and to serve, in their turn, as teachers and examples. . . . Even most of the old-fogy chiefs, who have clung most tenaciously to their traditional customs, very earnestly desire their children to receive that education for which they feel themselves too old. In one word, knowledge and skill are now in practical requisition among them, and the man who possesses these accomplishments is no longer ridiculed, but looked up to and envied. . . .

As the third thing necessary for the absorption of the Indians in the great body of American citizenship, I mentioned their individualization in the possession of property by their settlement in severalty upon small farm tracts with a fee-simple title. When the Indians are so settled, and have become individual property owners, holding their farms by the same title under the law by which white men hold theirs, they will feel more readily inclined to part with such of their lands as they cannot themselves cultivate, and from which they can derive profit only if they sell them, either in lots or in bulk, for a fair equivalent in money or in annuities. This done, the Indians will occupy no more ground than so many white people; the large reservations will gradually be opened to general settlement and enterprise, and the Indians, with their possessions, will cease to stand in the way of the "development of the country." The difficulty which has provoked so many encroachments and conflicts will then no longer exist. When the Indians are individual owners of real property, and as individuals enjoy the protection of the laws, their tribal cohesion will necessarily relax, and gradually disappear. They will have advanced an immense step in the direction of the "white man's way."

Is this plan practicable? In this respect we are not entirely without experience. Allotments of farm tracts to Indians and their settlement in severalty have already been attempted under special laws or treaties with a few tribes; in some instances, with success; in others, the Indians, when they had acquired individual title to their land, and before they had learned to appreciate its value, were induced to dispose of it, or were tricked out of it by unscrupulous white men, who took advantage of their ignorance. They were thus impoverished again, and some of them fell back upon the government for support. This should be guarded against, as much as it can be, by a legal provision making the title to their farm tracts inalienable for a certain period, say twenty-five years, during which the Indians will have sufficient opportunity to acquire more provident habits, to become somewhat acquainted with the ways of the world and to learn to take care of themselves. . . .

The question whether and how far the Indians generally are prepared for so great a change in their habits as their settlement in severalty involves, is certainly a very important one. . . . Appeals to the government from Indians of that class for the allotment of farm tracts to heads of families and for "the white man's paper," have been very frequent of late, and in many instances very urgent. . . .

It must be kept in mind that the settlement of the Indians in severalty is one of those things for which the Indians and the government are not always permitted to choose their own time. The necessity of immediate action may now and then present itself suddenly. Take the case of the Utes. Living in a country where game was still comparatively abundant down to a recent time, they were less inclined than other "wild" tribes to recognize the necessity of a change in their mode of life. But the pressure of mining enterprise in the direction of the Ute reservation was great. . . . Fights and massacres occurred on the Ute reservation, which are still fresh in our memory. . . . Negotiations were opened, and the Utes agreed to be settled in severalty upon the lands designated for that purpose, and to cede to the United States the whole of their reservation, except some small tracts of agricultural and grazing lands, in consideration of certain ample equivalents in various forms. . . .

It is, therefore, of the utmost importance to the Indians, as well as to the country generally, that a policy be adopted which will secure to them and their descendants the safe possession of such tracts of land as they can cultivate, and a fair compensation for the rest; and that such a policy be proceeded with before the protection of their present large possessions by the government becomes too precarious—that is to say, before conflicts are precipitated upon them which the government is not always able to prevent, and by which they may be in danger of losing their lands, their compensation, and even their lives, at the same time. It would undoubtedly be better if they could be carefully prepared for such a change of condition, so that they might clearly appreciate all its requirements and the consequences which are to follow. But those intrusted with the management of Indian affairs must not forget that, with regard to some Indian tribes and reservations at least, the matter is pressing; that the government cannot control circumstances but is rather apt to be controlled by them, and that it must not only devise the necessary preparations for the change in the condition of the Indians with forecast and wisdom, but must push them with the greatest possible expedition and energy if untoward accidents are to be avoided. . . .

I am aware that I have not discussed here all points of importance connected with the Indian problem, such, for instance, as the necessity of extending the jurisdiction of the courts over Indian reservations, bringing the red men under the protection as well as the restraints of the law; and the question of how the service should be organized to secure to the Indians intelligent, honest, and humane management, etc. It has been my purpose merely to set forth those important points which, in the practical management of Indian affairs, should be steadily kept in view. I will recapitulate them:

1. The greatest danger hanging over the Indian race arises from the fact that, with their large and valuable territorial possessions which are lying waste, they stand in the way of what is commonly called "the development of the country."

2. A rational Indian policy will make it its principal object to avert that danger from the red men, by doing what will be most beneficial to them, as well as to the whole people: namely, by harmonizing the habits, occupations, and interests of the Indians with that "development of the country."

3. To accomplish this object, it is of pressing necessity to set the Indians to work, to educate their youth of both sexes, to make them small proprietors of land, with the right of individual ownership under the protection of the law, and to induce them to make that part of their lands which they do not need for cultivation, profitable to themselves in the only possible way, by selling it at a just rate of compensation, thus opening it to general settlement and enterprise.

The policy here outlined is apt to be looked upon with disfavor by two classes of people: on the one hand, those who think that "the only good Indian is a dead Indian," . . . and, on the other hand, that class of philanthropists who, in their treatment of the Indian question, pay no regard to surrounding circumstances and suspect every policy contemplating a reduction of the Indian reservations of being a scheme of spoliation and robbery, gotten up by speculators and "land-grabbers." With the first class it seems useless to reason. As to the second, they do not themselves believe, if they are sensible, that twenty-five years hence millions of acres of valuable land will, in any part of the country, still be kept apart as Indian hunting grounds. The question is, whether the Indians are to be exposed to the danger of hostile collisions, and of being robbed of their lands in consequence, or whether they are to be induced by proper and fair means to sell that which, as long as they keep it, is of no advantage to anybody, but which, as soon as they part with it for a just compensation, will be a great advantage to themselves and their white neighbors alike. No true friend of the Indian will hesitate to choose the latter line of policy as one in entire accord with substantial justice, humanity, the civilization and welfare of the red men, and the general interests of the country.

Source: Originally published in *North American Review* CXXXIII, 296 (July 1881): 1–24. Reprinted in *Speeches, Correspondence, and Political Papers of Carl Schurz*, ed. Frederic Bancroft (New York: G. P. Putnam's Sons, 1913), 4:116–46.

CHAPTER 26

What Social Classes Owe to Each Other, William Graham Sumner, 1883

William Graham Sumner was an influential academic who published in a variety of disciplines and is often considered the father of "social Darwinism" in America. He was the first to teach a course in sociology, and a staunch advocate of laissez-faire free-market capitalism. His book *What Social Classes Owe to Each Other*, published in 1883, clearly outlined what social classes did *not* owe each other and formed the basis for the traditionalist opposition to communism and socialism, which were gaining hold in the United States with the new wave of immigrants from Europe. Within the next two decades, populism would give way to socialism, and Sumner would take a leading role in opposing the new ideology. He offered a view of social harmony that entailed a certain amount of common sense: those who have in abundance should voluntarily help those who have nothing, both for reasons of civic peace and to ensure that government does not force redistribution. Volunteerism and charity had been ingrained in American culture since early colonial times, as settlers worked together to protect themselves from Indian attacks and the hardships of taming the land, and Sumner's work was a logical extension of that experience. By Sumner's time, however, the demographics were changing.

With the rapid industrialization taking place in the United States during this time, social Darwinism was used by giant corporations to justify policies of low wages, long working hours, and company towns, particularly companies involved in textiles, steel, coal, copper and iron ore mining, and railroads. These same industries were the first to become unionized and the first to experience strikes and labor unrest. Sumner felt that since employment was voluntary, workers could always vote with their feet and go elsewhere, thereby automatically forcing companies into more labor-friendly practices. American Indians, with their history of being mobile, would indeed leave when mistreated, but recent immigrants tended to herd together and, with many unable to speak English or understand the American political or legal system, to view both job and employer as essentially permanent. In many European countries, a person's job was almost part of their name, and certainly governed their economic and social status. In the United States, a person could have many jobs or careers, and if he disliked one, he was free to choose another. Even today in Europe, that is often not an option, and social and geographic mobility are limited.

Sumner's thesis tended to describe people born in America as better than recent immigrants, probably exacerbated the conflict between social classes, and confirmed immigrants' assumption that the United States was little different from their mother countries. The reader should consider whether another approach would have been more appropriate to avoid European-type militant unions, socialism, and job ownership. Obviously, Sumner did a poor job of selling American exceptionalism to newcomers, and progressivism jolted into being by European-style anarchists was the result.

From *What Social Classes Owe to Each Other*

IT IS COMMONLY ASSERTED THAT THERE ARE IN THE UNITED States no classes, and any allusion to classes is resented. On the other hand, we constantly read and hear discussions of social topics in which the existence of social classes is assumed as a simple fact. "The poor," "the weak," "the laborers," are expressions which are used as if they had exact and well-understood definition. Discussions are made to bear upon the assumed rights, wrongs, and misfortunes of certain social classes; and all public speaking and writing consists, in a large measure, of the discussion of general plans for meeting the wishes of classes of people who have not been able to satisfy their own desires. These classes are sometimes discontented, and sometimes not. Sometimes they do not know that anything is amiss with them until the "friends of humanity" come to them with offers of aid. Sometimes they are discontented and envious. They do not take their achievements as a fair measure of their rights. They do not blame themselves or their parents for their lot, as compared with that of other people. Sometimes they claim that they have a right to everything of which they feel the need for their happiness on earth. To make such a claim against God or nature would, of course, be only to say that we claim a right to live on earth if we can. But . . . we are absolutely shut up to the need and duty, if we would learn how to live happily, of investigating the laws of nature, and deducing the rules of right living in the world as it is. These are very wearisome and commonplace tasks. They consist in labor and self-denial repeated over and over again in learning and doing. When the people whose claims we are considering are told to apply themselves to these tasks, they become irritated and feel almost insulted. They formulate their claims as rights against society—that is, against some other men. In their view they have a right, not only to pursue happiness, but to get it; and if they fail to get it, they think they have a claim to the aid of other men—that is, to the labor and self-denial of other men—to get it for them. They find orators and poets who tell them that they have grievances, so long as they have unsatisfied desires.

Now, if there are groups of people who have a claim to other people's labor and self-denial, and if there are other people whose labor and self-denial are liable to be claimed by the first groups, then there certainly are "classes," and classes of the oldest and most vicious type.

For a man who can command another man's labor and self-denial for the support of his own existence is a privileged person of the highest species conceivable on earth. Princes and paupers meet on this plane, and no other men are on it at all. On the other hand, a man whose labor and self-denial may be diverted from his maintenance to that of some other man is not a free man, and approaches more or less toward the position of a slave. Therefore we shall find that, in all the notions which we are to discuss, this elementary contradiction, that there are classes and that there are not classes, will produce repeated confusion and absurdity. We shall find that, in our efforts to eliminate the old vices of class government, we are impeded and defeated by new products of the worst class theory. We shall find that all the schemes for producing equality and obliterating the organization of society produce a new differentiation based on the worst possible distinction—the right to claim and the duty to give one man's effort for another man's satisfaction. We shall find that every effort to realize equality necessitates a sacrifice of liberty. . . .

Certain ills belong to the hardships of human life. They are natural. They are part of the struggle with nature for existence. We cannot blame our fellow men for our share of these. My neighbor and I are both struggling to free ourselves from these ills. The fact that my neighbor has succeeded in this struggle better than I constitutes no grievance for me. Certain other ills are due to the malice of men, and to the imperfections or errors of civil institutions. . . . The distinction here made between the ills which belong to the struggle for existence and those which are due to the faults of human institutions is of prime importance.

It will also be important, in order to clear up our ideas about the notions which are in fashion, to note the relation of the economic to the political significance of assumed duties of one class to another. That is to say, we may discuss the question whether one class owes duties to another by reference to the economic effects which will be produced on the classes and society; or we may discuss the political expediency of formulating and enforcing rights and duties respectively between the parties. In the former case we might assume that the givers of aid were willing to give it, and we might discuss the benefit or mischief of their activity. In the other case we must assume that some at least of those who were forced to give aid did so unwillingly. Here, then, there would be a question of rights. The question whether voluntary charity is mischievous or not is one thing; the question whether legislation which forces one man to aid another is right and wise, as well as economically beneficial, is quite another question. Great confusion and consequent error is produced by allowing these two questions to become entangled in the discussion.

Especially we shall need to notice the attempts to apply legislative methods of reform to the ills which belong to the order of nature. . . .

Under the names of the poor and the weak, the negligent, shiftless, inefficient, silly, and imprudent are fastened upon the industrious and prudent as a responsibility and a duty. On the one side, the terms are extended to cover the idle, intemperate, and vicious, who, by the combination, gain credit which they do not deserve, and which they could not get if they stood alone. On the other hand, the terms are extended to include wage receivers of the humblest rank, who are degraded by the combination. The reader who desires to guard himself against fallacies should always scrutinize the terms "poor" and "weak" as used, so as to see which or how many of these classes they are made to cover. . . .

When I have read certain of these [humanitarian] discussions I have thought that it must be quite disreputable to be respectable, quite dishonest to own property, quite unjust to go one's own way and earn one's own living, and that the only really admirable person was the good-for-nothing. The man who by his own effort raises himself above poverty appears, in these discussions, to be of no account. The man who has done nothing to raise himself above poverty finds that the social doctors flock about him, bringing the capital which they have collected from the other class, and promising him the aid of the state to give him what the other had to work for. In all these schemes and projects the organized intervention of society through the state is either planned or hoped for, and the state is thus made to become the protector and guardian of certain classes.

The agents who are to direct the state action are, of course, the reformers and philanthropists. Their schemes, therefore, may always be reduced to this type—that A and B decide what C shall do for D. . . .

In all the discussions attention is concentrated on A and B, the noble social reformers, and on D, the "poor man." I call C the Forgotten Man, because I have never seen that any notice was taken of him in any of the discussions. When we have disposed of A, B, and D, we can better appreciate the case of C, and I think that we shall find that he deserves our attention, for the worth of his character and the magnitude of his unmerited burdens. Here it may suffice to observe that, on the theories of the social philosophers to whom I have referred, we should get a new maxim of judicious living: Poverty is the best policy. If you get wealth, you will have to support other people; if you do not get wealth, it will be the duty of other people to support you. . . .

Every man and woman in society has one big duty. That is, to take care of his or her own self. This is a social duty. For, fortunately, the matter stands so that the duty of making the best of one's self individually is not a separate thing from the duty of filling one's place in society, but the two are one, and the latter is accomplished when the former is done. The common notion, however, seems to be that one has a duty to society, as a special and separate thing, and that this duty consists in considering and deciding what other people ought to do.

Now, the man who can do anything for or about anybody else than himself is fit to be head of a family; and when he becomes head of a family he has duties to his wife and his children, in addition to the former big duty. Then, again, any man who can take care of himself and his family is in a very exceptional position, if he does not find in his immediate surroundings people who need his care and have some sort of a personal claim upon him. If, now, he is able to fulfill all this, and to take care of anybody outside his family and his dependents, he must have a surplus of energy, wisdom, and moral virtue beyond what he needs for his own business. No man has this; for a family is a charge which is capable of infinite development, and no man could suffice to the full measure of duty for which a family may draw upon him. Neither can a man give to society so advantageous an employment of his services, whatever they are, in any other way as by spending them on his family. Upon this, however, I will not insist. I recur to the observation that a man who proposes to take care of other people must have himself and his family taken care of, after some sort of a fashion, and must have an as yet unexhausted store of energy.

The danger of minding other people's business is twofold. First, there is the danger that a man may leave his own business unattended to; and, second, there is the danger of an impertinent interference with another's affairs. The "friends of humanity" almost always run into both dangers. I am one of humanity, and I do not want any volunteer friends. I regard friendship as mutual, and I want to have my say about it. I suppose that other components of humanity feel in the same way about it. If so, they must regard anyone who assumes the role of a friend of humanity as impertinent. The reference of the friend of humanity back to his own business is obviously the next step. . . .

The amateur social doctors are like the amateur physicians—they always begin with the question of remedies, and they go at this without any diagnosis or any knowledge of the anatomy or physiology of society. They never have any doubt of the efficacy of their remedies. They never take account of any ulterior effects which may be apprehended from the remedy itself. It generally troubles them not a whit that their remedy implies a complete reconstruction of society, or even a reconstitution of human nature. Against all such social quackery the obvious injunction to the quacks is, to mind their own business.

The social doctors enjoy the satisfaction of feeling themselves to be more moral or more enlightened than their fellow men. They are able to see what other men ought to do when the other men do not see it. An examination of the work of the social doctors, however, shows that they are only more ignorant and more presumptuous than other people. We have a great many social difficulties and hardships to contend with. Poverty, pain, disease, and misfortune surround our existence. We fight against them all the time.

The individual is a center of hopes, affections, desires, and sufferings. When he dies, life changes its form, but does not cease. That means that the person—the center of all the hopes, affections, etc.—after struggling as long as he can, is sure to succumb at last. We would, therefore, as far as the hardships of the human lot are concerned, go on struggling to the best of our ability against them but for the social doctors, and we would endure what we could not cure.

But we have inherited a vast number of social ills which never came from nature. They are the complicated products of all the tinkering, muddling, and blundering of social doctors in the past. These products of social quackery are now buttressed by habit, fashion, prejudice, platitudinarian thinking, and new quackery in political economy and social science. . . . All this mischief has been done by men who sat down to consider the problem (as I heard an apprentice of theirs once express it), "What kind of a society do we want to make?" When they had settled this question a priori to their satisfaction, they set to work to make their ideal society, and today we suffer the consequences. Human society tries hard to adapt itself to any conditions in which it finds itself, and we have been warped and distorted until we have got used to it, as the foot adapts itself to an ill-made boot. Next, we have come to think that that is the right way for things to be; and it is true that a change to a sound and normal condition would for a time hurt us, as a man whose foot has been distorted would suffer if he tried to wear a well-shaped boot. Finally, we have produced a lot of economists and social philosophers who have invented sophisms for fitting our thinking to the distorted facts.

Society, therefore, does not need any care or supervision. If we can acquire a science of society, based on observation of phenomena and study of forces, we may hope to gain some ground slowly toward the elimination of old errors and the reestablishment of a sound and natural social order. Whatever we gain that way will be by growth, never in the world by any reconstruction of society on the plan of some enthusiastic social architect. The latter is only repeating the old error over again, and postponing all our chances of real improvement.

Society needs first of all to be freed from these meddlers—that is, to be let alone. Here we are, then, once more back at the old doctrine—laissez-faire. Let us translate it into blunt English, and it will read, "Mind your own business." It is nothing but the doctrine of liberty. Let every man be happy in his own way. If his sphere of action and interest impinges on that of any other man, there will have to be compromise and adjustment. Wait for the occasion. Do not attempt to generalize those interferences or to plan for them a priori. We have a body of laws and institutions which have grown up as occasion has occurred for adjusting rights. Let the same process go on. Practice the utmost reserve possible in your interferences even of this kind, and by no means seize occasion for interfering with natural adjustments. Try first long and patiently whether the natural adjustment will not come about through the play of interests and the voluntary concessions of the parties. . . .

What, now, is the reason why we should help each other? . . . We may philosophize as coolly and correctly as we choose about our duties and about the laws of right living; no one of us lives up to what he knows. The man struck by the falling tree has, perhaps, been careless. We are all careless. Environed as we are by risks and perils, which befall us as misfortunes, no man of us is in a position to say, "I know all the laws, and am sure to obey them all; therefore I shall never need aid and sympathy.". . .

Men, therefore, owe to men, in the chances and perils of this life, aid and sympathy, on account of the common participation in human frailty and folly. This observation, however, puts aid and sympathy in the field of private and personal relations, under the regulation of reason and conscience, and gives no ground for mechanical and impersonal schemes.

We may, then, distinguish four things:

1. The function of science is to investigate truth. Science is colorless and impersonal. It investigates the force of gravity, and finds out the laws of that force, and has nothing to do with the weal or woe of men under the operation of the law.
2. The moral deductions as to what one ought to do are to be drawn by the reason and conscience of the individual man who is instructed by science. Let him take note of the force of gravity, and see to it that he does not walk off a precipice or get in the way of a falling body.
3. On account of the number and variety of perils of all kinds by which our lives are environed, and on account of ignorance, carelessness, and folly, we all neglect to obey the moral deductions which we have learned, so that, in fact, the wisest and the best of us act foolishly and suffer.
4. The law of sympathy, by which we share each others' burdens, is to do as we would be done by. It is not a scientific principle, and does not admit of such generalization or interpretation that A can tell B what this law enjoins on B to do. Hence the relations of sympathy and sentiment are essentially limited to two persons only, and they cannot be made a basis for the relations of groups of persons, or for discussion by any third party.

Social improvement is not to be won by direct effort. It is secondary, and results from physical or economic improvements. That is the reason why schemes of direct social amelioration always have an arbitrary, sentimental, and artificial character, while true social advance must be a product and a growth. The efforts which are being put forth for every kind of progress in the arts and sciences are, therefore, contributing to true social progress. Let anyone learn what hardship was involved, even for a wealthy person, a century ago, in crossing the Atlantic, and then let him compare that hardship even with a steerage passage at the present time, considering time and money cost.

This improvement in transportation by which "the poor and weak" can be carried from the crowded centers of population to the new land is worth more to them than all the schemes of all the social reformers. An improvement in surgical instruments or in anesthetics really does more for those who are not well off than all the declamations of the orators and pious wishes of the reformers. Civil service reform would be a greater gain to the laborers than innumerable factory acts and eight-hour laws. Free trade would be a greater blessing to "the poor man" than all the devices of all the friends of humanity if they could be realized. If the economists could satisfactorily solve the problem of the regulation of paper currency, they would do more for the wage-earning class than could be accomplished by all the artificial doctrines about wages which they seem to feel bound to encourage. If we could get firm and good laws passed for the management of savings banks, and then refrain from the amendments by which those laws are gradually broken down, we should do more for the noncapitalist class than by volumes of laws against "corporations" and the "excessive power of capital.". . .

Now, the aid which helps a man to help himself is not in the least akin to the aid which is given in charity. If alms are given, or if we "make work" for a man, or "give him employment," or "protect" him, we simply take a product from one and give it to another. If we help a man to help himself, by opening the chances around him, we put him in a position to add to the wealth of the community by putting new powers in operation to produce. It would seem that the difference between getting something already in existence from the one who has it, and producing a new thing by applying new labor to natural materials, would be so plain as never to be forgotten; but the fallacy of confusing the two is one of the commonest in all social discussions.

We have now seen that the current discussions about the claims and rights of social classes on each other are radically erroneous and fallacious, and we have seen that an analysis of the general obligations which we all have to each other leads us to nothing but an emphatic repetition of old but well-acknowledged obligations to perfect our political institutions. We have been led to restriction, not extension, of the functions of the state, but we have also been led to see the necessity of purifying and perfecting the operation of the state in the functions which properly belong to it. If we refuse to recognize any classes as existing in society when, perhaps, a claim might be set up that the wealthy, educated, and virtuous have acquired special rights and precedence, we certainly cannot recognize any classes when it is attempted to establish such distinctions for the sake of imposing burdens and duties on one group for the benefit of others. The men who have not done their duty in this world never can be equal to those who have done their duty more or less well.

If words like wise and foolish, thrifty and extravagant, prudent and negligent, have any meaning in language, then it must make some difference how people behave in this world, and the difference will appear in the position they acquire in the body of society, and in relation to the chances of life. They may, then, be classified in reference to these facts. Such classes always will exist; no other social distinctions can endure. If, then, we look to the origin and definition of these classes, we shall find it impossible to deduce any obligations which one of them bears to the other. The class distinctions simply result from the different degrees of success with which men have availed themselves of the chances which were presented to them. Instead of endeavoring to redistribute the acquisitions which have been made between the existing classes, our aim should be to increase, multiply, and extend the chances.

Such is the work of civilization. Every old error or abuse which is removed opens new chances of development to all the new energy of society. Every improvement in education, science, art, or government expands the chances of man on earth. Such expansion is no guarantee of equality. On the contrary, if there be liberty, some will profit by the chances eagerly and some will neglect them altogether. Therefore, the greater the chances the more unequal will be the fortune of these two sets of men. So it ought to be, in all justice and right reason. The yearning after equality is the offspring of envy and covetousness, and there is no possible plan for satisfying that yearning which can do aught else than rob A to give to B; consequently all such plans nourish some of the meanest vices of human nature, waste capital, and overthrow civilization. But if we can expand the chances, we can count on a general and steady growth of civilization and advancement of society by and through its best members. In the prosecution of these chances we all owe to each other goodwill, mutual respect, and mutual guarantees of liberty and security. Beyond this nothing can be affirmed as a duty of one group to another in a free state.

Source: Excerpted from William Graham Sumner, *What Social Classes Owe to Each Other* (New York: Harper and Brothers, 1883), 13–24, 113–21, 157–68.

CHAPTER 27

Booker T. Washington's Atlanta Compromise Speech, 1895

Booker T. Washington was a Negro or black educator and leader of the Tuskegee Institute in Alabama who by 1890 had become highly regarded as an administrator and spokesman for educated blacks. In 1893 he spoke at a Christian Workers meeting in Atlanta, and his reception there prompted the governor of Georgia, Rufus Bullock, to invite him to speak at the opening of the Cotton States and International Exposition in Atlanta on September 18, 1895. Surpassing all expectations, he delivered a resounding speech to a predominately white audience and was greeted by thundering applause and a standing ovation. He called for shared responsibility between blacks and whites, and stressed education and the employment of the Protestant work ethic. He did not blame whites for slavery or black problems, and that was the key to his acceptance—rather than looking backward, he asked everyone to start from where they were and move forward. His Atlanta Compromise address, as it came to be called, was widely hailed as one of the most important and influential speeches in American history, and the editor of the *Atlanta Constitution* even took the speaker's stand to proclaim the speech as the beginning of a moral revolution in America. With this speech, Washington became the foremost black leader in the nation and held that position until his death in 1915.

The reader should ask himself why Washington is almost forgotten today. Is this because schools fail to teach history, people have short memories, or because his style was cooperative rather than confrontational? He sought to improve the education and training of African Americans, to prepare them for the day when they could be full partners with whites, politically and economically. Reconstruction had failed to establish equality between the races, so Washington chose to earn equality like the Catholic Irish and other persecuted peoples before him. Would a confrontational approach at the time have achieved results faster or simply alienated whites and been counterproductive? Marcus Garvey's alternative "return to Africa" movement was hardly successful, but would it have been a better long-term solution? What would Martin Luther King Jr. have done in Washington's stead?

The 1895 Atlanta Compromise Speech

MR. PRESIDENT AND GENTLEMEN OF THE BOARD OF DIRECtors and Citizens:

One-third of the population of the South is of the Negro race. No enterprise seeking the material, civil, or moral welfare of this section can disregard this element of our population and reach the highest success. I but convey to you, Mr. President and Directors, the sentiment of the masses of my race when I say that in no way have the value and manhood of the American Negro been more fittingly and generously recognized than by the managers of this magnificent exposition at every stage of its progress. It is a recognition that will do more to cement the friendship of the two races than any occurrence since the dawn of our freedom.

Not only this, but the opportunity here afforded will awaken among us a new era of industrial progress. Ignorant and inexperienced, it is not strange that in the first years of our new life we began at the top instead of at the bottom; that a seat in Congress or the state legislature was more sought than real estate or industrial skill; that the political convention or stump speaking had more attractions than starting a dairy farm or truck garden.

A ship lost at sea for many days suddenly sighted a friendly vessel. From the mast of the unfortunate vessel was seen a signal, "Water, water; we die of thirst!" The answer from the friendly vessel at once came back, "Cast down your bucket where you are." A second time the signal, "Water, water; send us water!" ran up from the distressed vessel, and was answered, "Cast down your bucket where you are." And a third and fourth signal for water was answered, "Cast down your bucket where you are." The captain of the distressed vessel, at last heeding the injunction, cast down his bucket, and it came up full of fresh, sparkling water from the mouth of the Amazon River. To those of my race who depend on bettering their condition in a foreign land or who underestimate the importance of cultivating friendly relations with the southern white man, who is their next-door neighbor, I would say: "Cast down your bucket where you are"—cast it down in making friends in every manly way of the people of all races by whom we are surrounded.

Cast it down in agriculture, mechanics, in commerce, in domestic service, and in the professions. And in this connection it is well to bear in mind that whatever other sins the South may be called to bear, when it comes to business, pure and simple, it is in the South that the Negro is given a man's chance in the commercial world, and in nothing is this exposition more eloquent than in emphasizing this chance. Our greatest danger is that in the great leap from slavery to freedom we may overlook the fact that the masses of us are to live by the productions of our hands, and fail to keep in mind that we shall prosper in proportion as we learn to dignify and glorify common labor, and put brains and skill into the common occupations of life; shall prosper in proportion as we learn to draw the line between the superficial and the substantial, the ornamental gewgaws of life and the useful. No race can prosper till it learns that there is as much dignity in tilling a field as in writing a poem. It is at the bottom of life we must begin, and not at the top. Nor should we permit our grievances to overshadow our opportunities.

To those of the white race who look to the incoming of those of foreign birth and strange tongue and habits for the prosperity of the South, were I permitted I would repeat what I say to my own race, "Cast down your bucket where you are."

Cast it down among the eight millions of Negroes whose habits you know, whose fidelity and love you have tested in days when to have proved treacherous meant the ruin of your firesides. Cast down your bucket among these people who have, without strikes and labor wars, tilled your fields, cleared your forests, built your railroads and cities, and brought forth treasures from the bowels of the earth, and helped make possible this magnificent representation of the progress of the South. Casting down your bucket among my people, helping and encouraging them as you are doing on these grounds, and to education of head, hand, and heart, you will find that they will buy your surplus land, make blossom the waste places in your fields, and run your factories. While doing this, you can be sure in the future, as in the past, that you and your families will be surrounded by the most patient, faithful, law-abiding, and unresentful people that the world has seen. As we have proved our loyalty to you in the past, in nursing your children, watching by the sickbed of your mothers and fathers, and often following them with tear-dimmed eyes to their graves, so in the future, in our humble way, we shall stand by you with a devotion that no foreigner can approach, ready to lay down our lives, if need be, in defense of yours, interlacing our industrial, commercial, civil, and religious life with yours in a way that shall make the interests of both races one. In all things that are purely social we can be as separate as the fingers, yet one as the hand in all things essential to mutual progress.

There is no defense or security for any of us except in the highest intelligence and development of all. If anywhere there are efforts tending to curtail the fullest growth of the Negro, let these efforts be turned into stimulating, encouraging, and making him the most useful and intelligent citizen. Effort or means so invested will pay a thousand percent interest. These efforts will be twice blessed—blessing him that gives and him that takes.

There is no escape through law of man or God from the inevitable:

The laws of changeless justice bind oppressor with oppressed;
And close as sin and suffering joined we march to fate abreast. . . .

Nearly sixteen millions of hands will aid you in pulling the load upward, or they will pull against you the load downward. We shall constitute one-third and more of the ignorance and crime of the South, or one-third of its intelligence and progress; we shall contribute one-third to the business and industrial prosperity of the South, or we shall prove a veritable body of death, stagnating, depressing, retarding every effort to advance the body politic.

Gentlemen of the exposition, as we present to you our humble effort at an exhibition of our progress, you must not expect overmuch. Starting thirty years ago with ownership here and there in a few quilts and pumpkins and chickens (gathered from miscellaneous sources), remember the path that has led from these to the inventions and production of agricultural implements, buggies, steam engines, newspapers, books, statuary, carving, paintings, the management of drug stores and banks, has not been trodden without contact with thorns and thistles. While we take pride in what we exhibit as a result of our independent efforts, we do not for a moment forget that our part in this exhibition would fall far short of your expectations but for the constant help that has come to our educational life, not only from the southern states, but especially from northern philanthropists, who have made their gifts a constant stream of blessing and encouragement.

The wisest among my race understand that the agitation of questions of social equality is the most extreme folly, and that progress in the enjoyment of all the privileges that will come to us must be the result of severe and constant struggle rather than of artificial forcing. No race that has anything to contribute to the markets of the world is long in any degree ostracized. It is important and right that all privileges of the law be ours, but it is vastly more important that we be prepared for the exercise of these privileges. The opportunity to earn a dollar in a factory just now is worth infinitely more than the opportunity to spend a dollar in an opera house.

In conclusion, may I repeat that nothing in thirty years has given us more hope and encouragement, and drawn us so near to you of the white race, as this opportunity offered by the exposition; and here bending, as it were, over the altar that represents the results of the struggles of your race and mine, both starting practically empty-handed three decades ago, I pledge that in your effort to work out the great and intricate problem which God has laid at the doors of the South, you shall have at all times the patient, sympathetic help of my race; only let this be constantly in mind, that, while from representations in these buildings of the product of field, of forest, of mine, of factory, letters, and art, much good will come, yet far above and beyond material benefits will be that higher good, that, let us pray God, will come, in a blotting out of sectional differences and racial animosities and suspicions, in a determination to administer absolute justice, in a willing obedience among all classes to the mandates of law. This, coupled with our material prosperity, will bring into our beloved South a new heaven and a new earth.

Source: *The Booker T. Washington Papers*, ed. Louis R. Harlan (Urbana: University of Illinois Press, 1974), 583–7.

CHAPTER 28

Plessy v. Ferguson, 1896

The landmark case of *Homer A. Plessy v. Ferguson*, 163 U.S. 537 (No. 210), was argued April 18, 1896, and the decision rendered May 18, 1896. If the *Dred Scott* decision was the worst in American judicial history, *Plessy* wasn't far behind. Henry Billings Brown issued the majority opinion of the Court, in its seven-to-one decision, while John Marshall Harlan wrote the dissent. The case was actually a designed test, whereby the New Orleans Comité des Citoyens (Citizens Committee) arranged for the plaintiff, Homer Plessy, to be arrested in order to test the constitutionality of a Louisiana statute. He chose to ride in a railroad car that was designated as "white only" and refused to move to a "colored" car. At issue was no less than the entire concept of segregation and jim crow laws whereby the races could be required to use separate facilities without such statutes running afoul of the U.S. Constitution, particularly the Thirteenth and Fourteenth Amendments.

The court held that the offering of "separate but equal" facilities, the basis for segregation in the South, was entirely constitutional—and this decision remained in force until overturned in 1953 in the case of *Brown v. Board of Education of Topeka* (Kansas). In his *Plessy* dissent, Justice Harlan provided the basis for the 1953 decision that "separate but equal" was inconsistent with full individual liberty, enabling legislative intervention to ensure the full enjoyment of the blessings of freedom. Before 1953, however, Congress and southern states had massively curtailed individual liberty through jim crow segregation laws and acts such as the Espionage and Sedition Acts during World War I, which the Supreme Court upheld as being in the public interest. With unequal rights deemed by the Court to be in the public interest, there seemed to be no limits on the legislature or executive in curtailing liberty or the blessings of freedom. The Bill of Rights apparently was not to be applied to everyone. How can these situations be handled without constitutional amendments or repudiating the Constitution as the law of the land? Certainly the founders intended that neither Congress nor the courts could curtail liberty beyond a certain point. But where that line is drawn remains a matter of debate. In times of war, conscription for military service has generally been held as a legitimate intrusion on personal freedom, even when applied unequally based on intelligence, physical capabilities, religion, occupation, and other factors. Can some laws be exceptions to the Constitution and others not? Should private clubs—country clubs, for example—be forced to admit women? *Plessy v. Ferguson* demonstrates that there are times when even the Supreme Court can be terribly wrong. And in such cases, should its rulings be obeyed?

(Note: case and page citations have been removed in the interest of brevity.)

Plessy v. Ferguson

MR. JUSTICE [HENRY BILLINGS] BROWN, AFTER STATING THE case, delivered the opinion of the Court.

This case turns upon the constitutionality of an act of the General Assembly of the State of Louisiana, passed in 1890, providing for separate railway carriages for the white and colored races.

The first section of the statute enacts "that all railway companies carrying passengers in their coaches in this state shall provide equal but separate accommodations for the white and colored races by providing two or more passenger coaches for each passenger train, or by dividing the passenger coaches by a partition so as to secure separate accommodations: Provided, That this section shall not be construed to apply to street railroads. No person or persons, shall be admitted to occupy seats in coaches other than the ones assigned to them on account of the race they belong to."

By the second section, it was enacted "that the officers of such passenger trains shall have power and are hereby required to assign each passenger to the coach or compartment used for the race to which such passenger belongs; any passenger insisting on going into a coach or compartment to which by race he does not belong shall be liable to a fine of twenty-five dollars, or in lieu thereof to imprisonment for a period of not more than twenty days in the parish prison, and any officer of any railroad insisting on assigning a passenger to a coach or compartment other than the one set aside for the race to which said passenger belongs shall be liable to a fine of twenty-five dollars, or in lieu thereof to imprisonment for a period of not more than twenty days in the parish prison; and should any passenger refuse to occupy the coach or compartment to which he or she is assigned by the officer of such railway, said officer shall have power to refuse to carry such passenger on his train, and for such refusal neither he nor the railway company which he represents shall be liable for damages in any of the courts of this state."

The third section provides penalties for the refusal or neglect of the officers, directors, conductors, and employees of railway companies to comply with the act, with a proviso that "nothing in this act shall be construed as applying to nurses attending children of the other race." The fourth section is immaterial.

The information filed in the criminal District Court charged in substance that Plessy, being a passenger between two stations within the state of Louisiana, was assigned by officers of the company to the coach used for the race to which he belonged, but he insisted upon going into a coach used by the race to which he did not belong. Neither in the information nor plea was his particular race or color averred. The petition for the writ of prohibition averred that petitioner was seven-eighths Caucasian and one eighth African blood; that the mixture of colored blood was not discernible in him, and that he was entitled to every right, privilege, and immunity secured to citizens of the United States of the white race; and that, upon such theory, he took possession of a vacant seat in a coach where passengers of the white race were accommodated, and was ordered by the conductor to vacate said coach and take a seat in another assigned to persons of the colored race, and, having refused to comply with such demand, he was forcibly ejected with the aid of a police officer, and imprisoned in the parish jail to answer a charge of having violated the above act.

The constitutionality of this act is attacked upon the ground that it conflicts both with the Thirteenth Amendment of the Constitution, abolishing slavery, and the Fourteenth Amendment, which prohibits certain restrictive legislation on the part of the States.

1. That it does not conflict with the Thirteenth Amendment, which abolished slavery and involuntary servitude, except as a punishment for crime, is too clear for argument. Slavery implies involuntary servitude—a state of bondage; the ownership of mankind as a chattel, or at least the control of the labor and services of one man for the benefit of another, and the absence of a legal right to the disposal of his own person, property and services. This amendment was said in the *Slaughterhouse Cases*, to have been intended primarily to abolish slavery as it had been previously known in this country, and that it equally forbade Mexican peonage or the Chinese coolie trade when they amounted to slavery or involuntary servitude, and that the use of the word "servitude" was intended to prohibit the use of all forms of involuntary slavery, of whatever class or name. It was intimated, however, in that case that this amendment was regarded by the statesmen of that day as insufficient to

protect the colored race from certain laws which had been enacted in the southern states, imposing upon the colored race onerous disabilities and burdens and curtailing their rights in the pursuit of life, liberty, and property to such an extent that their freedom was of little value; and that the Fourteenth Amendment was devised to meet this exigency.

So, too, in the *Civil Rights Cases*, it was said that the act of a mere individual, the owner of an inn, a public conveyance, or place of amusement, refusing accommodations to colored people cannot be justly regarded as imposing any badge of slavery or servitude upon the applicant, but only as involving an ordinary civil injury, properly cognizable by the laws of the state and presumably subject to redress by those laws until the contrary appears. "It would be running the slavery argument into the ground," said Mr. Justice Bradley, "to make it apply to every act of discrimination which a person may see fit to make as to the guests he will entertain, or as to the people he will take into his coach or cab or car, or admit to his concert or theater, or deal with in other matters of intercourse or business." . . .

2. By the Fourteenth Amendment, all persons born or naturalized in the United States and subject to the jurisdiction thereof are made citizens of the United States and of the State wherein they reside, and the States are forbidden from making or enforcing any law which shall abridge the privileges or immunities of citizens of the United States, or shall deprive any person of life, liberty, or property without due process of law, or deny to any person within their jurisdiction the equal protection of the laws.

The proper construction of this amendment was first called to the attention of this court in the *Slaughterhouse Cases* which involved, however, not a question of race, but one of exclusive privileges. The case did not call for any expression of opinion as to the exact rights it was intended to secure to the colored race, but it was said generally that its main purpose was to establish the citizenship of the Negro, to give definitions of citizenship of the United States and of the states, and to protect from the hostile legislation of the states the privileges and immunities of citizens of the United States, as distinguished from those of citizens of the states.

The object of the amendment was undoubtedly to enforce the absolute equality of the two races before the law, but, in the nature of things, it could not have been intended to abolish distinctions based upon color, or to enforce social, as distinguished from political, equality, or a commingling of the two races upon terms unsatisfactory to either. Laws permitting, and even requiring, their separation in places where they are liable to be brought into contact do not necessarily imply the inferiority of either race to the other, and have been generally, if not universally, recognized as within the competency of the state legislatures in the exercise of their police power. The most common instance of this is connected with the establishment of separate schools for white and colored children, which has been held to be a valid exercise of the legislative power even by courts of states where the political rights of the colored race have been longest and most earnestly enforced.

One of the earliest of these cases is that of *Roberts v. City of Boston*, in which the Supreme Judicial Court of Massachusetts held that the general school committee of Boston had power to make provision for the instruction of colored children in separate schools established exclusively for them, and to prohibit their attendance upon the other schools. "The great principle," said Chief Justice Shaw, "advanced by the learned and eloquent advocate for the plaintiff" (Mr. Charles Sumner), "is that, by the constitution and laws of Massachusetts, all persons without distinction of age or sex, birth or color, origin or condition, are equal before the law. . . . But when this great principle comes to be applied to the actual and various conditions of persons in society, it will not warrant the assertion that men and women are legally clothed with the same civil and political powers, and that children and adults are legally to have the same functions and be subject to the same treatment, but only that the rights of all, as they are settled and regulated by law, are equally entitled to the paternal consideration and protection of the law for their maintenance and security."

It was held that the powers of the committee extended to the establishment of separate schools for children of different ages, sexes, and colors, and that they might also establish special schools for poor and neglected children, who have become too old to attend the primary school and yet have not acquired the rudiments of learning to enable them to enter the ordinary schools. Similar laws have been enacted by Congress under its general power of legislation over the District of Columbia, as well as by the legislatures of many of the states, and have been generally, if not uniformly, sustained by the courts. . . .

Laws forbidding the intermarriage of the two races may be said in a technical sense to interfere with the freedom of contract, and yet have been universally recognized as within the police power of the state. . . .

The distinction between laws interfering with the political equality of the Negro and those requiring the separation of the two races in schools, theaters, and railway carriages has been frequently drawn by this court. Thus, in *Strauder v. West Virginia*, it was held that a law of West Virginia limiting to white male persons, twenty-one years of age and citizens of the state, the right to sit upon juries was a discrimination which implied a legal inferiority in civil society, which lessened the security of the right of the colored race, and was a step toward reducing them to a condition of servility. Indeed, the right of a colored man that, in the selection of jurors to pass upon his life, liberty, and property, there shall be no exclusion of his race and no discrimination against them because of color has been asserted in a number of cases. . . . So, where the laws of a particular locality or the charter of a particular railway corporation has provided that no person shall be excluded from the cars on account of color, we have held that this meant that persons of color should travel in the same car as white ones, and that the enactment was not satisfied by the company's providing cars assigned exclusively to people of color, though they were as good as those which they assigned exclusively to white persons. . . .

Upon the other hand, where a statute of Louisiana required those engaged in the transportation of passengers among the states to give to all persons traveling within that state, upon vessels employed in that business, equal rights and privileges in all parts of the vessel, without distinction on account of race or color, and subjected to an action for damages the owner of such a vessel, who excluded colored passengers on account of their color from the cabin set aside by him for the use of whites, it was held to be, so far as it applied to interstate commerce, unconstitutional and void. *Hall v. De Cuir.* The court in this case, however, expressly disclaimed that it had anything whatever to do with the statute as a regulation of internal commerce, or affecting anything else than commerce among the States.

In the *Civil Rights Case,* 109 U.S. 3, it was held that an act of Congress entitling all persons within the jurisdiction of the United States to the full and equal enjoyment of the accommodations, advantages, facilities, and privileges of inns, public conveyances, on land or water, theaters, and other places of public amusement, and made applicable to citizens of every race and color, regardless of any previous condition of servitude, was unconstitutional and void upon the ground that the Fourteenth Amendment was prohibitory upon the states only, and the legislation authorized to be adopted by Congress for enforcing it was not direct legislation on matters respecting which the states were prohibited from making or enforcing certain laws, or doing certain acts, but was corrective legislation such as might be necessary or proper for counteracting and redressing the effect of such laws or acts. In delivering the opinion of the court, Mr. Justice Bradley observed that the Fourteenth Amendment "does not invest Congress with power to legislate upon subjects that are within the domain of state legislation, but to provide modes of relief against state legislation or state action of the kind referred to. It does not authorize Congress to create a code of municipal law for the regulation of private rights, but to provide modes of redress against the operation of state laws and the action of state officers, executive or judicial, when these are subversive of the fundamental rights specified in the amendment. Positive rights and privileges are undoubtedly secured by the Fourteenth Amendment, but they are secured by way of prohibition against state laws and state proceedings affecting those rights and privileges, and by power given to Congress to legislate for the pur-

pose of carrying such prohibition into effect, and such legislation must necessarily be predicated upon such supposed state laws or state proceedings, and
be directed to the correction of their operation and effect."

Much nearer, and, indeed, almost directly in point is the case of the *Lou-
isville, New Orleans etc. Railway v. Mississippi*, wherein the railway company
was indicted for a violation of a statute of Mississippi enacting that all railroads
carrying passengers should provide equal but separate accommodations for
the white and colored races by providing two or more passenger cars for each
passenger train, or by dividing the passenger cars by a partition so as to secure
separate accommodations. The case was presented in a different aspect from
the one under consideration, inasmuch as it was an indictment against the
railway company for failing to provide the separate accommodations, but
the question considered was the constitutionality of the law. In that case, the
Supreme Court of Mississippi, 66 Mississippi 662, had held that the statute
applied solely to commerce within the state, and that, being the construction
of the state statute by its highest court, was accepted as conclusive. "If it be a
matter," said the court, "respecting commerce wholly within a state, and not
interfering with commerce between the states, then obviously there is no
violation of the commerce clause of the Federal Constitution. . . . No question
arises under this section as to the power of the state to separate in different
compartments interstate passengers or affect in any manner the privileges and
rights of such passengers. All that we can consider is whether the state has the
power to require that railroad trains within her limits shall have separate
accommodations for the two races; that affecting only commerce within the
state is no invasion of the power given to Congress by the commerce clause."

A like course of reasoning applies to the case under consideration, since the
Supreme Court of Louisiana in the case of the *State ex rel. Abbott v. Hicks,
Judge, et al.*, held that the statute in question did not apply to interstate passengers, but was confined in its application to passengers traveling exclusively
within the borders of the state. The case was decided largely upon the authority of *Railway Co. v. State*, 66 Mississippi 662, and affirmed by this court. In the
present case, no question of interference with interstate commerce can possibly
arise, since the East Louisiana Railway appears to have been purely a local line,
with both its termini within the state of Louisiana. Similar statutes for the
separation of the races upon public conveyances were held to be constitutional.

While we think the enforced separation of the races, as applied to the
internal commerce of the state, neither abridges the privileges or immunities
of the colored man, deprives him of his property without due process of law,
nor denies him the equal protection of the laws within the meaning of the
Fourteenth Amendment, we are not prepared to say that the conductor, in
assigning passengers to the coaches according to their race, does not act at his

peril, or that the provision of the second section of the act that denies to the passenger compensation in damages for a refusal to receive him into the coach in which he properly belongs is a valid exercise of the legislative power. Indeed, we understand it to be conceded by the state's attorney that such part of the act as exempts from liability the railway company and its officers is unconstitutional. The power to assign to a particular coach obviously implies the power to determine to which race the passenger belongs, as well as the power to determine who, under the laws of the particular state, is to be deemed a white and who a colored person. This question, though indicated in the brief of the plaintiff in error, does not properly arise upon the record in this case, since the only issue made is as to the unconstitutionality of the act so far as it requires the railway to provide separate accommodations and the conductor to assign passengers according to their race.

It is claimed by the plaintiff in error that, in any mixed community, the reputation of belonging to the dominant race, in this instance the white race, is property in the same sense that a right of action or of inheritance is property. Conceding this to be so for the purposes of this case, we are unable to see how this statute deprives him of, or in any way affects his right to, such property. If he be a white man and assigned to a colored coach, he may have his action for damages against the company for being deprived of his so-called property. Upon the other hand, if he be a colored man and be so assigned, he has been deprived of no property, since he is not lawfully entitled to the reputation of being a white man.

In this connection, it is also suggested by the learned counsel for the plaintiff in error that the same argument that will justify the state legislature in requiring railways to provide separate accommodations for the two races will also authorize them to require separate cars to be provided for people whose hair is of a certain color, or who are aliens, or who belong to certain nationalities, or to enact laws requiring colored people to walk upon one side of the street and white people upon the other, or requiring white men's houses to be painted white and colored men's black, or their vehicles or business signs to be of different colors, upon the theory that one side of the street is as good as the other, or that a house or vehicle of one color is as good as one of another color. The reply to all this is that every exercise of the police power must be reasonable, and extend only to such laws as are enacted in good faith for the promotion for the public good, and not for the annoyance or oppression of a particular class. Thus, in *Yick Wo v. Hopkins*, it was held by this court that a municipal ordinance of the city of San Francisco to regulate the carrying on of public laundries within the limits of the municipality violated the provisions of the Constitution of the United States if it conferred upon the municipal authorities arbitrary power, at their own will and without regard to discretion, in the legal sense of the term, to give or withhold consent as to persons or places without regard to the competency of the persons applying or the propriety of the places selected for the carrying on of the business. It was held to be a covert attempt on the part of the municipality to make an arbitrary and unjust discrimination against the Chinese race. While this was the case of a municipal ordinance, a like principle has been held to apply to acts of a state legislature passed in the exercise of the police power. . . .

So far, then, as a conflict with the Fourteenth Amendment is concerned, the case reduces itself to the question whether the statute of Louisiana is a reasonable regulation, and, with respect to this, there must necessarily be a large discretion on the part of the legislature. In determining the question of reasonableness, it is at liberty to act with reference to the established usages, customs, and traditions of the people, and with a view to the promotion of their comfort and the preservation of the public peace and good order. Gauged by this standard, we cannot say that a law which authorizes or even requires the separation of the two races in public conveyances is unreasonable, or more obnoxious to the Fourteenth Amendment than the acts of Congress requiring separate schools for colored children in the District of Columbia, the constitutionality of which does not seem to have been questioned, or the corresponding acts of state legislatures.

We consider the underlying fallacy of the plaintiff's argument to consist in the assumption that the enforced separation of the two races stamps the colored race with a badge of inferiority. If this be so, it is not by reason of anything found in the act, but solely because the colored race chooses to put that construction upon it. The argument necessarily assumes that if, as has been more than once the case and is not unlikely to be so again, the colored race should become the dominant power in the state legislature, and should enact a law in precisely similar terms, it would thereby relegate the white race to an inferior position. We imagine that the white race, at least, would not acquiesce in this assumption. The argument also assumes that social prejudices may be overcome by legislation, and that equal rights cannot be secured to the Negro except by an enforced commingling of the two races. We cannot accept this proposition. If the two races are to meet upon terms of social equality, it must be the result of natural affinities, a mutual appreciation of each other's merits, and a voluntary consent of individuals. As was said by the Court of Appeals of New York in *People v. Gallagher*, "this end can neither be accomplished nor promoted by laws which conflict with the general sentiment of the community upon whom they are designed to operate. When the government, therefore, has secured to each of its citizens equal rights before the law and equal opportunities for improvement and progress, it has accomplished the end for which it was organized, and performed all of the functions respecting social advantages with which it is endowed."

Legislation is powerless to eradicate racial instincts or to abolish distinctions based upon physical differences, and the attempt to do so can only result in accentuating the difficulties of the present situation. If the civil and political rights of both races be equal, one cannot be inferior to the other civilly or politically. If one race be inferior to the other socially, the Constitution of the United States cannot put them upon the same plane.

It is true that the question of the proportion of colored blood necessary to constitute a colored person, as distinguished from a white person, is one upon which there is a difference of opinion in the different states, some holding that any visible admixture of black blood stamps the person as belonging to the colored race; others that it depends upon the preponderance of blood; and still others that the predominance of white blood must only be in the proportion of three-fourths. But these are questions to be determined under the laws of each state, and are not properly put in issue in this case. Under the allegations of his petition, it may undoubtedly become a question of importance whether, under the laws of Louisiana, the petitioner belongs to the white or colored race.

The judgment of the court below is, therefore, affirmed.

Source: Cornell University Law School, Legal Information Institute, *Plessy v. Ferguson*, 163 U.S. 537 (No. 210). Retrieved May 20, 2010, from http://www.law.cornell.edu/supct/html/historics/USSC_CR_0163_0537_ZO.html.

CHAPTER 29

William Jennings Bryan's "Cross of Gold" Speech, 1896

On July 9, 1896, thirty-six-year-old William Jennings Bryan, a former congressman from Nebraska, delivered the final speech in defense of the Democratic Party platform at the party's national convention. It demanded a bimetallic standard with unlimited coinage of both silver and gold, whereas the Republican platform called for continuing adherence to the gold standard as the base for all U.S. currency. The bimetallic standard was to be at a ratio of sixteen to one, in the value of silver to gold. The idea was to increase the money supply and inflate the currency to help the strapped and debt-ridden farmers and workers in Middle America. It was the Populists' primary economic measure in the 1896 election.

Although young and relatively inexperienced, Bryan had been lobbying extensively behind the scenes for the presidential nomination. His speech, however, almost totally by itself catapulted Bryan to national prominence, and he was nominated the following day on the fifth ballot. Bryan electrified the delegates with his dramatic oratory eloquence, possibly the most effective delivery style in American history, and the convention dissolved into a frenzy. The listeners tore off their coats and hats, flung them into the air, and screamed in ecstasy as if in an old-fashioned religious revival. The phrase, "You shall not crucify mankind upon a cross of gold" became the Democratic slogan in the election. Bryan was defeated by William McKinley, and his speech became the final hurrah for the bimetallic standard and the "free silver" movement. It also marked the end of the Populist movement—a generally lower-class western and southern agrarian revolt—and the rise of the new Progressive movement, with its upper-class, elite, urban influences.

In Bryan's time there was no radio or TV, so only Democratic stalwarts heard the original speech, and with only a few months to campaign, he was unable to dazzle enough voters to win. Bryan spoke to a specific issue and was heard by thousands. Style and content of political speeches have been changed radically by the media, but for its time, the "cross of gold" address was the epitome of political speech making.

Address to the Democratic National Convention

I WOULD BE PRESUMPTUOUS, INDEED, TO PRESENT MYSELF against the distinguished gentlemen to whom you have listened if this were but a measuring of ability; but this is not a contest among persons. The humblest citizen in all the land when clad in the armor of a righteous cause is stronger than all the whole hosts of error that they can bring. I come to speak to you in defense of a cause as holy as the cause of liberty—the cause of humanity. When this debate is concluded, a motion will be made to lay upon the table the resolution offered in commendation of the administration and also the resolution in condemnation of the administration. I shall object to bringing this question down to a level of persons. The individual is but an atom; he is born, he acts, he dies; but principles are eternal; and this has been a contest of principle.

Never before in the history of this country has there been witnessed such a contest as that through which we have passed. Never before in the history of American politics has a great issue been fought out as this issue has been by the voters themselves.

On the 4th of March, 1895, a few Democrats, most of them members of Congress, issued an address to the Democrats of the nation asserting that the money question was the paramount issue of the hour; asserting also the right of a majority of the Democratic Party to control the position of the party on this paramount issue; concluding with the request that all believers in free coinage of silver in the Democratic Party should organize and take charge of and control the policy of the Democratic Party. Three months later, at Memphis, an organization was perfected, and the silver Democrats went forth openly and boldly and courageously proclaiming their belief and declaring that if successful they would crystallize in a platform the declaration which they had made; and then began the conflict with a zeal approaching the zeal which inspired the crusaders who followed Peter the Hermit. Our silver Democrats went forth from victory unto victory, until they are assembled now, not to discuss, not to debate, but to enter up the judgment rendered by the plain people of this country.

But in this contest, brother has been arrayed against brother, and father against son. The warmest ties of love and acquaintance and association have been disregarded. Old leaders have been cast aside when they refused to give expression to the sentiments of those whom they would lead, and new leaders have sprung up to give direction to this cause of freedom. Thus has the contest been waged, and we have assembled here under as binding and solemn instructions as were ever fastened upon the representatives of a people.

We do not come as individuals. Why, as individuals we might have been glad to compliment the gentleman from New York [Senator Hill], but we knew that the people for whom we speak would never be willing to put him in a position where he could thwart the will of the Democratic Party. I say it was not a question of persons; it was a question of principle; and it is not with gladness, my friends, that we find ourselves brought into conflict with those who are now arrayed on the other side. The gentleman who just preceded me [Governor Russell] spoke of the old state of Massachusetts. Let me assure him that not one person in all this convention entertains the least hostility to the people of the state of Massachusetts.

But we stand here representing people who are the equals before the law of the largest cities in the state of Massachusetts. When you come before us and tell us that we shall disturb your business interests, we reply that you have disturbed our business interests by your action. We say to you that you have made too limited in its application the definition of a businessman. The man who is employed for wages is as much a businessman as his employer. The attorney in a country town is as much a businessman as the corporation counsel in a great metropolis. The merchant at the crossroads store is as much a businessman as the merchant of New York. The farmer who goes forth in the morning and toils all day, begins in the spring and toils all summer, and by the application of brain and muscle to the natural resources of this country creates wealth, is as much a businessman as the man who goes upon the board of trade and bets upon the price of grain. The miners who go one thousand feet into the earth or climb two thousand feet upon the cliffs and bring forth from their hiding places the precious metals to be poured in the channels of trade are as much businessmen as the few financial magnates who in a back room corner the money of the world.

We come to speak for this broader class of businessmen. Ah, my friends, we say not one word against those who live upon the Atlantic coast; but those hardy pioneers who braved all the dangers of the wilderness, who have made the desert to blossom as the rose—those pioneers away out there, rearing their children near to nature's heart, where they can mingle their voices with the voices of the birds—out there where they have erected schoolhouses for the education of their children and churches where they praise their Creator, and the cemeteries where sleep the ashes of their dead—are as deserving of the consideration of this party as any people in this country.

It is for these that we speak. We do not come as aggressors. Our war is not a war of conquest. We are fighting in the defense of our homes, our families, and posterity. We have petitioned, and our petitions have been scorned. We have entreated, and our entreaties have been disregarded. We have begged, and they have mocked when our calamity came.

We beg no longer; we entreat no more; we petition no more. We defy them! The gentleman from Wisconsin has said he fears a Robespierre. My friend, in this land of the free you need fear no tyrant who will spring up from among the people. What we need is an Andrew Jackson to stand as Jackson stood, against the encroachments of aggregated wealth.

They tell us that this platform was made to catch votes. We reply to them that changing conditions make new issues; that the principles upon which rest democracy are as everlasting as the hills; but that they must be applied to new conditions as they arise. Conditions have arisen and we are attempting to meet those conditions. They tell us that the income tax ought not to be brought in here; that is not a new idea. They criticize us for our criticism of the Supreme Court of the United States. My friends, we have made no criticism. We have simply called attention to what you know. If you want criticisms, read the dissenting opinions of the Court. That will give you criticisms.

They say we passed an unconstitutional law. I deny it. The income tax was not unconstitutional when it was passed. It was not unconstitutional when it went before the Supreme Court for the first time. It did not become unconstitutional until one judge changed his mind; and we cannot be expected to know when a judge will change his mind.

The income tax is a just law. It simply intends to put the burdens of government justly upon the backs of the people. I am in favor of an income tax. When I find a man who is not willing to pay his share of the burden of the government which protects him, I find a man who is unworthy to enjoy the blessings of a government like ours.

He says that we are opposing the national bank currency. It is true. If you will read what Thomas Benton [senator from Missouri] said, you will find that he said that in searching history he could find but one parallel to Andrew Jackson. That was Cicero, who destroyed the conspiracies of Cataline and saved Rome. He did for Rome what Jackson did when he destroyed the bank conspiracy and saved America.

We say in our platform that we believe that the right to coin money and issue money is a function of government. We believe it. We believe it is a part of sovereignty and can no more with safety be delegated to private individuals than can the power to make penal statutes or levy laws for taxation.

Mr. Jefferson, who was once regarded as good Democratic authority, seems to have a different opinion from the gentleman who has addressed us on the part of the minority. Those who are opposed to this proposition tell us that the issue of paper money is a function of the bank and that the government ought to go out of the banking business. I stand with Jefferson rather than with them, and tell them, as he did, that the issue of money is a function of the government and that the banks should go out of the governing business.

They complain about the plank which declares against the life tenure in office. They have tried to strain it to mean that which it does not mean. What we oppose in that plank is the life tenure that is being built up in Washington which establishes an office-holding class and excludes from participation in the benefits the humbler members of our society. . . .

Let me call attention to two or three great things. The gentleman from New York says that he will propose an amendment providing that this change in our law shall not affect contracts which, according to the present laws, are made payable in gold. But if he means to say that we cannot change our monetary system without protecting those who have loaned money before the change was made, I want to ask him where, in law or in morals, he can find authority for not protecting the debtors when the act of 1873 was passed when he now insists that we must protect the creditor. He says he also wants to amend this platform so as to provide that if we fail to maintain the parity within a year that we will then suspend the coinage of silver. We reply that when we advocate a thing which we believe will be successful we are not compelled to raise a doubt as to our own sincerity by trying to show what we will do if we are wrong.

I ask him, if he will apply his logic to us, why he does not apply it to himself. He says that he wants this country to try to secure an international agreement. Why doesn't he tell us what he is going to do if they fail to secure an international agreement. There is more reason for him to do that than for us to expect to fail to maintain the parity. They have tried for thirty years—thirty years—to secure an international agreement, and those are waiting for it most patiently who don't want it at all.

Now, my friends, let me come to the great paramount issue. If they ask us here why it is we say more on the money question than we say upon the tariff question, I reply that if protection has slain its thousands the gold standard has slain its tens of thousands. If they ask us why we did not embody all these things in our platform which we believe, we reply to them that when we have restored the money of the Constitution, all other necessary reforms will be possible, and that until that is done there is no reform that can be accomplished.

Why is it that within three months such a change has come over the sentiments of the country? Three months ago, when it was confidently asserted that those who believed in the gold standard would frame our platforms and nominate our candidates, even the advocates of the gold standard did not think that we could elect a president; but they had good reasons for the suspicion, because there is scarcely a state here today asking for the gold standard that is not within the absolute control of the Republican Party.

But note the change. Mr. McKinley was nominated at St. Louis upon a platform that declared for the maintenance of the gold standard until it should be changed into bimetallism by an international agreement. Mr. McKinley was the most popular man among the Republicans; and everybody three months ago in the Republican Party prophesied his election. How is it today? Why, that man who used to boast that he looked like Napoleon, that man shudders today when he thinks that he was nominated on the anniversary of the Battle of Waterloo. Not only that, but as he listens he can hear with ever increasing distinctness the sound of the waves as they beat upon the lonely shores of St. Helena.

Why this change? Ah, my friends, is not the change evident to anyone who will look at the matter? It is because no private character, however pure, no personal popularity, however great, can protect from the avenging wrath of an indignant people the man who will either declare that he is in favor of fastening the gold standard upon this people, or who is willing to surrender the right of self-government and place legislative control in the hands of foreign potentates and powers. . . .

We go forth confident that we shall win. Why? Because upon the paramount issue in this campaign there is not a spot of ground upon which the enemy will dare to challenge battle. Why, if they tell us that the gold standard is a good thing, we point to their platform and tell them that their platform pledges the party to get rid of a gold standard and substitute bimetallism. If the gold standard is a good thing, why try to get rid of it? If the gold standard, and I might call your attention to the fact that some of the very people who are in this convention today and who tell you that we ought to declare in favor of international bimetallism and thereby declare that the gold standard is wrong and that the principles of bimetallism are better—these very people four months ago were open and avowed advocates of the gold standard and telling us that we could not legislate two metals together even with all the world.

I want to suggest this truth, that if the gold standard is a good thing we ought to declare in favor of its retention and not in favor of abandoning it; and if the gold standard is a bad thing, why should we wait until some other nations are willing to help us to let it go?

Here is the line of battle. We care not upon which issue they force the fight. We are prepared to meet them on either issue or on both. If they tell us that the gold standard is the standard of civilization, we reply to them that this, the most enlightened of all nations of the earth, has never declared for a gold standard, and both the parties this year are declaring against it. If the gold standard is the standard of civilization, why, my friends, should we not have it? So if they come to meet us on that, we can present the history of our nation. More than that, we can tell them this, that they will search the pages of history in vain to find a single instance in which the common people of any land ever declared themselves in favor of a gold standard. They can find where the holders of fixed investments have.

Mr. Carlisle [John G. Carlisle, secretary of the treasury] said in 1878 that this was a struggle between the idle holders of idle capital and the struggling masses who produce the wealth and pay the taxes of the country; and my friends, it is simply a question that we shall decide upon which side shall the Democratic Party fight. Upon the side of the idle holders of idle capital, or upon the side of the struggling masses? That is the question that the party must answer first; and then it must be answered by each individual hereafter. The sympathies of the Democratic Party, as described by the platform, are on the side of the struggling masses, who have ever been the foundation of the Democratic Party.

There are two ideas of government. There are those who believe that if you just legislate to make the well-to-do prosperous, that their prosperity will leak through on those below. The Democratic idea has been that if you legislate to make the masses prosperous their prosperity will find its way up and through every class that rests upon it.

You come to us and tell us that the great cities are in favor of the gold standard. I tell you that the great cities rest upon these broad and fertile prairies. Burn down your cities and leave our farms, and your cities will spring up again as if by magic. But destroy our farms and the grass will grow in the streets of every city in the country.

My friends, we shall declare that this nation is able to legislate for its own people on every question without waiting for the aid or consent of any other nation on earth, and upon that issue we expect to carry every single state in the Union.

I shall not slander the fair state of Massachusetts nor the state of New York by saying that when citizens are confronted with the proposition, "Is this nation able to attend to its own business?" I will not slander either one by saying that the people of those states will declare our helpless impotency as a nation to attend to our own business. It is the issue of 1776 over again. Our ancestors, when but three million, had the courage to declare their political independence of every other nation upon earth. Shall we, their descendants, when we have grown to seventy million, declare that we are less independent than our forefathers? No, my friends, it will never be the judgment of this people.

Therefore, we care not upon what lines the battle is fought. If they say bimetallism is good but we cannot have it till some nation helps us, we reply that, instead of having a gold standard because England has, we shall restore bimetallism, and then let England have bimetallism because the United States have.

If they dare to come out in the open field and defend the gold standard as a good thing, we shall fight them to the uttermost, having behind us the producing masses of the nation and the world. Having behind us the commercial interests and the laboring interests and all the toiling masses, we shall answer their demands for a gold standard by saying to them, you shall not press down upon the brow of labor this crown of thorns. You shall not crucify mankind upon a cross of gold!

Source: *Official Proceedings of the Democratic National Convention Held in Chicago, Illinois, July 7, 8, 9, 10, and 11, 1896* (Logansport, Indiana, 1896), 226–34. Reprinted in *The Annals of America* (Chicago: Encyclopedia Britannica, Inc., 1968), 12: 100–105.

CHAPTER 30

On Academic Freedom: William Harper, 1902, and the American Association of University Professors, 1915

In 1892 the University of Chicago was opened under its first president, William Rainey Harper, with funding primarily from John D. Rockefeller. Harper attracted many prominent educators to the faculty, including John Dewey, and rapidly built a world-class institution. Almost immediately some of these distinguished faculty members offended midwestern sensibilities, and Harper developed a policy with respect to academic freedom of speech, in part based on the principles of academic freedom historically enjoyed in German universities. In 1902 he issued a statement on this policy in the university's decennial report, which, particularly given the presence of Dewey on the faculty, was at the time widely understood to be the correct position for a university to take. His stance, along with that of presidents of Harvard and Columbia, set the standard with respect to academic freedom.

The evolution of faculty responsibilities and privileges continued, and in 1915 the American Association of University Professors was formed. Edwin R. A. Seligman, a progressive political economist championing the income tax at Columbia (where Dewey was then employed) headed a committee to draw up the principles of academic freedom as seen by faculty. As Seligman was involved with radicals and leaned toward Marxist economics, he, along with many faculty members, wished to limit administrative interference in faculty research, teaching, and other activities. He came from a tradition of Jewish liberal humanism and a wealthy banking family, and throughout his life strove to use state power to address social ills. He also pushed for the concept of tenure wherein a faculty member is granted lifetime employment. This principle would not become formalized until 1940.

The reader should consider whether anyone should be granted a sinecure for life and be secure from economic factors unless he commits some crime or moral outrage. The idea that a faculty member is free to inquire into any line of study is at the heart of academic freedom, but often it is used as an excuse to say and teach anything an individual desires. Only in the public school system do administrators, taxpayers, or benefactors have control over what is taught, and then it is through textbook selection and predetermined curricula. National standards infringe on local control and effectively remove taxpayers from consideration, and forcing compliance through testing has proven ineffective because teachers teach the tests. At the university level, individual faculty members or academic departments choose textbooks and determine course content unfettered by external influences. The reader should consider the role of academic freedom in public schools, as well its effects in universities.

As American education began to fail on a widespread basis in the late twentieth century, and President George W. Bush's No Child Left Behind Act (whose details were largely written by Senator Edward Kennedy) imposed an unprecedented federal involvement in local education—even with the best of intentions—the entire place of public education in American society has been questioned. By some estimates, more than 15 percent of American children (K–12) are homeschooled or in private schools, and the number dropping out of the public systems has increased annually. In states like Arkansas where homeschooling through high school is allowed without certification, large numbers of parents with means homeschool their children, lowering public school educational scores and compromising enormously expensive federal programs. The transformation of education in the early 1900s had a great deal to do with the system that came into being later in the century.

On Academic Freedom, William Rainey Harper, 1902

I AM MOVED TO MAKE A STATEMENT OF FACT AND OPINION concerning two related subjects which quite recently have attracted some attention in the public mind. The first of these if the freedom of opinion enjoyed in these days by members of the university. The second is the use and abuse of this right by professors of the university faculty.

Concerning the first, I may be permitted to present a statement adopted unanimously by the members of the congregation of the university on June 30, 1899:

Resolved:

1. That the principle of complete freedom of speech on all subjects has from the beginning been regarded as fundamental in the University of Chicago, as has been shown both by the attitude of the president and the board of trustees and by the actual practice of the president and the professors.

2. That this principle can neither now nor at any future time be called in question.

3. That it is desirable to have it clearly understood that the university, as such, does not appear as a disputant on either side upon any public question; and that the utterances which any professor may make in public are to be regarded as representing his opinions only. . . .

When, for any reason, in a university on private foundation, or in a university supported by public money, the administration of the institution or the instruction in any of its departments is changed by an influence from without; when an effort is made to dislodge an officer or a professor because the political sentiment or the religious sentiment of the majority has undergone a change, at that moment the institution has ceased to be a university; and it cannot again take its place in the rank of universities so long as there continues to exist to any appreciable extent the factor of coercion. Neither an individual, nor a state, nor the church has the right to interfere with the search for truth or with its promulgation when found. Individuals, or the state, or the church may found schools for propagating certain special kinds of instruction, but such schools are not universities and may not be so denominated.

A donor has the privilege of ceasing to make his gifts to an institution if, in his opinion, for any reason, the work of the institution is not satisfactory; but as donor he has no right to interfere with the administration or the instruction of the university. The trustees in an institution in which such interference has taken place may not maintain their self-respect and remain trustees. They owe it to themselves and to the cause of liberty of thought to resign their places rather than to yield a principle the significance of which rises above all else in comparison. . . .

Concerning the second subject, the use and abuse of the right of free expression by officers of the university staff: As I have said, an instructor in a university has an absolute right to express his opinion. If such an instructor is on an appointment for two or three or four years, and if during these years he exercises his right in such a way as to do himself and the institution serious injury, it is of course the privilege of the university to allow his appointment to lapse at the end of the term for which it was originally made. If an officer on permanent appointment abuses his privilege as a professor, the university must suffer and it is proper that it should suffer. This is only the direct and inevitable consequence of the lack of foresight and wisdom involved in the original appointment.

The injury thus accruing to the university is, moreover, far less serious than would follow if, for an expression of opinion differing from that of the majority of the faculty, or from that of the board of trustees, or from that of the president of the university, a permanent officer were asked to present his res-ignation. The greatest single element necessary for the cultivation of the aca-demic spirit is the feeling of security from interference. It is only those who have this feeling that are able to do work which in the highest sense will be beneficial to humanity. Freedom of expression must be given the members of a university faculty, even though it be abused; for, as has been said, the abuse of it is not so great an evil as the restriction of such liberty.

But it may be asked: In what way may the professor abuse his privilege of freedom or expression? Or, to put the question more largely: In what way does a professor bring reproach and injury to himself and to his institution? I answer: A professor is guilty of an abuse of his privilege who promulgates as truth ideas or opinions which have not been tested scientifically by his colleagues in the same department of research or investigation. A professor has no right to pro-claim to the public a truth discovered which is yet unsettled and uncertain. A professor abuses his privilege who takes advantage of a classroom exercise to propagate the partisan views of one or another of the political parties. The university is no place for partisanship. From the teacher's desk should emanate the discussion of principles, the judicial statement of arguments from various points of view, and not the one-sided representations of a partisan character.

A professor abuses his privilege who in any way seeks to influence his pupils or the public by sensational methods. A professor abuses his privilege of expression or opinion when, although a student and perhaps an authority in one department or group of departments, he undertakes to speak authorita-tively on subjects which have no relationship to the department in which he was appointed to give instruction. A professor abuses his privilege in many cases when, although shut off in large measure from the world and engaged within a narrow field of investigation, he undertakes to instruct his colleagues or the public concerning matters in the world at large in connection with which he has had little or no experience.

A professor abuses his privilege of freedom of expression when he fails to exercise that quality ordinarily called common sense, which, it must be con-fessed, in some cases the professor lacks. A professor ought not to make such an exhibition of his weakness, or to make an exhibition of his weakness so many times, that the attention of the public at large is called to the fact. In this respect he has no larger liberty than other men.

But may a professor do all these things and yet remain an officer in the university? Yes. The professor in most cases is only an ordinary man. Perfec-tion is not to be expected of him. Like men in other professions, professors have their weaknesses. But will a professor under any circumstances be asked to withdraw from the university? Yes. His resignation will be demanded, and will be accepted, when, in the opinion of those in authority, he has been guilty of immorality, or when for any reason he has proved himself to be incompetent to perform the service called for.

The public should be on its guard in two particulars: The utterance of a professor, however wise or foolish, is not the utterance of the university. No individual, no group of individuals, can speak for the university. A statement, by whomsoever made, is the statement of an individual. . . .

I may sum up the point in three sentences: (1) college and university professors do make mistakes, and sometimes serious ones; but (2) these are to be attributed to the professor and not to the university; and (3) in a large majority of instances the mistake, as published to the world, is misrepresented, exaggerated, or, at least, presented in such a form as to do the professor, the university, and the cause of truth itself gross injustice.

Proposals for Academic Freedom, American Association of University Professors, 1915

THE ENDS TO BE ACCOMPLISHED ARE CHIEFLY THREE:

First: To safeguard freedom of inquiry and of teaching against both covert and overt attacks, by providing suitable judicial bodies, composed of members of the academic profession, which may be called into action before university teachers are dismissed or disciplined, and may determine in what cases the question of academic freedom is actually involved.

Second: By the same means, to protect college executives and governing boards against unjust charges of infringement of academic freedom, or of arbitrary and dictatorial conduct—charges which, when they gain wide currency and belief, are highly detrimental to the good repute and the influence of universities.

Third: To render the profession more attractive to men of high ability and strong personality by insuring the dignity, the independence, and the reasonable security of tenure of the professional office.

The measures which it is believed to be necessary for our universities to adopt to realize these ends—measures which have already been adopted in part by some institutions—are four:

1. Action by faculty committees of reappointments: Official action relating to reappointments and refusals or reappointment should be taken only with the advice and consent of some board or committee representative of the faculty. Your committee does not desire to make at this time any suggestion as to the manner of selection of such boards.

2. Definition of tenure of office: In every institution there should be an unequiv-
ocal understanding as to the term of each appointment; and the tenure of
professorships and associate professorships, and of all positions above the
grade of instructor after ten years of service, should be permanent (subject
to the provisions hereinafter given for removal upon charges). In those state
universities which are legally incapable of making contracts for more than a
limited period, the governing boards should announce their policy with
respect to the presumption of reappointment in the several classes of position, and such announcements, though not legally enforceable, should be
regarded as morally binding. No university teacher of any rank should, except
in cases of grave moral delinquency, receive notice of dismissal or of refusal
of reappointment later than three months before the close of any academic
year, and in the case of teachers above the grade of instructor, one year's
notice should be given.

3. Formulation of grounds for dismissal: In every institution the grounds which
will be regarded as justifying the dismissal of members of the faculty should
be formulated with reasonable definiteness; and in the case of instructions
which impose upon their faculties doctrinal standards of a sectarian or partisan character, these standards should be clearly defined and the body or
individual having authority to interpret them, in case of controversy, should
be designated. Your committee does not think it best at this time to attempt
to enumerate the legitimate grounds for dismissal, believing it to be preferable that individual institutions should take the initiative in this.

4. Judicial hearings before dismissal: Every university or college teacher should
be entitled, before dismissal or demotion, to have the charges against him
stated in writing in specific terms and to have a fair trial on those charges
before a special or permanent judicial committee chosen by the faculty at
large. At such trial the teacher accused should have full opportunity to present evidence, and, if the charge is one of professional incompetency, a formal
report upon his work should be first made in writing by the teachers of his
own department and of cognate departments in the university, and, if the
teacher concerned so desires, by a committee of his fellow specialists from
other institutions, appointed by some competent authority.

Sources: William Rainey Harper, "The President's Report" in *The Decennial Publications of the University of Chicago*, First Series (Chicago: University of Chicago Press,
1902), 1: 21–4. The excerpt from the American Association of University Professors'
"1915 Declaration of Principles on Academic Freedom and Academic Tenure" appears
below the heading "Practical Proposals" and was retrieved June 4, 2010, from http://
www.aaup.org/AAUP/pubsres/policydocs/contents/1915.htm.

CHAPTER 31

Eugene V. Debs's Presidential Nomination Acceptance Speech, 1908

E ugene V. Debs was a first-generation American, born to French immigrants from Alsace in Terre Haute, Indiana, in 1855. The family was prosperous, but Debs dropped out of school at fourteen to work in the railroad yards. He became a founding member of the Brotherhood of Locomotive Firemen and dedicated himself to union activities. In prison after the Pullman strike in 1894, Debs studied the writings of Karl Marx and thereafter was a devoted Socialist. The following speech was given in the square of Girard, Kansas, where he was living when informed of his nomination as the Socialist Party of America's candidate for president of the United States. It was an impromptu talk, and one held in high regard by American Socialists as coming from his heart instead of his mind. Debs went on to garner only 420,980 votes in the 1908 election, compared to the 7,677,788 for Taft and 6,407,982 for Bryan.

In this speech, now known as "The Issue," Debs outlined the general pie-in-the-sky utopia that would be realized through a Socialist victory. He had fallen in with radicals fresh from Europe who blamed all human failure on the capitalist system and the environment in which people were raised. His defense of collectivism and socialism and his stance toward private property reflected thinking that is still prevalent today. Even an individual's salvation required a collective salvation through collective actions promoting social justice to be realized. Although he recognized that marvels of science and industry had been accomplished under capitalism, he was against giving the system any credit for these advances. Such ideas resonated with recent immigrants from eastern and central Europe, and among working-class people who felt trapped in low-paying jobs. He made them feel privileged and cultured by emphasizing classical music, literature, and art—a theme stressed by American Communists and Socialists throughout the twentieth century, though contradictory to the very notion of collectivism and economic equality. Debs was jailed and permanently disenfranchised for his opposition to military conscription during World War I but continued to oppose the United States' form of government and social system to the last.

(Note: the document's frequent descriptive subheadings have not been retained.)

Speech at Girard, Kansas, May 23, 1908

COMRADES, LADIES, AND GENTLEMEN: WHEN I MADE SOME inquiry a few moments ago as to the cause of this assembling, I was told that it was the beginning of another street fair. I am quite surprised, and agreeably so, to find myself the central attraction. Allow me in the very beginning to express my heartiest appreciation of the more than kind and generous words which have been spoken here for me this afternoon. . . .

The honor to which reference has been made has come to me through no fault of my own. It has been said that some are born great, some achieve greatness, and some have greatness thrust upon them. It is even so with what are called honors. Some have honors thrust upon them. I find myself in that class. I did what I could to prevent myself from being nominated by the convention now in session at Chicago, but the nomination sought me out, and in spite of myself I stand in your presence this afternoon the nominee of the Socialist Party for the presidency of the United States. Long, long ago I made up my mind never again to be a candidate for any political office within the gift of the people. But I have had to violate that vow, because when I joined the Socialist Party I was taught that the wish of the individual was subordinate to the party will, and that when the party commanded it was my duty to obey. . . .

Now, my friends, I am opposed to the system of society in which we live today, not because I lack the natural equipment to do for myself, but because I am not satisfied to make myself comfortable knowing that there are thousands upon thousands of my fellow men who suffer for the barest necessities of life. We were taught under the old ethic that man's business upon this earth was to look out for himself. That was the ethic of the jungle, the ethic of the wild beast. Take care of yourself, no matter what may become of your fellow man. Thousands of years ago the question was asked: "Am I my brother's keeper?" That question has never yet been answered in a way that is satisfactory to civilized society. Yes, I am my brother's keeper. I am under a moral obligation to him, inspired, not by any maudlin sentimentality, but by the higher duty I owe to myself. What would you think of me if I were capable of seating myself at a table and gorging myself with food and saw about me the children of my fellow beings starving to death? . . .

I am in revolt against capitalism because I love my fellow men, and if I am opposing you it is for what I believe to be your good, and though you spat upon me with contempt I would still oppose you to the extent of my power.

I don't hate the workingman because he has turned against me. I know the poor fellow is too ignorant to understand his own interest, and I know that as a rule the workingman is the friend of his enemy and the enemy of his friend. He votes for men who represent a system in which labor is simply merchandise; in which the man who works the hardest and longest has the least to show for it. If there is a man on earth who is entitled to all the comforts and luxuries of life in abundance it is the man whose labor produces them. If he is not, who is? Does he get them in the present system? . . .

. . . I am not satisfied with things as they are, and I know that no matter what administration is in power, even were it a Socialist administration, there will be no material change in the condition of the people until we have a new social system based upon the mutual economic interests of the people: until you and I and all of us collectively own those things that we collectively need and use.

As long as a relatively few men own the railroads, the telegraph, the telephone, the oil fields, and the gas fields and the steel mills and the sugar refineries and the leather tanneries—own, in short, the sources and means of life—they will corrupt our politics; they will enslave the working class; they will impoverish and debase society; they will do all things that are needful to perpetuate their power as the economic masters and the political rulers of the people. Not until these great agencies are owned and operated by the people can the people hope for any material, improvement in their social condition.

Is the condition fair today, and satisfactory to any thinking man? . . .

Now, there has been a revolution in industry during the last fifty years, but the trouble with most people is that they haven't kept pace with it. They don't know anything about it and they are especially innocent in regard to it in the small western cities and states where the same old conditions of a century ago still largely prevail. Your grandfather could help himself anywhere. All he needed was some cheap, simple, primitive tools and he could then apply his labor to the resources of nature and produce what he needed. That era in our history produced some of our greatest men. Lincoln himself sprang from this primitive state of society. People have said, "Why, he had no chance. See how great he became." Yes, but Lincoln had for his comrades great green-plumed forest monarchs. He could put his arms about them and hear their heart-throbs, as they said: "Go on, Abe, a great destiny awaits you." He was in partnership with nature. He mingled with the birds and bees and flowers in the green fields and he heard the rippling music of the laughing brooks and streams. Nature took him to her bosom. Nature nourished him and from his unpolluted heart there sprang his noble aspirations.

Had Lincoln been born in a sweatshop he would never have been heard of.

How is it with the babe that is born on Mott Street, or in the lower Bowery, in the east side of New York City? That is where thousands, tens of thousands and hundreds of thousands of babes are born who are to constitute our future generations. . . .

You have seen your beehive—just fancy a human beehive of which yours is the miniature, and you have the social hive under capitalism. If you have never seen this condition, you are perhaps excusable for not being a Socialist. Come to New York, Chicago, San Francisco with me; remain with me just twenty-four hours, and then look into my face as I shall look into yours when I ask: "What about Socialism now?" These children by hundreds and thousands are born in subcellars where a whole grown family is crowded together in one room, where modesty between the sexes is absolutely impossible. They are surrounded by filth and vermin. From their birth they see nothing but ill morality and vice and crime. They are tainted in the cradle. They are inoculated by their surroundings and they are doomed from the beginning. This system takes their lives just as certainly as if a dagger were thrust into their quivering little hearts, and let me say to you that it were better for many thousands of them if they had never seen the light of day.

Now I submit, my friends, that such a condition as this is indefensible in the twentieth century. . . .

Nature's storehouse is full to the surface of the earth. All of the raw materials are deposited here in abundance. We have the most marvelous machinery the world has ever known. Man has long since become master of the natural forces and made them work for him. Now he has but to touch a button and the wheels begin to spin and the machinery to whir, and wealth is produced on every hand in increasing abundance. Why should any man, woman, or child suffer for food, clothing, or shelter? Why? The question cannot be answered. Don't tell me that some men are too lazy to work. Suppose they are too lazy to work, what do you think of a social system that produces men too lazy to work? If a man is too lazy to work, don't treat him with contempt. Don't look down upon him with scorn as if you were a superior being. If there is a man too lazy to work, there is something the matter with him; he wasn't born right or he was perverted in this system. You could not, if you tried, keep a normal man inactive, and if you did he would go stark mad. Go to any penitentiary and you will find the men there begging for the privilege of doing work.

I know by very close study of the question exactly how men become idle. I don't repel them when I meet them. I have never yet seen the tramp I was not able to receive with open arms. He is less fortunate than I. He is made the same as I am made. He is the child of the same Father. Had I been born in his environment, had I been subjected to the same things he was, I should be where he is. . . .

Your material interest and mine in the society of the future will be the same. Instead of having to fight each other like animals, as we do today, and seeking to glorify the brute struggle for existence—of which every civilized human being ought to be ashamed—instead of this, our material interests are going to be mutual. We are going to jointly own these mammoth machines, and we are going to operate them as joint partners and we are going to divide the products among ourselves.

We are not going to send our surplus to the Jim Hills, Goulds, and Vanderbilts of New York. We are not going to pile up a billion of dollars in John D. Rockefeller's hands—a vast pyramid from the height of which he can look down with scorn and contempt upon the "common herd." John D. Rockefeller's great fortune is built upon your ignorance. When you know enough to know what your interest is, you will support the party that is organized upon the basis of the collective ownership of the means of life. This party will sweep into power upon the issue of wage slavery just as republicanism swept into power upon the issue of chattel slavery half a century ago.

In the meantime, don't have any fear of us Socialists. We don't mean any harm! Many of you have been taught to look upon us as dangerous people. It is amazing to what extent this prejudice has struck root. The capitalist press tells you of a good many things that we Socialists are going to do that we do not intend to do. They tell you we are going to break up the home. Great heavens! What about the homes of the four million tramps that are looking for work today? How about the thousands and thousands of miserable shacks in New York and every great city where humanity festers? It would be a good thing if they were torn down and obliterated completely, for they are not fit for human habitation. No, we are not going to destroy the home, but we are going to make the home possible for all for the first time in history.

You may think you are very comfortable. You may not agree with me. I don't expect you to and don't ask you to. I am going to ask you to remember what I say this afternoon and perhaps before I am elected president of the United States you will know it is true. Now there are those of you who are fairly comfortable under the present standard. Isn't it amazing to you how little the average man is satisfied with? You go out here to the edge of town and you will find a small farmer who has a cabin with just room enough to keep himself and wife and two or three children, which has a mortgage on it, and he works early and late and gets just enough in net returns, to keep him in working order, and he will enthuse about the wonderful prosperity of the country.

He is satisfied, and that is his calamity.

Now the majority of you would say that is his good fortune. "It is a blessing that he is satisfied." As a matter of fact it is a curse to him and to society that he is satisfied.

If it had not been for the discontent of the few fellows who have not been satisfied with their condition, you would still be living in caves. You never would have emerged from the jungle. Intelligent discontent is the mainspring of civilization.

Progress is born of agitation. It is agitation or stagnation. I have taken my choice. . . .

You may have plenty of money. The poorest people on this earth are those who have most money. A man is said to be poor when he has none, but he is a pauper who has nothing else. Now this farmer, what does he know about literature? After his hard day's work, he sits in his little shack. He is fed and his animal wants are satisfied. It is at this time that a man ought to begin to live. It is not while you work and slave that you live. It is when you have done your work honestly, when you have contributed your share to the common fund, that you begin to live. Then, as Whitman said, you take out your soul; you can commune with yourself; you can take a comrade by the hand and you can look into his eyes and down into his soul, and in that communion you live. And if you don't know what that is, or if you are not at least on the edge of it, it is denied you to even look into the promised land.

Now this farmer knows nothing about the literature of the world. All its libraries are sealed to him. So far as he is concerned, Homer and Dante and Dickens might as well not have lived; Beethoven, Liszt and Wagner, and all those musicians whose art makes the common atmosphere rich with melody, never have been for this farmer. He knows nothing about literature or art. Never rises above the animal plane. Within fifteen minutes after he has ceased to live, he is forgotten; the next generation doesn't know his name, and the world doesn't know he ever lived. This is life under the present standard.

You tell me this is all the farmer is fit for? What do I propose to do for that farmer? Nothing. I simply want to awaken that farmer to the fact that he is robbed every day in the week, and if I can do that he will fall into line with the Socialist movement, and will march to the polls on election day, and, instead of casting his vote to fasten the shackles upon his limb more firmly, he will vote for his emancipation. All I have to do is to show that farmer, that day laborer, that tramp, that they are victims of this system, that their interests are identical, that they constitute the millions and that the millions have the votes. The Rockefellers have the dollars, but we have the votes; and when we have sense enough to know how to use the votes, we will have not only the votes but the dollars for all the children of men.

This seems quite visionary to some of you, and especially to those of you who know absolutely nothing about economics. I could not begin to tell you the story of social evolution this afternoon; of how these things are doing day by day, of how the world is being pushed into Socialism, and how it is bound to arrive, no matter whether you are for it or against it. It is the next inevitable phase of civilization. It isn't a scheme; it isn't a contrivance. It isn't anything that is made to order. The day is coming when you will be pushed into it by unseen hands whether you will or not.

I venture the prophecy that within the next few years you will be almost completely dispossessed. You are howling against the trusts, and the trusts are laughing at you. You keep on voting in the same old way, and the trusts will keep on getting what you produce. You say Congress will give you relief. Good heavens! Who will save us from Congress? Don't you know that Congress is made up almost wholly of trust lawyers and corporation attorneys? I don't happen to have the roll of this one, but with few exceptions they are all lawyers. Now, in the competitive system the lawyer sells himself to the highest bidder, the same as the workingman does. Who is the highest bidder? The corporation, of course. So the trust buys the best lawyer and the common herd gets the worst one. . . .

Now, we Socialists propose that society in its collective capacity shall produce, not for profit, but in abundance to satisfy all human wants; that every man shall have the inalienable right to work, and receive the full equivalent of what he produces; that every man may stand fearlessly erect in the pride and majesty of his own manhood; that every man and every woman shall be economically free.

We are not going to destroy private property. We are going to so establish private property that every worker may have all the private property necessary to house and keep him in comfort and satisfy all his physical wants. Eighty percent of the people in the United States have little or no property of any kind today. A few have got it all. They have dispossessed the people, and when we get into power we will dispossess them. We will reduce the work day and give every man a chance. We will go to the parks and we will have music because we will have time for music and inclination to enjoy it. . . .

Competition was natural and constructive once, but do you think you are competing today? Many of you think you are. Against whom? Against Rockefeller? About as I would if I had a wheelbarrow and competed with the Santa Fe from here to Kansas City. That is about the way you are competing, but your boys will not have even that chance if capitalism lives. You hear of the "late" panic. It is very late. It is going to be very late. This panic will be with us five years from now, and will continue from now till then.

When we have stopped clutching each others' throats, when we have stopped enslaving each other, we will stand together, hands clasped, and be friends. We will be comrades, we will be brothers, and we will begin the march to the grandest civilization the human race has ever known. . . .

Source: Eugene V. Debs, "The Issue" in *Debs: His Life, Writings and Speeches,* 3rd ed. (Chicago: Charles H. Kerr & Company Co-operative, 1910), 473–91. As transcribed December 2006 by Robert Bills and David Walters (for the Socialist Labor Party of America) on the E. V. Debs Internet Archive. Retrieved April 13, 2010, from http:// www.marxists.org/archive/debs/works/1908/issue.htm.

CHAPTER 32

Woodrow Wilson's Address for a Declaration of War, 1917

In 1916 Woodrow Wilson was reelected on the campaign slogan that "he kept us out of the war," but less than six months later he called upon Congress for a declaration of war. Before its direct involvement in the First World War, the United States had lent the Allies billions of dollars, and American industry had sold massive amounts of supplies and war materials to them too. None of this aid or material went to the Central powers, which were effectively cut off from the United States by Britain's blockade. But while honoring the British blockade, Wilson demanded the right for American ships to sail unmolested anywhere in the world, including the war zone where they were at risk of attack by German submarines. The Germans indeed sank numerous commercial vessels, killed civilians—many of them American—and their responses to Wilson's protests were unsatisfactory. Germany's employment of risky and unreliable submarine warfare ensured that its captains—however well-intentioned—would eventually make serious errors and attack civilian ships.

In 1917 two events caused Wilson to seek war: Germany's declaration of the resumption of unrestricted submarine warfare on February 1, 1917, in hopes of winning the war before the blockade effectively destroyed its will to fight; and an intercepted telegram in which the German foreign secretary, Arthur Zimmerman, proposed an alliance between Germany and Mexico. What broke the camel's back was that Zimmermann promised to support Mexico's claims to recovering the American Southwest at the conclusion of the war. As usual, Wilson couched his message in moral terms: America's rights as a neutral country, he claimed, had been grossly violated, and "the world must be made safe for democracy." Wilson pledged to stamp out all disloyal factions "with a firm hand of stern repression"—a pledge made real with the Espionage and Sedition Acts, which jailed thousands of Americans in the most high-handed suppression of civil liberties ever experienced in the United States. Congress declared war four days after

Wilson's speech, but there was widespread opposition to becoming involved in a European war.

More recent scholarship has indicated that had the United States not intervened on the side of the Allies a negotiated peace might have resulted between the belligerents, since both sides were reaching exhaustion. Whether this would have prevented the rise of Adolf Hitler is of course a matter of dispute: recent studies also suggest that conflicts that end without a clear victor are usually resumed until one is determined. Consider whether Wilson had sufficient grounds for declaring war, contrasting the reluctance of James Madison in the War of 1812 with the belligerence of Thomas Jefferson in the Barbary Coast Wars. Or were the accidental (according to the Germans) deaths on civilian liners to be laid at the door of the United States for insisting on sailing in a war zone in the first place? And if so, was Britain justified for the same reason in its impressment of captured Americans in the War of 1812?

Joint Address to Congress for a Declaration of War, April 2, 1917

GENTLEMEN OF THE CONGRESS:

I have called the Congress into extraordinary session because there are serious, very serious, choices of policy to be made, and made immediately, which it was neither right nor constitutionally permissible that I should assume the responsibility of making.

On the third of February last I officially laid before you the extraordinary announcement of the imperial German government that on and after the first day of February it was its purpose to put aside all restraints of law or of humanity and use its submarines to sink every vessel that sought to approach either the ports of Great Britain and Ireland or the western coasts of Europe or any of the ports controlled by the enemies of Germany within the Mediterranean. That had seemed to be the object of the German submarine warfare earlier in the war, but since April of last year the imperial government had somewhat restrained the commanders of its undersea craft in conformity with its promise then given to us that passenger boats should not be sunk and that due warning would be given to all other vessels which its submarines might seek to destroy when no resistance was offered or escape attempted, and care taken that their crews were given at least a fair chance to save their lives in their open boats. The precautions taken were meager and haphazard enough, as was proved in distressing instance after instance in the progress of the cruel and unmanly business, but a certain degree of restraint was observed. The new policy has swept every restriction aside. Vessels of every kind, whatever their flag, their character, their cargo, their destination, their errand, have been ruthlessly sent to the bottom: without warning and without thought of help or mercy for those on board, the vessels of friendly neutrals along with those of belligerents. Even hospital ships and ships carrying relief to the sorely bereaved and stricken people of Belgium, though the latter were provided with safe conduct through the proscribed areas by the German government itself and were distinguished by unmistakable marks of identity, have been sunk with the same reckless lack of compassion or of principle. I was for a little while unable to believe that such things would in fact be done by any government that had hitherto subscribed to the humane practices of civilized nations. International law had its origin in the attempt to set up some law which would be respected and observed upon the seas, where no nation had right of dominion and where lay the free highways of the world. . . . This minimum of right the German government has swept aside under the plea of retaliation and necessity and because it had no weapons which it could use at sea except these which it is impossible to employ as it is employing them without throwing to the winds all scruples of humanity or of respect for the understandings that were supposed to underlie the intercourse of the world. I am not now thinking of the loss of property involved, immense and serious as that is, but only of the wanton and wholesale destruction of the lives of noncombatants, men, women, and children, engaged in pursuits which have always, even in the darkest periods of modern history, been deemed innocent and legitimate. Property can be paid for; the lives of peaceful and innocent people cannot be. The present German submarine warfare against commerce is a warfare against mankind.

It is a war against all nations. American ships have been sunk, American lives taken, in ways which it has stirred us very deeply to learn of, but the ships and people of other neutral and friendly nations have been sunk and overwhelmed in the waters in the same way. There has been no discrimination. The challenge is to all mankind. Each nation must decide for itself how it will meet it. The choice we make for ourselves must be made with a moderation of counsel and a temperateness of judgment befitting our character and our motives as a nation. We must put excited feeling away. Our motive will not be revenge or the victorious assertion of the physical might of the nation, but only the vindication of right, of human right, of which we are only a single champion.

When I addressed the Congress on the twenty-sixth of February last I thought that it would suffice to assert our neutral rights with arms, our right to use the seas against unlawful interference, our right to keep our people safe against unlawful violence. But armed neutrality, it now appears, is impracticable. Because submarines are in effect outlaws when used as the German submarines have been used against merchant shipping, it is impossible to defend ships against their attacks as the law of nations has assumed that merchantmen would defend themselves against privateers or cruisers, visible craft giving chase upon the open sea. It is common prudence in such circumstances, grim necessity indeed, to endeavor to destroy them before they have shown their own intention. They must be dealt with upon sight, if dealt with at all. The German government denies the right of neutrals to use arms at all within the areas of the sea which it has proscribed, even in the defense of rights which no modern publicist has ever before questioned their right to defend. The intimation is conveyed that the armed guards which we have placed on our merchant ships will be treated as beyond the pale of law and subject to be dealt with as pirates would be. Armed neutrality is ineffectual enough at best; in such circumstances and in the face of such pretensions it is worse than ineffectual: it is likely only to produce what it was meant to prevent; it is practically certain to draw us into the war without either the rights or the effectiveness of belligerents. There is one choice we cannot make, we are incapable of making: we will not choose the path of submission and suffer the most sacred rights of our nation and our people to be ignored or violated. The wrongs against which we now array ourselves are no common wrongs; they cut to the very roots of human life.

With a profound sense of the solemn and even tragic character of the step I am taking and of the grave responsibilities which it involves, but in unhesitating obedience to what I deem my constitutional duty, I advise that the Congress declare the recent course of the imperial German government to be in fact nothing less than war against the government and people of the United States; that it formally accept the status of belligerent which has thus been thrust upon it, and that it take immediate steps not only to put the country in a more thorough state of defense but also to exert all its power and employ all its resources to bring the government of the German empire to terms and end the war.

What this will involve is clear. It will involve the utmost practicable cooperation in counsel and action with the governments now at war with Germany, and, as incident to that, the extension to those governments of the most liberal financial credit, in order that our resources may so far as possible be added to theirs. It will involve the organization and mobilization of all the material resources of the country to supply the materials of war and serve the incidental needs of the nation in the most abundant and yet the most economical and efficient way possible. It will involve the immediate full equipment of the navy in all respects but particularly in supplying it with the best means of dealing with the enemy's submarines. It will involve the immediate addition to the armed forces of the United States already provided for by law in case of war at least five hundred thousand men, who should, in my opinion, be chosen upon the principle of universal liability to service, and also the authorization of subsequent additional increments of equal force so soon as they may be needed and can be handled in training. It will involve also, of course, the granting of adequate credits to the government, sustained, I hope, so far as they can equitably be sustained by the present generation, by well-conceived taxation. I say sustained so far as may be equitable by taxation because it seems to me that it would be most unwise to base the credits which will now be necessary entirely on money borrowed. It is our duty, I most respectfully urge, to protect our people so far as we may against the very serious hardships and evils which would be likely to arise out of the inflation which would be produced by vast loans.

In carrying out the measures by which these things are to be accomplished we should keep constantly in mind the wisdom of interfering as little as possible in our own preparation and in the equipment of our own military forces with the duty—for it will be a very practical duty—of supplying the nations already at war with Germany with the materials which they can obtain only from us or by our assistance. They are in the field and we should help them in every way to be effective there.

I shall take the liberty of suggesting, through the several executive departments of the government, for the consideration of your committees, measures for the accomplishment of the several objects I have mentioned. I hope that it will be your pleasure to deal with them as having been framed after very careful thought by the branch of the government upon which the responsibility of conducting the war and safeguarding the nation will most directly fall.

While we do these things, these deeply momentous things, let us be very clear, and make very clear to all the world what our motives and our objects are. My own thought has not been driven from its habitual and normal course by the unhappy events of the last two months, and I do not believe that the thought of the nation has been altered or clouded by them. I have exactly the same things in mind now that I had in mind when I addressed the Senate on the twenty-second of January last, the same that I had in mind when I addressed the Congress on the third of February and on the twenty-sixth of February. Our object now, as then, is to vindicate the principles of peace and justice in the life of the world as against selfish and autocratic power and to set up amongst the really free and self-governed peoples of the world such a concert of purpose and of action as will henceforth insure the observance of those principles. Neutrality is no longer feasible or desirable where the peace of the world is involved and the freedom of its peoples, and the menace to that peace and freedom lies in the existence of autocratic governments backed by organized force which is controlled wholly by their will, not by the will of their people. We have seen the last of neutrality in such circumstances. We are at the beginning of an age in which it will be insisted that the same standards of conduct and of responsibility for wrong done shall be observed among nations and their governments that are observed among the individual citizens of civilized states.

We have no quarrel with the German people. We have no feeling towards them but one of sympathy and friendship. It was not upon their impulse that their government acted in entering this war. It was not with their previous knowledge or approval. It was a war determined upon as wars used to be determined upon in the old, unhappy days when peoples were nowhere consulted by their rulers and wars were provoked and waged in the interest of dynasties or of little groups of ambitious men who were accustomed to use their fellow men as pawns and tools.

Self-governed nations do not fill their neighbor states with spies or set the course of intrigue to bring about some critical posture of affairs which will give them an opportunity to strike and make conquest. Such designs can be successfully worked out only under cover and where no one has the right to ask questions. Cunningly contrived plans of deception or aggression, carried, it may be, from generation to generation, can be worked out and kept from the light only within the privacy of courts or behind the carefully guarded confidences of a narrow and privileged class. They are happily impossible where public opinion commands and insists upon full information concerning all the nation's affairs.

A steadfast concert for peace can never be maintained except by a partnership of democratic nations. No autocratic government could be trusted to keep faith within it or observe its covenants. It must be a league of honor, a partnership of opinion. Intrigue would eat its vitals away; the plottings of inner circles who could plan what they would and render account to no one would be a corruption seated at its very heart. Only free people can hold their purpose and their honor steady to a common end and prefer the interests of mankind to any narrow interest of their own.

Does not every American feel that assurance has been added to our hope for the future peace of the world by the wonderful and heartening things that have been happening within the last few weeks in Russia? Russia was known by those who knew it best to have been always in fact democratic at heart, in all the vital habits of her thought, in all the intimate relationships of her people that spoke their natural instinct, their habitual attitude towards life. The autocracy that crowned the summit of her political structure, long as it had stood and terrible as was the reality of its power, was not in fact Russian in origin, character, or purpose; and now it has been shaken off and the great, generous Russian people have been added in all their naive majesty and might to the forces that are fighting for freedom in the world, for justice, and for peace. Here is a fit partner for a league of honor.

One of the things that has served to convince us that the Prussian autocracy was not and could never be our friend is that from the very outset of the present war it has filled our unsuspecting communities and even our offices of government with spies and set criminal intrigues everywhere afoot against our national unity of counsel, our peace within and without, our industries and our commerce. Indeed it is now evident that its spies were here even before the war began; and it is unhappily not a matter of conjecture but a fact proved in our courts of justice that the intrigues which have more than once come perilously near to disturbing the peace and dislocating the industries of the country have been carried on at the instigation, with the support, and even under the personal direction of official agents of the imperial government accredited to the government of the United States. Even in checking these things and trying to extirpate them we have sought to put the most generous interpretation possible upon them because we knew that their source lay, not in any hostile feeling or purpose of the German people towards us (who were, no doubt, as ignorant of them as we ourselves were), but only in the selfish designs of a government that did what it pleased and told its people nothing. But they have played their part in serving to convince us at last that that government entertains no real friendship for us and means to act against our peace and security at its convenience. That it means to stir up enemies against us at our very doors the intercepted note to the German minister at Mexico City is eloquent evidence.

We are accepting this challenge of hostile purpose because we know that in such a government, following such methods, we can never have a friend; and that in the presence of its organized power, always lying in wait to accomplish we know not what purpose, there can be no assured security for the democratic governments of the world. We are now about to accept gauge of battle with this natural foe to liberty and shall, if necessary, spend the whole force of the nation to check and nullify its pretensions and its power. We are glad, now that we see the facts with no veil of false pretense about them to fight thus for the ultimate peace of the world and for the liberation of its peoples, the German peoples included: for the rights of nations great and small and the privilege of men everywhere to choose their way of life and of obedience. The world must be made safe for democracy. Its peace must be planted upon the tested foundations of political liberty. We have no selfish ends to serve.

We desire no conquest, no dominion. We seek no indemnities for ourselves, no material compensation for the sacrifices we shall freely make. We are but one of the champions of the rights of mankind. We shall be satisfied when those rights have been made as secure as the faith and the freedom of nations can make them. Just because we fight without rancor and without selfish object, seeking nothing for ourselves but what we shall wish to share with all free peoples, we shall, I feel confident, conduct our operations as belligerents without passion and ourselves observe with proud punctilio the principles of right and of fair play we profess to be fighting for. . . .

. . . We enter this war only where we are clearly forced into it because there are no other means of defending our rights.

It will be all the easier for us to conduct ourselves as belligerents in a high spirit of right and fairness because we act without animus, not in enmity towards a people or with the desire to bring any injury or disadvantage upon them, but only in armed opposition to an irresponsible government which has thrown aside all considerations of humanity and of right and is running amuck. We are, let me say again, the sincere friends of the German people, and shall desire nothing so much as the early reestablishment of intimate relations of mutual advantage between us—however hard it may be for them, for the time being, to believe that this is spoken from our hearts. We have borne with their present government through all these bitter months because of that friendship—exercising a patience and forbearance which would otherwise have been impossible. We shall, happily, still have an opportunity to prove that friendship in our daily attitude and actions towards the millions of men and women of German birth and native sympathy who live amongst us and share our life, and we shall be proud to prove it towards all who are in fact loyal to their neighbors and to the government in the hour of test. They are, most of them, as true and loyal Americans as if they had never known any other fealty or allegiance. They will be prompt to stand with us in rebuking and restraining the few who may be of a different mind and purpose. If there should be disloyalty, it will be dealt with a firm hand of stern repression; but, if it lifts its head at all, it will lift it only here and there and without countenance except from a lawless and malignant few.

It is a distressing and oppressive duty, Gentlemen of the Congress, which I have performed in thus addressing you. There are, it may be, many months of fiery trial and sacrifice ahead of us. It is a fearful thing to lead this great peaceful people into war, into the most terrible and disastrous of all wars, civilization itself seeming to be in the balance.

But the right is more precious than peace, and we shall fight for the things which we have always carried nearest our hearts—for democracy, for the right of those who submit to authority to have a voice in their own governments, for the rights and liberties of small nations, for a universal dominion of right by such a concert of free peoples as shall bring peace and safety to all nations and make the world itself at last free. To such a task we can dedicate our lives and our fortunes, every thing that we are and everything that we have, with the pride of those who know that the day has come when America is privileged to

spend her blood and her might for the principles that gave her birth and happiness and the peace which she has treasured. God helping her, she can do no
other.

Source: National Archives and Records Administration. Retrieved May 20, 2010,
from http://www.ourdocuments.gov/doc.php?doc=61&page=transcript.

CHAPTER 33

William E. Borah's Speech
on the League of Nations, 1919

William Borah was a progressive Republican senator from Idaho who once said, "America has risen to a position where she is respected and admired by the whole world. She did this by minding her own business . . . the American and European systems do not agree." Senator Borah railed against Wilson's intervention in Russia when he sent American troops to support the White Russian armies in Arkhangel against the Bolsheviks in 1918 and 1919, perhaps the most feckless expenditure of American lives ever engineered by a president.* The leader of the "irreconcilables" in the Senate, he was an outspoken opponent of Wilson's policy of intervention outside of the Western Hemisphere and strongly opposed ratification of the 1919 Treaty of Versailles as well as America's participation in the League of Nations. His eloquent speech made on November 19, 1919, helped swing enough senators to his side and keep the United States out of the league. Many Americans became isolationist in sentiment as a result, later blaming the Treaty of Versailles for causing World War II, due to its overly harsh treatment of Germany, and opposing U.S. involvement in the war until the attack on Pearl Harbor.

History has tended to support Senator Borah's condemnation of the Treaty of Versailles—certainly in terms of abusing the Central powers without there being a clear and defined victory on the battlefield. Many historians point to it as a major contributory factor for the rise of Nazi Germany and the outbreak of World War II. No doubt Senator Borah would also condemn the American intervention across the entire globe that we have experienced since the Civil War. The tendency of the United Nations to enthusiastically send troops on "peacekeeping" missions where self-defense is difficult would certainly be opposed vigorously, especially since the UN is reluctant to commit armed forces to defeat tyrants. Since Senator Borah was opposed to the League of Nations, an organization that

---

* E. M. Halliday, *The Ignorant Armies* (New York: Award Books, 1964), 1–304 passim.

proved to be effective only when action was detrimental to the Western republics, one hardly needs to wonder what he would say about the United Nations.

Speech on the League of Nations

WHEN THE LEAGUE SHALL HAVE BEEN FORMED, WE SHALL BE a member of what is known as the council of the league. Our accredited representative will sit in judgment with the accredited representatives of the other members of the league to pass upon the concerns not only of our country but of all Europe and all Asia and the entire world. Our accredited representatives will be members of the assembly. They will sit there to represent the judgment of these 110,000,000 people just as we are accredited here to represent our constituencies. We cannot send our representatives to sit in council with the representatives of the other great nations of the world with mental reservations as to what we shall do in case their judgment shall not be satisfactory to us. If we go to the council or to the assembly with any other purpose than that of complying in good faith and in absolute integrity with all upon which the council or the assembly may pass, we shall soon return to our country with our self-respect forfeited and the public opinion of the world condemnatory.

Why need you gentlemen across the aisle worry about a reservation here or there when we are sitting in the council and in the assembly and bound by every obligation in morals, which the president said was supreme above that of law, to comply with the judgment which our representatives and the other representatives finally form? Shall we go there, Mr. President, to sit in judgment, and in case that judgment works for peace join with our allies, but in case it works for war withdraw our cooperation? How long would we stand as we now stand a great republic commanding the respect and holding the leadership of the world, if we should adopt any such course?. . .

We have said, Mr. President, that we would not send our troops abroad without the consent of Congress. Pass by now for a moment the legal proposition. If we create executive functions, the executive will perform those functions without the authority of Congress. Pass that question by and go to the other question. Our members of the council are there. Our members of the assembly are there. Article 11 is complete, and it authorizes the league, a member of which is our representative, to deal with matters of peace and war, and the league through its council and its assembly deals with the matter, and our accredited representative joins with the others in deciding upon a certain course, which involves a question of sending troops. What will the Congress of the United States do? What right will it have left, except the bare technical right to refuse, which as a moral proposition it will not dare to exercise? Have we not been told day by day for the last nine months that the Senate of the United States, a coordinate part of the treaty-making power, should accept this league as it was written because the wise men sitting at Versailles had so written it, and has not every possible influence and every source of power in public opinion been organized and directed against the Senate to compel it to do that thing? How much stronger will be the moral compulsion upon the Congress of the United States when we ourselves have endorsed the proposition of sending our accredited representatives there to vote for us?

Ah, but you say that there must be unanimous consent, and that there is vast protection in unanimous consent.

I do not wish to speak disparagingly; but has not every division and dismemberment of every nation which has suffered dismemberment taken place by unanimous consent for the last three hundred years? Did not Prussia and Austria and Russia by unanimous consent divide Poland? Did not the United States and Great Britain and Japan and Italy and France divide China and give Shandong to Japan? Was that not a unanimous decision? Close the doors upon the diplomats of Europe, let them sit in secret, give them the material to trade on, and there always will be unanimous consent. . . .

Mr. President, if you have enough territory, if you have enough material, if you have enough subject peoples to trade upon and divide, there will be no difficulty about unanimous consent.

Do our Democratic friends ever expect any man to sit as a member of the council or as a member of the assembly equal in intellectual power and in standing before the world with that of our representative at Versailles? Do you expect a man to sit in the council who will have made more pledges, and I shall assume made them in sincerity, for self-determination and for the rights of small peoples, than had been made by our accredited representative? And yet, what became of it? The unanimous consent was obtained nevertheless.

But take another view of it. We are sending to the council one man. That one man represents 110,000,000 people.

Here, sitting in the Senate, we have two from every state in the Union, and over in the other house we have representatives in accordance with population, and the responsibility is spread out in accordance with our obligations to our constituency. But now we are transferring to one man the stupendous power of representing the sentiment and convictions of 110,000,000 people in tremendous questions which may involve the peace or may involve the war of the world. . . .

What is the result of all this? We are in the midst of all of the affairs of Europe. We have entangled ourselves with all European concerns. We have joined in alliance with all the European nations which have thus far joined the league, and all nations which may be admitted to the league. We are sitting there dabbling in their affairs and intermeddling in their concerns. In other words, Mr. President—and this comes to the question which is fundamental with me—we have forfeited and surrendered, once and for all, the great policy of "no entangling alliances" upon which the strength of this republic has been founded for 150 years.

My friends of reservations, tell me where is the reservation in these articles which protects us against entangling alliances with Europe?

Those who are differing over reservations, tell me what one of them protects the doctrine laid down by the Father of his Country. That fundamental proposition is surrendered, and we are a part of the European turmoils and conflicts from the time we enter this league. . . .

Lloyd George is reported to have said just a few days before the conference met at Versailles that Great Britain could give up much, and would be willing to sacrifice much, to have America withdraw from that policy. That was one of the great objects of the entire conference at Versailles, so far as the foreign representatives were concerned. Clemenceau and Lloyd George and others like them were willing to make any reasonable sacrifice which would draw America away from her isolation and into the internal affairs and concerns of Europe. This league of nations, with or without reservations, whatever else it does or does not do, does surrender and sacrifice that policy; and once having surrendered and become a part of the European concerns, where, my friends, are you going to stop?

You have put in here a reservation upon the Monroe Doctrine. I think that, in so far as language could protect the Monroe Doctrine, it has been protected. But as a practical proposition, as a working proposition, tell me candidly, as men familiar with the history of your country and of other countries, do you think that you can intermeddle in European affairs; and, secondly, never to permit Europe to [interfere in our affairs].

We cannot protect the Monroe Doctrine unless we protect the basic principle upon which it rests, and that is the Washington policy. I do not care how earnestly you may endeavor to do so, as a practical working proposition your league will come to the United States. . . .

Mr. President, there is another and even a more commanding reason why I shall record my vote against this treaty. It imperils what I conceive to be the underlying, the very first principles of this republic. It is in conflict with the right of our people to govern themselves free from all restraint, legal or moral, of foreign powers. . . .

Sir, since the debate opened months ago those of us who have stood against this proposition have been taunted many times with being little Americans. Leave us the word American, keep that in your presumptuous impeachment, and no taunt can disturb us, no gibe discompose our purposes. Call us little Americans if you will, but leave us the consolation and the pride which the term American, however modified, still imparts. . . . We have sought nothing save the tranquility of our own people and the honor and independence of our own republic. No foreign flattery, no possible world glory and power have disturbed our poise or come between us and our devotion to the traditions which have made us a people or the policies which have made us a nation, unselfish and commanding. If we have erred we have erred out of too much love for those things which from childhood you and we together have been taught to revere—yes, to defend even at the cost of limb and life. If we have erred it is because we have placed too high an estimate upon the wisdom of Washington and Jefferson, too exalted an opinion upon the patriotism of the sainted Lincoln. . . .

Senators, even in an hour so big with expectancy we should not close our eyes to the fact that democracy is something more, vastly more, than a mere form of government by which society is restrained into free and orderly life. It is a moral entity, a spiritual force, as well. And these are things which live only and alone in the atmosphere of liberty. The foundation upon which democracy rests is faith in the moral instincts of the people. Its ballot boxes, the franchise, its laws, and constitutions are but the outward manifestations of the deeper and more essential thing—a continuing trust in the moral purposes of the average man and woman. When this is lost or forfeited your outward forms, however democratic in terms, are a mockery. Force may find expression through institutions democratic in structure equal with the simple and more direct processes of a single supreme ruler. These distinguishing virtues of a real republic you cannot commingle with the discordant and destructive forces of the Old World and still preserve them. You cannot yoke a government whose fundamental maxim is that of liberty to a government whose first law is that of force and hope to preserve the former. These things are in eternal war, and one must ultimately destroy the other. You may still keep for a time the outward form, you may still delude yourself, as others have done in the past, with appearances and symbols, but when you shall have committed this republic to a scheme of world control based upon force, upon the combined military force of the four great nations of the world, you will have soon destroyed the atmosphere of freedom, of confidence in the self-governing capacity of the masses, in which alone a democracy may thrive. We may become one of the four dictators of the world, but we shall no longer be master of our own spirit. And what shall it profit us as a nation if we shall go forth to the domination of the earth and share with others the glory of world control and lose that fine sense of confidence in the people, the soul of democracy?

Look upon the scene as it is now presented. Behold the task we are to assume, and then contemplate the method by which we are to deal with this task. Is the method such as to address itself to a government "conceived in liberty and dedicated to the proposition that all men are created equal"? When this league, this combination, is formed four great powers representing the dominant people will rule one-half of the inhabitants of the globe as subject peoples—rule by force, and we shall be a party to the rule of force. There is no other way by which you can keep people in subjection. You must either give them independence, recognize their rights as nations to live their own life and to set up their own form of government, or you must deny them these things by force. That is the scheme, the method proposed by the league. It proposes no other. We will in time become inured to its inhuman precepts and its soulless methods strange as this doctrine now seems to a free people. If we stay with our contract, we will come in time to declare with our associates that force—force, the creed of the Prussian military oligarchy—is after all the true foundation upon which must rest all stable governments. Korea, despoiled and bleeding at every pore; India, sweltering in ignorance and burdened with inhuman taxes after more than one hundred years of dominant rule; Egypt, trapped and robbed of her birthright; Ireland, with seven hundred years of sacrifice for independence—this is the task, this is the atmosphere, and this is the creed in and under which we are to keep alive our belief in the moral purposes and self-governing capacity of the people, a belief without which the republic must disintegrate and die. The maxim of liberty will soon give way to the rule of blood and iron. We have been pleading here for our Constitution. Conform this league, it has been said, to the technical terms of our charter, and all will be well. But I declare to you that we must go further and conform to those sentiments and passions for justice and freedom which are essential to the existence of democracy. . . .

Sir, we are told that this treaty means peace. Even so, I would not pay the price. Would you purchase peace at the cost of any part of our independence? We could have had peace in 1776—the price was high, but we could have had it. James Otis, Sam Adams, Hancock, and Warren were surrounded by those who urged peace and British rule. All through that long and trying struggle, particularly when the clouds of adversity lowered upon the cause, there was a cry of peace—let us have peace. We could have had peace in 1860; Lincoln was counseled by men of great influence and accredited wisdom to let our brothers—and, thank heaven, they are brothers—depart in peace. But the tender, loving Lincoln, bending under the fearful weight of impending civil war, an apostle of peace, refused to pay the price, and a reunited country will praise his name forevermore—bless it because he refused peace at the price of national honor and national integrity. Peace upon any other basis than national independence, peace purchased at the cost of any part of our national integrity, is fit only for slaves, and even when purchased at such a price it is a delusion, for it cannot last.

But your treaty does not mean peace—far, very far, from it. If we are to judge the future by the past, it means war. Is there any guaranty of peace other than the guaranty which comes of the control of the war-making power by the people? Yet what great rule of democracy does the treaty leave unassailed? The people in whose keeping alone you can safely lodge the power of peace or war nowhere, at no time and in no place, have any voice in this scheme for world peace. Autocracy which has bathed the world in blood for centuries reigns supreme. Democracy is everywhere excluded. This, you say, means peace.

Can you hope for peace when love of country is disregarded in your scheme, when the spirit of nationality is rejected, even scoffed at? Yet what law of that moving and mysterious force does your treaty not deny? With a ruthlessness unparalleled your treaty in a dozen instances runs counter to the divine law of nationality. Peoples who speak the same language, kneel at the same ancestral tombs, moved by the same traditions, animated by a common hope, are torn asunder, broken in pieces, divided, and parceled out to antagonistic nations. And this you call justice. This, you cry, means peace. Peoples who have dreamed of independence, struggled and been patient, sacrificed and been hopeful, peoples who were told that through this peace conference they should realize the aspirations of centuries, have again had their hopes dashed to earth. One of the most striking and commanding figures in this war, soldier and statesmen, turned away from the peace table at Versailles declaring to the world, "The promise of the new life, the victory of the great humane ideals for which the peoples have shed their blood and their treasure without stint, the fulfillment of their aspirations toward a new international order and a fairer and better world, are not written into the treaty." No, your treaty means injustice. It means slavery. It means war. And to all this you ask this republic to become a party. You ask it to abandon the creed under which it has grown to power and accept the creed of autocracy, the creed of repression and force.

Source: MultiEducator, Inc., "William E. Borah—Speech On The League of Nations, Nov. 19, 1919," Retrieved May 15, 2010, from http://www.historycentral.com/documents/Borah.html.

CHAPTER 34

On the Principles of Progressive Education, Association for the Advancement of Progressive Education, 1919

In 1919 the Association for the Advancement of Progressive Education (AAPE) was formed to promote the ideas and principles of the American atheist philosopher John Dewey. The intent was to form an educational resource and political pressure group to reform the American educational system, starting with the public schools. Not the least of its precepts, although normally unstated, was the elimination of religion from the educational process. Hegelian dialectics were adapted for classroom teaching, and education was intended, not just to impart knowledge, but to teach students how to live. Students were to be allowed to progress at their own pace, encouraged rather than discouraged through testing, and teachers were to be facilitators in the learning process rather than stern instructors. By the 1940s some school districts no longer assigned grades on the old A, B, C, D, F system but rather gave out evaluations in three designations: PN for "progressing normally," N for "normal," and U for "unsatisfactory progress." Behavior was rated S for "satisfactory" progress and U for "unsatisfactory."* Parents, however, equated the notations to A, C, and F. Other schools reverted to the "little red schoolhouse" concept of having no separate classrooms, with teachers instructing circles of students who moved from circle to circle in accordance with their progress.† In most cases competition between students was shunned as counterproductive and antisocial. This trend evolved to its highest form in the 1990s, when some schools ceased having valedictorians lest other students feel inferior.

The result of such innovations was to dramatically lower the educational attainments of students in public schools and force colleges to offer remedial courses before they could be admitted. Community colleges took up the slack and offered both adult and remedial education, sometimes going as far back as

---

* Denver, Colorado, public schools, 1948–52: author's personal experience.
† Mentor, Ohio, public schools, 1970–74: author's personal experience.

third-grade concepts. Educational departments in universities were seen as dumping grounds for the less able, and academic degrees in education were considered far below those of other academic disciplines. Progressive education principles are still in vogue today, and the federal government has thrown billions into programs to increase learning, with little effect. The principles below were adopted by the AAPE shortly after its creation. The reader should match these principles to those in effect in classrooms today. In addition, Dewey's concept of teaching students how to live presupposes a standard humanistic value system that is universally in effect. One could challenge such educational goals as being inconsistent with individual liberty and the principles of a representative democracy.

Statement of Progressive Educational Principles

1. The conduct of the pupil should be self-governed according to the social needs of his community rather than by arbitrary laws. This does not mean that liberty should be allowed to become license, or that the teacher should not exercise authority when it proves necessary. Full opportunity for initiative and self-expression should be provided, together with an environment rich in interesting material that is available for the free use of every pupil.

2. Interest should be satisfied and developed through: (1) direct and indirect contact with the world and its activities, and use of the experience thus gained; (2) application of knowledge gained, and correlation between different subjects; (3) the consciousness of achievement.

3. It is important that teachers believe in the aims and general principles of progressive education. They should be thoroughly prepared for the profession of teaching, and should have latitude for the development of initiative and originality. They should be possessed of personality and character, and should be as much at home in all the activities of the school, such as the pupils' play, their dramatic productions, and their social gatherings, as they are in the classroom. Ideal teaching conditions demand that classes be small, especially in the elementary school years.

   Progressive teachers will encourage the use of all the senses, training the pupils in both observation and judgment; and, instead of hearing recitations only, will spend most of the time teaching how to use various sources of information, including life activities as well as books; how to reason about the information thus acquired; and how to express forcefully and logically the conclusions reached. Teachers will inspire a desire for knowledge and will serve as guides in the investigations undertaken, rather than taskmasters.

To be a proper inspiration to their pupils, teachers must have ample opportunity and encouragement for self-improvement and for the development of broad interests.

4. School records should not be confined to the marks given by the teachers to show the advancement of the pupils in their study of subjects, but should also include both objective and subjective reports on those physical, mental, moral, and social characteristics which affect both school and adult life, and which can be influenced by the school and the home.

   Such records should be used as a guide for the treatment of each pupil, and should also serve to focus the attention of the teacher on the all-important work of development rather than on simply teaching subject matter.

5. One of the first considerations of progressive education is the health of the pupils. Much more room in which to move about, better light and air, clean and well-ventilated buildings, easier access to the out-of-doors and greater use of it are all necessary. There should be frequent use of adequate playgrounds.

   The teachers should observe closely the physical condition of each pupil in cooperation with a school physician, who should examine the children at stated intervals.

6. The school should provide, with the home, as much as possible of all that the natural interests and activities of the child demand, especially during the elementary school years. It should give opportunity for manual experience for both boys and girls, for homemaking, and for healthful recreation of various kinds. Most, if not all, of a child's studying should be done at the school and such extra-curriculum studies as a child may take should be at the school or home, so that there will be no unnecessary dissipation of energy.

   These conditions can come about only through intelligent cooperation between parents and teachers. It is the duty of the parents to know what the school is doing and why, and to find out the most effective way to cooperate. It is the duty of the school to help the parents to a broader outlook on education and to make available all the resources of the school that can give information or help to the home.

7. The progressive school should be a leader in educational movements. It should be a laboratory where new ideas, if worthy, meet encouragement; where tradition alone does not rule, but the best of the past is leavened with the discoveries of today and the result is freely added to the sum of educational knowledge.

Source: Lawrence A. Cremin, *The Transformation of the School: Progressivism in American Education, 1876–1957* (New York: Vintage Books, 1961), 243–5.

V

THE ROARING TWENTIES, NEW DEAL, AND WORLD WAR II

As the low-tax, small-government policies of presidents Warren G. Harding and Calvin Coolidge and secretary of the treasury Andrew Mellon aided the economic boom that buoyed the era known as the Roaring Twenties, America moved into a golden decade. It was terminated by the stunning and severe crash of the stock market in 1929—which some argue was triggered by the Smoot-Hawley Tariff Act, which raised taxes on hundreds of imported items, some substantially, clearing a key committee vote in Congress—and became a recession due to contributing Federal Reserve policies.* President Herbert Hoover, a superb engineer and good organizer, was over his head in attempting to deal with the Great Depression that followed. His instinct was to follow Progressive solutions of "more government," and his programs only worsened the economic distress. It is a myth that Franklin D. Roosevelt, elected in 1932, "saved" American capitalism—indeed, his programs made the depression worse; the nation was little different in 1939 than in 1933. Military spending in 1940 began to revive some industries, but military goods were only useful in a war. Roosevelt also pursued social legislation such as creating Social Security, the National Labor Relations Board and labor laws, taxation rates of 90 percent, and government programs to manage the economy. The ravages of the Depression and disgust over European perfidy prevented Americans from confronting the rise of Nazi Germany. Roosevelt relocated the Pacific Fleet to Hawaii in 1940, funded a doubling of the Navy's tonnage, and initiated trade restrictions and finally an embargo in efforts to curb Japanese aggression, all of which finally culminated

---

* Liaquat Ahamed, *Lords of Finance: The Bankers Who Broke the World* (New York: Penguin Press, 2009), 275–6; Jude Wanniski, *The Way the World Works* (New York: Basic Books, 1978); Douglas A. Irwin, *Against the Tide: An Intellectual History of Free Trade* (Princeton, NJ: Princeton University Press, 1996).

in the attack on Pearl Harbor. While a shock to the American public, the Japanese had (in the apocryphal words) "awakened a sleeping giant." America already—without the provocation of war—could outproduce Japan many times over in any single industrial good. With the incentive of military victory over a treacherous foe, the Americans would prove unstoppable.

Even before the end of World War II, it was clear that world hegemony would be split between the Soviet Union and the United States, but Roosevelt continued to push for additional social legislation such as that indicated by his "second Bill of Rights." The Yalta Agreement created the postwar spheres of influence for the winners, and like it or not America now had worldwide responsibilities. The United States had come a long way from barely attaining a draw in the War of 1812, 132 years earlier, and now stood as one of only two superpowers in the world.

CHAPTER 35

On Policies in the Regulation of Business, Herbert Hoover, 1924

Perhaps the only American to return from the negotiations resulting in the Treaty of Versailles with his reputation enhanced, Herbert Hoover, the head of the American Relief Administration, was a favorite for political office. Both the Republican and Democratic parties sought him as a candidate, but Hoover declared himself a Republican and became secretary of commerce in the Harding and Coolidge administrations. A brilliant mining engineer, who developed new methods for the extraction and production of copper, Hoover had proven adept in all the managerial posts to which he was appointed. Unluckily, Hoover was elected president in 1928 just before the crash, and his progressive fiscal policies, which actually differed little, if at all, from those of his successor, Franklin D. Roosevelt, proved ineffectual to stop the slide into economic depression while the Federal Reserve kept the country on the gold standard.

On May 7, 1924, Hoover gave a speech at the annual meeting of the U.S. Chamber of Commerce in Cleveland, Ohio, on unfair competition and business ethics. A Quaker, Hoover operated possibly on a higher moral plane than even Wilson, and he believed businessmen should be held to a higher standard than politicians since their activities were strictly voluntary. Hoover's stewardship as president during the stock market crash and Great Depression defined his place in American history. Wedded to Progressive doctrines of higher taxes and government activism, Hoover made an already bad situation worse. The reader should consider Hoover's very modern approach toward the regulation of business with legislation and the imposition of standards that is evident in this speech, excerpted below. These ideas and principles ultimately came to be commonplace in American business, and instead of government promulgating new laws and regulations without business involvement, we see that Hoover's call for joint government and business efforts was well heeded. The result was special-interest lobbies and industry representatives writing legislation. In many respects, this speech was truly Hoover's main legacy to the United States. Has it led to positive developments, and was it what Hoover intended?

Address at the Annual Meeting of the U.S. Chamber of Commerce, May 7, 1924

THE ADVANCEMENT OF SCIENCE AND OUR INCREASING POPU-lation require constantly new standards of conduct and breed an increasing multitude of new rules and regulations. The basic principles laid down in the Ten Commandments and the Sermon on the Mount are as applicable today as when they were declared, but they require a host of subsidiary clauses. The ten ways to evil in the time of Moses have increased to ten thousand now. . . .

A whole host of rules and regulations are necessary to maintain human rights with this amazing transformation into an industrial era. Ten people in a whole country, with a plow apiece, did not elbow each other very much. But when we put seven million people in a country with the tools of electric, steam, thirty-floor buildings, telephones, miscellaneous noises, streetcars, railways, motors, stock exchanges, and what not, then we do jostle each other in a multitude of directions. Thereupon our lawmakers supply the demand by the ceaseless piling up of statutes. . . .

Moreover, with increasing education our sense become more offended and our moral discriminations increase; for all of which we discover new things to remedy. In one of our states over one thousand laws and ordinances have been added in the last eight months. It is also true that a large part of them will sleep peacefully in the statute book.

The question we need to consider is whether these rules and regulations are to be developed solely by government or whether they cannot be in some large part developed out of voluntary forces in the nation. In other words, can the abuses which give rise to government in business be eliminated by the systematic and voluntary action of commerce and industry itself? . . .

National character cannot be built by law. It is the sum of the moral fiber of its individuals. When abuses which rise from our growing system are cured by live individual conscience, by initiative in the creation of voluntary standards, then is the growth of moral perceptions fertilized in every individual character.

No one disputes the necessity for constantly new standards of conduct in relation to all these tools and inventions. Even our latest great invention—radio—has brought a host of new questions. No one disputed that much of these subsidiary additions to the Ten Commandments must be made by leg-islation. Our public utilities are wasteful and costly unless we give them a privilege more or less monopolistic. At once when we have business affected with monopoly we must have regulation by law. Much of even this phase might have been unnecessary had there been a higher degree of responsibility to the public, higher standards of business practice among those who dominated these agencies in years gone by. . . .

When legislation penetrates the business world it is because there is abuse somewhere. A great deal of this legislation is due rather to the inability of business hitherto to so organize as to correct abuses than to any lack of desire to have it done. Sometimes the abuses are more apparent than real, but anything is a handle for demagoguery. In the main, however, the public acts only when it has lost confidence in the ability or willingness of business to correct its own abuses.

Legislative action is always clumsy—it is incapable of adjustment to shifting needs. It often enough produces new economic currents more abusive than those intended to be cured. Government too often becomes the persecutor instead of the regulator.

The thing we all need to searchingly consider is the practical question of the method by which the business world can develop and enforce its own standards and thus stem the tide of governmental regulation. The cure does not lie in mere opposition. It lies in the correction of abuse. It lies in an adaptability to changing human outlook.

The problem of business ethics as a prevention of abuse is of two categories: those where the standard must be one of individual moral perceptions, and those where we must have a determination of standards of conduct for a whole group in order that there may be a basis for ethics.

The standards of honesty, of a sense of mutual obligation, and of service were determined two thousand years ago. They may require at times to be recalled. And the responsibility for them increases infinitely in high places either in business or government, for there rests the high responsibility for leadership in fineness of moral perception. Their failure is a blow at the repute of business and at confidence in government itself.

The second field, and the one which I am primarily discussing, is the great area of indirect economic wrong and unethical practices that spring up under the pressures of competition and habit. There is also the great field of economic waste through destructive competition, through strikes, booms and slumps, unemployment, through the failure of our different industries to synchronize, and a hundred other causes which directly lower our productivity and employment. Waste may be abstractly unethical, but in any event it can be remedied by economic action.

If we are to find solutions to these collective issues outside of government regulation, we must meet two practical problems:

First, there must be organization in such form as can establish the standards of conduct in this vast complex of shifting invention, production, and use. There is no existing basis to check the failure of service or the sacrifice of public interest. Someone must determine such standards. They must be determined and held flexibly in tune with the intense technology of trade.

Second, there must be some sort of enforcement. There is the perpetual difficulty of a small minority who will not play the game. They too often bring disrepute upon the vast majority; they drive many others to adopt unfair competitive methods which all deplore; their abuses give rise to public indignation and clamor which breed legislative action.

I believe we now for the first time have the method at hand for voluntarily organized determination of standards and their adoption. I would go further; I believe we are in the presence of a new era in the organization of industry and commerce in which, if properly directed, lie forces pregnant with infinite possibilities of moral progress. I believe that we are, almost unnoticed, in the midst of a great revolution—or perhaps a better word, a transformation in the whole superorganization of our economic life. We are passing from a period of extremely individualistic action into a period of associational activities.

Practically our entire American working world is now organized into some form of economic association. We have trade associations and trade institutes embracing particular industries and occupations. We have chambers of commerce embracing representatives of different industries and commerce. We have the labor unions representing the different crafts. We have associations embracing all the different professions—law, engineering, medicine, banking, real estate, and what not. We have farmers' associations, and we have the enormous growth of farmers' cooperatives for actual dealing in commodities. Of indirect kin to this is the great increase in ownership of industries by their employees and customers, and again we have a tremendous expansion of mutualized insurance and banking.

Associational activities are, I believe, driving upon a new road where the objectives can be made wholly and vitally of public interest. . . .

Three years of study and intimate contact with the associations of economic groups, whether in production, distribution, labor, or finance, convince me that there lies within them a great moving impulse toward betterment.

If these organizations accept as their primary purpose the lifting of standards, if they will cooperate together for voluntary enforcement of high standards, we shall have proceeded far along the road of the elimination of government from business. . . .

The test of our whole economic and social system is its capacity to cure it own abuses. New abuses and new relationships to the public interest will occur as long as we continue to progress. If we are to be wholly dependent upon government to cure these abuses, we shall by this very method have created an enlarged and deadening abuse through the extension of bureaucracy and the clumsy and incapable handling of delicate economic forces. . . .

American business needs a lifting purpose greater than the struggle of materialism. Nor can it lie in some evanescent, emotional, dramatic crusade. It lies in the higher pitch of economic life, in a finer regard for the rights of others, a stronger devotion to obligations of citizenship that will assure an improved leadership in every community and the nation; it lies in the organization of the forces of our economic life so that they may product happier individual lives, more secure in employment and comfort, wider in the possibilities of enjoyment of nature, larger in its opportunities of intellectual life.

Source: *The Hoover Policies*, ed. Ray Lyman Wilbur and Arthur Mastick Hyde (New York: Charles Scribner's Sons, 1937), 301–4.

CHAPTER 36

On Principles of Taxation, Andrew W. Mellon, 1924

Andrew William Mellon was the son of Scots-Irish immigrants and head of the Mellon banking family of Pittsburgh, Pennsylvania. Very early in life he showed great aptitude for finance and in 1921 was made secretary of the treasury, a post he held until 1932. He was the first proponent of the idea that lowering taxes stimulated business and therefore resulted in increased tax revenues. In 1924 Mellon wrote a book, based on a series of earlier essays outlining his opinions on taxation, called *Taxation: The People's Business*, the first chapter of which, "Fundamental Principles," is excerpted here. His policies did much to create the prosperity of the 1920s, and as Treasury secretary he was able to reduce the debt piled up under Wilson by almost 40 percent. From a tax rate of 73 percent on incomes over $300,000 producing 20 percent of federal revenue, in 1926 a 25 percent rate on such incomes accounted for 65 percent of the revenue. Lower taxes meant more revenue, and Mellon intuitively knew that it was the private sector, not government, which was the engine of economic growth.

Later Mellon was demonized by the Roosevelt administration as one of the architects of the Great Depression, although that honor actually belonged to the Federal Reserve chairman as well as to Herbert Hoover and FDR himself. Roosevelt initiated a vicious smear campaign against Mellon and intensely audited his tax returns. A grand jury refused to indict Mellon, and a civil trial exonerated him. Roosevelt's actions were most likely politically motivated since FDR raised tax rates to 80 percent on the highest incomes by 1935 and to 90 percent by 1940—actions directly opposite to Mellon's in the 1920s. Mellon's policies were vindicated under John F. Kennedy, Ronald Reagan, and George W. Bush but are under attack again today as "tax cuts for the rich." A graduated income tax seems inevitable now under all circumstances, and the reader is invited to determine what might be fair and what might yield the most revenue. The question of taxation now seems to be more political than economic, particularly when attempting to pay down the national debt. How does Mellon see the role of taxes in the economy?

From *Taxation: The People's Business*

THE PROBLEM OF THE GOVERNMENT IS TO FIX RATES WHICH will bring in a maximum amount of revenue to the Treasury and at the same time bear not too heavily on the taxpayer or on business enterprises. A sound tax policy must take into consideration three factors. It must produce sufficient revenue for the government; it must lessen, so far as possible, the burden of taxation on those least able to bear it; and it must also remove those influences which might retard the continued steady development of business and industry on which, in the last analysis, so much of our prosperity depends. Furthermore, a permanent tax system should be designed, not merely for one or two years nor for the effect it may have on any given class of taxpayers but should be worked out with regard to conditions over a long period and with a view to its ultimate effect on the prosperity of the country as a whole. These are the principles on which the Treasury's tax policy is based, and any revision of taxes which ignores these fundamental principles will prove merely a makeshift and must eventually be replaced by a system based on economic rather than political considerations. . . .

I have never viewed taxation as a means of rewarding one class of taxpayers or punishing another. If such a point of view ever controls our public policy, the traditions of freedom, justice, and equality of opportunity, which are the distinguishing characteristics of our American civilization, will have disappeared and in their place we shall have class legislation with all its attendant evils. . . . Any man of energy and initiative in this country can get what he wants out of life. But when that initiative is crippled by legislation or by a tax system which denies him the right to receive a reasonable share of his earnings, then he will no longer exert himself and the country will be deprived of the energy on which its continued greatness depends.

This condition has already begun to make itself felt as a result of the present unsound basis of taxation. The existing tax system is an inheritance from the war. During that time the highest taxes ever levied by any country were borne uncomplainingly by the American people for the purpose of defraying the unusual and ever increasing expenses incident to the successful conduct of a great war. Normal tax rates were increased, and a system of surtaxes was evolved in order to make the man of large income pay more proportionately than the smaller taxpayer. If he had twice as much income, he paid not twice as much but three or four times as much tax. For a short time the surtaxes yielded a large revenue.

But since the close of the war people have come to look upon them as a business expense and have treated them accordingly by avoiding payment as much as possible. The history of taxation shows that taxes which are inherently excessive are not paid. The high rates inevitably put pressure upon the taxpayer to withdraw his capital from productive business and invest it in tax-exempt securities or to find other lawful methods of avoiding the realization of taxable income. The result is that the sources of taxation are drying up; wealth is failing to carry its share of the tax burden; and capital is being diverted into channels which yield neither revenue to the government nor profit to the people. . . .

Adam Smith, in his great work *Wealth of Nations*, laid down as the first maxim of taxation that "The subjects of every state ought to contribute toward the support of the government, as nearly as possible, in proportion to their respective abilities," and in his fourth and last maxim, that "Every tax ought to be so contrived as both to take out and to keep out of the pockets of the people as little as possible over and above what it brings into the public treasury of the state," citing as one of the ways by which this last maxim is violated a tax which "may obstruct the industry of the people, and discourage them from applying to certain branches of business which might give maintenance and employment to great multitudes. . . . While it obliges the people to pay, it may thus diminish, or perhaps destroy, some of the funds, which might enable them more easily to do so."

The further experience of 150 years since this was written has emphasized the truth of these maxims, but those who argue against a reduction of surtaxes to more nearly peacetime figures cite only the first maxim and ignore the fourth. The principle that a man should pay taxes in accordance with his "ability to pay" is sound but, like all other statements, and when, as a result of an excessive or unsound basis of taxation, it becomes evident that the source of taxation is drying up and wealth is being diverted into unproductive channels. . . . then it is time to readjust our basis of taxation upon sound principles.

It seems difficult for some to understand that high rates of taxation do not necessarily mean large revenue to the government and that more revenue may often be obtained by lower rates. . . .

Experience has shown that the present high rates of surtax are bringing in each year progressively less revenue to the government. This means that the price is too high to the large taxpayer and he is avoiding a taxable income by the many ways which are available to him. What rates will bring in the largest revenue to the government experience has not yet developed, but it is estimated that by cutting the surtaxes in half, the government, when the full effect of the reduction is felt, will receive more revenue from the owners of large incomes at the lower rates of tax than it would have received at the higher rates. . . .

If we consider, however, the far more important subject of the effect of the present high surtax rates on the development and prosperity of our country, then the necessity for a change is more apparent. The most noteworthy characteristic of the American people is their initiative. It is this spirit which has developed America, and it was the same spirit in our soldiers which made our armies successful abroad. If the spirit of business adventure is killed, this country will cease to hold the foremost position in the world. And yet it is this very spirit which excessive surtaxes are now destroying. Anyone at all in touch with affairs knows of his own knowledge of buildings which have not been built, of businesses which have not been started, and of new projects which have been abandoned, all for one reason—high surtaxes. If failure attends, the loss is borne exclusively by the adventurer, but if success ensures, the government takes more than half of the profits. People argue the risk is not worth the return.

With the open invitation to all men who have wealth to be relieved from taxation by the simple expedient of investing in the more that $12 billion of tax-exempt securities now available, and which would be unaffected by any constitutional amendment, the rich need not pay taxes. We violate Adam Smith's first maxim. Where these high surtaxes do bear is not on the man who has acquired and holds available wealth but on the man who, through his own initiative, is making wealth. The idle man is relieved; the producer is penalized. We violate the fourth maxim. We do not reach the people in proportion to their ability to pay and we destroy the initiative which produces the wealth in which the whole country should share and which is the source of revenue to the government. . . .

High taxation, even it levied upon an economic basis, affects the prosperity of the country, because in its ultimate analysis the burden of all taxes rests only in part upon the individual or property taxed. It is largely borne by the ultimate consumer. High taxation means a high price level and high cost of living. A reduction in taxes, therefore, results not only in an immediate saving to the individual or property directly affected but an ultimate saving to all people in the country.

It can safely be said that a reduction in the income tax reduces expenses not only of the income taxpayers but of the entire 110 million people in the United States. It is for this basic reason that the present question of tax reform is not how much each individual taxpayer reduces his direct contribution . . . ; the real problem to determine is what plan results in the least burden to the people and the most revenue to the government.

Source: Andrew W. Mellon, *Taxation: The People's Business* (New York: The Macmillan Company, 1924), 9–22. Reprinted with the permission of Scribner, a division of Simon & Schuster, Inc., from TAXATION: THE PEOPLE'S BUSINESS by Andrew W. Mellon. Copyright © 1952 by Nora McMullen Mellon. All rights reserved.

CHAPTER 37

On Social Security, Franklin D. Roosevelt, 1935

In 1932 the Democrats had included planks in their campaign platform for old-age relief and unemployment benefits to offset some of the effects of the Depression. As drafted in 1934 by the President's Committee on Economic Security, payments to retirees and relief for the elderly were to be managed by a new federal program, while unemployment compensation, aid to dependent children, child welfare, public health services, and assistance to the blind would be handled by the states with federal funding. Franklin D. Roosevelt introduced the initiative to Congress in the speech below on January 17, 1935, and Congress voted Social Security into law on August 14, 1935. The new law was soon tested for constitutionality, and unlike the Agricultural Adjustment Act, the National Industrial Recovery Act, and the Railroad Retirement Act, Social Security passed the Court's muster as falling within the purview of the Constitution's general welfare clause (article 1, section 8: "The Congress shall have Power To . . . provide for the . . . general Welfare of the United States. . . .").

The program, in which retirees would receive benefits paid for by those still working, was held by the Court as not qualifying as an annuity, and no one paying money into the system earned a right to receive back his paid-in money. The benefit grew to become the largest government benefit program in the world, representing well over 20 percent of the federal budget. Although an accounting fiction of a "trust fund" was set up, every dollar contributed to the Social Security program was immediately put into the general revenue fund and spent by Congress on whatever it desired at the time. Although estimates vary (depending on the definition of payees and recipients), at the time it was instituted Social Security saw between ten and fourteen workers paying into the system for every recipient receiving a check. In 2010, the ratio was about three to one, and within twenty years, some forecasts anticipate that the ratio will be one to three.

Curiously, Social Security coverage was not at first generally extended to women and minorities: about two-thirds of working blacks were not covered as well as almost half of all employed women. Agricultural workers were excluded in the act, and married women usually received benefits only through their husbands or because of their children. In selling his program, FDR promised that no worker would ever pay more than 1 percent of his income in Social Security tax. By 2010, self-employed persons would be paying 15.3 percent of their income in "self-employment tax," which covers both Social Security and Medicare. Is this a case of the camel's nose getting in the tent? Is Social Security, as critics suggest, a Ponzi scheme? Why are federal employees and certain other occupations excluded from paying into Social Security? FDR argued for the government system to eventually be supplanted by private accounts, yet that did not happen. What institutional barriers did Roosevelt intentionally or unintentionally create that prevented this private retirement system from developing?

Message to Congress on Social Security, January 17, 1935

IN ADDRESSING YOU ON JUNE 8, 1934, I SUMMARIZED THE MAIN objectives of our American program. Among these was, and is, the security of the men, women, and children of the nation against certain hazards and vicissitudes of life. This purpose is an essential part of our task. In my annual message to you I promised to submit a definite program of action. This I do in the form of a report to me by a Committee on Economic Security, appointed by me for the purpose of surveying the field and of recommending the basis of legislation.

I am gratified with the work of this committee and of those who have helped it: The Technical Board on Economic Security drawn from various departments of the government, the Advisory Council on Economic Security, consisting of informed and public-spirited private citizens, and a number of other advisory groups, including a committee on actuarial consultants, a medical advisory board, a dental advisory committee, a hospital advisory committee, a public health advisory committee, a child welfare committee, and an advisory committee on employment relief. All of those who participated in this notable task of planning this major legislative proposal are ready and willing, at any time, to consult with and assist in any way the appropriate congressional committees and members, with respect to detailed aspects.

It is my best judgment that this legislation should be brought forward with a minimum of delay. Federal action is necessary to, and conditioned upon, the action of states. Forty-four legislatures are meeting or will meet soon. In order that the necessary state action may be taken promptly it is important that the federal government proceed speedily.

The detailed report of the committee sets forth a series of proposals that will appeal to the sound sense of the American people. It has not attempted the impossible, nor has it failed to exercise sound caution and consideration of all of the factors concerned: the national credit, the rights and responsibilities of states, the capacity of industry to assume financial responsibilities, and the fundamental necessity of proceeding in a manner that will merit the enthusiastic support of citizens of all sorts.

It is overwhelmingly important to avoid any danger of permanently discrediting the sound and necessary policy of federal legislation for economic security by attempting to apply it on too ambitious a scale before actual experience has provided guidance for the permanently safe direction of such efforts. The place of such a fundamental in our future civilization is too precious to be jeopardized now by extravagant action. It is a sound idea—a sound ideal. Most of the other advanced countries of the world have already adopted it and their experience affords the knowledge that social insurance can be made a sound and workable project.

Three principles should be observed in legislation on this subject. First, the system adopted, except for the money necessary to initiate it, should be self-sustaining in the sense that funds for the payment of insurance benefits should not come from the proceeds of general taxation. Second, excepting in old-age insurance, actual management should be left to the states subject to standards established by the federal government. Third, sound financial management of the funds and the reserves, and protection of the credit structure of the nation, should be assured by retaining federal control over all funds through trustees in the Treasury of the United States.

At this time, I recommend the following types of legislation looking to economic security:

1. Unemployment compensation.
2. Old-age benefits, including compulsory and voluntary annuities.
3. Federal aid to dependent children through grants to states for the support of existing mothers' pension systems and for services for the protection and care of homeless, neglected, dependent, and crippled children.
4. Additional federal aid to state and local public health agencies and the strengthening of the federal Public Health Service. I am not at this time recommending the adoption of so called "health insurance," although groups representing the medical profession are cooperating with the federal government in the further study of the subject and definite progress is being made.

With respect to unemployment compensation, I have concluded that the most practical proposal is the levy of a uniform federal payroll tax, 90 percent of which should be allowed as an offset to employers contributing under a compulsory state unemployment compensation act. The purpose of this is to afford a requirement of a reasonably uniform character for all states cooperating with the federal government and to promote and encourage the passage of unemployment compensation laws in the states. The 10 percent not thus offset should be used to cover the costs of federal and state administration of this broad system. Thus, states will largely administer unemployment compensation, assisted and guided by the federal government. An unemployment compensation system should be constructed in such a way as to afford every practicable aid and incentive toward the larger purpose of employment stabilization. This can be helped by the intelligent planning of both public and private employment. It also can be helped by correlating the system with public employment so that a person who has exhausted his benefits may be eligible for some form of public work as is recommended in this report. Moreover, in order to encourage the stabilization of private employment, federal legislation should not foreclose the states from establishing means for inducing industries to afford an even greater stabilization of employment.

In the important field of security for our old people, it seems necessary to adopt three principles:

First, noncontributory old-age pensions for those who are now too old to build up their own insurance. It is, of course, clear that for perhaps thirty years to come funds will have to be provided by the states and the federal government to meet these pensions.

Second, compulsory contributory annuities which in time will establish a self-supporting system for those now young and for future generations.

Third, voluntary contributory annuities by which individual initiative can increase the annual amounts received in old age. It is proposed that the federal government assume one-half of the cost of the old-age pension plan, which ought ultimately to be supplanted by self-supporting annuity plans.

The amount necessary at this time for the initiation of unemployment compensation, old-age security, children's aid, and the promotion of public health, as outlined in the report of the Committee on Economic Security, is approximately $100 million.

The establishment of sound means toward a greater future economic security of the American people is dictated by a prudent consideration of the hazards involved in our national life. No one can guarantee this country against the dangers of future depressions but we can reduce these dangers. We can eliminate many of the factors that cause economic depressions, and we can provide the means of mitigating their results. This plan for economic security is at once a measure of prevention and a method of alleviation.

We pay now for the dreadful consequence of economic insecurity—and dearly. This plan presents a more equitable and infinitely less expensive means of meeting these costs. We cannot afford to neglect the plain duty before us. I strongly recommend action to attain the objectives sought in this report.

Source: Social Security Administration. Retrieved May 22, 2010, from http://www.ssa.gov/history/fdrstmts.html#message2.

CHAPTER 38

Schechter Poultry v. United States, 1935

Following his election in 1932, Franklin Roosevelt immediately took dramatic steps to impact the American economy through government intervention in business and banking. One of his programs was the National Industrial Recovery Act (NIRA) of 1933, which established a great deal of government control over business by fixing prices, wage rates, work hours, and imposing standards to which businesses in the various industries must adhere. Schechter Poultry Corporation was hardly a corporation at all—it was comprised of the five Schechter brothers, all recent immigrants, who slaughtered chickens and sold them in two kosher butcher shops. The "corporation" possessed no formal agreement, minutes book, or stockholders. The brothers purchased live chickens locally and slaughtered them on demand for customers, either retailers or families. Their great sin was that they set prices daily according to the wholesale prices they paid, which sometimes was less than that set by the Live Poultry Code under the NIRA. Occasionally, they paid less than the minimum wage set by the NIRA, allowing their *shochtim*, Jewish ritual slaughterers, to work more than forty hours per week. Worst of all (at least in the eyes of the federal government), they allowed their customers to select which chickens they wanted to buy.

Taken to court by the federal government, the Schechters lost their case and were given fines and jail terms. They then lost their appeal in the circuit court. When *A. L. A Schechter Poultry Corporation, et al. v. United States*, 295 U.S. 495 (1935), was argued before the U.S. Supreme Court in May of 1935, the justices practically ridiculed the government's case and voted unanimously that the NIRA was unconstitutional on two counts: Congress could not delegate the function of creating laws regulating commerce to the executive branch, and the case being adjudicated did not fall under the scope of interstate commerce. FDR had severely overreached in establishing the NIRA, which attempted to keep prices and wages high by law. In this, the first attempt in U.S. history to set wage and price controls over a wide range of industries, FDR tried to exercise an unprecedented level of government control over the American economy. The Court saw this as a serious and unwarranted extension of executive power. Yet in 2009, President Obama, through the takeover of General Motors and Chrysler—as well as the bailout of many large investment banks—clearly told executives what salaries they could earn. Are there, according to the Constitution, instances when the government has the authority to dictate economic practices?

Schechter Poultry v. United States

MR. CHIEF JUSTICE [CHARLES EVANS] HUGHES DELIVERED the opinion of the Court.

Petitioners in No. 854 were convicted in the District Court of the United States for the Eastern District of New York on eighteen counts of an indictment charging violations of what is known as the "Live Poultry Code," and on an additional count for conspiracy to commit such violations. By demurrer to the indictment and appropriate motions on the trial, the defendants contended (1) that the code had been adopted pursuant to an unconstitutional delegation by Congress of legislative power; (2) that it attempted to regulate intrastate transactions which lay outside the authority of Congress; and (3) that in certain provisions it was repugnant to the due process clause of the Fifth Amendment. . . .

The "Live Poultry Code" was promulgated under section 3 of the National Industrial Recovery Act. . . .

The president approved the code by an executive order (No. 6675-A) in which he found that the application for his approval had been duly made in accordance with the provisions of title I of the National Industrial Recover Act. . . .

Of the eighteen counts of the indictment upon which the defendants were convicted, aside from the count for conspiracy, two counts charged violation of the minimum wage and maximum hour provisions of the code, and ten counts were for violation of the requirement (found in the "trade practice provisions") of "straight killing." This requirement was really one of "straight" selling. The term "straight killing" was defined in the code as "the practice of requiring persons purchasing poultry for resale to accept the run of any half coop, coop, or coops, as purchased by slaughterhouse operators, except for culls." The charges in the ten counts, respectively, were that the defendants in selling to retail dealers and butchers had permitted "selections of individual chickens taken from particular coops and half coops."

Of the other six counts, one charged the sale to a butcher of an unfit chicken; two counts charged the making of sales without having the poultry inspected or approved in accordance with regulations or ordinances of the City of New York; two counts charged the making of false reports or the failure to make reports relating to the range of daily prices and volume of sales for certain periods; and the remaining count was for sales to slaughterers or dealers who were without licenses required by the ordinances and regulations of the City of New York.

First. Two preliminary points are stressed by the government with respect to the appropriate approach to the important questions presented. We are told that the provision of the statute authorizing the adoption of codes must be viewed in the light of the grave national crisis with which Congress was confronted. Undoubtedly, the conditions to which power is addressed are always to be considered when the exercise of power is challenged. Extraordinary conditions may call for extraordinary remedies. But the argument necessarily stops short of an attempt to justify action which lies outside the sphere of constitutional authority. Extraordinary conditions do not create or enlarge constitutional power. The Constitution established a national government with powers deemed to be adequate, as they have proved to be both in war and peace, but these powers of the national government are limited by the constitutional grants. Those who act under these grants are not at liberty to transcend the imposed limits because they believe that more or different power is necessary. . . .

Second. The question of the delegation of legislative power. . . . The Constitution provides that "All legislative powers herein granted shall be vested in a Congress of the United States, which shall consist of a Senate and House of Representatives." And the Congress is authorized "To make all Laws which shall be necessary and proper for carrying into Execution" its general powers. The Congress is not permitted to abdicate or to transfer to others the essential legislative functions with which it is thus vested. . . .

. . . Unfairness in competition has been predicated on acts which lie outside the ordinary course of business and are tainted by fraud or coercion or conduct otherwise prohibited by law. But it is evident that in its widest range, "unfair competition," as it has been understood in the law, does not reach the objectives of the codes which are authorized by the National Industrial Recovery Act. The codes may, indeed, cover conduct which existing law condemns, but they are not limited to conduct of that sort. The government does not contend that the act contemplates such a limitation. It would be opposed both to the declared purposes of the act and to its administrative construction.

The Federal Trade Commission Act introduced the expression "unfair methods of competition," which were declared to be unlawful. That was an expression new in the law. Debate apparently convinced the sponsors of the legislation that the words "unfair competition," in the light of their meaning at common law, were too narrow. We have said that the substituted phrase has a broader meaning, that it does not admit of precise definition; its scope being left to judicial determination as controversies arise. What are "unfair methods of competition" are thus to be determined in particular instances, upon evidence, in the light of particular competitive conditions and of what is found to be a specific and substantial public interest. To make this possible, Congress set up a special procedure. A commission, a quasi-judicial body, was created. Provision was made for formal complaint, for notice and hearing, for appropriate findings of fact supported by adequate evidence, and for judicial review to give assurance that the action of the commission is taken within its statutory authority.

In providing for codes, the National Industrial Recovery Act dispenses with this administrative procedure and with any administrative procedure of an analogous character. But the difference between the code plan of the Recovery Act and the scheme of the Federal Trade Commission Act lies not only in procedure but in subject matter. We cannot regard the "fair competition" of the codes as antithetical to the "unfair methods of competition" of the Federal Trade Commission Act. The "fair competition" of the codes has a much broader range and a new significance. The Recovery Act provides that it shall not be construed to impair the powers of the Federal Trade Commission, but, when a code is approved, its provisions are to be the "standards of fair competition" for the trade or industry concerned, and any violation of such standards in any transaction in or affecting interstate or foreign commerce is to be deemed "an unfair method of competition" within the meaning of the Federal Trade Commission Act. . . .

The question, then, turns upon the authority which section 3 of the Recovery Act vests in the president to approve or prescribe. If the codes have standing as penal statutes, this must be due to the effect of the executive action. But Congress cannot delegate legislative power to the president to exercise an unfettered discretion to make whatever laws he thinks may be needed or advisable for the rehabilitation and expansion of trade or industry.

Accordingly we turn to the Recovery Act to ascertain what limits have been set to the exercise of the president's discretion:

First, the president, as a condition of approval, is required to find that the trade or industrial associations or groups which propose a code "impose no inequitable restrictions on admission to membership" and are "truly representative." That condition, however, relates only to the status of the initiators of the new laws and not to the permissible scope of such laws.

Second, the president is required to find that the code is not "designed to promote monopolies or to eliminate or oppress small enterprises and will not operate to discriminate against them." And to this is added a proviso that the code "shall not permit monopolies or monopolistic practices." But these restrictions leave virtually untouched the field of policy envisaged by section 1, and, in that wide field of legislative possibilities, the proponents of a code, refraining from monopolistic designs, may roam at will, and the president may approve or disapprove their proposals as he may see fit. That is the precise effect of the further finding that the president is to make—that the code "will tend to effectuate the policy of this title." While this is called a finding, it is really but a statement of an opinion as to the general effect upon the promotion of trade or industry of a scheme of laws. These are the only findings which Congress has made essential in order to put into operation a legislative code having the aims described in the "Declaration of Policy." . . .

. . . The act provides for the creation by the president of administrative agencies to assist him, but the action or reports of such agencies, or of his other assistants—their recommendations and findings in relation to the making of codes—have no sanction beyond the will of the president, who may accept, modify, or reject them as he pleases. Such recommendations or findings in no way limit the authority which section 3 undertakes to vest in the president with no other conditions than those there specified. And this authority relates to a host of different trades and industries, thus extending the president's discretion to all the varieties of laws which he may deem to be beneficial in dealing with the vast array of commercial and industrial activities throughout the country.

Such a sweeping delegation of legislative power finds no support in the decisions upon which the government especially relies.

To summarize and conclude upon this point: Section 3 of the Recovery Act is without precedent. It supplies no standards for any trade, industry, or activity. It does not undertake to prescribe rules of conduct to be applied to particular states of fact determined by appropriate administrative procedure. Instead of prescribing rules of conduct, it authorizes the making of codes to prescribe them. For that legislative undertaking, section 3 sets up no standards, aside from the statement of the general aims of rehabilitation, correction, and expansion described in section 1. In view of the scope of that broad declaration and of the nature of the few restrictions that are imposed, the discretion of the president in approving or prescribing codes, and thus enacting laws for the government of trade and industry throughout the country, is virtually unfettered. We think that the code-making authority thus conferred is an unconstitutional delegation of legislative power.

Third. The question of the application of the provisions of the Live Poultry Code to intrastate transactions. Although the validity of the codes (apart from the question of delegation) rests upon the commerce clause of the Constitution, section 3(a) of the act is not in terms limited to interstate and foreign commerce. From the generality of its terms, and from the argument of the government at the bar, it would appear that section 3(a) was designed to authorize codes without that limitation. But under section 3(f) of the act penalties are confined to violations of a code provision "in any transaction in or affecting interstate or foreign commerce." This aspect of the case presents the question whether the particular provisions of the Live Poultry Code, which the defendants were convicted for violating and for having conspired to violate, were within the regulating power of Congress.

These provisions relate to the hours and wages of those employed by defendants in their slaughterhouses in Brooklyn and to the sales there made to retail dealers and butchers.

Were these transactions "in" interstate commerce? Much is made of the fact that almost all the poultry coming to New York is sent there from other states. But the code provisions, as here applied, do not concern the transportation of the poultry from other states to New York, or the transactions of the commission men or others to whom it is consigned, or the sales made by such consignees to defendants. When defendants had made their purchases, whether at the West Washington Market in New York City or at the railroad terminals serving the city, or elsewhere, the poultry was trucked to their slaughterhouses in Brooklyn for local disposition. The interstate transactions in relation to that poultry then ended. Defendants held the poultry at their slaughterhouse markets for slaughter and local sale to retail dealers and butchers who in turn sold directly to consumers. Neither the slaughtering nor the sales by defendants were transactions in interstate commerce. . . .

. . . Defendants have been convicted, not upon direct charges of injury to interstate commerce or of interference with persons engaged in that commerce, but of violations of certain provisions of the Live Poultry Code and of conspiracy to commit these violations. Interstate commerce is brought in only upon the charge that violations of these provisions—as to hours and wages of employees and local sales— "affected" interstate commerce.

In determining how far the federal government may go in controlling intrastate transactions upon the ground that they "affect" interstate commerce, there is a necessary and well-established distinction between direct and indirect effects. The precise line can be drawn only as individual cases arise, but the distinction is clear in principle. Direct effects are illustrated by the railroad cases . . . , as, e.g., the effect of failure to use prescribed safety appliances on railroads which are the highways of both interstate and intrastate commerce, injury to an employee engaged in interstate transportation by the negligence of an employee engaged in an intrastate movement, the fixing of rates for intrastate transportation which unjustly discriminate against interstate commerce. But where the effect of intrastate transactions upon interstate commerce is merely indirect, such transactions remain within the domain of state power. If the commerce clause were construed to reach all enterprises and transactions which could be said to have an indirect effect upon interstate commerce, the federal authority would embrace practically all the activities of the people, and the authority of the state over its domestic concerns would exist only by sufferance of the federal government. Indeed, on such a theory, even the development of the state's commercial facilities would be subject to federal control. . . .

The distinction between direct and indirect effects has been clearly recognized in the application of the Antitrust Act. Where a combination or conspiracy is formed, with the intent to restrain interstate commerce or to monopolize any part of it, the violation of the statute is clear. But, where that intent is absent, and the objectives are limited to intrastate activities, the fact that there may be an indirect effect upon interstate commerce does not subject the parties to the federal statute, notwithstanding its broad provisions. . . .

. . . Otherwise, as we have said, there would be virtually no limit to the federal power, and for all practical purposes we should have a completely centralized government. We must consider the provisions here in question in the light of this distinction.

The question of chief importance relates to the provisions of the code as to the hours and wages of those employed in defendants' slaughterhouse markets. It is plain that these requirements are imposed in order to govern the details of defendants' management of their local business. The persons employed in slaughtering and selling in local trade are not employed in interstate commerce. Their hours and wages have no direct relation to interstate commerce. The question of how many hours these employees should work and what they should be paid differs in no essential respect from similar questions in other local businesses which handle commodities brought into a state and there dealt in as a part of its internal commerce. This appears from an examination of the considerations urged by the government with respect to conditions in the poultry trade. Thus, the government argues that hours and wages affect prices; that slaughterhouse men sell at a small margin above operating costs; that labor represents 50 to 60 percent of these costs; that a slaughterhouse operator paying lower wages or reducing his cost by exacting long hours of work translates his saving into lower prices; that this results in demands for a cheaper grade of goods: and that the cutting of prices brings about a demoralization of the price structure. Similar conditions may be adduced in relation to other businesses. The argument of the government proves too much. If the federal government may determine the wages and hours of employees in the internal commerce of a state, because of their relation to cost and prices and their indirect effect upon interstate commerce, it would seem that a similar control might be exerted over other elements of cost, also affecting prices, such as the number of employees, rents, advertising, methods of doing business, etc. All the processes of production and distribution that enter into cost could likewise be controlled. If the cost of doing an intrastate business is in itself the permitted object of federal control, the extent of the regulation of cost would be a question of discretion and not of power.

The government also makes the point that efforts to enact state legislation establishing high labor standards have been impeded by the belief that, unless similar action is taken generally, commerce will be diverted from the states adopting such standards, and that this fear of diversion has led to demands for federal legislation on the subject of wages and hours. The apparent implication is that the federal authority under the commerce clause should be deemed to extend to the establishment of rules to govern wages and hours in intrastate trade and industry generally throughout the country, thus overriding the authority of the states to deal with domestic problems arising from labor conditions in their internal commerce.

It is not the province of the Court to consider the economic advantages or disadvantages of such a centralized system. It is sufficient to say that the federal Constitution does not provide for it. Our growth and development have called for wide use of the commerce power of the federal government in its control over the expanded activities of interstate commerce and in protecting that commerce from burdens, interferences, and conspiracies to restrain and monopolize it. But the authority of the federal government may not be pushed to such an extreme as to destroy the distinction, which the commerce clause itself establishes, between commerce "among the several States" and the internal concerns of a state. The same answer must be made to the contention that is based upon the serious economic situation which led to the passage of the Recovery Act—the fall in prices, the decline in wages and employment, and the curtailment of the market for commodities. Stress is laid upon the great importance of maintaining wage distributions which would provide the necessary stimulus in starting "the cumulative forces making for expanding commercial activity." Without in any way disparaging this motive, it is enough to say that the recuperative efforts of the federal government must be made in a manner consistent with the authority granted by the Constitution.

We are of the opinion that the attempt through the provisions of the code to fix the hours and wages of employees of defendants in their intrastate business was not a valid exercise of federal power.

The other violations for which defendants were convicted related to the making of local sales. Ten counts, for violation of the provision as to "straight killing," were for permitting customers to make "selections of individual chickens taken from particular coops and half coops." Whether or not this practice is good or bad for the local trade, its effect, if any, upon interstate commerce was only indirect. The same may be said of violations of the code by intrastate transactions consisting of the sale "of an unfit chicken" and of sales which were not in accord with the ordinances of the City of New York. The requirement of reports as to prices and volumes of defendants' sales was incident to the effort to control their intrastate business. In view of these conclusions, we find it unnecessary to discuss other questions which have been raised as to the validity of certain provisions of the code under the due process clause of the Fifth Amendment.

On both the grounds we have discussed, the attempted delegation of legislative power and the attempted regulation of intrastate transactions which affect interstate commerce only indirectly, we hold the code provisions here in question to be invalid and that the judgment of conviction must be reversed.

Source: Yale Law School, Lillian Goldman Law Library's Avalon Project: Documents in Law, History and Diplomacy. Retrieved May 20, 2010, from http://caselaw.lp .findlaw.com/scripts/getcase.pl?court=US&vol=295&invol=495.

CHAPTER 39

On Problems in New Deal Policies, Robert A. Taft, 1939

"Mr. Republican," Senator Robert A. Taft was an outspoken critic of Roosevelt's New Deal, and when unemployment once again reached 20 percent in the late 1930s, Taft went on the offensive. FDR's policies had failed to lift the United States out of the Depression, and later analysts would conclude that his policies actually extended it while he tinkered with social engineering. On July 14, 1939, Taft spoke to a meeting at the Institute of Public Affairs at the University of Virginia and outlined what he considered to be problems in New Deal policies that were causing the United States harm. Although establishing himself as the leader of the conservative faction of the Republican Party, Taft influenced progressive Republicans like Wendell Willkie, who adopted some of Taft's points in his 1940 campaign for president.

Many of Taft's points and arguments are just as applicable in the twenty-first century as they were in 1939. During the past seventy years, Congress and the presidents have solved literally none of the problems Taft pointed out—in fact the problems have gotten worse as the federal government has grown. Taft had a strong and vocal base of national support, but it represented the minority. Were there specific conditions that caused Americans to submit to New Deal programs or even welcome them? In the long term, Congress has not balanced its budget, and while the American spirit of enterprise resurrected itself to fight World War II, it has languished of late under government regulation and the stress on private-public partnerships—an organizational form Taft opposed. FDR's policies failed to lower unemployment, yet identical approaches are still widely promoted today.

Address to the Institute of Public Affairs, University of Virginia

THE NEW DEAL PROGRAM HAS CREATED A VAST NUMBER OF new problems for government. Every activity creates a new problem, and usually an interesting one. Some are well administered; some are hopelessly inefficient; all are experimental and subject to a continual change of policy. Little public attention is paid to them. Few men even in Congress have a comprehensive idea of the countless activities of government. A good many more problems have been created than solved.

But there are two great problems whose solution, in my opinion, is essential if the nation is to survive. I wish to suggest what those problems are, and how the Republicans propose to meet them.

The first and most important problem is that of unemployment. The question is how we can encourage again in the United States the tremendous volume of private enterprise which existed in the twenties. . . .

Whatever else has resulted from the great increase in government activity . . . it has certainly had the effect of checking private enterprise completely. This country was built up by the constant establishment of new business and the expansion of old businesses. In every city and every village throughout the country, men were constantly starting out on their own initiative to improve on the enterprises of others, or develop a new product. They put a few men to work. If successful, they expanded to employ ten or a hundred or thousands. If unsuccessful, they passed from the picture without the need of government subsidy.

New methods of production were found, and small industries expanded into large industries. Men were willing to spend their time and their money in order that they might provide more completely for themselves and their family in their old age, in order that they might rise above the average standard of living and enjoy a little more luxury or a little more power. In the last six years this process has come to an end because of government regulation and the development of a tax system which penalizes hard work and success. We must and can resume the progress which returned us to prosperity after every depression, but it can only be done by a radical change in government policy.

The policy of fixing the prices of basic commodities has been frequently attempted in history, and has always failed in the end, usually resulting in lower prices for those whom it attempted to benefit. I believe that most of the laws attempting to regulate prices and wages should be repealed, although I believe in a minimum wage law to protect unorganized employees against oppression where the right of collective bargaining cannot be made effective.

Laws attempting to dictate the amount of production and the method of operating agriculture and business should be repealed. Those resulting from some definite abuse should be confined to the cure of that abuse.

The SEC [Securities and Exchange Commission] should confine itself to the prevention of fraud in the sale of securities. The NLRB [National Labor Relations Board] should confine itself to seeing that the employees of each employer obtain, through collective bargaining, what they themselves really desire.

The limitation of farm production and the making of unsound loans on crops for the sole purpose of maintaining prices should come to an end.

Government competition with private industry should be confined to its present limits, and assurance given that it will not be expanded into other fields.

The government should gradually withdraw from the business of lending money and leave that function to private capital under proper regulation.

The whole tax system should be reformed to put a premium on expansion of industry and the risking of private money in the development of new and old enterprises.

The capital gains tax should be substantially modified, so that such risks as result in profit may not be subjected to high surtaxes.

Above all, the laws must be administered with a constant effort to encourage the development of private industry. There must be a real sympathy with its success, a real desire to relieve it from unnecessary harassment and discouragement. There must be a recognition of the fact that the making of profits is not a crime; that the average businessman, making a success in his own business, is an essential cog in the national machine, and ought to be encouraged, as long as it does not cost the taxpayer any money.

I am convinced that we can restore prosperity . . . but it cannot be done by government regulation of agriculture and commerce and industry.

The other new problem which must be solved is that of adjusting our expenses to our income. How can we maintain the humanitarian measures I have described within a tax system that does not completely bog down the industrial machine? If anything is certain, it is that a continuation of the present policy of reckless expenditure, without regard to taxes, can only lead to bankruptcy, repudiation, and a breakdown of our entire economic life. No government has ever continued a deficit policy without ultimate repudiation. Sooner or later the time will come when the burden of debt is so great that the people refuse to meet the expense of the interest. The temptation to pay in paper money becomes politically irresistible. Leading as it must to inflated prices, it wipes out the savings of the people and bears down most heavily on the groups with fixed income, to the benefit only of successful speculators. If we ever reach the point which Germany reached after the world war, it is doubtful if we could ever reestablish a system based on thrift and saving and investment of funds in private enterprise. The American system as we know it would not survive. . . .

The only people who can support men and women who do not work are those who are working. Obviously the humanitarian measures must be administered as economically as possible. Pensions cannot be carelessly increased, as the Congress has just increased the old-age pension from $30 to $40, unless a majority of the people are willing to pay the taxes necessary to pay the increase. I was shocked by the fact that Wednesday a dozen senators voted a pension which would cost the people $5 billion without the slightest suggestion of any way in which the money could possibly be raised. There must be an utter repudiation of that point of view.

Furthermore, these laws should be administered so that the recipients of government assistance are not placed in a better position through that assistance than the other workmen with private jobs, who have saved their own money and have to provide the taxes. There has been too much tendency on the part of each department to look only at its own job, and try to please its wards by a liberal administration in its particular field. The man who lives in government housing should not be better off than the man who has built his own home out of his own savings. The man who gets an old-age pension should not be better off than he who has spent his life in making provision for his own old age. In short, measures to assist the lower-income groups must be administered with just as much consideration for the middle-income groups, who have to do the paying, as for the lower-income groups.

The budget can be balanced. Economy can be secured even in relief without decreasing its efficiency. If administration were returned to the localities, with full discretion to administer both work relief and direct relief in the manner best suited to local conditions, the federal government would pay less, even though it supplied two-thirds of the entire cost. There would be far more equal treatment of those on relief; more liberal treatment for direct relief clients than today. Housing can be cheaper, and there does not need to be the large subsidy required by the present program. . . .

It is no easy task to economize. It cannot be done effectively over the opposition of the executive, for many federal policies can be changed only by affirmative legislation, which the executive can block. For instance, until the relief policy is completely changed, we must go on voting the appropriations required by the present WPA [Works Progress Administration] system. Economy cannot be secured piecemeal, for each project has its appeal, and often a very attractive appeal. Some leadership must develop a plan for balancing the budget within two years and hold Congress to it.

This is the proper function of the executive, but if the executive will not do it, Congress will have to create a budget committee of its own. The findings of such a committee can only be carried through with a strong leadership for economy, backed by a majority of the members in both houses of Congress. I feel confident that expenses can be reduced by several billions of dollars, that a tax system can produce the necessary income in a way that will not destroy the very income which is to provide the taxes. It can be done, but it cannot be done by neglecting the fundamental principles of common sense.

Source: Robert A. Taft, *A Republican Program; Speeches and Broadcasts* (Cleveland, OH: D. S. Ingalls, 1939), 21–34.

CHAPTER 40

Franklin D. Roosevelt's "Date Which Will Live in Infamy" Speech, 1941

One of the most controversial topics for World War II historians concerns Japan's attack on Pearl Harbor. Did President Roosevelt know it was coming? Did he maneuver the Japanese government into a situation in which it felt it had no other options? Why weren't the Hawaiian commanders better prepared—particularly after having been given a "war warning" less than two weeks before the attack? While documents showing the radio and cryptanalysis traffic confirm that Roosevelt was not informed of a Japanese strike force on its way to Pearl Harbor, some historians contend that Roosevelt's transfer of the Pacific Fleet to Hawaii and series of economic sanctions against Japan, including the machine-tool and oil embargoes, were actions designed to provoke the Japanese and force them into a corner, pushing Japan to withdraw from China or fight.* The situation in Europe was grim: only England stood outside Nazi Germany's reach, and in late 1941 the Germans were literally at the gates of Moscow. Should the USSR have collapsed, England—and then America—were next. Hitler's Amerika Bomber (on the drawing boards) did not bear that name for nothing. It cannot be forgotten or ignored that Japan struck first—deceptively, brutally, and entirely unexpectedly—by bombing the U.S. naval base at Pearl Harbor. Until that moment, American isolationism prevented Roosevelt from involving the country in another of Europe's wars, but shortly thereafter Germany declared war on the United States and, as some critics complained, America entered the European war through the "back door" of Japan. Yet Japan, and a week later Germany, had flung the back door wide open.

Roosevelt was aghast at the magnitude of the disaster and genuinely outraged. His address here, asking for a declaration of war against Japan was perhaps

---

* Discussed at length in Edward S. Miller, *Bankrupting the Enemy* (Annapolis: Naval Institute Press, 2007); James W. Morley, *Japan's Road to the Pacific War: The Final Confrontation* (New York: Columbia University Press, 1994); Jonathan Marshall, *To Have and Have Not: Southeast Asian Raw Materials and the Origins of the Pacific War* (Berkeley: University of California Press, 1995).

the most stirring speech the American public had heard on radio to that point. Although Roosevelt misled Congress somewhat with respect to warnings of war, Congress immediately voted unanimously to declare war (Jeannette Rankin reversed her negative vote after making a telephone call), and Japan would soon regret its decision to attack the United States. The reader might consider why unprovoked attacks before Pearl Harbor, such as on the *Panay* by the Japanese or on the *Reuben James* by the Nazis, were not considered sufficient for a declaration of war. The political response to Roosevelt's speech was important, and there is no doubt that prior to Pearl Harbor the American public was substantially against any overseas military involvement. In the wake of World War I, were the reasons for this hesitancy understandable or dangerous?

Joint Address to Congress, December 8, 1941

MR. VICE PRESIDENT, AND MR. SPEAKER, AND MEMBERS OF the Senate and House of Representatives:

Yesterday, December 7, 1941—a date which will live in infamy—the United States of America was suddenly and deliberately attacked by naval and air forces of the empire of Japan.

The United States was at peace with that nation and, at the solicitation of Japan, was still in conversation with its government and its emperor looking toward the maintenance of peace in the Pacific. Indeed, one hour after Japanese air squadrons had commenced bombing in the American island of Oahu, the Japanese ambassador to the United States and his colleague delivered to our secretary of state a formal reply to a recent American message. And while this reply stated that it seemed useless to continue the existing diplomatic negotiations, it contained no threat or hint of war or of armed attack.

It will be recorded that the distance of Hawaii from Japan makes it obvious that the attack was deliberately planned many days or even weeks ago. During the intervening time the Japanese government has deliberately sought to deceive the United States by false statements and expressions of hope for continued peace.

The attack yesterday on the Hawaiian Islands has caused severe damage to American naval and military forces. I regret to tell you that very many American lives have been lost. In addition American ships have been reported torpedoed on the high seas between San Francisco and Honolulu.

Yesterday the Japanese government also launched an attack against Malaya.

Last night Japanese forces attacked Hong Kong.

Last night Japanese forces attacked Guam.

Last night Japanese forces attacked the Philippine Islands.

Last night the Japanese attacked Wake Island. And this morning the Japanese attacked Midway Island.

Japan has, therefore, undertaken a surprise offensive extending throughout the Pacific area. The facts of yesterday and today speak for themselves. The people of the United States have already formed their opinions and well understand the implications to the very life and safety of our nation.

As commander in chief of the army and navy I have directed that all measures be taken for our defense.

But always will our whole nation remember the character of the onslaught against us.

No matter how long it may take us to overcome this premeditated invasion, the American people in their righteous might will win through to absolute victory. I believe that I interpret the will of the Congress and of the people when I assert that we will not only defend ourselves to the uttermost but will make it very certain that this form of treachery shall never again endanger us.

Hostilities exist. There is no blinking at the fact that our people, our territory, and our interests are in grave danger.

With confidence in our armed forces—with the unbounded determination of our people—we will gain the inevitable triumph—so help us God.

I ask that the Congress declare that since the unprovoked and dastardly attack by Japan on Sunday, December 7, 1941, a state of war has existed between the United States and the Japanese Empire.

Source: Franklin D. Roosevelt Presidential Library and Museum. Retrieved June 3, 2010, from http://docs.fdrlibrary.marist.edu/oddec7.html.

CHAPTER 41

Franklin D. Roosevelt's State of the Union Address, 1944

On January 11, 1944, President Roosevelt delivered his annual State of the Union address in which he not only implored Americans to redouble their efforts to win the war but also unveiled a "second Bill of Rights." FDR did not agree with the idea as stated in the Declaration of Independence that all human rights came from God, and instead of seeking amendments to the Constitution for his new rights the president intended to implement them politically through new federal laws and executive action. Many people thought Roosevelt had fallen victim to his own hubris and set himself up as equal to the Almighty, but over time the Democratic Party came to embrace many of these "rights," such as the freedom from want or the "right" to a job, as deserving of legislative support. The idea that a "right" given to man by a government can also be taken away by that same government was, of course, not included in arguments supporting these initiatives. Recall also that Thomas Paine, among many, had insisted that genuine rights could only come from God.

FDR also recognized that efforts on the home front were beginning to flag as rationing and shortages made life more difficult. Politically, Roosevelt was still pursuing New Deal policies in economic control, and domestic opposition was building against him before the coming election in the fall. Promising new social legislation for prosperity and security was an effective political strategy, and coupled with the successful invasion of France and the expectation that the war in Europe would be over by Christmas, it secured the president a fourth term. Perhaps more than any other initiative, this "second Bill of Rights" promoted the development of the welfare state through the expectation of unemployment relief, minimum wages, and Social Security. The immediate effect of this "second Bill of Rights" was not to ensure an economy that was "fair to all" but rather to ensure a political system that for the next half century stacked the deck in the Democrats' favor through an alliance with unions, the poor, and the elderly. It also bankrupted the country and pushed it toward the waiting arms of

European-style socialism—threatening to sound the death knell for American exceptionalism.

State of the Union Message to Congress, January 11, 1944

TO THE CONGRESS:

This nation in the past two years has become an active partner in the world's greatest war against human slavery.

We have joined with like-minded people in order to defend ourselves in a world that has been gravely threatened with gangster rule.

But I do not think that any of us Americans can be content with mere survival. Sacrifices that we and our allies are making impose upon us all a sacred obligation to see to it that out of this war we and our children will gain something better than mere survival.

We are united in determination that this war shall not be followed by another interim which leads to new disaster—that we shall not repeat the tragic errors of ostrich isolationism—that we shall not repeat the excesses of the wild twenties when this nation went for a joyride on a roller coaster which ended in a tragic crash. . . .

And right here I want to address a word or two to some suspicious souls who are fearful that Mr. Hull [the secretary of state] or I have made "commitments" for the future which might pledge this nation to secret treaties, or to enacting the role of Santa Claus. To such suspicious souls—using a polite terminology—I wish to say that Mr. Churchill, and Marshal Stalin, and Generalissimo Chiang Kai-shek are all thoroughly conversant with the provisions of our Constitution. And so is Mr. Hull. And so am I.

Of course we made some commitments. We most certainly committed ourselves to very large and very specific military plans which require the use of all Allied forces to bring about the defeat of our enemies at the earliest possible time. But there were no secret treaties or political or financial commitments.

The one supreme objective for the future, which we discussed for each nation individually, and for all the United Nations, can be summed up in one word: security.

And that means not only physical security which provides safety from attacks by aggressors. It means also economic security, social security, moral security—in a family of nations.

In the plain down-to-earth talks that I had with the generalissimo and Marshal Stalin and Prime Minister Churchill, it was abundantly clear that they are all most deeply interested in the resumption of peaceful progress by their own peoples—progress toward a better life. All our allies want freedom to develop their lands and resources, to build up industry, to increase education and individual opportunity, and to raise standards of living.

All our allies have learned by bitter experience that real development will not be possible if they are to be diverted from their purpose by repeated wars—or even threats of war.

China and Russia are truly united with Britain and America in recognition of this essential fact:

The best interests of each nation, large and small, demand that all freedom-loving nations shall join together in a just and durable system of peace. In the present world situation, evidenced by the actions of Germany, Italy, and Japan, unquestioned military control over disturbers of the peace is as necessary among nations as it is among citizens in a community. And an equally basic essential to peace is a decent standard of living for all individual men and women and children in all nations. Freedom from fear is eternally linked with freedom from want. . . .

Overconfidence and complacency are among our deadliest enemies. Last spring—after notable victories at Stalingrad and in Tunisia and against the U-boats on the high seas—overconfidence became so pronounced that war production fell off. In two months, June and July 1943, more than a thousand airplanes that could have been made and should have been made were not made. Those who failed to make them were not on strike. They were merely saying, "The war's in the bag—so let's relax."

That attitude on the part of anyone—government or management or labor—can lengthen this war. It can kill American boys.

Let us remember the lessons of 1918. In the summer of that year the tide turned in favor of the Allies. But this Government did not relax. In fact, our national effort was stepped up. In August 1918 the draft age limits were broadened from twenty-one to thirty-one to eighteen to forty-five. The president called for "force to the utmost," and his call was heeded. And in November, only three months later, Germany surrendered.

That is the way to fight and win a war—all out—and not with half an eye on the battlefronts abroad and the other eye and a half on personal, selfish, or political interests here at home.

Therefore, in order to concentrate all our energies and resources on winning the war, and to maintain a fair and stable economy at home, I recommend that the Congress adopt:

1. A realistic tax law—which will tax all unreasonable profits, both individual and corporate, and reduce the ultimate cost of the war to our sons and

daughters. The tax bill now under consideration by the Congress does not begin to meet this test.

2. A continuation of the law for the renegotiation of war contracts—which will prevent exorbitant profits and assure fair prices to the government. For two long years I have pleaded with the Congress to take undue profits out of war.

3. A cost of food law—which will enable the government (a) to place a reasonable floor under the prices the farmer may expect for his production; and (b) to place a ceiling on the prices a consumer will have to pay for the food he buys. This should apply to necessities only; and will require public funds to carry out. It will cost in appropriations about one percent of the present annual cost of the war.

4. Early reenactment of the stabilization statute of October 1942. This expires June 30, 1944, and if it is not extended well in advance, the country might just as well expect price chaos by summer. We cannot have stabilization by wishful thinking. We must take positive action to maintain the integrity of the American dollar.

5. A national service law—which, for the duration of the war, will prevent strikes, and, with certain appropriate exceptions, will make available for war production or for any other essential services every able-bodied adult in this nation.

These five measures together form a just and equitable whole. I would not recommend a national service law unless the other laws were passed to keep down the cost of living, to share equitably the burdens of taxation, to hold the stabilization line, and to prevent undue profits.

The federal government already has the basic power to draft capital and property of all kinds for war purposes on a basis of just compensation.

As you know, I have for three years hesitated to recommend a national service act. Today, however, I am convinced of its necessity. Although I believe that we and our allies can win the war without such a measure, I am certain that nothing less than total mobilization of all our resources of manpower and capital will guarantee an earlier victory, and reduce the toll of suffering and sorrow and blood.

I have received a joint recommendation for this law from the heads of the War Department, the Navy Department, and the Maritime Commission. These are the men who bear responsibility for the procurement of the necessary arms and equipment, and for the successful prosecution of the war in the field. They say:

"When the very life of the nation is in peril the responsibility for service is common to all men and women. In such a time there can be no discrimination between the men and women who are assigned by the government to its defense at the battlefront and the men and women assigned to producing the vital materials essential to successful military operations. A prompt enactment of a national service law would be merely an expression of the universality of this responsibility."

I believe the country will agree that those statements are the solemn truth.

National service is the most democratic way to wage a war. Like selective service for the armed forces, it rests on the obligation of each citizen to serve his nation to his utmost where he is best qualified. . . .

It is my conviction that the American people will welcome this win-the-war measure which is based on the eternally just principle of "fair for one, fair for all."

It will give our people at home the assurance that they are standing four-square behind our soldiers and sailors. And it will give our enemies demoralizing assurance that we mean business—that we, 130,000,000 Americans, are on the march to Rome, Berlin, and Tokyo.

I hope that the Congress will recognize that, although this is a political year, national service is an issue which transcends politics. Great power must be used for great purposes.

As to the machinery for this measure, the Congress itself should determine its nature—but it should be wholly nonpartisan in its makeup. . . .

It is our duty now to begin to lay the plans and determine the strategy for the winning of a lasting peace and the establishment of an American standard of living higher than ever before known. We cannot be content, no matter how high that general standard of living may be, if some fraction of our people—whether it be one-third or one-fifth or one-tenth—is ill fed, ill clothed, ill housed, and insecure.

This republic had its beginning, and grew to its present strength, under the protection of certain inalienable political rights—among them the right of free speech, free press, free worship, trial by jury, freedom from unreasonable searches and seizures. They were our rights to life and liberty. As our nation has grown in size and stature, however—as our industrial economy expanded—these political rights proved inadequate to assure us equality in the pursuit of happiness.

We have come to a clear realization of the fact that true individual freedom cannot exist without economic security and independence. "Necessitous men are not free men." People who are hungry and out of a job are the stuff of which dictatorships are made.

In our day these economic truths have become accepted as self-evident. We have accepted, so to speak, a second Bill of Rights under which a new basis of security and prosperity can be established for all regardless of station, race, or creed.

Among these are:

The right to a useful and remunerative job in the industries or shops or farms or mines of the nation;

The right to earn enough to provide adequate food and clothing and recreation;

The right of every farmer to raise and sell his products at a return which will give him and his family a decent living;

The right of every businessman, large and small, to trade in an atmosphere of freedom from unfair competition and domination by monopolies at home or abroad;

The right of every family to a decent home;

The right to adequate medical care and the opportunity to achieve and enjoy good health;

The right to adequate protection from the economic fears of old age, sickness, accident, and unemployment;

The right to a good education.

All of these rights spell security. And after this war is won we must be prepared to move forward, in the implementation of these rights, to new goals of human happiness and well-being.

America's own rightful place in the world depends in large part upon how fully these and similar rights have been carried into practice for our citizens. For unless there is security here at home there cannot be lasting peace in the world. . . .

I ask the Congress to explore the means for implementing this economic bill of rights—for it is definitely the responsibility of the Congress so to do. Many of these problems are already before committees of the Congress in the form of proposed legislation. I shall from time to time communicate with the Congress with respect to these and further proposals. In the event that no adequate program of progress is evolved, I am certain that the nation will be conscious of the fact.

Our fighting men abroad—and their families at home—expect such a program and have the right to insist upon it. It is to their demands that this government should pay heed rather than to the whining demands of selfish pressure groups who seek to feather their nests while young Americans are dying. The foreign policy that we have been following—the policy that guided us at Moscow, Cairo, and Teheran—is based on the commonsense principle which was best expressed by Benjamin Franklin on July 4, 1776: "We must all hang together, or assuredly we shall all hang separately."

I have often said that there are no two fronts for America in this war. There is only one front. There is one line of unity which extends from the hearts of the people at home to the men of our attacking forces in our farthest outposts.

When we speak of our total effort, we speak of the factory and the field, and the mine as well as of the battleground—we speak of the soldier and the civilian, the citizen and his government.

Each and every one of us has a solemn obligation under God to serve this nation in its most critical hour—to keep this nation great—to make this nation greater in a better world.

Source: Franklin D. Roosevelt Presidential Library and Museum. Retrieved June 6, 2010, from http://www.fdrlibrary.marist.edu/archives/address_text.html.

CHAPTER 42

The Yalta Agreement, 1945

The Yalta, or Crimea, Conference between the three primary Allied leaders in World War II was held to develop an agreement on the restructuring of Europe following Germany's expected surrender later in the spring. The Soviet dictator, Joseph Stalin, had an aversion to flying or leaving the Soviet Union, so the conference was held on the Crimean peninsula near the vacation resort of Yalta from February 4 to 11, 1945. President Roosevelt, crippled since 1921 from polio, was visibly declining in health, and later the agreements that favored the Soviet Union were said to be a result of his failing health and lack of support from Winston Churchill, the third participant. Some of the protocols, such as degrees of interest in the various countries, were secret and disclosed only years later when public support of the agreements was no longer needed. A substantial number of senior officials in the Roosevelt administration were actually Soviet agents, as later exposed in the Venona project, a major American code-breaking effort dealing with Soviet spy traffic, and postwar institutions such as the United Nations, financial structures, and political alliances were generally constructed by Soviet officials in and outside the Soviet Union. The American representative most involved with forming the UN was Alger Hiss, code named "Ales," and Harry Dexter White, another Soviet agent, was the chief American delegate to the Bretton Woods Conference that set up the International Monetary Fund, General Agreement on Tariffs and Trade, and the International Bank for Reconstruction and Development. The Venona project uncovered over three hundred high-level Soviet agents in the Roosevelt administration, and their influence, beyond the damage caused by their spying activities, was enormous. Even Harry Hopkins, Roosevelt's closest confidant, may have been a Soviet agent, although the evidence is not conclusive beyond all doubt.[*]

---

[*] Herbert Romerstein and Eric Breindel, *The Venona Secrets, Exposing Soviet Espionage and America's Traitors* (Washington: Regnery, 2001), and John Earl Haynes and Harvey Klehr, *Venona: Decoding Soviet Espionage in America* (New Haven: Yale University Press, 2000).

In the end, Stalin failed to honor most of the agreement, particularly the parts ensuring free elections in countries under his control, and established satellite communist governments throughout Eastern Europe. Although the subject is still controversial, there is evidence that Soviet forces liberated some 55,000 British and American soldiers from German POW camps and held them in Siberia instead of repatriating them as required. Supposedly Stalin feared that the Allies would renege on the Yalta Agreement, so held these men as hostages, but when the agreement was honored and such pressure proved unnecessary, Stalin did away with the hostages to avoid exposure.* The fate of these men has never been investigated by the American or British governments. The following is the full text of the primary protocols and the pertinent section of the POW agreement. Yalta was probably the nadir of American diplomacy and made the cold war inevitable. Clearly Eastern Europe could not be saved from communism through this agreement, and Stalin's much sought Manchurian attack against Japan actually worked to America's great disadvantage. Roosevelt's agreement relied almost entirely on Soviet promises and failed as a guarantor of the liberties of the occupied countries. He included no enforcement mechanisms and few actual processes to follow, and in the end Yalta merely echoed Lenin's phrase that "promises are like piecrusts, made to be broken."

Protocol of Proceedings of Crimea Conference

THE CRIMEA CONFERENCE OF THE HEADS OF THE GOVERNments of the United States of America, the United Kingdom, and the Union of Soviet Socialist Republics, came to the following conclusions:

I. WORLD ORGANIZATION

It was decided:

1. That a United Nations conference on the proposed world organization should be summoned for Wednesday, 25 April 1945, and should be held in the United States of America.
2. The nations to be invited to this conference should be:
   a. The United Nations as they existed on 8 Feb., 1945; and
   b. Such of the Associated Nations [the eight Associated Nations and Turkey] as have declared war on the common enemy by 1 March 1945. When

---

* James Sanders, Mark Sauter, and R. Cort Kirkwood, *Soldiers of Misfortune* (Washington, DC: National Press Books, 1992), 1–137, passim.

the conference on world organization is held, the delegates of the United Kingdom and United State of America will support a proposal to admit to original membership two Soviet Socialist Republics, i.e., the Ukraine and White Russia.

3. That the United States government, on behalf of the three powers, should consult the government of China and the French provisional government in regard to decisions taken at the present conference concerning the proposed world organization.

4. That the text of the invitation to be issued to all the nations which would take part in the United Nations conference should be as follows: "The government of the United States of America, on behalf of itself and of the governments of the United Kingdom, the Union of Soviet Socialistic Republics and the Republic of China and of the provisional government of the French Republic invite the government of——to send representatives to a conference to be held on 25 April 1945, or soon thereafter, at San Francisco, in the United States of America, to prepare a charter for a general international organization for the maintenance of international peace and security.

"The above-named governments suggest that the conference consider as affording a basis for such a charter the proposals for the establishment of a general international organization which were made public last October as a result of the Dumbarton Oaks conference and which have now been supplemented by the following provisions for section C of chapter VI:

"C. Voting

"1. Each member of the Security Council should have one vote.

"2. Decisions of the Security Council on procedural matters should be made by an affirmative vote of seven members.

"3. Decisions of the Security Council on all matters should be made by an affirmative vote of seven members, including the concurring votes of the permanent members; provided that, in decisions under chapter VIII, section A and under the second sentence of paragraph 1 of chapter VIII, section C, a party to a dispute should abstain from voting.

"Further information as to arrangements will be transmitted subsequently. In the event that the government of——desires in advance of the conference to present views or comments concerning the proposals, the government of the United States of America will be pleased to transmit such views and comments to the other participating governments."

Territorial trusteeship:

It was agreed that the five nations which will have permanent seats on the Security Council should consult each other prior to the United Nations conference on the question of territorial trusteeship. The acceptance of this recommendation is subject to its being made clear that territorial trusteeship will only apply to:

a. Existing mandates of the League of Nations;
b. Territories detached from the enemy as a result of the present war;
c. Any other territory which might voluntarily be placed under trusteeship; and
d. No discussion of actual territories is contemplated at the forthcoming United Nations conference or in the preliminary consultations, and it will be a matter for subsequent agreement which territories within the above categories will be place under trusteeship.

II. DECLARATION OF LIBERATED EUROPE

The following declaration has been approved:

The premier of the Union of Soviet Socialist Republics, the prime minister of the United Kingdom, and the president of the United States of America have consulted with each other in the common interests of the people of their countries and those of liberated Europe. They jointly declare their mutual agreement to concert during the temporary period of instability in liberated Europe the policies of their three governments in assisting the peoples liberated from the domination of Nazi Germany and the peoples of the former Axis satellite states of Europe to solve by democratic means their pressing political and economic problems.

The establishment of order in Europe and the rebuilding of national economic life must be achieved by processes which will enable the liberated peoples to destroy the last vestiges of Nazism and Fascism and to create democratic institutions of their own choice. This is a principle of the Atlantic Charter—the right of all people to choose the form of government under which they will live—the restoration of sovereign rights and self-government to those peoples who have been forcibly deprived to them by the aggressor nations.

To foster the conditions in which the liberated people may exercise these rights, the three governments will jointly assist the people in any European liberated state or former Axis state in Europe where, in their judgment conditions require,

a. to establish conditions of internal peace;
b. to carry out emergency relief measures for the relief of distressed peoples;
c. to form interim governmental authorities broadly representative of all democratic elements in the population and pledged to the earliest possible establishment through free elections of governments responsive to the will of the people; and
d. to facilitate where necessary the holding of such elections.

The three governments will consult the other United Nations and provisional authorities or other governments in Europe when matters of direct interest to them are under consideration.

When, in the opinion of the three governments, conditions in any European liberated state or former Axis satellite in Europe make such action necessary, they will immediately consult together on the measure necessary to discharge the joint responsibilities set forth in this declaration.

By this declaration we reaffirm our faith in the principles of the Atlantic Charter, our pledge in the Declaration by the United Nations and our determination to build in cooperation with other peace-loving nations world order, under law, dedicated to peace, security, freedom, and general well-being of all mankind.

In issuing this declaration, the three powers express the hope that the provisional government of the French Republic may be associated with them in the procedure suggested.

III. DISMEMBERMENT OF GERMANY

It was agreed that article 12 (a) of the surrender terms for Germany should be amended to read as follows:

"The United Kingdom, the United States of America, and the Union of Soviet Socialist Republics shall possess supreme authority with respect to Germany. In the exercise of such authority they will take such steps, including the complete dismemberment of Germany, as they deem requisite for future peace and security."

The study of the procedure of the dismemberment of Germany was referred to a committee consisting of Mr. Anthony Eden, Mr. John Winant, and Mr. Fedor T. Gusev. This body would consider the desirability of associating with it a French representative.

IV. ZONE OF OCCUPATION FOR THE FRENCH AND CONTROL COUNCIL FOR GERMANY

It was agreed that a zone in Germany, to be occupied by the French forces, should be allocated France. This zone would be formed out of the British and American zones and its extent would be settled by the British and Americans in consultation with the French provisional government.

It was also agreed that the French provisional government should be invited to become a member of the Allied Control Council for Germany.

V. REPARATION

The following protocol has been approved:

Protocol on the Talks Between the Heads of Three Governments

at the Crimean Conference on the Question of the German Reparations in Kind

1. Germany must pay in kind for the losses caused by her to the Allied nations in the course of the war. Reparations are to be received in the first instance by those countries which have borne the main burden of the war, have suffered the heaviest losses, and have organized victory over the enemy.
2. Reparation in kind is to be exacted from Germany in three following forms:
    a. Removals within two years from the surrender of Germany or the cessation of organized resistance from the national wealth of Germany located on the territory of Germany herself as well as outside her territory (equipment, machine tools, ships, rolling stock, German investments abroad, shares of industrial, transport, and other enterprises in Germany, etc.), these removals to be carried out chiefly for the purpose of destroying the war potential of Germany.
    b. Annual deliveries of goods from current production for a period to be fixed.
    c. Use of German labor.
3. For the working out on the above principles of a detailed plan for exaction of reparation from Germany an Allied reparation commission will be set up in Moscow. It will consist of three representatives—one from the Union of Soviet Socialist Republics, one from the United Kingdom, and one from the United States of America.
4. With regard to the fixing of the total sum of the reparation as well as the distribution of it among the countries which suffered from the German aggression, the Soviet and American delegations agreed as follows:

"The Moscow reparation commission should take in its initial studies as a basis for discussion the suggestion of the Soviet government that the total sum of the reparation in accordance with the points (a) and (b) of the paragraph 2 should be 22 billion dollars and that 50 percent should go to the Union of Soviet Socialist Republics."

The British delegation was of the opinion that, pending consideration of the reparation question by the Moscow reparation commission, no figures of reparation should be mentioned.

The above Soviet-American proposal has been passed to the Moscow reparation commission as one of the proposals to be considered by the commission.

VI. MAJOR WAR CRIMINALS

The conference agreed that the question of the major war criminals should be the subject of inquiry by the three foreign secretaries for report in due course after the close of the conference.

VII. POLAND

The following declaration on Poland was agreed by the conference:

"A new situation has been created in Poland as a result of her complete liberation by the Red Army. This calls for the establishment of a Polish provisional government which can be more broadly based than was possible before the recent liberation of the western part of Poland. The provisional government which is now functioning in Poland should therefore be reorganized on a broader democratic basis with the inclusion of democratic leaders from Poland itself and from Poles abroad. This new government should then be called the Polish Provisional Government of National Unity.

"M. Molotov, Mr. Harriman, and Sir A. Clark Kerr are authorized as a commission to consult in the first instance in Moscow with members of the present provisional government and with other Polish democratic leaders from within Poland and from abroad, with a view to the reorganization of the present government along the above lines. This Polish Provisional Government of National Unity shall be pledged to the holding of free and unfettered elections as soon as possible on the basis of universal suffrage and secret ballot. In these elections all democratic and anti-Nazi parties shall have the right to take part and to put forward candidates.

"When a Polish Provisional Government of National Unity has been properly formed in conformity with the above, the government of the USSR, which now maintains diplomatic relations with the present provisional government of Poland, and the government of the United Kingdom and the government of the United States of America will establish diplomatic relations with the new Polish Provisional Government of National Unity, and will exchange Ambassadors by whose reports the respective governments will be kept informed about the situation in Poland.

"The three heads of government consider that the eastern frontier of Poland should follow the Curzon Line with digressions from it in some regions of five to eight kilometers in favor of Poland. They recognize that Poland must receive substantial accessions in territory in the north and west. They feel that the opinion of the new Polish Provisional Government of National Unity should be sought in due course of the extent of these accessions and that the final delimitation of the western frontier of Poland should thereafter await the peace conference."

VIII. YUGOSLAVIA

It was agreed to recommend to Marshal Tito and to Dr. Ivan Subasitch:

a. That the Tito-Subasitch agreement should immediately be put into effect and a new government formed on the basis of the agreement.

b. That as soon as the new government has been formed it should declare;

    I. That the Anti-Fascist Assembly of the National Liberation (AVNOJ) will be extended to include members of the last Yugoslav Skupstina who have not compromised themselves by collaboration with the enemy, thus forming a body to be known as a temporary Parliament and

    II. That legislative acts passed by the Anti-Fascist Assembly of the National Liberation (AVNOJ) will be subject to subsequent ratification by a constituent assembly; and that this statement should be published in the communiqué of the conference.

IX. ITALO-YUGOSLAV FRONTIER—ITALO-AUSTRIAN FRONTIER

Notes on these subjects were put in by the British delegation and the American and Soviet delegations agreed to consider them and give their views later.

X. YUGOSLAV-BULGARIAN RELATIONS

There was an exchange of views between the foreign secretaries on the question of the desirability of a Yugoslav-Bulgarian pact of alliance. The question at issue was whether a state still under an armistice regime could be allowed to enter into a treaty with another state. Mr. Eden suggested that the Bulgarian and Yugoslav governments should be informed that this could not be approved. Mr. Stettinius suggested that the British and American ambassadors should discuss the matter further with Mr. Molotov in Moscow. Mr. Molotov agreed with the proposal of Mr. Stettinius.

XI. SOUTHEASTERN EUROPE

The British delegation put in notes for the consideration of their colleagues on the following subjects:

a. The Control Commission in Bulgaria.
b. Greek claims upon Bulgaria, more particularly with reference to reparations.
c. Oil equipment in Romania.

XII. IRAN

Mr. Eden, Mr. Stettinius, and Mr. Molotov exchanged views on the situation in Iran. It was agreed that this matter should be pursued through the diplomatic channel.

XIII. MEETINGS OF THE THREE FOREIGN SECRETARIES

The conference agreed that permanent machinery should be set up for consultation between the three foreign secretaries; they should meet as often as necessary, probably about every three or four months.

These meetings will be held in rotation in the three capitals, the first meeting being held in London.

XIV. THE MONTREAUX CONVENTION AND THE STRAITS

It was agreed that at the next meeting of the three foreign secretaries to be held in London, they should consider proposals which it was understood the Soviet government would put forward in relation to the Montreaux Convention, and report to their governments. The Turkish government should be informed at the appropriate moment.

The forgoing protocol was approved and signed by the three foreign secretaries at the Crimean Conference Feb. 11, 1945.

E. R. Stettinius Jr., M. Molotov, Anthony Eden

AGREEMENT REGARDING JAPAN

The leaders of the three great powers—the Soviet Union, the United States of America, and Great Britain—have agreed that in two or three months after Germany has surrendered and the war in Europe is terminated, the Soviet Union shall enter into war against Japan on the side of the Allies on condition that:

1. The status quo in Outer Mongolia (the Mongolian People's Republic) shall be preserved.
2. The former rights of Russia violated by the treacherous attack of Japan in 1904 shall be restored, viz.:
   a. The southern part of Sakhalin as well as the islands adjacent to it shall be returned to the Soviet Union;
   b. The commercial port of Dairen shall be internationalized, the preeminent interests of the Soviet Union in this port being safeguarded, and the lease of Port Arthur as a naval base of the USSR restored;
   c. The Chinese-Eastern Railroad and the South Manchurian Railroad, which provide an outlet to Dairen, shall be jointly operated by the establishment of a joint Soviet-Chinese company, it being understood that the preeminent interests of the Soviet Union shall be safeguarded and that China shall retain sovereignty in Manchuria;
3. The Kuril Islands shall be handed over to the Soviet Union.

It is understood that the agreement concerning Outer Mongolia and the ports and railroads referred to above will require concurrence of Generalissimo Chiang Kai-shek. The president will take measures in order to maintain this concurrence on advice from Marshal Stalin.

The heads of the three great powers have agreed that these claims of the Soviet Union shall be unquestionably fulfilled after Japan has been defeated.

For its part, the Soviet Union expresses it readiness to conclude with the national government of China a pact of friendship and alliance between the USSR and China in order to render assistance to China with its armed forces for the purpose of liberating China from the Japanese yoke.

Joseph Stalin, Franklin D. Roosevelt, Winston S. Churchill

Agreement Relating to Prisoners of War and Civilians Liberated by Forces Operating Under Soviet Command and Forces Operating Under United States of America Command; February 11, 1945

The government of the United States of America on the one hand and the government of the Union of Soviet Socialist Republics on the other hand, wishing to make arrangements for the care and repatriation of United States citizens freed by forces operating under Soviet command and for Soviet citizens freed by forces operating under United States command, have agreed as follows:

Article 1

All Soviet citizens liberated by the forces operating under United States command and all United States citizens liberated by the forces operating under Soviet command will, without delay after their liberation, be separated from enemy prisoners of war and will be maintained separately from them in camps or points of concentration until they have been handed over to the Soviet or United States authorities, as the case may be, at places agreed upon between those authorities.

United States and Soviet military authorities will respectively take the necessary measures for protection of camps, and points of concentration from enemy bombing, artillery fire, etc. . . .

[Articles 2–9 covered details]

Done at the Crimea in duplicate and in the English and Russian languages, both being equally authentic, this eleventh day of February, 1945.

For the government of the United States of America:

John R. Deane, Major General, USA

For the government of the Union of Soviet Socialist Republics:

Lieutenant General Gryzlov

Sources: The proceedings are taken from *The Yalta Conference*, 2nd ed., ed. Richard Fenno Jr. (Lexington, MA: D. C. Heath, 1972), 46–55. The prisoner of war agreement is from *Treaties and Other International Agreements of the United States of America 1776–1949* (Department of State Publication 8484), ed. Charles I. Bevans (Washington, DC: Government Printing Office, 1969), at the Yale Law School, Lillian Goldman Law Library's Avalon Project: Documents in Law, History and Diplomacy. Retrieved June 10, 2010, from http://avalon.law.yale.edu/20th_century/sov007.asp.

VI

HUMAN RIGHTS AND DOMESTIC ISSUES

The America that emerged from World War II had liberated millions, and partly because of that success both domestically and abroad the nation committed itself to a new era of human rights. At home, the long-ignored social and political status of African Americans finally came fully before the public with the school-integration case of *Brown v. the Board of Education*, and a decade later large-scale civil rights marches finally achieved in legislation the promises of Reconstruction. But the government rarely stops at merely ensuring an equal starting line, and the Great Society legislation of Lyndon Johnson soon went far beyond the intentions of many of its originators (including his own vice president, Hubert Humphrey) to attempt to legislate an equality of outcome. The language of civil rights was also applied to women in the *Roe v. Wade* case, where an arguably nonexistent "right to privacy" was ruled to trump the lives of the unborn. At this moment of civil unrest, racial tensions, the rise of radical feminism, and the ever-expansive power of government, Richard Nixon stretched executive power even further in an illegal attempt to ensure his reelection. Far from being an episode removed from the events of the 1960s, which are often treated positively by historians, Nixon's actions arguably fit right in with the period's amoral and increasingly pervasive view that government power was all that mattered and that any one person's values were as good as another's.

To a large degree these trends reflected the rise of secularism and the reduction in the role of religion in American society. The progressivism promulgated by atheist John Dewey in the schools continued to gain popularity, and with God increasingly replaced by the federal government, human rights became confused with government programs. The Supreme Court tended to marginalize religion, especially Christianity, in a series of landmark decisions that effectively removed God and religion from schools and public property. Minor attempts, with popular support, were made to restore traditional religious authority such as adding "under God" to the Pledge of Allegiance, but the trends would deepen through the end of the century. Becoming ever more activist, the Supreme Court also severely restricted applications of the Tenth Amendment in support of state sovereignty. Justice Black's opinion in *Everson v. Board of Education* (1947) clearly gave the Court's approval for the federal government to insert itself in state, local, and individual affairs, altering the system of checks and balances forever.

CHAPTER 43

Everson v. Board of Education, 1947

The case of *Arch R. Everson v. Board of Education of the Township of Ewing, et al.*, 330 US 1 (1947), argued November 20, 1946, and decided February 10, 1947, was the first Supreme Court decision that used the due process clause in the Fourteenth Amendment to make other amendments applicable to states as well as to Congress or the federal government. To say that Hugo Black's opinion for the majority in the five to four decision stretched historical facts would be an understatement. Justice Black's rendition of the rise of sentiment for religious freedom was overwrought, inaccurate, and strictly designed to support his preconception of colonial times. He concentrated his historical study on a single state, Virginia, where the established high Anglican church was loyalist and under attack from patriots, and several writings by only two founders, Thomas Jefferson (who was not at the Constitutional Convention) and James Madison. He ignored contrary evidence and other writings by Madison and Jefferson as well as their actions while in office that stood in opposition to his opinion. At the time the First Amendment was ratified, a majority of the states recognized Christianity or some denomination thereof as their state religion in one form or other, and the amendment was designed only to ensure that the federal government could not institute a national religion. Black used Jefferson's phrase "separation between church and state" multiple times, although Jefferson used it only once in his volumes of writings, and that in a private letter to a group that was formerly his client when he was a practicing attorney. While president, both Jefferson and Madison regularly attended church services in the chambers of the House of Representatives. No doubt they would have been aghast at Black's analysis, particularly his statement that "These practices [official religions in individual colonies] became so commonplace as to shock the freedom-loving colonials into a feeling of abhorrence."

Black's faulty reading of history aside, he blithely applied the due process clause of the Fourteenth Amendment to another part of the Constitution. On his logic, Black is silent—apparently he considered the due process clause a green light to apply all federal law to the states. Unfortunately, he set a precedent, without supporting or clarifying argument, that has been followed by later courts in applying the Constitution's restrictions on Congress to the states, thereby also contravening the Tenth Amendment. This is the feature that makes this case a landmark and a major turning point in moving the United States from being an essentially Christian nation to a secular one. What had the founders said about Christianity in public education? Why had they established public schools in the first place? Why did the framers of the Constitution not envision an activist Supreme Court such as those of modern times (or even the Taney court with its decision in the *Dred Scott* case)?

(Note: case citations have been removed for brevity.)

Everson v. Board of Education

MR. JUSTICE [HUGO] BLACK DELIVERED THE OPINION OF THE Court.

A New Jersey statute authorizes its local school districts to make rules and contracts for the transportation of children to and from schools. The appellee, a township board of education, acting pursuant to this statute authorized reimbursement to parents of money expended by them for the bus transportation of their children on regular buses operated by the public transportation system. Part of this money was for the payment of transportation of some children in the community to Catholic parochial schools. These church schools give their students, in addition to secular education, regular religious instruction conforming to the religious tenets and modes of worship of the Catholic faith. The superintendent of these schools is a Catholic priest.

The appellant, in his capacity as a district taxpayer, filed suit in a state court challenging the right of the board to reimburse parents of parochial school students. He contended that the statute and the resolution passed pursuant to it violated both the state and the federal constitutions. That court held that the legislature was without power to authorize such payment under the state constitution.

The New Jersey Court of Errors and Appeals reversed, holding that neither the statute nor the resolution passed pursuant to it was in conflict with the state constitution or the provisions of the federal Constitution in issue.

Since there has been no attack on the statute on the ground that a part of its language excludes children attending private schools operated for profit from enjoying state payment for their transportation, we need not consider this exclusionary language; it has no relevancy to any constitutional question here presented. Furthermore, if the exclusion clause had been properly challenged, we do not know whether New Jersey's highest court would construe its statutes as precluding payment of the school transportation of any group of pupils, even those of a private school run for profit. Consequently, we put to one side the question as to the validity of the statute against the claim that it does not authorize payment for the transportation generally of school children in New Jersey.

The only contention here is that the state statute and the resolution, insofar as they authorized reimbursement to parents of children attending parochial schools, violate the federal Constitution in these two respects, which to some extent, overlap. First, they authorize the state to take by taxation the private property of some and bestow it upon others, to be used for their own private purposes. This, it is alleged, violates the due process clause of the Fourteenth Amendment. Second, the statute and the resolution forced inhabitants to pay taxes to help support and maintain schools which are dedicated to, and which regularly teach, the Catholic faith. This is alleged to be a use of state power to support church schools contrary to the prohibition of the First Amendment which the Fourteenth Amendment made applicable to the states.

First. The due process argument that the state law taxes some people to help others carry out their private purposes is framed in two phases. The first phase is that a state cannot tax A to reimburse B for the cost of transporting his children to church schools. This is said to violate the due process clause because the children are sent to these church schools to satisfy the personal desires of their parents, rather than the public's interest in the general education of all children. This argument, if valid, would apply equally to prohibit state payment for the transportation of children to any nonpublic school, whether operated by a church, or any other nongovernment individual or group. But, the New Jersey legislature has decided that a public purpose will be served by using tax-raised funds to pay the bus fares of all school children, including those who attend parochial schools. The New Jersey Court of Errors and Appeals has reached the same conclusion. The fact that a state law, passed to satisfy a public need, coincides with the personal desires of the individuals most directly affected is certainly an inadequate reason for us to say that a legislature has erroneously appraised the public need.

It is true that this Court has, in rare instances, struck down state statutes on the ground that the purpose for which tax-raised funds were to be expended was not a public one. But the Court has also pointed out that this far-reaching authority must be exercised with the most extreme caution. Otherwise, a state's power to legislate for the public welfare might be seriously curtailed, a power which is a primary reason for the existence of states. Changing local conditions create new local problems which may lead a state's people and its local authorities to believe that laws authorizing new types of public services are necessary to promote the general well-being of the people. The Fourteenth Amendment did not strip the states of their power to meet problems previously left for individual solution.

It is much too late to argue that legislation intended to facilitate the opportunity of children to get a secular education serves no public purpose. The same thing is no less true of legislation to reimburse needy parents, or all parents, for payment of the fares of their children so that they can ride in public busses to and from schools rather than run the risk of traffic and other hazards incident to walking or "hitchhiking." Nor does it follow that a law has a private rather than a public purpose because it provides that tax-raised funds will be paid to reimburse individuals on account of money spent by them in a way which furthers a public program. Subsidies and loans to individuals such as farmers and home owners, and to privately owned transportation systems, as well as many other kinds of businesses, have been commonplace practices in our state and national history.

Insofar as the second phase of the due process argument may differ from the first, it is by suggesting that taxation for transportation of children to church schools constitutes support of a religion by the state. But if the law is invalid for this reason, it is because it violates the First Amendment's prohibition against the establishment of religion by law. This is the exact question raised by appellant's second contention, to consideration of which we now turn.

Second. The New Jersey statute is challenged as a "law respecting an establishment of religion." The First Amendment, as made applicable to the states by the Fourteenth, commands that a state "shall make no law respecting an establishment of religion, or prohibiting the free exercise thereof." These words of the First Amendment reflected in the minds of early Americans a vivid mental picture of conditions and practices which they fervently wished to stamp out in order to preserve liberty for themselves and for their posterity. Doubtless their goal has not been entirely reached; but so far has the nation moved toward it that the expression "law respecting an establishment of religion," probably does not so vividly remind present-day Americans of the evils, fears, and political problems that caused that expression to be written into our Bill of Rights. Whether this New Jersey law is one respecting the "establishment of religion" requires an understanding of the meaning of that language, particularly with respect to the imposition of taxes.

Once again, therefore, it is not inappropriate briefly to review the background and environment of the period in which that constitutional language was fashioned and adopted.

A large proportion of the early settlers of this country came here from Europe to escape the bondage of laws which compelled them to support and attend government favored churches. The centuries immediately before and contemporaneous with the colonization of America had been filled with turmoil, civil strife, and persecutions, generated in large part by established sects determined to maintain their absolute political and religious supremacy. With the power of government supporting them, at various times and places, Catholics had persecuted Protestants, Protestants had persecuted Catholics, Protestant sects had persecuted other Protestant sects, Catholics of one shade of belief had persecuted Catholics of another shade of belief, and all of these had from time to time persecuted Jews. In efforts to force loyalty to whatever religious group happened to be on top and in league with the government of a particular time and place, men and women had been fined, cast in jail, cruelly tortured, and killed. Among the offenses for which these punishments had been inflicted were such things as speaking disrespectfully of the views of ministers of government-established churches, nonattendance at those churches, expressions of nonbelief in their doctrines, and failure to pay taxes and tithes to support them.

These practices of the Old World were transplanted to and began to thrive in the soil of the new America. The very charters granted by the English Crown to the individuals and companies designated to make the laws which would control the destinies of the colonials authorized these individuals and companies to erect religious establishments which all, whether believers or nonbelievers, would be required to support and attend. An exercise of this authority was accompanied by a repetition of many of the Old World practices and persecutions. Catholics found themselves hounded and proscribed because of their faith; Quakers who followed their conscience went to jail; Baptists were peculiarly obnoxious to certain dominant Protestant sects; men and women of varied faiths who happened to be in a minority in a particular locality were persecuted because they steadfastly persisted in worshipping God only as their own consciences dictated. And all of these dissenters were compelled to pay tithes and taxes to support government-sponsored churches whose ministers preached inflammatory sermons designed to strengthen and consolidate the established faith by generating a burning hatred against dissenters.

These practices became so commonplace as to shock the freedom-loving colonials into a feeling of abhorrence. The imposition of taxes to pay ministers' salaries and to build and maintain churches and church property aroused their indignation. It was these feelings which found expression in the First Amendment. No one locality and no one group throughout the colonies can rightly be given entire credit for having aroused the sentiment that culminated in adoption of the Bill of Rights' provisions embracing religious liberty. But Virginia, where the established church had achieved a dominant influence in political affairs and where many excesses attracted wide public attention, provided a great stimulus and able leadership for the movement. The people there, as elsewhere, reached the conviction that individual religious liberty could be achieved best under a government which was stripped of all power to tax, to support, or otherwise to assist any or all religions, or to interfere with the beliefs of any religious individual or group.

The movement toward this end reached its dramatic climax in Virginia in 1785–6 when the Virginia legislative body was about to renew Virginia's tax levy for the support of the established church. Thomas Jefferson and James Madison led the fight against this tax. Madison wrote his great "Memorial and Remonstrance" against the law. In it, he eloquently argued that a true religion did not need the support of law; that no person, either believer or nonbeliever, should be taxed to support a religious institution of any kind; that the best interest of a society required that the minds of men always be wholly free; and that cruel persecutions were the inevitable result of government-established religions. Madison's "Remonstrance" received strong support throughout Virginia, and the assembly postponed consideration of the proposed tax measure until its next session. When the proposal came up for consideration at that session, it not only died in committee, but the assembly enacted the famous "Virginia Bill for Religious Liberty" [Virginia Act for Establishing Religious Freedom] originally written by Thomas Jefferson.

The preamble to that bill stated among other things that "Almighty God hath created the mind free; that all attempts to influence it by temporal punishments, or burthens, or by civil incapacitations, tend only to beget habits of hypocrisy and meanness, and are a departure from the plan of the Holy author of our religion who being Lord both of body and mind, yet chose not to propagate it by coercions on either . . . ; that to compel a man to furnish contributions of money for the propagation of opinions which he disbelieves, is sinful and tyrannical; that even the forcing him to support this or that teacher of his own religious persuasion, is depriving him of the comfortable liberty of giving his contributions to the particular pastor, whose morals he would make his pattern. . . ." And the statute itself enacted "That no man shall be compelled to frequent or support any religious worship, place, or ministry whatsoever, nor shall be enforced, restrained, molested, or burthened, in his body or goods, nor shall otherwise suffer on account of his religious opinions or belief. . . ."

This Court has previously recognized that the provisions of the First Amendment, in the drafting and adoption of which Madison and Jefferson played such leading roles, had the same objective and were intended to provide the same protection against governmental intrusion on religious liberty as the Virginia statute.

Prior to the adoption of the Fourteenth Amendment, the First Amendment did not apply as a restraint against the states. Most of them did soon provide similar constitutional protections for religious liberty. But some states persisted for about half a century in imposing restraints upon the free exercise of religion and in discriminating against particular religious groups. In recent years, so far as the provision against the establishment of a religion is concerned, the question has most frequently arisen in connection with proposed state aid to church schools and efforts to carry on religious teachings in the public schools in accordance with the tenets of a particular sect. Some churches have either sought or accepted state financial support for their schools. Here again the efforts to obtain state aid or acceptance of it have not been limited to any one particular faith. The state courts, in the main, have remained faithful to the language of their own constitutional provisions designed to protect religious freedom and to separate religions and governments. Their decisions, however, show the difficulty in drawing the line between tax legislation which provides funds for the welfare of the general public and that which is designed to support institutions which teach religion.

The meaning and scope of the First Amendment, preventing establishment of religion or prohibiting the free exercise thereof, in the light of its history and the evils it was designed forever to suppress, have been several times elaborated by the decisions of this Court prior to the application of the First Amendment to the states by the Fourteenth. The broad meaning given the amendment by these earlier cases has been accepted by this Court in its decisions concerning an individual's religious freedom rendered since the Fourteenth Amendment was interpreted to make the prohibitions of the First applicable to state action abridging religious freedom. There is every reason to give the same application and broad interpretation to the "establishment of religion" clause. The interrelation of these complementary clauses was well summarized in a statement of the Court of Appeals of South Carolina, quoted with approval by this Court, in *Watson v. Jones*: "The structure of our government has, for the preservation of civil liberty, rescued the temporal institutions from religious interference. On the other hand, it has secured religious liberty from the invasions of the civil authority."

The "establishment of religion" clause of the First Amendment means at least this: Neither a state nor the federal government can set up a church. Neither can pass laws which aid one religion, aid all religions, or prefer one religion over another. Neither can force nor influence a person to go to or to remain away from church against his will or force him to profess a belief or disbelief in any religion. No person can be punished for entertaining or professing religious beliefs or disbeliefs, for church attendance or nonattendance. No tax in any amount, large or small, can be levied to support any religious activities or institutions, whatever they may be called, or whatever form they may adopt to teach or practice religion. Neither a state nor the federal government can, openly or secretly, participate in the affairs of any religious organizations or groups and vice versa. In the words of Jefferson, the clause against establishment of religion by law was intended to erect "a wall of separation between church and state."

We must consider the New Jersey statute in accordance with the foregoing limitations imposed by the First Amendment. But we must not strike that state statute down if it is within the state's constitutional power even though it approaches the verge of that power. New Jersey cannot consistently with the "establishment of religion" clause of the First Amendment contribute tax-raised funds to the support of an institution which teaches the tenets and faith of any church. On the other hand, other language of the amendment commands that New Jersey cannot hamper its citizens in the free exercise of their own religion. Consequently, it cannot exclude individual Catholics, Lutherans, Mohammedans, Baptists, Jews, Methodists, nonbelievers, Presbyterians, or the members of any other faith, because of their faith, or lack of it, from receiving the benefits of public welfare legislation. While we do not mean to intimate that a state could not provide transportation only to children attending public schools, we must be careful, in protecting the citizens of New Jersey against state-established churches, to be sure that we do not inadvertently prohibit New Jersey from extending its general state law benefits to all its citizens without regard to their religious belief.

Measured by these standards, we cannot say that the First Amendment prohibits New Jersey from spending tax-raised funds to pay the bus fares of parochial school pupils as a part of a general program under which it pays the fares of pupils attending public and other schools. It is undoubtedly true that children are helped to get to church schools. There is even a possibility that some of the children might not be sent to the church schools if the parents were compelled to pay their children's bus fares out of their own pockets when transportation to a public school would have been paid for by the state. The same possibility exists where the state requires a local transit company to provide reduced fares to school children including those attending parochial schools, or where a municipally owned transportation system undertakes to carry all school children free of charge. Moreover, state-paid policemen, detailed to protect children going to and from church schools from the very real hazards of traffic, would serve much the same purpose and accomplish much the same result as state provisions intended to guarantee free transportation of a kind which the state deems to be best for the school children's welfare. And parents might refuse to risk their children to the serious danger of traffic accidents going to and from parochial schools, the approaches to which were not protected by policemen. Similarly, parents might be reluctant to permit their children to attend schools which the state had cut off from such general government services as ordinary police and fire protection, connections for sewage disposal, public highways, and sidewalks. Of course, cutting off church schools from these services, so separate and so indisputably marked off from the religious function, would make it far more difficult for the schools to operate. But such is obviously not the purpose of the First Amendment.

That amendment requires the state to be a neutral in its relations with groups of religious believers and nonbelievers; it does not require the state to be their adversary. State power is no more to be used so as to handicap religions, than it is to favor them.

This Court has said that parents may, in the discharge of their duty under state compulsory education laws, send their children to a religious rather than a public school if the school meets the secular educational requirements which the state has power to impose. It appears that these parochial schools meet New Jersey's requirements. The state contributes no money to the schools. It does not support them. Its legislation, as applied, does no more than provide a general program to help parents get their children, regardless of their religion, safely and expeditiously to and from accredited schools.

The First Amendment has erected a wall between church and state. That wall must be kept high and impregnable. We could not approve the slightest breach. New Jersey has not breached it here. Affirmed.

Source: FindLaw: For Legal Professionals, *Everson v. Board of Education of Ewing TP*, 330 US 1 (1947). Retrieved April 30, 2010, from http://caselaw.lp.findlaw.com/scripts/getcase.pl?court=us&vol=330&invol=1.

CHAPTER 44

Brown v. Board of Education, 1954

The landmark case of *Oliver Brown et al. v. Board of Education of Topeka et al.*, 347 U.S. 583 (1954), was arranged by the National Association for the Advancement of Colored People to test the constitutionality of segregation in public schools. Segregation was still being practiced throughout the South and other states under the "separate but equal" doctrine established in *Plessy v. Ferguson* in 1896. In 1951 thirteen black parents filed in the class action suit on behalf of their twenty children who were refused enrollment in neighborhood schools and directed to a segregated school for only blacks. By the time the case reached the Supreme Court, it was combined with four other cases from Washington, D.C.; Virginia; Delaware; and South Carolina.

The cases were argued on December 9, 1952, but the Court was deeply divided and no opinion was reached. Chief Justice Fred Vinson passed away in September 1953, and President Eisenhower appointed Governor Earl Warren as the new chief justice. The case was reargued a year later, starting on December 8, 1953, and this time the Court issued a unanimous decision on May 17, 1954. *Plessy v. Ferguson* was reversed, and "separate but equal" was ruled to be inherently unequal. The entire principle of segregation in public facilities was now free to be attacked, and jim crow laws were at risk. Pressure from civil rights organizations continued to mount until the 1960s when federal civil rights legislation swept jim crow into the dustbin. *Brown v. Board* was a decision whose time had come. Could it have come earlier, in another case? What did this decision mean for America? Were there instances where private clubs could be sued as public facilities, and if so, were there any protections left for the concept of "private association"?

(Note: case citations have been removed for brevity.)

Brown v. Board of Education

MR. CHIEF JUSTICE WARREN DELIVERED THE OPINION OF THE Court.

These cases come to us from the States of Kansas, South Carolina, Virginia, and Delaware. They are premised on different facts and different local conditions, but a common legal question justifies their consideration together in this consolidated opinion.

In each of the cases, minors of the Negro race, through their legal representatives, seek the aid of the courts in obtaining admission to the public schools of their community on a nonsegregated basis. In each instance, they had been denied admission to schools attended by white children under laws requiring or permitting segregation according to race.

This segregation was alleged to deprive the plaintiffs of the equal protection of the laws under the Fourteenth Amendment. In each of the cases other than the Delaware case, a three-judge federal district court denied relief to the plaintiffs on the so-called "separate but equal" doctrine announced by this Court in *Plessy v. Ferguson*. Under that doctrine, equality of treatment is accorded when the races are provided substantially equal facilities, even though these facilities be separate. In the Delaware case, the Supreme Court of Delaware adhered to that doctrine, but ordered that the plaintiffs be admitted to the white schools because of their superiority to the Negro schools.

The plaintiffs contend that segregated public schools are not "equal" and cannot be made "equal," and that hence they are deprived of the equal protection of the laws. Because of the obvious importance of the question presented, the Court took jurisdiction. Argument was heard in the 1952 term, and reargument was heard this term on certain questions propounded by the Court.

Reargument was largely devoted to the circumstances surrounding the adoption of the Fourteenth Amendment in 1868. It covered exhaustively consideration of the amendment in Congress, ratification by the states, then-existing practices in racial segregation, and the views of proponents and opponents of the amendment. This discussion and our own investigation convince us that, although these sources cast some light, it is not enough to resolve the problem with which we are faced. At best, they are inconclusive. The most avid proponents of the postwar amendments undoubtedly intended them to remove all legal distinctions among "all persons born or naturalized in the United States." Their opponents, just as certainly, were antagonistic to both the letter and the spirit of the amendments and wished them to have the most limited effect. What others in Congress and the state legislatures had in mind cannot be determined with any degree of certainty.

An additional reason for the inconclusive nature of the amendment's history with respect to segregated schools is the status of public education at that time. In the South, the movement toward free common schools, supported by general taxation, had not yet taken hold. Education of white children was largely in the hands of private groups. Education of Negroes was almost nonexistent, and practically all of the race were illiterate. In fact, any education of Negroes was forbidden by law in some states. Today, in contrast, many Negroes have achieved outstanding success in the arts and sciences, as well as in the business and professional world. It is true that public school education at the time of the amendment had advanced further in the North, but the effect of the amendment on northern states was generally ignored in the congressional debates. Even in the North, the conditions of public education did not approximate those existing today. The curriculum was usually rudimentary; ungraded schools were common in rural areas; the school term was but three months a year in many states, and compulsory school attendance was virtually unknown. As a consequence, it is not surprising that there should be so little in the history of the Fourteenth Amendment relating to its intended effect on public education.

In the first cases in this Court construing the Fourteenth Amendment, decided shortly after its adoption, the Court interpreted it as proscribing all state-imposed discriminations against the Negro race. The doctrine of "separate but equal" did not make its appearance in this Court until 1896 in the case of *Plessy v. Ferguson*, involving not education but transportation. American courts have since labored with the doctrine for over half a century. In this Court, there have been six cases involving the "separate but equal" doctrine in the field of public education. In *Cumming v. County Board of Education*, and *Gong Lum v. Rice*, the validity of the doctrine itself was not challenged. In more recent cases, all on the graduate school level, inequality was found in that specific benefits enjoyed by white students were denied to Negro students of the same educational qualifications. In none of these cases was it necessary to reexamine the doctrine to grant relief to the Negro plaintiff. And in *Sweatt v. Painter*, the Court expressly reserved decision on the question of whether *Plessy v. Ferguson* should be held inapplicable to public education.

In the instant cases, that question is directly presented. Here, unlike *Sweatt v. Painter*, there are findings below that the Negro and white schools involved have been equalized, or are being equalized, with respect to buildings, curricula, qualifications and salaries of teachers, and other "tangible" factors. Our decision, therefore, cannot turn on merely a comparison of these tangible factors in the Negro and white schools involved in each of the cases. We must look instead to the effect of segregation itself on public education.

In approaching this problem, we cannot turn the clock back to 1868, when the amendment was adopted, or even to 1896, when *Plessy v. Ferguson* was written. We must consider public education in the light of its full development and its present place in American life throughout the nation. Only in this way can it be determined if segregation in public schools deprives these plaintiffs of the equal protection of the laws.

Today, education is perhaps the most important function of state and local governments. Compulsory school attendance laws and the great expenditures for education both demonstrate our recognition of the importance of education to our democratic society. It is required in the performance of our most basic public responsibilities, even service in the armed forces. It is the very foundation of good citizenship. Today it is a principal instrument in awakening the child to cultural values, in preparing him for later professional training, and in helping him to adjust normally to his environment. In these days, it is doubtful that any child may reasonably be expected to succeed in life if he is denied the opportunity of an education. Such an opportunity, where the state has undertaken to provide it, is a right which must be made available to all on equal terms.

We come then to the question presented: Does segregation of children in public schools solely on the basis of race, even though the physical facilities and other "tangible" factors may be equal, deprive the children of the minority group of equal educational opportunities? We believe that it does.

In *Sweatt v. Painter,* in finding that a segregated law school for Negroes could not provide them equal educational opportunities, this Court relied in large part on "those qualities which are incapable of objective measurement but which make for greatness in a law school." In *McLaurin v. Oklahoma State Regents,* the Court, in requiring that a Negro admitted to a white graduate school be treated like all other students, again resorted to intangible considerations: ". . . his ability to study, to engage in discussions and exchange views with other students, and, in general, to learn his profession." Such considerations apply with added force to children in grade and high schools. To separate them from others of similar age and qualifications solely because of their race generates a feeling of inferiority as to their status in the community that may affect their hearts and minds in a way unlikely ever to be undone. The effect of this separation on their educational opportunities was well stated by a finding in the Kansas case by a court which nevertheless felt compelled to rule against the Negro plaintiffs: "Segregation of white and colored children in public schools has a detrimental effect upon the colored children. The impact is greater when it has the sanction of the law, for the policy of separating the races is usually interpreted as denoting the inferiority of the Negro group. A sense of inferiority affects the motivation of a child to learn."

Segregation with the sanction of law, therefore, has a tendency to [retard] the educational and mental development of Negro children and to deprive them of some of the benefits they would receive in a racially integrated school system.

Whatever may have been the extent of psychological knowledge at the time of *Plessy v. Ferguson*, this finding is amply supported by modern authority. Any language in *Plessy v. Ferguson* contrary to this finding is rejected.

We conclude that, in the field of public education, the doctrine of "separate but equal" has no place. Separate educational facilities are inherently unequal. Therefore, we hold that the plaintiffs and others similarly situated for whom the actions have been brought are, by reason of the segregation complained of, deprived of the equal protection of the laws guaranteed by the Fourteenth Amendment. This disposition makes unnecessary any discussion whether such segregation also violates the due process clause of the Fourteenth Amendment.

Because these are class actions, because of the wide applicability of this decision, and because of the great variety of local conditions, the formulation of decrees in these cases presents problems of considerable complexity. On reargument, the consideration of appropriate relief was necessarily subordinated to the primary question—the constitutionality of segregation in public education. We have now announced that such segregation is a denial of the equal protection of the laws. In order that we may have the full assistance of the parties in formulating decrees, the cases will be restored to the docket, and the parties are requested to present further argument on questions 4 and 5 previously propounded by the Court for the reargument this term. The attorney general of the United States is again invited to participate. The attorneys general of the states requiring or permitting segregation in public education will also be permitted to appear as amici curiae upon request to do so by September 15, 1954, and submission of briefs by October 1, 1954.

It is so ordered.

Source: The National Center for Public Policy Research, *Brown v. Board of Education*, 347 US 483 (1954) (USSC+). Retrieved April 30, 2010, from http://nationalcenter .org/brown.html.

CHAPTER 45

John F. Kennedy's Inaugural Address, 1961

The election of Senator John F. Kennedy to the presidency in 1960 was widely hailed as a turning point in American history because, not only was Kennedy youthfully attractive, but he was also the first Roman Catholic elected to the office and the first of Irish Catholic ancestry.

Kennedy surprised many with his inaugural address, which was written by Ted Sorenson, but, as he would prove during his short time in office, he believed in latitudinarianism and that human rights came from God. With his religious equanimity, he disappointed Catholics but put Protestant fears to rest, and he did not follow FDR's authoritarian lead in creating new "human rights" though expanded government programs. His speech was widely hailed as striking just the right tone, and although the shortest inaugural speech in modern times, it ushered in the 1960s as a decade during which all things were possible. Unfortunately, Kennedy's performance as president fell short of the promise inherent in his speech. The Vietnam conflict, which escalated under his administration, radicalized a significant part of the baby boom generation, with consequences that became fully apparent only in the twenty-first century. Where did Kennedy fail to fulfill his promises and what were the consequences? Was it true then—and is it true today—that the United States is willing to "bear any burden" and "pay any price" for freedom? What would Kennedy's party, the Democrats, think of this speech in the twenty-first century?

Inaugural Address, January 20, 1961

VICE PRESIDENT JOHNSON, MR. SPEAKER, MR. CHIEF JUSTICE, President Eisenhower, Vice President Nixon, President Truman, Reverend Clergy, fellow citizens:

We observe today not a victory of party, but a celebration of freedom—symbolizing an end, as well as a beginning—signifying renewal, as well as change. For I have sworn before you and Almighty God the same solemn oath our forebears prescribed nearly a century and three-quarters ago.

The world is very different now. For man holds in his mortal hands the power to abolish all forms of human poverty and all forms of human life. And yet the same revolutionary beliefs for which our forebears fought are still at issue around the globe—the belief that the rights of man come not from the generosity of the state but from the hand of God.

We dare not forget today that we are the heirs of that first revolution. Let the word go forth from this time and place, to friend and foe alike, that the torch has been passed to a new generation of Americans—born in this century, tempered by war, disciplined by a hard and bitter peace, proud of our ancient heritage—and unwilling to witness or permit the slow undoing of those human rights to which this nation has always been committed, and to which we are committed today at home and around the world.

Let every nation know, whether it wishes us well or ill, that we shall pay any price, bear any burden, meet any hardship, support any friend, oppose any foe, in order to assure the survival and the success of liberty.

This much we pledge—and more.

To those old allies whose cultural and spiritual origins we share, we pledge the loyalty of faithful friends. United, there is little we cannot do in a host of cooperative ventures. Divided, there is little we can do—for we dare not meet a powerful challenge at odds and split asunder.

To those new states whom we welcome to the ranks of the free, we pledge our word that one form of colonial control shall not have passed away merely to be replaced by a far more iron tyranny. We shall not always expect to find them supporting our view. But we shall always hope to find them strongly supporting their own freedom—and to remember that, in the past, those who foolishly sought power by riding the back of the tiger ended up inside.

To those peoples in the huts and villages across the globe struggling to break the bonds of mass misery, we pledge our best efforts to help them help themselves, for whatever period is required—not because the communists may be doing it, not because we seek their votes, but because it is right. If a free society cannot help the many who are poor, it cannot save the few who are rich.

To our sister republics south of our border, we offer a special pledge—to convert our good words into good deeds—in a new alliance for progress—to assist free men and free governments in casting off the chains of poverty. But this peaceful revolution of hope cannot become the prey of hostile powers. Let all our neighbors know that we shall join with them to oppose aggression or subversion anywhere in the Americas. And let every other power know that this hemisphere intends to remain the master of its own house.

To that world assembly of sovereign states, the United Nations, our last best hope in an age where the instruments of war have far outpaced the instruments of peace, we renew our pledge of support—to prevent it from becoming merely a forum for invective—to strengthen its shield of the new and the weak—and to enlarge the area in which its writ may run.

Finally, to those nations who would make themselves our adversary, we offer not a pledge but a request: that both sides begin anew the quest for peace, before the dark powers of destruction unleashed by science engulf all humanity in planned or accidental self-destruction.

We dare not tempt them with weakness. For only when our arms are sufficient beyond doubt can we be certain beyond doubt that they will never be employed.

But neither can two great and powerful groups of nations take comfort from our present course—both sides overburdened by the cost of modern weapons, both rightly alarmed by the steady spread of the deadly atom, yet both racing to alter that uncertain balance of terror that stays the hand of mankind's final war.

So let us begin anew—remembering on both sides that civility is not a sign of weakness, and sincerity is always subject to proof. Let us never negotiate out of fear. But let us never fear to negotiate.

Let both sides explore what problems unite us instead of belaboring those problems which divide us.

Let both sides, for the first time, formulate serious and precise proposals for the inspection and control of arms—and bring the absolute power to destroy other nations under the absolute control of all nations.

Let both sides seek to invoke the wonders of science instead of its terrors. Together let us explore the stars, conquer the deserts, eradicate disease, tap the ocean depths, and encourage the arts and commerce.

Let both sides unite to heed in all corners of the earth the command of Isaiah—to "undo the heavy burdens . . . and to let the oppressed go free."

And if a beachhead of cooperation may push back the jungle of suspicion, let both sides join in creating a new endeavor, not a new balance of power, but a new world of law, where the strong are just and the weak secure and the peace preserved.

All this will not be finished in the first hundred days. Nor will it be finished in the first thousand days, nor in the life of this administration, nor even perhaps in our lifetime on this planet. But let us begin.

In your hands, my fellow citizens, more than in mine, will rest the final success or failure of our course. Since this country was founded, each generation of Americans has been summoned to give testimony to its national loyalty.

The graves of young Americans who answered the call to service surround the globe.

Now the trumpet summons us again—not as a call to bear arms, though arms we need; not as a call to battle, though embattled we are—but a call to bear the burden of a long twilight struggle, year in and year out, "rejoicing in hope, patient in tribulation"—a struggle against the common enemies of man: tyranny, poverty, disease, and war itself.

Can we forge against these enemies a grand and global alliance, North and South, East and West, that can assure a more fruitful life for all mankind? Will you join in that historic effort?

In the long history of the world, only a few generations have been granted the role of defending freedom in its hour of maximum danger. I do not shrink from this responsibility—I welcome it. I do not believe that any of us would exchange places with any other people or any other generation. The energy, the faith, the devotion which we bring to this endeavor will light our country and all who serve it—and the glow from that fire can truly light the world.

And so, my fellow Americans: ask not what your country can do for you— ask what you can do for your country.

My fellow citizens of the world: ask not what America will do for you, but what together we can do for the freedom of man.

Finally, whether you are citizens of America or citizens of the world, ask of us the same high standards of strength and sacrifice which we ask of you.

With a good conscience our only sure reward, with history the final judge of our deeds, let us go forth to lead the land we love, asking His blessing and His help, but knowing that here on earth God's work must truly be our own.

Source: John F. Kennedy Presidential Library and Museum quoting the National Archives and Records Administration. Retrieved June 3, 2010, from http://www .ourdocuments.gov/doc.php?flash=true&doc=91&page=transcript.

CHAPTER 46

The Civil Rights Act, 1964

In 1957, President Eisenhower introduced a civil rights bill to ensure voting rights for all citizens and to monitor and report on civil rights abuses. The Democratic leadership, headed by Senator Lyndon Johnson, extensively modified the bill so that Johnson could claim the credit for passing a civil rights bill (the first in eighty-two years) while at the same time taking credit for "killing" the more substantive bill that Eisenhower wanted. The door was opened, however, and civil rights leaders like Martin Luther King Jr. took to the streets and over the next seven years built a juggernaut of support for more effective legislation, through nonviolent protests and attempts to increase black voter registration.

In 1963, President Kennedy issued another call for civil rights legislation, but the Democrats effectively kept the bill in committees until his assassination. The new president, Lyndon Johnson, saw that the civil rights surge could not be held back any longer and maneuvered the bill through Congress as a tribute to Kennedy. Accordingly, the Civil Rights Act of 1964 was passed on July 2, over filibustering Democrats, with substantial Republican help (a fact largely ignored today), and was strengthened in 1965 with the passage of the Voting Rights Act and again in 1968 with another civil rights act, commonly called the Fair Housing Act. How did these acts change the political parties and the American electorate?

Civil Rights Act of 1964

AN ACT

To enforce the constitutional right to vote, to confer jurisdiction upon the district courts of the United States to provide injunctive relief against discrimination in public accommodations, to authorize the attorney general to institute suits to protect constitutional rights in public facilities and public education, to extend the Commission on Civil Rights, to prevent discrimination in federally assisted programs, to establish a Commission on Equal Employment Opportunity, and for other purposes.

Be it enacted by the Senate and House of Representatives of the United States of America in Congress assembled, That this Act may be cited as the "Civil Rights Act of 1964."

TITLE I—VOTING RIGHTS

SEC. 101. . . .

(2) No person acting under color of law shall—

(a) in determining whether any individual is qualified under state law or laws to vote in any federal election, apply any standard, practice, or procedure different from the standards, practices, or procedures applied under such law or laws to other individuals within the same county, parish, or similar political subdivision who have been found by state officials to be qualified to vote;

(b) deny the right of any individual to vote in any federal election because of an error or omission on any record or paper relating to any application, registration, or other act requisite to voting, if such error or omission is not material in determining whether such individual is qualified under state law to vote in such election; or

(c) employ any literacy test as a qualification for voting in any federal election unless (i) such test is administered to each individual and is conducted wholly in writing, and (ii) a certified copy of the test and of the answers given by the individual is furnished to him within twenty-five days of the submission of his request. . . .

TITLE II—INJUNCTIVE RELIEF AGAINST DISCRIMINATION IN PLACES OF PUBLIC ACCOMMODATION

SEC. 201. (a) All persons shall be entitled to the full and equal enjoyment of the goods, services, facilities, and privileges, advantages, and accommodations of any place of public accommodation, as defined in this section, without discrimination or segregation on the ground of race, color, religion, or national origin. . . .

SEC. 202. All persons shall be entitled to be free, at any establishment or place, from discrimination or segregation of any kind on the ground of race, color, religion, or national origin, if such discrimination or segregation is or purports to be required by any law, statute, ordinance, regulation, rule, or order of a state or any agency or political subdivision thereof.

SEC. 203. No person shall (a) withhold, deny, or attempt to withhold or deny, or deprive or attempt to deprive, any person of any right or privilege secured by section 201 or 202, or (b) intimidate, threaten, or coerce, or attempt to intimidate, threaten, or coerce any person with the purpose of interfering with any right or privilege secured by section 201 or 202, or (c) punish or attempt to punish any person for exercising or attempting to exercise any right or privilege secured by section 201 or 202.

SEC. 204. (a) Whenever any person has engaged or there are reasonable grounds to believe that any person is about to engage in any act or practice prohibited by section 203, a civil action for preventive relief, including an application for a permanent or temporary injunction, restraining order, or other order, may be instituted by the person aggrieved and, upon timely application, the court may, in its discretion, permit the attorney general to intervene in such civil action if he certifies that the case is of general public importance. Upon application by the complainant and in such circumstances as the court may deem just, the court may appoint an attorney for such complainant and may authorize the commencement of the civil action without the payment of fees, costs, or security. . . .

TITLE III—DESEGREGATION OF PUBLIC FACILITIES

SEC. 301. (a) Whenever the attorney general receives a complaint in writing signed by an individual to the effect that he is being deprived of or threatened with the loss of his right to the equal protection of the laws, on account of his race, color, religion, or national origin, by being denied equal utilization of any public facility which is owned, operated, or managed by or on behalf of any state or subdivision thereof, other than a public school or public college as defined in section 401 of title IV hereof, and the attorney general believes the complaint is meritorious and certifies that the signer or signers of such complaint are unable, in his judgment, to initiate and maintain appropriate legal proceedings for relief and that the institution of an action will materially further the orderly progress of desegregation in public facilities, the attorney general is authorized to institute for or in the name of the United States a civil action in any appropriate district court of the United States against such parties and for such relief as may be appropriate, and such court shall have and shall exercise jurisdiction of proceedings instituted pursuant to this section. . . .

TITLE IV—DESEGREGATION OF PUBLIC EDUCATION
DEFINITIONS. . . .

SURVEY AND REPORT OF EDUCATIONAL OPPORTUNITIES

SEC. 402. The commissioner shall conduct a survey and make a report to the president and the Congress, within two years of the enactment of this title, concerning the lack of availability of equal educational opportunities for individuals by reason of race, color, religion, or national origin in public educational institutions at all levels in the United States, its territories and possessions, and the District of Columbia.

TECHNICAL ASSISTANCE

SEC. 403. The commissioner is authorized, upon the application of any school board, state, municipality, school district, or other governmental unit legally responsible for operating a public school or schools, to render technical assistance to such applicant in the preparation, adoption, and implementation of plans for the desegregation of public schools. . . .

TRAINING INSTITUTES

SEC. 404. The commissioner is authorized to arrange, through grants or contracts, with institutions of higher education for the operation of short-term or regular session institutes for special training designed to improve the ability of teachers, supervisors, counselors, and other elementary or secondary school personnel to deal effectively with special educational problems occasioned by desegregation. . . .

SUITS BY THE ATTORNEY GENERAL

SEC. 407. (a) Whenever the attorney general receives a complaint in writing—

(1) signed by a parent or group of parents to the effect that his or their minor children, as members of a class of persons similarly situated, are being deprived by a school board of the equal protection of the laws, or

(2) signed by an individual, or his parent, to the effect that he has been denied admission to or not permitted to continue in attendance at a public college by reason of race, color, religion, or national origin, and the attorney general believes the complaint is meritorious and certifies that the signer or signers of such complaint are unable, in his judgment, to initiate and maintain appropriate legal proceedings for relief and that the institution of an action will materially further the orderly achievement of desegregation in public education, the attorney general is authorized, after giving notice of such complaint to the appropriate school board or college authority and after certifying that he is satisfied that such board or authority has had a reasonable time to adjust the conditions alleged in such complaint, to institute for or in the name of the United States a civil action in any appropriate district court of the United States against such parties and for such relief as may be appropriate, and such court shall have and shall exercise jurisdiction of proceedings instituted pursuant to this section, provided that nothing herein shall empower any official or court of the United States to issue any order seeking to achieve a racial balance in any school by requiring the transportation of pupils or students from one school to another or one school district to another in order to achieve such racial balance, or otherwise enlarge the existing power of the court to insure compliance with constitutional standards. . . .

TITLE V—COMMISSION ON CIVIL RIGHTS. . . .

DUTIES OF THE COMMISSION

SEC. 104. (a) The commission shall—

(1) investigate allegations in writing under oath or affirmation that certain citizens of the United States are being deprived of their right to vote and have that vote counted by reason of their color, race, religion, or national origin; which writing, under oath or affirmation, shall set forth the facts upon which such belief or beliefs are based;

(2) study and collect information concerning legal developments constituting a denial of equal protection of the laws under the Constitution because of race, color, religion or national origin or in the administration of justice;

(3) appraise the laws and policies of the federal government with respect to denials of equal protection of the laws under the Constitution because of race, color, religion, or national origin or in the administration of justice;

(4) serve as a national clearinghouse for information in respect to denials of equal protection of the laws because of race, color, religion, or national origin, including but not limited to the fields of voting, education, housing, employment, the use of public facilities, and transportation or in the administration of justice;

(5) investigate allegations, made in writing and under oath or affirmation, that citizens of the United States are unlawfully being accorded or denied the right to vote, or to have their votes properly counted, in any election of presidential electors, members of the United States Senate, or of the House of Representatives, as a result of any patterns or practice of fraud or discrimination in the conduct of such election. . . .

TITLE VI—NONDISCRIMINATION IN FEDERALLY ASSISTED PROGRAMS

SEC. 601. No person in the United States shall, on the ground of race, color, or national origin, be excluded from participation in, be denied the benefits of, or be subjected to discrimination under any program or activity receiving federal financial assistance. . . .

TITLE VII—EQUAL EMPLOYMENT OPPORTUNITY. . . .

DISCRIMINATION BECAUSE OF RACE, COLOR, RELIGION, SEX, OR NATIONAL ORIGIN

SEC. 703. (a) It shall be an unlawful employment practice for an employer—

(1) to fail or refuse to hire or to discharge any individual, or otherwise to discriminate against any individual with respect to his compensation, terms,

conditions, or privileges of employment, because of such individual's race, color, religion, sex, or national origin; or

(2) to limit, segregate, or classify his employees in any way which would deprive or tend to deprive any individual of employment opportunities or otherwise adversely affect his status as an employee, because of such individual's race, color, religion, sex, or national origin.

(b) It shall be an unlawful employment practice for an employment agency to fail or refuse to refer for employment, or otherwise to discriminate against, any individual because of his race, color, religion, sex, or national origin, or to classify or refer for employment any individual on the basis of his race, color, religion, sex, or national origin.

(c) It shall be an unlawful employment practice for a labor organization—

(1) to exclude or to expel from its membership, or otherwise to discriminate against, any individual because of his race, color, religion, sex, or national origin;

(2) to limit, segregate, or classify its membership, or to classify or fail or refuse to refer for employment any individual, in any way which would deprive or tend to deprive any individual of employment opportunities, or would limit such employment opportunities or otherwise adversely affect his status as an employee or as an applicant for employment, because of such individual's race, color, religion, sex, or national origin; or

(3) to cause or attempt to cause an employer to discriminate against an individual in violation of this section.

(d) It shall be an unlawful employment practice for any employer, labor organization, or joint labor-management committee controlling apprenticeship or other training or retraining, including on-the-job training programs, to discriminate against any individual because of his race, color, religion, sex, or national origin in admission to, or employment in, any program established to provide apprenticeship or other training. . . .

(j) Nothing contained in this title shall be interpreted to require any employer, employment agency, labor organization, or joint labor-management committee subject to this title to grant preferential treatment to any individual or to any group because of the race, color, religion, sex, or national origin of such individual or group on account of an imbalance which may exist with respect to the total number or percentage of persons of any race, color, religion, sex, or national origin employed by any employer, referred or classified for employment by any employment agency or labor organization, admitted to membership or classified by any labor organization, or admitted to, or employed in, any apprenticeship or other training program, in comparison with the total number or percentage of persons of such race, color, religion, sex, or national origin in any community, state, section, or other area, or in the available workforce in any community, state, section, or other area. . . .

EQUAL EMPLOYMENT OPPORTUNITY COMMISSION

SEC. 705. (a) There is hereby created a commission to be known as the Equal Employment Opportunity Commission, which shall be composed of five members, not more than three of whom shall be members of the same political party, who shall be appointed by the president by and with the advice and consent of the Senate. . . .

(g) The commission shall have power—

(1) to cooperate with and, with their consent, utilize regional, state, local, and other agencies, both public and private, and individuals;

(2) to pay to witnesses whose depositions are taken or who are summoned before the commission or any of its agents the same witness and mileage fees as are paid to witnesses in the courts of the United States;

(3) to furnish to persons subject to this title such technical assistance as they may request to further their compliance with this title or an order issued thereunder;

(4) upon the request of (i) any employer, whose employees or some of them, or (ii) any labor organization, whose members or some of them, refuse or threaten to refuse to cooperate in effectuating the provisions of this title, to assist in such effectuation by conciliation or such other remedial action as is provided by this title;

(5) to make such technical studies as are appropriate to effectuate the purposes and policies of this title and to make the results of such studies available to the public;

(6) to refer matters to the attorney general with recommendations for intervention in a civil action brought by an aggrieved party under section 706, or for the institution of a civil action by the attorney general under section 707, and to advise, consult, and assist the attorney general on such matters. . . .

TITLE IX—INTERVENTION AND PROCEDURE AFTER REMOVAL IN CIVIL RIGHTS CASES. . . .

SEC. 902. Whenever an action has been commenced in any court of the United States seeking relief from the denial of equal protection of the laws under the fourteenth amendment to the Constitution on account of race, color, religion, or national origin, the attorney general for or in the name of the United States may intervene in such action upon timely application if the attorney general certifies that the case is of general public importance. In such action the United States shall be entitled to the same relief as if it had instituted the action. . . .

Source: Retrieved September 1, 2010, from http://www.ourdocuments.gov/doc.php?flash=true&doc=97&page=transcript.

CHAPTER 47

Executive Order on Equal Employment Opportunity, 1965

On March 6, 1961, President Kennedy issued Executive Order 10925, which created a Committee on Equal Employment Opportunity and also required contractors receiving federal grants and contracts to "take affirmative action" to make sure that Negroes and Negro businesses were not discriminated against in projects and contracts funded by the federal government. This was the first time the term "affirmative action" was used, but lacking congressional action, enforcement, and appropriate guidelines, the initiative had almost no practical effect. Following Kennedy's death, President Johnson pursued his predecessor's program in Congress, and the resultant Civil Rights Act of 1964 created the Equal Employment Opportunity Commission (EEOC). Enforcement was still lacking, however, so on September 28, 1965, Johnson issued Executive Order 11246, which established affirmative action in federal employment and contracts with the proper enforcement mechanisms.

In 1968 gender was added to race, creed, color, and national origin as an illegal discriminatory factor, and the order was modified or superseded in 1969, 1973, and 1978. Of note is the fact that the term "affirmative action" appears only once in the order (the original, unmodified order appears here). The concept of affirmative action, to redress past wrongs by advantaging minorities that were formerly discriminated against, has been enhanced greatly by the EEOC and labor commissions since 11246 was issued, and has become firmly established. The order's supporters, especially Senator Hubert Humphrey (D-MN), were adamant that it would never mean quotas—yet within a few years, that was precisely what affirmative action came to mean. Is the concept of affirmative action valid to redress a previous wrong, especially when the recipient himself has not suffered discrimination? Is this reverse discrimination? Are there other solutions? Has affirmative action created more opportunities for minorities? Should there be an end to affirmative action at some point? Is there any way to have affirmative action without quotas?

Executive Order 11246: Equal Employment Opportunity

UNDER AND BY VIRTUE OF THE AUTHORITY VESTED IN ME AS president of the United States by the Constitution and statutes of the United States, it is ordered as follows:

PART I—NONDISCRIMINATION IN GOVERNMENT EMPLOYMENT

Section 101. It is the policy of the government of the United States to provide equal opportunity in federal employment for all qualified persons, to prohibit discrimination in employment because of race, creed, color, or national origin, and to promote the full realization of equal employment opportunity through a positive, continuing program in each executive department and agency. The policy of equal opportunity applies to every aspect of federal employment policy and practice.

Sec. 102. The head of each executive department and agency shall establish and maintain a positive program of equal employment opportunity for all civilian employees and applicants for employment within his jurisdiction in accordance with the policy set forth in section 101.

Sec. 103. The Civil Service Commission shall supervise and provide leadership and guidance in the conduct of equal employment opportunity programs for the civilian employees of and applications for employment within the executive departments and agencies and shall review agency program accomplishments periodically. In order to facilitate the achievement of a model program for equal employment opportunity in the federal service, the commission may consult from time to time with such individuals, groups, or organizations as may be of assistance in improving the federal program and realizing the objectives of this part.

Sec. 104. The Civil Service Commission shall provide for the prompt, fair, and impartial consideration of all complaints of discrimination in federal employment on the basis of race, creed, color, or national origin. Procedures for the consideration of complaints shall include at least one impartial review within the executive department or agency and shall provide for appeal to the Civil Service Commission.

Sec. 105. The Civil Service Commission shall issue such regulations, orders, and instructions as it deems necessary and appropriate to carry out its responsibilities under this part, and the head of each executive department and agency shall comply with the regulations, orders, and instructions issued by the commission under this part.

PART II—NONDISCRIMINATION IN EMPLOYMENT BY GOVERNMENT CONTRACTORS AND SUBCONTRACTORS

SUBPART A: DUTIES OF THE SECRETARY OF LABOR

Sec. 201. The secretary of labor shall be responsible for the administration of parts II and III of this order and shall adopt such rules and regulations and issue such orders as he deems necessary and appropriate to achieve the purposes thereof.

SUBPART B: CONTRACTORS' AGREEMENTS

Sec. 202. Except in contracts exempted in accordance with section 204 of this order, all government contracting agencies shall include in every government contract hereafter entered into the following provisions:

"During the performance of this contract, the contractor agrees as follows:

"(1) The contractor will not discriminate against any employee or applicant for employment because of race, creed, color, or national origin. The contractor will take affirmative action to ensure that applicants are employed, and that employees are treated during employment, without regard to their race, creed, color, or national origin. Such action shall include, but not be limited to the following: employment, upgrading, demotion, or transfer; recruitment or recruitment advertising; layoff or termination; rates of pay or other forms of compensation; and selection for training, including apprenticeship. The contractor agrees to post in conspicuous places, available to employees and applicants for employment, notices to be provided by the contracting officer setting forth the provisions of this nondiscrimination clause.

"(2) The contractor will, in all solicitations or advertisements for employees placed by or on behalf of the contractor, state that all qualified applicants will receive consideration for employment without regard to race, creed, color, or national origin.

"(3) The contractor will send to each labor union or representative of workers with which he has a collective bargaining agreement or other contract or understanding, a notice, to be provided by the agency contracting officer, advising the labor union or workers' representative of the contractor's commitments under section 202 of Executive Order No. 11246 of September 24, 1965, and shall post copies of the notice in conspicuous places available to employees and applicants for employment.

"(4) The contractor will comply with all provisions of Executive Order No. 11246 of September 24, 1965, and of the rules, regulations, and relevant orders of the secretary of labor.

"(5) The contractor will furnish all information and reports required by Executive Order No. 11246 of September 24, 1965, and by the rules, regulations, and orders of the secretary of labor, or pursuant thereto, and will permit access to his books, records, and accounts by the contracting agency and the secretary of labor for purposes of investigation to ascertain compliance with such rules, regulations, and orders.

"(6) In the event of the contractor's noncompliance with the nondiscrimination clauses of this contract or with any of such rules, regulations, or orders, this contract may be canceled, terminated, or suspended in whole or in part and the contractor may be declared ineligible for further government contracts in accordance with procedures authorized in Executive Order No. 11246 of September 24, 1965, and such other sanctions may be imposed and remedies invoked as provided in Executive Order No. 11246 of September 24, 1965, or by rule, regulation, or order of the secretary of labor, or as otherwise provided by law.

"(7) The contractor will include the provisions of paragraphs (1) through (7) in every subcontract or purchase order unless exempted by rules, regulations, or orders of the secretary of labor issued pursuant to section 204 of Executive Order No. 11246 of September 24, 1965, so that such provisions will be binding upon each subcontractor or vendor. The contractor will take such action with respect to any subcontract or purchase order as the contracting agency may direct as a means of enforcing such provisions including sanctions for noncompliance: Provided, however, That in the event the contractor becomes involved in, or is threatened with, litigation with a subcontractor or vendor as a result of such direction by the contracting agency, the contractor may request the United States to enter into such litigation to protect the interests of the United States."

Sec. 203. (a) Each contractor having a contract containing the provisions prescribed in section 202 shall file, and shall cause each of his subcontractors to file, Compliance Reports with the contracting agency or the secretary of labor as may be directed. Compliance Reports shall be filed within such times and shall contain such information as to the practices, policies, programs, and employment policies, programs, and employment statistics of the contractor and each subcontractor, and shall be in such form, as the secretary of labor may prescribe.

(b) Bidders or prospective contractors or subcontractors may be required to state whether they have participated in any previous contract subject to the provisions of this order, or any preceding similar executive order, and in that event to submit, on behalf of themselves and their proposed subcontractors, Compliance Reports prior to or as an initial part of their bid or negotiation of a contract.

(c) Whenever the contractor or subcontractor has a collective bargaining agreement or other contract or understanding with a labor union or an agency referring workers or providing or supervising apprenticeship or training for such workers, the Compliance Report shall include such information as to such labor union's or agency's practices and policies affecting compliance as the secretary of labor may prescribe: Provided, That to the extent such information is within the exclusive possession of a labor union or an agency referring workers or providing or supervising apprenticeship or training and such labor union or agency shall refuse to furnish such information to the contractor, the contractor shall so certify to the contracting agency as part of its Compliance Report and shall set forth what efforts he has made to obtain such information.

(d) The contracting agency or the secretary of labor may direct that any bidder or prospective contractor or subcontractor shall submit, as part of his Compliance Report, a statement in writing, signed by an authorized officer or agent on behalf of any labor union or any agency referring workers or providing or supervising apprenticeship or other training, with which the bidder or prospective contractor deals, with supporting information, to the effect that the signer's practices and policies do not discriminate on the grounds of race, color, creed, or national origin, and that the signer either will affirmatively cooperate in the implementation of the policy and provisions of this order or that it consents and agrees that recruitment, employment, and the terms and conditions of employment under the proposed contract shall be in accordance with the purposes and provisions of the order. In the event that the union, or the agency, shall refuse to execute such a statement, the Compliance Report shall so certify and set forth what efforts have been made to secure such a statement and such additional factual material as the contracting agency or the secretary of labor may require.

Sec. 204. The secretary of labor may, when he deems that special circumstances in the national interest so require, exempt a contracting agency from the requirement of including any or all of the provisions of section 202 of this order in any specific contract, subcontract, or purchase order. The secretary of labor may, by rule or regulation, also exempt certain classes of contracts, subcontracts, or purchase orders (1) whenever work is to be or has been performed outside the United States and no recruitment of workers within the limits of the United States is involved; (2) for standard commercial supplies or raw materials; (3) involving less than specified amounts of money or specified numbers or workers; or (4) to the extent that they involve subcontracts below a specified tier. The secretary of labor may also provide, by the rule, regulation, or order, for the exemption of facilities of a contractor which are in all respects separate and distinct from activities of the contractor related to the performance of the contract: Provided, That such an exemption will not interfere with or impede the effectuation of the purposes of this order: And provided further, That in the absence of such an exemption all facilities shall be covered by the provisions of this order.

SUBPART C: POWERS AND DUTIES OF THE SECRETARY OF LABOR AND THE CONTRACTING AGENCIES

Sec. 205. Each contracting agency shall be primarily responsible for obtaining compliance with the rules, regulations, and orders of the secretary of labor with respect to contracts entered into by such agency or its contractors. All contracting agencies shall comply with the rules of the secretary of labor in discharging their primary responsibility for securing compliance with the provisions of contracts and otherwise with the terms of this order and of the rules, regulations, and orders of the secretary of labor issued pursuant to this order. They are directed to cooperate with the secretary of labor and to furnish the secretary of labor such information and assistance as he may require in the performance of his functions under this order. They are further directed to appoint or designate, from among the agency's personnel, compliance officers. It shall be the duty of such officers to seek compliance with the objectives of this order by conference, conciliation, mediation, or persuasion.

Sec. 206. (a) The secretary of labor may investigate the employment practices of any government contractor or subcontractor, or initiate such investigation by the appropriate contracting agency, to determine whether or not the contractual provisions specified in section 202 of this order have been violated. Such investigation shall be conducted in accordance with the procedures established by the secretary of labor and the investigating agency shall report to the secretary of labor any action taken or recommended.

(b) The secretary of labor may receive and investigate or cause to be investigated complaints by employees or prospective employees of a government contractor or subcontractor which allege discrimination contrary to the contractual provisions specified in section of 202 of this order. If this investigation is conducted for the secretary of labor by a contracting agency, that agency shall report to the secretary what action has been taken or is recommended with regard to such complaints.

Sec. 207. The secretary of labor shall use his best efforts, directly and through contracting agencies, other interested federal, state, and local agencies, contractors, and all other available instrumentalities to cause any labor union engaged in work under government contracts or any agency referring workers or providing or supervising apprenticeship or training for or in the course of such work to cooperate in the implementation of the purposes of this order. The secretary of labor shall, in appropriate cases, notify the Equal Employment Opportunity Commission, the Department of Justice, or other appropriate federal agencies whenever it has reason to believe that the practices of any such labor organization or agency violate Title VI or Title VII of the Civil Rights Act of 1964 or other provision of federal law.

Sec. 208. (a) The secretary of labor, or any agency, officer, or employee in the executive branch of the government designated by rule, regulation, or order of the secretary, may hold such hearings, public or private, as the secretary may deem advisable for compliance, enforcement, or educational purposes.

(b) The secretary of labor may hold, or cause to be held, hearings in accordance with subsection (a) of this section prior to imposing, ordering, or recommending the imposition of penalties and sanctions under this order. No order for debarment of any contractor from further government contracts under section 209(a) (6) shall be made without affording the contractor an opportunity for a hearing.

SUBPART D: SANCTIONS AND PENALTIES

Sec. 209. (a) In accordance with such rules, regulations, or orders as the secretary of labor may issue or adopt, the secretary or the appropriate contracting agency may:

(1) Publish, or cause to be published, the names of contractors or unions which it has concluded have complied or have failed to comply with the provisions of this order or of the rules, regulations, and orders of the secretary of labor.

(2) Recommend to the Department of Justice that, in cases in which there is substantial or material violation or the threat of substantial or material violation of the contractual provisions set forth in section 202 of this order, appropriate proceedings be brought to enforce those provisions, including the enjoining, within the limitations of applicable law, of organizations, individuals, or groups who prevent directly or indirectly, or seek to prevent directly or indirectly, compliance with the provisions of this order.

(3) Recommend to the Equal Employment Opportunity Commission or the Department of Justice that appropriate proceedings be instituted under Title VII of the Civil Rights Act of 1964.

(4) Recommend to the Department of Justice that criminal proceedings be brought for the furnishing of false information to any contracting agency or to the secretary of labor as the case may be.

(5) Cancel, terminate, suspend, or cause to be canceled, terminated, or suspended, any contract, or any portion or portions thereof, for failure of the contractor or subcontractor to comply with the nondiscrimination provisions of the contract. Contracts may be canceled, terminated, or suspended absolutely or continuance of contracts may be conditioned upon a program for future compliance approved by the contracting agency.

(6) Provide that any contracting agency shall refrain from entering into further contracts, or extensions or other modifications of existing contracts, with any noncomplying contractor, until such contractor has satisfied the secretary of labor that such contractor has established and will carry out personnel and employment policies in compliance with the provisions of this order.

(b) Under rules and regulations prescribed by the secretary of labor, each contracting agency shall make reasonable efforts within a reasonable time limitation to secure compliance with the contract provisions of this order by methods of conference, conciliation, mediation, and persuasion before proceedings shall be instituted under subsection (a) (2) of this section, or before a contract shall be canceled or terminated in whole or in part under subsection (a) (5) of this section for failure of a contractor or subcontractor to comply with the contract provisions of this order.

Sec. 210. Any contracting agency taking any action authorized by this subpart, whether on its own motion, or as directed by the secretary of labor, or under the rules and regulations of the secretary, shall promptly notify the secretary of such action. Whenever the secretary of labor makes a determination under this section, he shall promptly notify the appropriate contracting agency of the action recommended. The agency shall take such action and shall report the results thereof to the secretary of labor within such time as the secretary shall specify.

Sec. 211. If the secretary shall so direct, contracting agencies shall not enter into contracts with any bidder or prospective contractor unless the bidder or prospective contractor has satisfactorily complied with the provisions of this order or submits a program for compliance acceptable to the secretary of labor or, if the secretary so authorizes, to the contracting agency.

Sec. 212. Whenever a contracting agency cancels or terminates a contract, or whenever a contractor has been debarred from further government contracts, under section 209(a) (6) because of noncompliance with the contract provisions with regard to nondiscrimination, the secretary of labor, or the contracting agency involved, shall promptly notify the comptroller general of the United States. Any such debarment may be rescinded by the secretary of labor or by the contracting agency which imposed the sanction.

SUBPART E: CERTIFICATES OF MERIT

Sec. 213. The secretary of labor may provide for issuance of a United States Government Certificate of Merit to employers or labor unions, or other agencies which are or may hereafter be engaged in work under government contracts, if the secretary is satisfied that the personnel and employment practices of the employer, or that the personnel, training, apprenticeship, membership, grievance and representation, upgrading, and other practices and policies of the labor union or other agency conform to the purposes and provisions of this order.

Sec. 214. Any Certificate of Merit may at any time be suspended or revoked by the secretary of labor if the holder thereof, in the judgment of the secretary, has failed to comply with the provisions of this order.

Sec. 215. The secretary of labor may provide for the exemption of any employer, labor union, or other agency from any reporting requirements imposed under or pursuant to this order if such employer, labor union, or other agency has been awarded a Certificate of Merit which has not been suspended or revoked.

PART III—NONDISCRIMINATION PROVISIONS IN FEDERALLY ASSISTED CONSTRUCTION CONTRACTS

Sec. 301. Each executive department and agency which administers a program involving federal financial assistance shall require as a condition for the approval of any grant, contract, loan, insurance, or guarantee thereunder, which may involve a construction contract, that the applicant for federal assistance undertake and agree to incorporate, or cause to be incorporated, into all construction contracts paid for in whole or in part with funds obtained from the federal government or borrowed on the credit of the federal government pursuant to such grant, contract, loan, insurance, or guarantee, or undertaken pursuant to any federal program involving such grant, contract, loan, insurance, or guarantee, the provisions prescribed for government contracts by section 202 of this order or such modification thereof, preserving in substance the contractor's obligations thereunder, as may be approved by the secretary of labor, together with such additional provisions as the secretary deems appropriate to establish and protect the interest of the United States in the enforcement of those obligations. Each such applicant shall also undertake and agree (1) to assist and cooperate actively with the administering department or agency and the secretary of labor in obtaining the compliance of contractors and subcontractors with those contract provisions and with the rules, regulations, and relevant orders of the secretary, (2) to obtain and to furnish to the administering department or agency and to the secretary of labor such information as they may require for the supervision of such compliance, (3) to carry out sanctions and penalties for violations of such obligations imposed upon contractors and subcontractors by the secretary of labor or the administering department or agency pursuant to part II, subpart D, of this order, and (4) to refrain from entering into any contract subject to this order, or extension or other modification of such a contract with a contractor debarred from government contracts under part II, subpart D, of this order.

Sec. 302. (a) "Construction contract" as used in this order means any contract for the construction, rehabilitation, alteration, conversion, extension, or repair of buildings, highways, or other improvements to real property.

(b) The provisions of part II of the order shall apply to such construction contracts, and for purposes of such application the administering department or agency shall be considered the contracting agency referred to therein.

(c) The term "applicant" as used in this order means an applicant for federal assistance or, as determined by agency regulation, other program participant, with respect to whom an application for any grant, contract, loan, insurance, or guarantee is not finally acted upon prior to the effective date of this part, and it includes such an applicant after he becomes a recipient of such federal assistance.

Sec. 303. (a) Each administering department or agency shall be responsible for obtaining the compliance of such applicants with their undertakings under this order. Each administering department and agency is directed to cooperate with the secretary of labor, and to furnish the secretary such information and assistance as he may require in the performance of his functions under this order.

(b) In the event an applicant fails and refuses to comply with his undertakings, the administering department or agency may take any or all of the following actions: (1) cancel, terminate, or suspend in whole or in part the agreement, contract, or other arrangement with such applicant with respect to which the failure and refusal occurred; (2) refrain for extending any further assistance to the applicant under the program with respect to which the failure or refusal occurred until satisfactory assurance of future compliance has been received from such applicant; and (3) refer the case to the Department of Justice for appropriate legal proceedings.

(c) Any action with respect to an applicant pursuant to subsection (b) shall be taken in conformity with section 602 of the Civil Rights Act of 1964 (and the regulations of the administering department or agency issued thereunder), to the extent applicable. In no case shall action be taken with respect to an applicant pursuant to clause (1) or (2) of subsection (b) without notice and opportunity for hearing before the administering department or agency.

Sec. 304. Any executive department or agency which imposes by rule, regulation or order requirements of nondiscrimination in employment, other than requirements imposed pursuant to this order, may delegate to the secretary of labor by agreement such responsibilities with respect to compliance standards, reports, and procedures as would tend to bring the administration of such requirements into conformity with the administration of requirements imposed under this order: Provided, That actions to effect compliance by recipients of federal financial assistance with requirements imposed pursuant to Title VI of the Civil Rights Act of 1964 shall be taken in conformity with the procedures and limitations prescribed in section 602 thereof and the regulations of the administering department or agency issued thereunder.

PART IV—MISCELLANEOUS

Sec. 401. The secretary of labor may delegate to any officer, agency, or employee in the executive branch of the government, any function or duty of the secretary under parts II and III of this order, except authority to promulgate rules and regulations of a general nature.

Sec. 402. The secretary of labor shall provide administrative support for the execution of the program known as the "Plans for Progress."

Sec. 403. (a) Executive Orders Nos. 10590 (January 19, 1955), 10722 (August 5, 1957), 10925 (March 6, 1961), 11114 (June 22, 1963), and 11162 (July 28, 1964), are hereby superseded and the President's Committee on Equal Employment Opportunity established by Executive Order No. 10925 is hereby abolished. All records and property in the custody of the committee shall be transferred to the Civil Service Commission and the secretary of labor, as appropriate.

(b) Nothing in this order shall be deemed to relieve any person of any obligation assumed or imposed under or pursuant to any executive order superseded by this order. All rules, regulations, orders, instructions, designations, and other directives issued by the President's Committee on Equal Employment Opportunity and those issued by the heads of various departments or agencies under or pursuant to any of the executive orders superseded by this order, shall, to the extent that they are not inconsistent with this order, remain in full force and effect unless and until revoked or superseded by appropriate authority. References in such directives to provisions of the superseded orders shall be deemed to be references to the comparable provisions of this order.

Sec. 404. The General Services Administration shall take appropriate action to revise the standard government contract forms to accord with the provisions of this order and of the rules and regulations of the secretary of labor.

Sec. 405. This order shall become effective thirty days after the date of this order.

Lyndon B. Johnson

Source: U.S. Equal Employment Opportunity Commission. Retrieved May 29, 2010, from http://www.eeoc.gov/eeoc/history/35th/thelaw/eo-11246.html.

CHAPTER 48

Roe v. Wade, 1973

Probably the most contentious Supreme Court decision since *Dred Scott, Jane Roe, et al. v. Henry Wade, District Attorney of Dallas County,* 410 U.S. 113 (1973) excites passionate hopes and fears that it might be overturned every time an individual is considered to fill a vacant spot on the U.S. Supreme Court bench. "Right to life" and "pro-choice" organizations exert constant influence on American public life, and the gulf between the represented points of view appears well-nigh unbridgeable. The case came to the Supreme Court after a pregnant woman, who was prohibited under state statute from seeking an abortion in her home state of Texas, filed suit. The case was argued on December 13, 1971; again on October 11, 1972; and the seven-to-two decision was rendered January 22, 1973.

The Court examined the history of the issue from ancient times and attempted to take many factors, some arguably not on point, into its decision. It sought a middle ground, which satisfied nobody but seemed relatively consistent with the legal trends and medical considerations involved. The insurmountable aspect of the problem concerns the point when life begins or, more appropriately, from a religious point of view, the point when the human soul or spirit is present in a developing fetus. For some this occurs at the time of conception, and for others when the baby is born. The Court elected to base its ruling on the term of pregnancy—for almost all citizens an arbitrary division of no theological significance. Moreover, the opinion cites a "right of personal privacy" that is not listed or, though it argues otherwise, even implied, in the U.S. Constitution. Can a ruling on this issue ever be made to satisfy everyone or even a majority? Do citizens have a right to privacy? Should what is essentially a question of religious belief be resolved in a court of law? If not, where should it be resolved and how? Are there similarities between the issues raised in this case and in the *Dred Scott* case one hundred years earlier?

Roe v. Wade

MR. JUSTICE [HAROLD A.] BLACKMUN DELIVERED THE OPINion of the Court.

THIS TEXAS FEDERAL APPEAL AND ITS GEORGIA COMPANION, *Doe v. Bolton*, present constitutional challenges to state criminal abortion legislation. The Texas statutes under attack here are typical of those that have been in effect in many states for approximately a century. The Georgia statutes, in contrast, have a modern cast and are a legislative product that, to an extent at least, obviously reflects the influences of recent attitudinal change, of advancing medical knowledge and techniques, and of new thinking about an old issue. We forthwith acknowledge our awareness of the sensitive and emotional nature of the abortion controversy, of the vigorous opposing views, even among physicians, and of the deep and seemingly absolute convictions that the subject inspires. One's philosophy, one's experiences, one's exposure to the raw edges of human existence, one's religious training, one's attitudes toward life and family and their values, and the moral standards one establishes and seeks to observe, are all likely to influence and to color one's thinking and conclusions about abortion.

In addition, population growth, pollution, poverty, and racial overtones tend to complicate and not to simplify the problem.

Our task, of course, is to resolve the issue by constitutional measurement, free of emotion and of predilection. We seek earnestly to do this, and, because we do, we have inquired into, and in this opinion place some emphasis upon, medical and medical-legal history and what that history reveals about man's attitudes toward the abortion procedure over the centuries. . . .

I

The Texas statutes . . . make it a crime to "procure an abortion," as therein defined, or to attempt one, except with respect to "an abortion procured or attempted by medical advice for the purpose of saving the life of the mother." Similar statutes are in existence in a majority of the states. . . .

II

Jane Roe, a single woman who was residing in Dallas County, Texas, instituted this federal action in March 1970 against the district attorney of the county. She sought a declaratory judgment that the Texas criminal abortion statutes were unconstitutional on their face, and an injunction restraining the defendant from enforcing the statutes.

Roe alleged that she was unmarried and pregnant; that she wished to terminate her pregnancy by an abortion "performed by a competent, licensed physician, under safe, clinical conditions"; that she was unable to get a "legal" abortion in Texas because her life did not appear to be threatened by the continuation of her pregnancy; and that she could not afford to travel to another jurisdiction in order to secure a legal abortion under safe conditions. She claimed that the Texas statutes were unconstitutionally vague and that they abridged her right of personal privacy, protected by the First, Fourth, Fifth, Ninth, and Fourteenth Amendments. By an amendment to her complaint Roe purported to sue "on behalf of herself and all other women" similarly situated. . . .

III

It might have been preferable if the defendant, pursuant to our Rule 20, had presented to us a petition for certiorari before judgment in the Court of Appeals. . . . those decisions do not foreclose our review of both the injunctive and the declaratory aspects of a case of this kind when it is properly here, as this one is, on appeal under 1253 from specific denial of injunctive relief, and the arguments as to both aspects are necessarily identical. . . .

IV

We are next confronted with issues of justiciability, standing, and abstention. [Has] Roe . . . established that "personal stake in the outcome of the controversy" that insures that "the dispute sought to be adjudicated will be presented in an adversary context and in a form historically viewed as capable of judicial resolution"? . . .

. . . Despite the use of the pseudonym, no suggestion is made that Roe is a fictitious person. For purposes of her case, we accept as true, and as established, her existence; her pregnant state, as of the inception of her suit in March 1970 and as late as May 21 of that year when she filed an alias affidavit with the District Court; and her inability to obtain a legal abortion in Texas.

Viewing Roe's case as of the time of its filing and thereafter until as late as May, there can be little dispute that it then presented a case or controversy and that, wholly apart from the class aspects, she, as a pregnant single woman thwarted by the Texas criminal abortion laws, had standing to challenge those statutes. Indeed, we do not read the appellee's brief as really asserting anything to the contrary. The "logical nexus between the status asserted and the claim sought to be adjudicated," and the necessary degree of contentiousness, are both present.

The appellee notes, however, that the record does not disclose that Roe was pregnant at the time of the District Court hearing on May 22, 1970, or on the following June 17 when the court's opinion and judgment were filed. And he suggests that Roe's case must now be moot because she and all other members of her class are no longer subject to any 1970 pregnancy. The usual rule in federal cases is that an actual controversy must exist at stages of appellate or certiorari review, and not simply at the date the action is initiated.

But when, as here, pregnancy is a significant fact in the litigation, the normal 266-day human gestation period is so short that the pregnancy will come to term before the usual appellate process is complete. If that termination makes a case moot, pregnancy litigation seldom will survive much beyond the trial stage, and appellate review will be effectively denied. Our law should not be that rigid. Pregnancy often comes more than once to the same woman, and in the general population, if man is to survive, it will always be with us. Pregnancy provides a classic justification for a conclusion of nonmootness. It truly could be "capable of repetition, yet evading review."

We, therefore, agree with the District Court that Jane Roe had standing to undertake this litigation, that she presented a justiciable controversy, and that the termination of her 1970 pregnancy has not rendered her case moot. . . .

V

The principal thrust of appellant's attack on the Texas statutes is that they improperly invade a right, said to be possessed by the pregnant woman, to choose to terminate her pregnancy. Appellant would discover this right in the concept of personal "liberty" embodied in the Fourteenth Amendment's due process clause; or in personal, marital, familial, and sexual privacy said to be protected by the Bill of Rights or its penumbras, or among those rights reserved to the people by the Ninth Amendment.

Before addressing this claim, we feel it desirable briefly to survey, in several aspects, the history of abortion, for such insight as that history may afford us, and then to examine the state purposes and interests behind the criminal abortion laws.

VI

It perhaps is not generally appreciated that the restrictive criminal abortion laws in effect in a majority of states today are of relatively recent vintage. Those laws, generally proscribing abortion or its attempt at any time during pregnancy except when necessary to preserve the pregnant woman's life, are not of ancient or even of common-law origin. Instead, they derive from statutory changes effected, for the most part, in the latter half of the nineteenth century.

1. Ancient attitudes. These are not capable of precise determination. . . .
3. The common law. It is undisputed that at common law, abortion performed before "quickening"—the first recognizable movement of the fetus in utero, appearing usually from the sixteenth to the eighteenth week of pregnancy— was not an indictable offense. . . .

   Whether abortion of a quick fetus was a felony at common law, or even a lesser crime, is still disputed.

4. The English statutory law. England's first criminal abortion statute, Lord Ellenborough's Act, came in 1803. It made abortion of a quick fetus a capital crime, but it provided lesser penalties for the felony of abortion before quickening, and thus preserved the "quickening" distinction. This contrast was continued in the general revision of 1828. It disappeared, however, together with the death penalty, in 1837, and did not reappear in the Offenses Against the Person Act of 1861, that formed the core of English antiabortion law until the liberalizing reforms of 1967. In 1929, the Infant Life (Preservation) Act, came into being. Its emphasis was upon the destruction of "the life of a child capable of being born alive." It made a willful act performed with the necessary intent a felony. It contained a proviso that one was not to be found guilty of the offense "unless it is proved that the act which caused the death of the child was not done in good faith for the purpose only of preserving the life of the mother." . . .

. . . The [1967] act permits a licensed physician to perform an abortion where two other licensed physicians agree (a) "that the continuance of the pregnancy would involve risk to the life of the pregnant woman, or of injury to the physical or mental health of the pregnant woman or any existing children of her family, greater than if the pregnancy were terminated," or (b) "that there is a substantial risk that if the child were born it would suffer from such physical or mental abnormalities as to be seriously handicapped." The act also provides that, in making this determination, "account may be taken of the pregnant woman's actual or reasonably foreseeable environment." It also permits a physician, without the concurrence of others, to terminate a pregnancy where he is of the good-faith opinion that the abortion "is immediately necessary to save the life or to prevent grave permanent injury to the physical or mental health of the pregnant woman."

5. The American law. In this country, the law in effect in all but a few states until mid-nineteenth century was the preexisting English common law. Connecticut, the first state to enact abortion legislation, adopted in 1821 that part of Lord Ellenborough's Act that related to a woman "quick with child." The death penalty was not imposed. Abortion before quickening was made a crime in that state only in 1860. In 1828, New York enacted legislation that, in two respects, was to serve as a model for early antiabortion statutes. First, while barring destruction of an unquickened fetus as well as a quick fetus, it made the former only a misdemeanor, but the latter second-degree manslaughter. Second, it incorporated a concept of therapeutic abortion by providing that an abortion was excused if it "shall have been necessary to preserve the life of such mother, or shall have been advised by two physicians to be necessary for such purpose." By 1840, when Texas had received the common law, only eight American states had statutes dealing with abortion. It was not until after the War Between the States that legislation began

generally to replace the common law. Most of these initial statutes dealt severely with abortion after quickening but were lenient with it before quickening. Most punished attempts equally with completed abortions. While many statutes included the exception for an abortion thought by one or more physicians to be necessary to save the mother's life, that provision soon disappeared and the typical law required that the procedure actually be necessary for that purpose.

Gradually, in the middle and late nineteenth century the quickening distinction disappeared from the statutory law of most states and the degree of the offense and the penalties were increased. By the end of the 1950's, a large majority of the jurisdictions banned abortion, however and whenever performed, unless done to save or preserve the life of the mother. The exceptions, Alabama and the District of Columbia, permitted abortion to preserve the mother's health. . . .

It is thus apparent that at common law, at the time of the adoption of our Constitution, and throughout the major portion of the nineteenth century, abortion was viewed with less disfavor than under most American statutes currently in effect. Phrasing it another way, a woman enjoyed a substantially broader right to terminate a pregnancy than she does in most states today. At least with respect to the early stage of pregnancy, and very possibly without such a limitation, the opportunity to make this choice was present in this country well into the nineteenth century. Even later, the law continued for some time to treat less punitively an abortion procured in early pregnancy.

6. The position of the American Medical Association. The antiabortion mood prevalent in this country in the late nineteenth century was shared by the medical profession. Indeed, the attitude of the profession may have played a significant role in the enactment of stringent criminal abortion legislation during that period. . . .

7. The position of the American Public Health Association. In October 1970, the executive board of the APHA adopted Standards for Abortion Services. These were five in number:

"a. Rapid and simple abortion referral must be readily available through state and local public health departments, medical societies, or other nonprofit organizations.

"b. An important function of counseling should be to simplify and expedite the provision of abortion services; it should not delay the obtaining of these services.

"c. Psychiatric consultation should not be mandatory. As in the case of other specialized medical services, psychiatric consultation should be sought for definite indications and not on a routine basis.

"d. A wide range of individuals from appropriately trained, sympathetic volunteers to highly skilled physicians may qualify as abortion counselors.

"e. Contraception and/or sterilization should be discussed with each abortion patient."

Among factors pertinent to life and health risks associated with abortion were three that "are recognized as important":

"a. the skill of the physician,

"b. the environment in which the abortion is performed, and above all

"c. the duration of pregnancy, as determined by uterine size and confirmed by menstrual history." . . .

8. The position of the American Bar Association. At its meeting in February 1972 the ABA House of Delegates approved, with seventeen opposing votes, the Uniform Abortion Act that had been drafted and approved the preceding August by the Conference of Commissioners on Uniform State Laws. . . .

VII

Three reasons have been advanced to explain historically the enactment of criminal abortion laws in the nineteenth century and to justify their continued existence.

It has been argued occasionally that these laws were the product of a Victorian social concern to discourage illicit sexual conduct. Texas, however, does not advance this justification in the present case, and it appears that no court or commentator has taken the argument seriously. The appellants and amici contend, moreover, that this is not a proper state purpose at all and suggest that, if it were, the Texas statutes are overbroad in protecting it since the law fails to distinguish between married and unwed mothers.

A second reason is concerned with abortion as a medical procedure. When most criminal abortion laws were first enacted, the procedure was a hazardous one for the woman. . . . Thus, it has been argued that a state's real concern in enacting a criminal abortion law was to protect the pregnant woman, that is, to restrain her from submitting to a procedure that placed her life in serious jeopardy.

Modern medical techniques have altered this situation. Appellants and various amici refer to medical data indicating that abortion in early pregnancy, that is, prior to the end of the first trimester, although not without its risk, is now relatively safe. Mortality rates for women undergoing early abortions, where the procedure is legal, appear to be as low as or lower than the rates for normal childbirth. . . . The prevalence of high mortality rates at illegal "abortion mills" strengthens, rather than weakens, the state's interest in regulating the conditions under which abortions are performed. Moreover, the risk to the woman increases as her pregnancy continues. Thus, the state retains a definite interest in protecting the woman's own health and safety when an abortion is proposed at a late stage of pregnancy.

The third reason is the state's interest—some phrase it in terms of duty—

in protecting prenatal life. Some of the argument for this justification rests on the theory that a new human life is present from the moment of conception. The state's interest and general obligation to protect life then extends, it is argued, to prenatal life. . . .

Parties challenging state abortion laws have sharply disputed in some courts the contention that a purpose of these laws, when enacted, was to protect prenatal life. Pointing to the absence of legislative history to support the contention, they claim that most state laws were designed solely to protect the woman. Because medical advances have lessened this concern, at least with respect to abortion in early pregnancy, they argue that with respect to such abortions the laws can no longer be justified by any state interest. There is some scholarly support for this view of original purpose. . . .

It is with these interests, and the weight to be attached to them, that this case is concerned.

VIII

The Constitution does not explicitly mention any right of privacy. In a line of decisions, however, going back perhaps as far as *Union Pacific R. Co. v. Botsford*, the Court has recognized that a right of personal privacy, or a guarantee of certain areas or zones of privacy, does exist under the Constitution. In varying contexts, the Court or individual justices have, indeed, found at least the roots of that right in the First Amendment, in the Fourth and Fifth Amendments, in the penumbras of the Bill of Rights, in the Ninth Amendment, or in the concept of liberty guaranteed by the first section of the Fourteenth Amendment. These decisions make it clear that only personal rights that can be deemed "fundamental" or "implicit in the concept of ordered liberty," are included in this guarantee of personal privacy. They also make it clear that the right has some extension to activities relating to marriage, procreation, contraception, family relationships, and child rearing and education.

This right of privacy, whether it be founded in the Fourteenth Amendment's concept of personal liberty and restrictions upon state action, as we feel it is, or, as the District Court determined, in the Ninth Amendment's reservation of rights to the people, is broad enough to encompass a woman's decision whether or not to terminate her pregnancy. The detriment that the state would impose upon the pregnant woman by denying this choice altogether is apparent. . . .

. . . [A]ppellant and some amici argue that the woman's right is absolute and that she is entitled to terminate her pregnancy at whatever time, in whatever way, and for whatever reason she alone chooses. With this we do not agree. Appellant's arguments that Texas either has no valid interest at all in regulating the abortion decision, or no interest strong enough to support any limitation upon the woman's sole determination, are unpersuasive. The Court's decisions recognizing a right of privacy also acknowledge that some state regulation in areas protected by that right is appropriate. As noted above, a state may properly assert important interests in safeguarding health, in maintaining medical standards, and in protecting potential life. At some point in pregnancy, these respective interests become sufficiently compelling to sustain regulation of the factors that govern the abortion decision. The privacy right involved, therefore, cannot be said to be absolute. In fact, it is not clear to us that the claim asserted by some amici that one has an unlimited right to do with one's body as one pleases bears a close relationship to the right of privacy previously articulated in the Court's decisions.

We, therefore, conclude that the right of personal privacy includes the abortion decision, but that this right is not unqualified and must be considered against important state interests in regulation. . . .

Where certain "fundamental rights" are involved, the Court has held that regulation limiting these rights may be justified only by a "compelling state interest," and that legislative enactments must be narrowly drawn to express only the legitimate state interests at stake. . . .

IX

The District Court held that the appellee failed to meet his burden of demonstrating that the Texas statute's infringement upon Roe's rights was necessary to support a compelling state interest, and that, although the appellee presented "several compelling justifications for state presence in the area of abortions," the statutes outstripped these justifications and swept "far beyond any areas of compelling state interest."

Appellant and appellee both contest that holding. Appellant, as has been indicated, claims an absolute right that bars any state imposition of criminal penalties in the area. Appellee argues that the state's determination to recognize and protect prenatal life from and after conception constitutes a compelling state interest. As noted above, we do not agree fully with either formulation.

A. The appellee and certain amici argue that the fetus is a "person" within the language and meaning of the Fourteenth Amendment. In support of this, they outline at length and in detail the well-known facts of fetal development. If this suggestion of personhood is established, the appellant's case, of course, collapses, for the fetus right to life would then be guaranteed specifically by the amendment. The appellant conceded as much on reargument. On the other hand, the appellee conceded on reargument that no case could be cited that holds that a fetus is a person within the meaning of the Fourteenth Amendment.

The Constitution does not define "person" in so many words. . . . But . . .

the use of the word is such that it has application only postnatally. None indicates, with any assurance, that it has any possible prenatal application.

All this, together with our observation, that throughout the major portion of the nineteenth century prevailing legal abortion practices were far freer than they are today, persuades us that the word "person," as used in the Fourteenth Amendment, does not include the unborn. This is in accord with the results reached in those few cases where the issue has been squarely presented. Indeed, our decision in *United States v. Vuitch* inferentially is to the same effect, for we there would not have indulged in statutory interpretation favorable to abortion in specified circumstances if the necessary consequence was the termination of life entitled to Fourteenth Amendment protection.

This conclusion, however, does not of itself fully answer the contentions raised by Texas, and we pass on to other considerations.

B. The pregnant woman cannot be isolated in her privacy. She carries an embryo and, later, a fetus, if one accepts the medical definitions of the developing young in the human uterus. . . .

Texas urges that, apart from the Fourteenth Amendment, life begins at conception and is present throughout pregnancy, and that, therefore, the state has a compelling interest in protecting that life from and after conception. We need not resolve the difficult question of when life begins. When those trained in the respective disciplines of medicine, philosophy, and theology are unable to arrive at any consensus, the judiciary, at this point in the development of man's knowledge, is not in a position to speculate as to the answer.

It should be sufficient to note briefly the wide divergence of thinking on this most sensitive and difficult question. There has always been strong support for the view that life does not begin until live birth. This was the belief of the Stoics. It appears to be the predominant, though not the unanimous, attitude of the Jewish faith. It may be taken to represent also the position of a large segment of the Protestant community, insofar as that can be ascertained; organized groups that have taken a formal position on the abortion issue have generally regarded abortion as a matter for the conscience of the individual and her family. As we have noted, the common law found greater significance in quickening. Physicians and their scientific colleagues have regarded that event with less interest and have tended to focus either upon conception, upon live birth, or upon the interim point at which the fetus becomes "viable," that is, potentially able to live outside the mother's womb, albeit with artificial aid.

Viability is usually placed at about seven months (twenty-eight weeks) but may occur earlier, even at twenty-four weeks. The Aristotelian theory of "mediate animation," that held sway throughout the Middle Ages and the Renaissance in Europe, continued to be official Roman Catholic dogma until the nineteenth century, despite opposition to this "ensoulment" theory from those in the church who would recognize the existence of life from the moment of conception. The latter is now, of course, the official belief of the Catholic Church. As one brief amicus discloses, this is a view strongly held by many non-Catholics as well, and by many physicians. Substantial problems for precise definition of this view are posed, however, by new embryological data that purport to indicate that conception is a "process" over time, rather than an event, and by new medical techniques such as menstrual extraction, the "morning-after" pill, implantation of embryos, artificial insemination, and even artificial wombs.

In areas other than criminal abortion, the law has been reluctant to endorse any theory that life, as we recognize it, begins before live birth or to accord legal rights to the unborn except in narrowly defined situations and except when the rights are contingent upon live birth. . . . In short, the unborn have never been recognized in the law as persons in the whole sense.

X

In view of all this, we do not agree that, by adopting one theory of life, Texas may override the rights of the pregnant woman that are at stake. We repeat, however, that the state does have an important and legitimate interest in preserving and protecting the health of the pregnant woman, whether she be a resident of the state or a nonresident who seeks medical consultation and treatment there, and that it has still another important and legitimate interest in protecting the potentiality of human life. These interests are separate and distinct. Each grows in substantiality as the woman approaches term and, at a point during pregnancy, each becomes "compelling."

With respect to the state's important and legitimate interest in the health of the mother, the "compelling" point, in the light of present medical knowledge, is at approximately the end of the first trimester. This is so because of the now-established medical fact, referred to above, that until the end of the first trimester mortality in abortion may be less than mortality in normal childbirth. It follows that, from and after this point, a state may regulate the abortion procedure to the extent that the regulation reasonably relates to the preservation and protection of maternal health. Examples of permissible state regulation in this area are requirements as to the qualifications of the person who is to perform the abortion; as to the licensure of that person; as to the facility in which the procedure is to be performed, that is, whether it must be a hospital or may be a clinic or some other place of less-than-hospital status; as to the licensing of the facility; and the like.

This means, on the other hand, that, for the period of pregnancy prior to this "compelling" point, the attending physician, in consultation with his patient, is free to determine, without regulation by the state, that, in his medical judgment, the patient's pregnancy should be terminated. If that decision is reached, the judgment may be effectuated by an abortion free of interference by the state.

With respect to the state's important and legitimate interest in potential life, the "compelling" point is at viability. This is so because the fetus then presumably has the capability of meaningful life outside the mother's womb. State regulation protective of fetal life after viability thus has both logical and biological justifications. If the state is interested in protecting fetal life after viability, it may go so far as to proscribe abortion during that period, except when it is necessary to preserve the life or health of the mother.

Measured against these standards, article 1196 of the Texas Penal Code, in restricting legal abortions to those "procured or attempted by medical advice for the purpose of saving the life of the mother," sweeps too broadly. The statute makes no distinction between abortions performed early in pregnancy and those performed later, and it limits to a single reason, "saving" the mother's life, the legal justification for the procedure. The statute, therefore, cannot survive the constitutional attack made upon it here.

This conclusion makes it unnecessary for us to consider the additional challenge to the Texas statute asserted on grounds of vagueness.

XI

To summarize and to repeat:

1. A state criminal abortion statute of the current Texas type, that excepts from criminality only a life-saving procedure on behalf of the mother, without regard to pregnancy stage and without recognition of the other interests involved, is violative of the due process clause of the Fourteenth Amendment.

   (a) For the stage prior to approximately the end of the first trimester, the abortion decision and its effectuation must be left to the medical judgment of the pregnant woman's attending physician.

   (b) For the stage subsequent to approximately the end of the first trimester, the state, in promoting its interest in the health of the mother, may, if it chooses, regulate the abortion procedure in ways that are reasonably related to maternal health.

   (c) For the stage subsequent to viability, the state in promoting its interest in the potentiality of human life may, if it chooses, regulate, and even proscribe, abortion except where it is necessary, in appropriate medical judgment, for the preservation of the life or health of the mother.

2. The state may define the term "physician," as it has been employed in the preceding paragraphs of this part XI of this opinion, to mean only a physician currently licensed by the state, and may proscribe any abortion by a person who is not a physician as so defined. . . .

XII

Our conclusion that article 1196 is unconstitutional means, of course, that the Texas abortion statutes, as a unit, must fall. . . .

It is so ordered.

Source: Findlaw: For Legal Professionals, *Roe, et al., v. Wade,* 410 U.S. 113 (1973). Retrieved May 22, 2010, from http://caselaw.lp.findlaw.com/cgi-bin/getcase.pl? court=us&vol=410&invol=113.

CHAPTER 49

Richard Nixon's Second Watergate Speech, 1973

In June 1972, five men were arrested for breaking into the Democratic National Committee headquarters at the Watergate apartment complex in Washington, D.C. An investigation revealed ties to the Committee to Re-elect the President, Richard Nixon's campaign committee. As the investigation unfolded, driven by a pair of reporters from the *Washington Post*, the question arose as to how high involvement in the break-in and ensuing cover-up went. President Nixon gave a televised address to the nation on August 15, 1973, in which he denied all knowledge of the break-in or any cover-up concerning the case. Nonetheless, the investigation continued, and it was discovered that several White House officials were involved, and that the presidential offices were routinely monitored by a tape-recording system. When the tapes were demanded by the special prosecutor on the case, Nixon resisted, citing executive privilege, and the investigation began to focus on Nixon's possible personal involvement.

The president released edited transcripts of the tapes in April 1974, but a storm of protest ensued, demanding access to the unedited tapes. When the U.S. Supreme Court ruled that the president had to hand over the complete, unedited tapes, Nixon complied on June 30, 1974. The tapes revealed that the president had been informed of the break-in and attempts to cover it up on March 31, 1973. Soon afterward, the "smoking gun" tape was released. It recorded a conversation on July 23, 1972, only a few days after the break-in, in which Nixon was briefed and essentially issued orders to manage the situation with a cover-up. Rather than be impeached and convicted, Nixon announced his resignation on August 8, 1974, a day after being visited by Republican members of the Senate, who explained to him that the votes existed to convict. The speech contains multiple lies and is a notable instance of a president looking the public in the eye and telling false-hoods. But since the first proven instance of a president lying to the public was

James Buchanan in his inaugural speech (about Mexico),* and it is probably true that the vast majority of presidents since that time have occasionally lied to the public, what makes the Nixon case so egregious? Was it worse than President Clinton's "I have not had sexual relations with that woman" speech? Are there times when a president should lie? If so, what are they? And what does it say about the American governmental structure that a president will simply walk away from the most powerful office in the world rather than violently resisting his removal?

President's Speech to the Nation, August 15, 1973

GOOD EVENING:

Now that most of the major witnesses in the Watergate phase of the Senate committee hearings on campaign practices have been heard, the time has come for me to speak out about the charges made and to provide a perspective on the issue for the American people.

For over four months, Watergate has dominated the news media. During the past three months, the three major networks have devoted an average of over twenty-two hours of television time each week to this subject. The Senate committee has heard over two million words of testimony.

This investigation began as an effort to discover the facts about the break-in and bugging of the Democratic National Headquarters and other campaign abuses.

But as the weeks have gone by, it has become clear that both the hearings themselves and some of the commentaries on them have become increasingly absorbed in an effort to implicate the president personally in the illegal activities that took place.

Because the abuses occurred during my administration, and in the campaign for my reelection, I accept full responsibility for them. I regret that these events took place, and I do not question the right of a Senate committee to investigate charges made against the president to the extent that this is relevant to legislative duties.

However, it is my constitutional responsibility to defend the integrity of this great office against false charges. I also believe that it is important to address the overriding question of what we as a nation can learn from this experience and what we should now do. I intend to discuss both of these subjects tonight.

The record of the Senate hearings is lengthy. The facts are complicated,

* See William W. Freehling, *The Road to Disunion* (New York: Oxford University Press, 2007), 2:117.

the evidence conflicting. It would not be right for me to try to sort out the evidence, to rebut specific witnesses, or to pronounce my own judgments about their credibility. That is for the committee and for the courts.

I shall not attempt to deal tonight with the various charges in detail. Rather, I shall attempt to put the events in perspective from the standpoint of the presidency.

On May 22, before the major witnesses had testified, I issued a detailed statement addressing the charges that had been made against the president.

I have today issued another written statement, which addresses the charges that have been made since then as they relate to my own conduct, and which describes the efforts that I made to discover the facts about the matter.

On May 22, I stated in very specific terms—and I state again to every one of you listening tonight these facts—I had no prior knowledge of the Watergate break-in; I neither took part in nor knew about any of the subsequent cover-up activities; I neither authorized nor encouraged subordinates to engage in illegal or improper campaign tactics. That was and that is the simple truth. In all of the millions of words of testimony, there is not the slightest suggestion that I had any knowledge of the planning for the Watergate break-in. As for the cover-up, my statement has been challenged by only one of the thirty-five witnesses who appeared—a witness who offered no evidence beyond his own impressions and whose testimony has been contradicted by every other witness in a position to know the facts.

Tonight, let me explain to you what I did about Watergate after the break-in occurred, so that you can better understand the fact that I also had no knowledge of the so-called cover-up.

From the time when the break-in occurred, I pressed repeatedly to know the facts, and particularly whether there was any involvement of anyone in the White House. I considered two things essential:

First, that the investigation should be thorough and aboveboard; and second, that if there were any higher involvement, we should get the facts out first. As I said at my August 29 press conference last year, "What really hurts in matters of this sort is not the fact that they occur, because overzealous people in campaigns do things that are wrong. What really hurts is if you try to cover it up." I believed that then, and certainly the experience of this last year has proved that to be true.

I know that the Justice Department and the FBI were conducting intensive investigations—as I had insisted that they should. The White House counsel, John Dean, was assigned to monitor these investigations, and particularly to check into any possible White House involvement. Throughout the summer of 1972, I continued to press the question, and I continued to get the same answer: I was told again and again that there was no indication that any persons were involved other than the seven who were known to have planned and carried out the operation, and who were subsequently indicted and convicted.

On September 12 at a meeting that I held with the cabinet, the senior White House staff, and a number of legislative leaders, Attorney General Kleindienst reported on the investigation. He told us it had been the most extensive investigation since the assassination of President Kennedy and that it had established that only those seven were involved.

On September 15, the day the seven were indicted, I met with John Dean, the White House counsel. He gave me no reason whatever to believe that any others were guilty; I assumed that the indictments of only the seven by the grand jury confirmed the reports he had been giving to that effect throughout the summer.

On February 16, I met with Acting Director Gray prior to submitting his name to the Senate for confirmation as permanent director of the FBI. I stressed to him that he would be questioned closely about the FBI's conduct of the Watergate investigation. I asked him if he still had full confidence in it. He replied that he did, that he was proud of its thoroughness and that he could defend it with enthusiasm before the committee.

Because I trusted the agencies conducting the investigations, because I believed the reports I was getting, I did not believe the newspaper accounts that suggested a cover-up. I was convinced there was no cover-up, because I was convinced that no one had anything to cover up.

It was not until March 21 of this year that I received new information from the White House counsel that led me to conclude that the reports I had been getting for over nine months were not true. On that day, I launched an intensive effort of my own to get the facts and to get the facts out. Whatever the facts might be, I wanted the White House to be the first to make them public.

At first, I entrusted the task of getting me the facts to Mr. Dean. When, after spending a week at Camp David, he failed to produce the written report I had asked for, I turned to John Ehrlichman and to the attorney general—while also making independent inquiries of my own. By mid-April, I had received Mr. Ehrlichman's report and also one from the attorney general based on new information uncovered by the Justice Department. These reports made it clear to me that the situation was far more serious than I had imagined. It at once became evident to me that the responsibility for the investigation in the case should be given to the Criminal Division of the Justice Department.

I turned over all the information I had to the head of that department, Assistant Attorney General Henry Petersen, a career government employee with an impeccable nonpartisan record, and I instructed him to pursue the matter thoroughly. I ordered all members of the administration to testify fully before the grand jury.

And with my concurrence, on May 18 Attorney General Richardson appointed a special prosecutor to handle the matter, and the case is now before the grand jury.

Far from trying to hide the facts, my effort throughout has been to discover the facts—and to lay those facts before the appropriate law enforcement authorities so that justice could be done and the guilty dealt with.

I relied on the best law enforcement agencies in the country to find and report the truth. I believed they had done so—just as they believed they had done so.

Many have urged that in order to help prove the truth of what I have said, I should turn over to the special prosecutor and the Senate committee recordings of conversations that I held in my office or on my telephone.

However, a much more important principle is involved in this question than what the tapes might prove about Watergate.

Each day, a president of the United States is required to make difficult decisions on grave issues. It is absolutely necessary, if the president is to be able to do his job as the country expects, that he be able to talk openly and candidly with his advisers about issues and individuals. This kind of frank discussion is only possible when those who take part in it know that what they say is in strictest confidence.

The presidency is not the only office that requires confidentiality. A member of Congress must be able to talk in confidence with his assistants; judges must be able to confer in confidence with their law clerks and with each other. For very good reasons, no branch of government has ever compelled disclosure of confidential conversations between officers of other branches of government and their advisers about government business would want to talk frankly about the congressional horse-trading that might get a vital bill passed. No one would want to speak bluntly about public figures here and abroad.

That is why I shall continue to oppose efforts which would set a precedent that would cripple all future presidents by inhibiting conversations between them and those they look to for advice.

This principle of confidentiality of presidential conversations is at stake in the question of these tapes. I must and I shall oppose any efforts to destroy this principle, which is so vital to the conduct of this great office.

Turning now to the basic issues which have been raised by Watergate, I recognize that merely answering the charges that have been made against the president is not enough. The word "Watergate" has come to represent a much broader set of concerns.

To most of us, Watergate has come to mean not just a burglary and bugging of party headquarters but a whole series of acts that either represent or appear to represent an abuse of trust. It has come to stand for excessive partisanship, for "enemy lists," for efforts to use the great institutions of government for partisan political purposes.

For many Americans, the term "Watergate" also has come to include a number of national security matters that have been brought into the investigation, such as those involved in my efforts to stop massive leaks of vital diplomatic and military secrets, and to counter the wave of bombings and burnings and other violent assaults of just a few years ago.

Let me speak first of the political abuses.

I know from long experience that a political campaign is always a hard and a tough contest. A candidate for high office has an obligation to his party, to his supporters, and to the cause he represents. He must always put forth his best efforts to win. But he also has an obligation to the country to conduct that contest within the law and within the limits of decency.

No political campaign ever justifies obstructing justice, or harassing individuals, or compromising those great agencies of government that should and must be above politics. To the extent that these things were done in the 1972 campaign, they were serious abuses, and I deplore them.

Practices of that kind do not represent what I believe government should be, or what I believe politics should be. In a free society, the institutions of government belong to the people. They must never be used against the people.

And in the future, my administration will be more vigilant in ensuring that such abuses do not take place and that officials at every level understand that they are not to take place.

And I reject the cynical view that politics is inevitably or even usually a dirty business. Let us not allow what a few overzealous people did in Watergate to tar the reputation of the millions of dedicated Americans of both parties who fought hard but clean for the candidates of their choice in 1972. By their unselfish efforts, these people make our system work and they keep America free.

I pledge to you tonight that I will do all that I can to ensure that one of the results of Watergate is a new level of political decency and integrity in America—in which what has been wrong in our politics no longer corrupts or demeans what is right in our politics.

Let me turn now to the difficult questions that arise in protecting the national security.

It is important to recognize that these are difficult questions and that reasonable and patriotic men and women may differ on how they should be answered.

Only last year, the Supreme Court said that implicit in the president's constitutional duty is "the power to protect our government against those who would subvert or overthrow it by unlawful means." How to carry out this duty is often a delicate question to which there is no easy answer. . . .

As we look at Watergate in a longer perspective, we can see that its abuses resulted from the assumption by those involved that their cause placed them beyond the reach of those rules that apply to other persons and that hold a free society together. . . .

The notion that the end justifies the means proved contagious. Thus, it is not surprising, even though it is deplorable, that some persons in 1972 adopted the morality that they themselves had rightly condemned and committed acts that have no place in our political system.

Those acts cannot be defended. Those who were guilty of abuses must be punished. But ultimately, the answer does not lie merely in the jailing of a few overzealous persons who mistakenly thought their cause justified their violations of the law. . . .

We must recognize that one excess begets another, and that the extremes of violence and discord in the 1960s contributed to the extremes of Watergate.

Both are wrong. Both should be condemned. No individual, no group, and no political party has a corner on the market on morality in America.

If we learn the important lessons of Watergate, if we do what is necessary to prevent such abuses in the future—on both sides—we can emerge from this experience a better and a stronger nation.

Let me turn now to an issue that is important above all else and that is critically affecting your life today and will affect your life and your children's life in the years to come.

After twelve weeks and two million words of televised testimony, we have reached a point at which a continued, backward looking obsession with Watergate is causing this nation to neglect matters of far greater importance to all of the American people.

We must not stay so mired in Watergate that we fail to respond to challenges of surpassing importance to America and the world. We cannot let an obsession with the past destroy our hopes for the future. . . .

The time has come to turn Watergate over to the courts, where the questions of guilt or innocence belong. The time has come for the rest of us to get on with the urgent business of our nation. . . .

If you share my belief in these goals—if you want the mandate you gave this administration to be carried out—then I ask for your help to ensure that those who would exploit Watergate in order to keep us from doing what we were elected to do will not succeed.

I ask tonight for your understanding, so that as a nation we can learn the lessons of Watergate and gain from that experience. . . .

And I ask for your support in getting on once again with meeting your problems, improving your life, building your future.

With your help, with God's help, we will achieve those great goals for America. Thank you and good evening.

Source: Miller Center of Public Affairs at the University of Virginia. Retrieved April 23, 2010, from http://millercenter.org/scripps/archive/speeches/detail/3886.

VII

RISE OF THE NEW
WORLD ORDER

I f the founders thought their nation exceptional, a much different attitude had engulfed many Americans by the second half of the twentieth century. This countertrend finds voice in the like of Jimmy Carter's famous "malaise" speech (he never used the word, yet certainly conveyed the sentiment) to Barack Obama's Cairo address, wherein he portrayed the United States as just another nation, with past mistakes for which it should apologize. There were beacons during that half century, to be sure. Ronald Reagan lifted the nation out of its funk, inspiring Americans to a "noble vision" that harkened back to the founders. After the terrorist attacks of 9/11, President George W. Bush captured both the sorrow and the anger of the nation and seemed to echo previous presidents' war messages by vowing that the war would end at a time and place of our choosing. But it was a speech we have not included, an address by President George H. W. Bush a decade before his son's, that introduced the ominous term "new world order," which seemed to suggest that the day of American exceptionalism was over, and that a global consortium of nations would somehow govern the world in the future. Whether Reagan's exceptionalist and individualist view or the darker outlook of Carter, Obama, and G. H. W. Bush will prevail is yet to be determined, but there can be little doubt that they are incompatible with each other.

Perhaps the agent of change that will drive the United States to a nonexceptional status, and possibly even a vastly reduced role in world leadership, is the United Nations' Agenda 21. Its principles are included here, but its goals also include the elimination of private property and free-market capitalism and the establishment of a true world government following socialist concepts. The United States is to pay reparations to developing countries for having consumed resources that otherwise would have been available to those countries, effectively practicing self-criticism and making amends for its putative past crimes.

Clearly, the United States faces many challenges in the future as resources decline while the world's population soars.

CHAPTER 50

Jimmy Carter's "Crisis of Confidence" Speech, 1979

E lected by a narrow margin in 1976, largely on the grounds that he was not Richard Nixon and did not have any ties to the Nixon administration, Jimmy Carter saw his approval ratings fall to 25 percent by June 1979—lower than Nixon's during the Watergate scandal. People no longer felt the future was bright; things just seemed to get worse and worse; the economy was in decline; gasoline prices and interest rates climbed to record levels; and everywhere pessimism had replaced optimism. Carter held a series of meetings at Camp David to address the problem, but his staff misread the situation. Pat Caddell, Carter's pollster, recommended that the president address the people and inspire them to overcome what he called "a crisis of confidence." Carter took the advice, but failed to understand that the problem was one of leadership—and that he was failing to provide it.

What resulted was a televised sermon, on July 15, 1979, in which the president, rather than blaming the policies that had led to the country to its current state, pointed the finger at the American people. The speech gave Republicans great ammunition. When a president is viewed as inept, blaming the people only intensifies the perception of weakness. Disappointed with the nation's reaction, Carter accepted the resignations of five members of his cabinet, but the misery index (which measures the combined unemployment and inflation rates) climbed from 13.57 percent in 1976 to 21.98 percent in 1980.* Interest rates on home mortgages topped 10 percent, personal credit card interest rates soared above 25 percent, and frustration abounded. Carter did nothing to stop the slide and was punished with a loss at the polls in November to Ronald Reagan. Although he never actually used the word in his address, Carter's misdirected effort became known as the "malaise" speech. Given the circumstances, what should Carter

---

* Retrieved from http://www.miseryindex.us. Based on data from the U.S. Department of Labor (www.dol.gov) and Financial Trends Forecaster (www.InflationData.com).

have done? Being unable to fulfill any of the initiatives mentioned in his speech, should he have taken another tack? Has any leader in history inspired a people to greatness by blaming them?

The "Crisis of Confidence" Speech

GOOD EVENING. THIS IS A SPECIAL NIGHT FOR ME. EXACTLY three years ago, on July 15, 1976, I accepted the nomination of my party to run for president of the United States.

I promised you a president who is not isolated from the people, who feels your pain, and who shares your dreams and who draws his strength and his wisdom from you.

During the past three years I've spoken to you on many occasions about national concerns, the energy crisis, reorganizing the government, our nation's economy, and issues of war and especially peace. But over those years the subjects of the speeches, the talks, and the press conferences have become increasingly narrow, focused more and more on what the isolated world of Washington thinks is important. Gradually, you've heard more and more about what the government thinks or what the government should be doing and less and less about our nation's hopes, our dreams, and our vision of the future.

Ten days ago I had planned to speak to you again about a very important subject—energy. For the fifth time I would have described the urgency of the problem and laid out a series of legislative recommendations to the Congress. But as I was preparing to speak, I began to ask myself the same question that I now know has been troubling many of you. Why have we not been able to get together as a nation to resolve our serious energy problem?

It's clear that the true problems of our nation are much deeper—deeper than gasoline lines or energy shortages, deeper even than inflation or recession. And I realize more than ever that as president I need your help. So I decided to reach out and listen to the voices of America.

I invited to Camp David people from almost every segment of our society— business and labor, teachers and preachers, governors, mayors, and private citizens. And then I left Camp David to listen to other Americans, men and women like you.

It has been an extraordinary ten days, and I want to share with you what I've heard. First of all, I got a lot of personal advice. Let me quote a few of the typical comments that I wrote down.

This from a southern governor: "Mr. President, you are not leading this nation—you're just managing the government."

"You don't see the people enough anymore."

"Some of your cabinet members don't seem loyal. There is not enough discipline among your disciples."

"Don't talk to us about politics or the mechanics of government, but about an understanding of our common good."

"Mr. President, we're in trouble. Talk to us about blood and sweat and tears."

"If you lead, Mr. President, we will follow." . . .

This kind of summarized a lot of other statements: "Mr. President, we are confronted with a moral and a spiritual crisis." . . .

And the last that I'll read: "When we enter the moral equivalent of war, Mr. President, don't issue us BB guns."

These ten days confirmed my belief in the decency and the strength and the wisdom of the American people, but it also bore out some of my long-standing concerns about our nation's underlying problems.

I know, of course, being president, that government actions and legislation can be very important. That's why I've worked hard to put my campaign promises into law—and I have to admit, with just mixed success. But after listening to the American people I have been reminded again that all the legislation in the world can't fix what's wrong with America. So, I want to speak to you first tonight about a subject even more serious than energy or inflation. I want to talk to you right now about a fundamental threat to American democracy.

I do not mean our political and civil liberties. They will endure. And I do not refer to the outward strength of America, a nation that is at peace tonight everywhere in the world, with unmatched economic power and military might.

The threat is nearly invisible in ordinary ways. It is a crisis of confidence. It is a crisis that strikes at the very heart and soul and spirit of our national will. We can see this crisis in the growing doubt about the meaning of our own lives and in the loss of a unity of purpose for our nation.

The erosion of our confidence in the future is threatening to destroy the social and the political fabric of America. The confidence that we have always had as a people is not simply some romantic dream or a proverb in a dusty book that we read just on the Fourth of July.

It is the idea which founded our nation and has guided our development as a people. Confidence in the future has supported everything else—public institutions and private enterprise, our own families, and the very Constitution of the United States. Confidence has defined our course and has served as a link between generations. We've always believed in something called progress.

We've always had a faith that the days of our children would be better than our own.

Our people are losing that faith, not only in government itself but in the ability as citizens to serve as the ultimate rulers and shapers of our democracy.

As a people we know our past and we are proud of it. Our progress has been part of the living history of America, even the world. We always believed that we were part of a great movement of humanity itself called democracy, involved in the search for freedom, and that belief has always strengthened us in our purpose. But just as we are losing our confidence in the future, we are also beginning to close the door on our past.

In a nation that was proud of hard work, strong families, close-knit com- munities, and our faith in God, too many of us now tend to worship self- indulgence and consumption. Human identity is no longer defined by what one does, but by what one owns. But we've discovered that owning things and consuming things does not satisfy our longing for meaning. We've learned that piling up material goods cannot fill the emptiness of lives which have no con- fidence or purpose.

The symptoms of this crisis of the American spirit are all around us. For the first time in the history of our country a majority of our people believe that the next five years will be worse than the past five years. Two-thirds of our people do not even vote. The productivity of American workers is actually dropping, and the willingness of Americans to save for the future has fallen below that of all other people in the Western world.

As you know, there is a growing disrespect for government and for churches and for schools, the news media, and other institutions.

This is not a message of happiness or reassurance, but it is the truth and it is a warning.

These changes did not happen overnight. They've come upon us gradually over the last generation, years that were filled with shocks and tragedy.

We were sure that ours was a nation of the ballot, not the bullet, until the murders of John Kennedy and Robert Kennedy and Martin Luther King Jr. We were taught that our armies were always invincible and our causes were always just, only to suffer the agony of Vietnam. We respected the presidency as a place of honor until the shock of Watergate. We remember when the phrase "sound as a dollar" was an expression of absolute dependability, until ten years of inflation began to shrink our dollar and our savings. We believed that our nation's resources were limitless until 1973, when we had to face a growing dependence on foreign oil.

These wounds are still very deep. They have never been healed. Looking for a way out of this crisis, our people have turned to the federal government and found it isolated from the mainstream of our nation's life. Washington, D.C., has become an island. The gap between our citizens and our government has never been so wide. The people are looking for honest answers, not easy answers; clear leadership, not false claims and evasiveness and politics as usual.

What you see too often in Washington and elsewhere around the country is a system of government that seems incapable of action. You see a Congress twisted and pulled in every direction by hundreds of well-financed and powerful special interests. You see every extreme position defended to the last vote, almost to the last breath by one unyielding group or another. You often see a balanced and a fair approach that demands sacrifice, a little sacrifice from everyone, abandoned like an orphan without support and without friends.

Often you see paralysis and stagnation and drift. You don't like it, and neither do I. What can we do?

First of all, we must face the truth, and then we can change our course. We simply must have faith in each other, faith in our ability to govern ourselves, and faith in the future of this nation. Restoring that faith and that confidence to America is now the most important task we face. It is a true challenge of this generation of Americans.

One of the visitors to Camp David last week put it this way: "We've got to stop crying and start sweating, stop talking and start walking, stop cursing and start praying. The strength we need will not come from the White House, but from every house in America." We know the strength of America. We are strong. We can regain our unity. We can regain our confidence. We are the heirs of generations who survived threats much more powerful and awesome than those that challenge us now. Our fathers and mothers were strong men and women who shaped a new society during the Great Depression, who fought world wars, and who carved out a new charter of peace for the world. . . .

Energy will be the immediate test of our ability to unite this nation, and it can also be the standard around which we rally. On the battlefield of energy we can win for our nation a new confidence, and we can seize control again of our common destiny. In little more than two decades we've gone from a position of energy independence to one in which almost half the oil we use comes from foreign countries, at prices that are going through the roof. Our excessive dependence on OPEC has already taken a tremendous toll on our economy and our people. This is the direct cause of the long lines which have made millions of you spend aggravating hours waiting for gasoline. It's a cause of the increased inflation and unemployment that we now face. This intolerable dependence on foreign oil threatens our economic independence and the very security of our nation. The energy crisis is real. It is worldwide. It is a clear and present danger to our nation. These are facts and we simply must face them.

What I have to say to you now about energy is simple and vitally important.

Point one: I am tonight setting a clear goal for the energy policy of the United States. Beginning this moment, this nation will never use more foreign oil than we did in 1977—never. From now on, every new addition to our demand for energy will be met from our own production and our own conservation. The generation-long growth in our dependence on foreign oil will be stopped dead in its tracks right now and then reversed as we move through the

1980s, for I am tonight setting the further goal of cutting our dependence on foreign oil by one-half by the end of the next decade—a saving of over 4.5 million barrels of imported oil per day.

Point two: To ensure that we meet these targets, I will use my presidential authority to set import quotas. I'm announcing tonight that for 1979 and 1980, I will forbid the entry into this country of one drop of foreign oil more than these goals allow. These quotas will ensure a reduction in imports even below the ambitious levels we set at the recent Tokyo summit.

Point three: To give us energy security, I am asking for the most massive peacetime commitment of funds and resources in our nation's history to develop America's own alternative sources of fuel—from coal, from oil shale, from plant products for gasohol, from unconventional gas, from the sun.

I propose the creation of an energy security corporation to lead this effort to replace 2.5 million barrels of imported oil per day by 1990. The corporation will issue up to $5 billion in energy bonds, and I especially want them to be in small denominations so that average Americans can invest directly in America's energy security.

Just as a similar synthetic rubber corporation helped us win World War II, so will we mobilize American determination and ability to win the energy war. Moreover, I will soon submit legislation to Congress calling for the creation of this nation's first solar bank, which will help us achieve the crucial goal of 20 percent of our energy coming from solar power by the year 2000.

These efforts will cost money, a lot of money, and that is why Congress must enact the windfall profits tax without delay. It will be money well spent. Unlike the billions of dollars that we ship to foreign countries to pay for foreign oil, these funds will be paid by Americans to Americans. These funds will go to fight, not to increase, inflation and unemployment.

Point four: I'm asking Congress to mandate, to require as a matter of law, that our nation's utility companies cut their massive use of oil by 50 percent within the next decade and switch to other fuels, especially coal, our most abundant energy source.

Point five: To make absolutely certain that nothing stands in the way of achieving these goals, I will urge Congress to create an energy mobilization board which, like the War Production Board in World War II, will have the responsibility and authority to cut through the red tape, the delays, and the endless roadblocks to completing key energy projects.

We will protect our environment. But when this nation critically needs a refinery or a pipeline, we will build it.

Point six: I'm proposing a bold conservation program to involve every state, county, and city and every average American in our energy battle. This effort will permit you to build conservation into your homes and your lives at a cost you can afford.

I ask Congress to give me authority for mandatory conservation and for standby gasoline rationing. To further conserve energy, I'm proposing tonight an extra $10 billion over the next decade to strengthen our public transportation systems. And I'm asking you for your good and for your nation's security to take no unnecessary trips, to use carpools or public transportation whenever you can, to park your car one extra day per week, to obey the speed limit, and to set your thermostats to save fuel. Every act of energy conservation like this is more than just common sense—I tell you it is an act of patriotism.

Our nation must be fair to the poorest among us, so we will increase aid to needy Americans to cope with rising energy prices. We often think of conservation only in terms of sacrifice. In fact, it is the most painless and immediate way of rebuilding our nation's strength. Every gallon of oil each one of us saves is a new form of production. It gives us more freedom, more confidence, that much more control over our own lives.

So, the solution of our energy crisis can also help us to conquer the crisis of the spirit in our country. It can rekindle our sense of unity, our confidence in the future, and give our nation and all of us individually a new sense of purpose.

You know we can do it. We have the natural resources. We have more oil in our shale alone than several Saudi Arabias. We have more coal than any nation on Earth. We have the world's highest level of technology. We have the most skilled work force, with innovative genius, and I firmly believe that we have the national will to win this war.

I do not promise you that this struggle for freedom will be easy. I do not promise a quick way out of our nation's problems, when the truth is that the only way out is an all-out effort. What I do promise you is that I will lead our fight, and I will enforce fairness in our struggle, and I will ensure honesty. And above all, I will act. We can manage the short-term shortages more effectively and we will, but there are no short-term solutions to our long-range problems. There is simply no way to avoid sacrifice.

Twelve hours from now I will speak again in Kansas City, to expand and to explain further our energy program. Just as the search for solutions to our energy shortages has now led us to a new awareness of our nation's deeper problems, so our willingness to work for those solutions in energy can strengthen us to attack those deeper problems.

I will continue to travel this country, to hear the people of America. You can help me to develop a national agenda for the 1980s. I will listen and I will act. We will act together. These were the promises I made three years ago, and I intend to keep them. Little by little we can and we must rebuild our confidence. We can spend until we empty our treasuries, and we may summon all the wonders of science. But we can succeed only if we tap our greatest resources—America's people, America's values, and America's confidence.

I have seen the strength of America in the inexhaustible resources of our people. In the days to come, let us renew that strength in the struggle for an energy secure nation.

In closing, let me say this: I will do my best, but I will not do it alone. Let your voice be heard. Whenever you have a chance, say something good about our country. With God's help and for the sake of our nation, it is time for us to join hands in America. Let us commit ourselves together to a rebirth of the American spirit. Working together with our common faith we cannot fail.

Thank you and good night.

Sources: PBS Online: *American Experience*, "Jimmy Carter," primary sources. Retrieved April 21, 2010, from http://www.pbs.org/wgbh/amex/carter/filmmore/ps_crisis.html.

CHAPTER 51

Ronald Reagan's "Our Noble Vision" Speech, 1984

Contrasted with President Carter's "crisis of confidence" speech, Ronald Reagan's "noble vision" speech stood out for its confidence, inspiration, and leadership. It was given almost five years after Carter's, on March 2, 1984, while the country rode a wave of economic expansion not seen since World War II. Reagan insisted that the United States still had a heroic destiny in the world. For all his successes, Reagan was persistently derided by academics since his days as the governor of California, when he said the state had no business subsidizing intellectual curiosity. Reagan never kissed the feet of the Ivy League and cared nothing about opinions from professors at Harvard or Yale. Nor did he need them. Although he employed competent speech writers, all his addresses were either written by him or so heavily edited by him as to be unrecognizable from the original drafts.

The speech here is no exception and presents an unvarnished look at the real Ronald Reagan during the middle of his two terms. His unabashed patriotism and optimism was infectious. In 1981 he had announced an economic program, derided as "Reaganomics," and stuck with it through a brief recession. By late 1983, America had turned the corner and was coming back. Ironically, the year 1984, with its Orwellian overtones, was little more than a triumphal procession for Reagan, ending with a sweeping reelection in which he carried forty-nine out of fifty states. He was certainly the most important president since Franklin Roosevelt in respect to the domestic economy and the cold war, and his policies continued to exert great influence for a decade and a half after his farewell speech. Why was Reagan so controversial when the 1980s were so much more prosperous for America than the 1970s? What role did he play in ending the cold war? And what was the "noble vision" of which he spoke?

Our Noble Vision: An Opportunity for All

MR. VICE PRESIDENT, MEMBERS OF CONGRESS, MEMBERS OF the Cabinet, and distinguished Ladies and Gentlemen. . . .

The mission of this [American Conservative Union] conference is a mission of principle: It is a mission of commitment, and it must and will be a mission of victory. Color our cause with courage and confidence. We offer an optimistic society. More than two hundred years after the patriots fired that first shot heard round the world, one revolutionary idea still burns in the hearts of men and women everywhere: A society where man is not beholden to government; government is beholden to man.

The difference between the path toward greater freedom or bigger government is the difference between success and failure; between opportunity and coercion; between faith in a glorious future and fear of mediocrity and despair; between respecting people as adults, each with a spark of greatness, and treating them as helpless children to be forever dependent; between a drab, materialistic world where Big Brother rules by promises to special interest groups, and a world of adventure where everyday people set their sights on impossible dreams, distant stars, and the Kingdom of God. We have the true message of hope for America.

In *Year of Decision: 1846*, Bernard DeVoto explained what drove our ancestors to conquer the West, create a nation, and open up a continent. If you take away the dream, you take away the power of the spirit. If you take away the belief in a greater future, you cannot explain America—that we're a people who believed there was a promised land; we were a people who believed we were chosen by God to create a greater world. . . .

I think America is better off than we were three years ago because we've stopped placing our faith in more government programs. We're restoring our faith in the greatest resource this nation has—the mighty spirit of free people under God. It was you who reminded Washington that we are a government of, by, and for the people, not the other way around. It was you who said it is time to put earnings back in the hands of the people, time to put trust back in the hands of the people, time to put America back in the hands of the people.

And this is what we're trying to do. Our critics are not pleased, but I hope we'll be forgiven this small observation: the spendthrifts who mangled America with the nightmare of double-digit inflation, record interest rates, unfair tax increases, too much regulation, credit controls, farm embargoes, gas lines, no growth at home, weakness abroad, and phony excuses about "malaise" are the last people who should be giving sermonettes about fairness and compassion. Their failures were not caused by erratic weather patterns, unusual rotations of the moon, or by the personality of my predecessor. They were caused by misguided policies and misunderstanding human nature. Believe me, you cannot create a desert, hand a person a cup of water, and call that compassion. You cannot pour billions of dollars into make-work jobs while destroying the economy that supports them and call that opportunity. And you cannot build up years of dependence on government and dare call that hope.

But apparently nothing bothers our liberal friends. The same expertise that told them their policies must succeed convinced them that our program spelled economic Armageddon. First they blamed the recession on our tax cuts. The trouble is, our tax cuts hadn't started yet. They also warned that when our tax program passed, America would face runaway inflation, record interest rates, and a collapse of confidence. Well, at least they got part of it right. Our program passed, and we witnessed a collapse all right. A collapse of inflation from 12.4 down to about 4 percent; a collapse of the prime interest rate from over 21 percent to 11; and a new surge of confidence in stocks and bonds.

They warned that decontrolling the price of oil would send the cost of gas at the pumps skyrocketing. We decontrolled, and the price is lower today than it was three years ago when we decontrolled.

And then they said that recovery couldn't come, or would be too feeble to notice. Well, from strong growth in housing to autos, construction, and high technology, from a rebirth of productivity to the fastest drop in unemployment in over thirty years, we have one of the strongest recoveries in decades. And we'll keep it strong if they'll get out of the way. . . .

But our critics moan the recovery can't last. Those awful tax cuts haven't sparked business investment; private borrowers are being crowded out of the capital markets. Well, if that's true, how did the venture capital industry raise four times as much capital in 1983 as it did in 1980? How could real, fixed business investment increase by a 13 percent rate last year, the fastest rate in any recovery in the past thirty years? And how could funds raised in the equity markets zoom from $16.8 billion in 1983—or in 1982, to $36.6 billion in 1983? Still another record.

Now, all this means more growth, more jobs, more opportunities, and a more competitive America. Now, lately, the pessimists have been sounding a new alarm: the dollar is so strong, they say, that exporters can't export, and we'll have no chance for lasting growth.

Well, the facts are—as Secretary [of the Treasury] Don Regan has pointed out—the dollar is strong because of people's confidence in our currency, our low rate of inflation, and the incentives to invest in the United States. No American should undermine confidence in the nation's currency. A strong dollar is one of our greatest weapons against inflation. Anyone who doubts the value of a strong currency should look at the postwar performances of Japan, Switzerland, and West Germany. . . .

The critics were wrong on inflation, wrong on interest rates, wrong on the recovery, and I believe they'll be wrong on the deficit, too, if the Congress will get spending under control. If optimism were a national disease, they'd be immune for life. Isn't it time that we said no to those who keep saying no to America? If the sourpuss set cannot believe in our nation and her people, then let them stand aside and we will get the job done.

In fairness, I'll admit our critics are worried sick about the future of the economy. They're worried it might keep getting better and better.

Now, those who deal in a world of numbers cannot predict the progress of the human mind, the drive and energy of the spirit, or the power of incentives. We're beginning an industrial renaissance which most experts never saw coming. It started with the 1978 capital gains tax reduction—passed over the objections of the last administration—and which was then made greater by our own tax reductions in 1981.

Incentives laid the seeds for the great growth in venture capital which helped set off the revolution in high technology. Sunrise industries, such as computers, micro-electronics, robotics, and fiber optics—all are creating a new world of opportunities. And as our knowledge expands, business investment is stimulated to modernize older industries with the newer technologies. . . .

An opportunity society awaits us. We need only believe in ourselves and give men and women of faith, courage, and vision the freedom to build it. Let others run down America and seek to punish success. Let them call you greedy for not wanting government to take more and more of your earnings. Let them defend their tombstone society of wage and price guidelines, mandatory quotas, tax increases, planned shortages, and shared sacrifices.

We want no part of that mess, thank you very much. We will encourage all Americans—men and women, young and old, individuals of every race, creed, and color—to succeed and be healthy, happy, and whole. This is our goal. We see America not falling behind, but moving ahead; our citizens not fearful and divided, but confident and united by shared values of faith, family, work, neighborhood, peace, and freedom.

An opportunity society begins with growth, and that means incentives. As I told the people of Iowa last week, my sympathies are with the taxpayers, not the tax spenders. I consider stopping them from taking more of your earnings an economic responsibility and a moral obligation. I will not permit an anti-growth coalition to jeopardize this recovery. If they get their way, they'll charge everything on your "Taxpayers Express Card." And believe me, they never leave home without it.

As good conservatives, we were brought up to oppose deficits. But sometimes I think some have forgotten why. We were against deficit spending. Those who would be heroes trying to reduce deficits by raising taxes are not heroes. They have not addressed the point I made in the State of the Union: whether government borrows or increases taxes, it will be taking the same amount of money from the private economy and, either way, that's too much. . . .

Combining spending restraints with another key reform will make America's economy the undisputed leader for innovation, growth, and opportunity. I'm talking about simplification of the entire tax system. We can make taxes more fair, easier to understand and, more important, we can greatly increase incentives by bringing personal tax rates down. If we can reduce personal tax rates as dramatically as we've reduced capital gains taxes, the underground economy will shrink, the whole world will beat a path to our door, and no one will hold America back. This is the real blueprint for a brighter future and declining deficits.

But economic opportunities can only flourish if the values at the foundation of our society and freedom remain strong and secure. Our families and friends must be able to live and work without always being afraid. Americans are sick and tired of law-abiding people getting mugged, robbed, and raped, while dangerous criminals get off scot-free.

We have a comprehensive crime bill to correct this. It would put an end to the era of coddling criminals, and it's been passed by the Senate. But the legislation is bottled up in the House. Now, maybe it's time they heard from a few of you—a few million of you. You know, you don't have to make them see the light; just make them feel the heat. I hope you realize that in my comments about some of the shortcomings of the Congress, believe me, tonight present company is excepted.

Strengthening values also demands a national commitment to excellence in education. If we are to pioneer a revolution in technology, meet challenges of the space age, and preserve values of courage, responsibility, integrity, and love, then we can't afford a generation of children hooked on cocaine and unable to read or write. Conservatives have pointed out for years that while federal spending on education was soaring, aptitude scores were going steadily down. Look at the case of New Hampshire. It ranks dead last in state spending on education, but its students have the highest SAT scores among those states where at least half the students take the test. And they've maintained that honor for more than ten years. America's schools don't need new spending programs; they need tougher standards, more homework, merit pay for teachers, discipline, and parents back in charge. Now there's another important reform to be voted on soon in the Senate. . . .

Let us come together, citizens of all faiths, to pray, march, and mobilize every force we have so the God who loves us can be welcomed back into our children's classrooms. I'm gratified that Congressman Newt Gingrich is organizing a rally on the Capitol steps in support of our prayer in school amendment.

Please be there if you can, and please send the message loud and clear that God never should have been expelled from America's schools in the first place. And maybe if we can get God and discipline back in our schools, we can get drugs and violence out.

Now, let me make it plain that we seek voluntary school prayer, not a moment of silence. We already have the right to remain silent; we can take the Fifth Amendment. But as we go on, we must redouble our efforts to redress a national tragedy. Since the *Roe v. Wade* decision, fifteen million unborn children have been lost—fifteen million children who will never laugh, never sing, never know the joy of human love, will never strive to heal the sick or feed the poor or make peace among nations. They've been denied the most basic of human rights, and we're all the poorer for their loss.

Not long ago I received a letter from a young woman named Kim. She was born with the birth defect spina bifida and given little chance to live. But her parents were willing to try a difficult and risky operation on her spine. It worked. And Kim wrote me: "I am now twenty-four years old. I do have some medical problems due to my birth defect. I have a lot of problems with my legs. But I'm walking. I can talk. I went to grade and high school, plus one year of college. I thank God every day for my parents and my life." And Kim said, "I wouldn't change it if I could."

Life was her greatest opportunity, and she's made the most of it. An opportunity society for all, reaching for its future with confidence, sustained by faith, fair play, and a conviction that good and courageous people flourish when they're free—this is the noble vision we share, a vision of a strong and prosperous America, at peace with itself and the world. Just as America has always been synonymous with freedom, so, too, should we become the symbol of peace across the Earth. I'm confident we can keep faith with that mission.

Peace with freedom is our highest aspiration—a lasting peace anchored by courage, realism, and unity. We've stressed our willingness to meet the Soviets halfway in talks on strategic weapons. But as commander in chief, I have an obligation to protect this country, and I will never allow political expediency to influence these crucial negotiations.

We should remember that our defense capability was allowed to deteriorate for many years. Only when our arms are certain beyond doubt can we be certain beyond doubt that they will never be used. President John F. Kennedy spoke those words in 1961. Too many who admired him have forgotten that the price of peace is dear. But some members of his party have not, and I am proud to have one of them, a brilliant patriot, Jeane Kirkpatrick, by my side.

And I deeply appreciate your patriotic support for rebuilding our defenses. We're just beginning to restore our capability to meet present and future security needs. I am open to suggestions for budget savings, but defense is not just another federal program. It is solely the responsibility of the federal government. It is its prime responsibility. So, our first responsibility is to keep America strong enough to remain free, secure, and at peace, and I intend to make sure that we do just that.

America's foreign policy supports freedom, democracy, and human dignity for all mankind, and we make no apologies for it. The opportunity society that we want for ourselves we also want for others, not because we're imposing our system on others but because those opportunities belong to all people as God-given birthrights and because by promoting democracy and economic opportunity we make peace more secure. . . .

Fellow citizens, fellow conservatives, our time has come again. This is our moment. Let us unite, shoulder to shoulder, behind one mighty banner for freedom. And let us go forward from here not with some faint hope that our cause is not yet lost; let us go forward confident that the American people share our values, and that together we will be victorious.

And in those moments when we grow tired, when our struggle seems hard, remember what Eric Liddell, Scotland's Olympic champion runner, said in *Chariots of Fire*: "So where does the power come from to see the race to its end? From within. God made me for a purpose, and I will run for His pleasure."

If we trust in Him, keep His word, and live our lives for His pleasure, He'll give us the power we need—power to fight the good fight, to finish the race and to keep the faith.

Thank you very much. God bless you and God bless America.

Sources: Reagan 2020, Publius Press, Inc. Retrieved May 14, 2010, from http://reagan2020.us/speeches/Our_Noble_Vision.asp.

CHAPTER 52

Rio Declaration on Environment and Development, 1992

In June of 1992 the United Nations Conference on Environment and Development was held in Rio de Janeiro, Brazil, and produced Agenda 21, a comprehensive plan to create a sustainable standard of living for all the earth's inhabitants, while depleting none of the planet's assets. President George H. W. Bush signed the agreement on behalf of the United States, and environmental agencies and organizations all over the world applauded the move. The concept of sustainable development was created, and much of the American way of life was declared to be unsustainable, with little actual proof being offered. In effect, this meant that the United States would have to give up its way of life and even pay reparations to developing countries for having used resources that otherwise would have been available to those countries. By 2010 these reparations were pegged as being from $15 trillion to $17 trillion. In section 8, for example ("To achieve sustainable development and a higher quality of life for all people, states should reduce and eliminate unsustainable patterns of production and consumption and promote appropriate demographic policies"), the "unsustainable patterns of production and consumption" was clearly code language for socialist/communal patterns and the "appropriate demographic policies" could easily, based on comments of leading UN figures, mean massive depopulation. While the code-phrasing of Agenda 21 avoided stating its real goals, to those who had listened with any degree of care to many of the proponents speak, "unsustainable" features clearly meant private property, capitalism, suburbs, the use of fossil fuels, animal husbandry of all grazing animals, paved roads, dams and reservoirs, heavy industry, metals production, electric transmission lines, and essentially everything commonly associated with the American lifestyle in the twentieth century. The world population was also to be reduced by several billion people, and a world government was to be established to ensure social justice and the equitable treatment of all humanity in a socialist setting.*

Within a few years it became obvious that Agenda 21 was the most serious threat to its prosperity and way of life that the United States had ever seen. Nonetheless, Agenda 21 was steadily promoted by the federal government and its initiatives forged ahead throughout the United States. Many cities pledged to become sustainable (green) communities. Schoolchildren were taught the principles established at Rio, without being told anything about the consequences for the country, their parents, or themselves. Included below is the Rio Declaration with its twenty-seven principles to bring about perpetually sustainable human activities. Does the government have a responsibility to protect the environment at the expense of its citizenry? What does the elimination of private property mean for individual liberties and freedom? Who would have to pay, and who would receive? What would the founders say about ceding American sovereignty to world bodies? The enormity of the program's details and impact as contained in the "Global Biodiversity Assessment" and "Agenda 21: Earth Summit: The United Nations Programme of Action from Rio" (New York, United Nations, 1993), boggles the mind, particularly when one considers Agenda 21 is generally dismissed by American media as a "conspiracy theory."

Rio Declaration on Environment and Development

THE UNITED NATIONS CONFERENCE ON ENVIRONMENT AND Development,

Having met at Rio de Janeiro from 3 to 14 June 1992,

Reaffirming the Declaration of the United Nations Conference on the Human Environment, adopted at Stockholm on 16 June 1972, and seeking to build upon it,

With the goal of establishing a new and equitable global partnership through the creation of new levels of cooperation among states, key sectors of societies, and people,

Working towards international agreements which respect the interests of all and protect the integrity of the global environmental and developmental system,

Recognizing the integral and interdependent nature of the Earth, our home,

Proclaims that:

---

* V. H. Heywood, ed., *Global Biodiversity Assessment* (Cambridge: United Nations Environment Programme, Cambridge University Press, 1996). This book also condemns "inappropriate social structures" and the attitudes toward nature found in Judeo-Christian-Islamic religions. See pages 766, 838.

PRINCIPLE 1

Human beings are at the center of concerns for sustainable development. They are entitled to a healthy and productive life in harmony with nature.

PRINCIPLE 2

States have, in accordance with the Charter of the United Nations and the principles of international law, the sovereign right to exploit their own resources pursuant to their own environmental and developmental policies, and the responsibility to ensure that activities within their jurisdiction or control do not cause damage to the environment of other states or of areas beyond the limits of national jurisdiction.

PRINCIPLE 3

The right of development must be fulfilled so as to equitably meet developmental and environmental needs of present and future generations.

PRINCIPLE 4

In order to achieve sustainable development, environmental protection shall constitute an integral part of the development process and cannot be considered in isolation from it.

PRINCIPLE 5

All states and all people shall cooperate in the essential task of eradicating poverty as an indispensable requirement for sustainable development, in order to decrease the disparities in standards of living and better meet the needs of the majority of the people of the world.

PRINCIPLE 6

The special situation and needs of developing countries, particularly the least developed and those most environmentally vulnerable, shall be given special priority. International actions in the field of environment and development should also address the interests and needs of all countries.

PRINCIPLE 7

States shall cooperate in a spirit of global partnership to conserve, protect, and restore the health and integrity of the Earth's ecosystem. In view of the different contributions to global environmental degradation, states have common but differentiated responsibilities. The developed countries acknowledge the responsibility that they bear to the international pursuit of sustainable development in view of the pressures their societies place on the global environment and of the technologies and financial resources they command.

PRINCIPLE 8

To achieve sustainable development and a higher quality of life for all people, states should reduce and eliminate unsustainable patterns of production and consumption and promote appropriate demographic policies.

PRINCIPLE 9

States should cooperate to strengthen endogenous capacity—building for sustainable development by improving scientific understanding through exchanges of scientific and technological knowledge, and by enhancing the development, adaptation, diffusion, and transfer of technologies, including new and innovative technologies.

PRINCIPLE 10

Environmental issues are best handled with the participation of all concerned citizens, at the relevant level. At the national level, each individual shall have appropriate access to information concerning the environment that is held by public authorities, including information on hazardous materials and activities in their communities, and the opportunity to participate in decision-making processes. States shall facilitate and encourage public awareness and participation by making information widely available. Effective access to judicial and administrative proceedings, including redress and remedy, shall be provided.

PRINCIPLE 11

States shall enact effective environmental legislation, environmental standards, management objectives, and priorities should reflect the environmental and development context to which they apply. Standards applied by some countries may be inappropriate and or unwarranted economic and social cost to other countries, in particular developing countries.

PRINCIPLE 12

States should cooperate to promote a supportive and open international economic system that would lead to economic growth and sustainable development in all countries, to better address the problems of environmental degradation. Trade policy measures for environmental purposes should not constitute a means of arbitrary or unjustifiable discrimination or a disguised restriction on international trade. Unilateral actions to deal with environmental challenges outside the jurisdiction of the importing country should be avoided. Environmental measures addressing transboundary or global environmental problems should, as far as possible, be based on an international consensus.

PRINCIPLE 13

States should develop national law regarding liability and compensation for the victims of pollution and other environmental damage. States shall also cooperate in an expeditious and more determined manner to develop further international law regarding liability and compensation for adverse effects of environmental damage caused by activities within their jurisdiction or control to areas beyond their jurisdiction.

PRINCIPLE 14

States should effectively cooperate to discourage or prevent the relocation and transfer to other states of any activities and substances that cause severe environmental degradation or are found to be harmful to human health.

PRINCIPLE 15

In order to protect the environment, the precautionary approach shall be widely applied by states according to their capabilities. Where there are threats of serious or irreversible damage, lack of full scientific certainty shall not be used as a reason for postponing cost-effective measures to prevent environmental degradation.

PRINCIPLE 16

National authorities should endeavor to promote the internalization of environmental costs and the use of economic instruments, taking into account the approach that the polluter should, in principle, bear the cost of pollution, with due regard to the public interest and without distorting international trade and investment.

PRINCIPLE 17

Environmental impact assessment, as a national instrument, shall be undertaken for proposed activities that are likely to have a significant adverse impact on the environment and are subject to a decision of a competent national authority.

PRINCIPLE 18

States shall immediately notify other states of any natural disasters or other emergencies that are likely to produce sudden harmful effects on the environment of those states. Every effort shall be made by the international community to help States so afflicted.

PRINCIPLE 19

States shall provide prior and timely notification and relevant information to potentially affected states on activities that may have a significant adverse transboundary environmental effect and shall consult with those states at an early stage and in good faith.

PRINCIPLE 20

Women have a vital role in environmental management and development. Their full participation is therefore essential to achieve sustainable development.

PRINCIPLE 21

The creativity, ideals, and courage of the youth of the world should be mobilized to forge a global partnership in order to achieve sustainable development and ensure a better future for all.

PRINCIPLE 22

Indigenous people and their communities and other local communities have a vital role in environmental management and development because of their knowledge and traditional practices. States should recognize and duly support their identity, culture, and interests and enable their effective participation in the achievement of sustainable development.

PRINCIPLE 23

The environment and natural resources of people under oppression, domination, and occupation shall be protected.

PRINCIPLE 24

Warfare is inherently destructive of sustainable development. States shall therefore respect international law providing protection for the environment in times of armed conflict and cooperate in its further development, as necessary.

PRINCIPLE 25

Peace, development, and environmental protection are interdependent and indivisible.

PRINCIPLE 26

States shall resolve all their environmental disputes peacefully and by appropriate means in accordance with the Charter of the United Nations.

PRINCIPLE 27

States and people shall cooperate in good faith and in a spirit of partnership in the fulfillment of the principles embodied in this declaration and in the further development of international law in the field of sustainable development.

Source: United Nations Department of Public Information, *Agenda 21: Programme of Action for Sustainable Development, The Final Text of Agreements Negotiated by Governments at the United Nations Conference on Environment and Development*, United Nations Publication: Sales No E.93.1.11 (Geneva: United Nations, 1993), 9–11.

CHAPTER 53

George W. Bush's National Cathedral Speech, 2001

On September 11, 2001, two commercial airliners were seized by radical Islamic terrorists and flown into the twin towers of the World Trade Center in New York City. A third airplane was flown into the Pentagon, and a fourth crashed into a field in Pennsylvania after passengers fought the terrorists on board, likely saving hundreds more lives and either the White House or Capitol building. Nevertheless, even with the heroic actions of the passengers aboard Flight 93, nearly three thousand American citizens and foreign nationals were killed and both World Trade Center towers collapsed into rubble. The nation was stunned at the unprovoked attack; however, since no specific government or country had made war on the United States, there was hardly a target for retaliation. Later it was determined that terrorists from al Qaeda (the Base), under Osama bin Laden, had trained in Afghanistan with approval from the Taliban government, and U.S. military efforts were directed against that government.

The usual rhetoric issued forth from those willing to blame America for everything, claiming that the attack was justified due to American imperialism and arrogance, and that the terrorists needed to be "understood." The American public had a much different view. Nonetheless, enlistments in the armed forces did not increase as they had following the attack on Pearl Harbor, and Americans were urged by leftists to control their anger and seek therapeutic help if necessary. Two days after the attack, President George W. Bush declared September 14 as a national day of prayer and remembrance, and on that day, after services honoring the dead at Washington National Cathedral, made the following speech. The attack ultimately involved the United States in wars in Afghanistan and Iraq, and opposition to the wars severely crippled Bush's presidency. Had the nation truly provoked such an attack? How did Bush characterize the attack in his speech? And how did his response differ—if at all—from that of Thomas Jefferson in his war on the Barbary pirates nearly two centuries earlier? Bush was ridiculed for his faith, and the notion that, ultimately, God is sovereign. In what passages does that faith emerge?

National Cathedral Speech, September 14, 2001

WE ARE HERE IN THE MIDDLE HOUR OF OUR GRIEF. SO MANY have suffered so great a loss, and today we express our nation's sorrow. We come before God to pray for the missing and the dead, and for those who loved them.

On Tuesday, our country was attacked with deliberate and massive cruelty. We have seen the images of fire and ashes and bent steel.

Now come the names, the list of casualties we are only beginning. They are the names of men and women who began their day at a desk or in an airport, busy with life. They are the names of people who faced death and in their last moments called home to say, be brave and I love you.

They are the names of passengers who defied their murderers and prevented the murder of others on the ground. They are the names of men and women who wore the uniform of the United States and died at their posts.

They are the names of rescuers—the ones whom death found running up the stairs and into the fires to help others. We will read all these names. We will linger over them and learn their stories, and many Americans will weep.

To the children and parents and spouses and families and friends of the lost, we offer the deepest sympathy of the nation. And I assure you, you are not alone. Just three days removed from these events, Americans do not yet have the distance of history, but our responsibility to history is already clear: to answer these attacks and rid the world of evil.

War has been waged against us by stealth and deceit and murder.

This nation is peaceful, but fierce when stirred to anger. This conflict was begun on the timing and terms of others; it will end in a way and at an hour of our choosing.

Our purpose as a nation is firm, yet our wounds as a people are recent and unhealed and lead us to pray. In many of our prayers this week, there's a searching and an honesty. At St. Patrick's Cathedral in New York, on Tuesday, a woman said, "I pray to God to give us a sign that he's still here."

Others have prayed for the same, searching hospital to hospital, carrying pictures of those still missing.

God's signs are not always the ones we look for. We learn in tragedy that his purposes are not always our own, yet the prayers of private suffering, whether in our homes or in this great cathedral, are known and heard and understood.

There are prayers that help us last through the day or endure the night. There are prayers of friends and strangers that give us strength for the journey, and there are prayers that yield our will to a will greater than our own.

This world He created is of moral design. Grief and tragedy and hatred are only for a time. Goodness, remembrance, and love have no end, and the Lord of life holds all who die and all who mourn.

It is said that adversity introduces us to ourselves. This is true of a nation as well. In this trial, we have been reminded and the world has seen that our fellow Americans are generous and kind, resourceful and brave.

We see our national character in rescuers working past exhaustion, in long lines of blood donors, in thousands of citizens who have asked to work and serve in any way possible. And we have seen our national character in eloquent acts of sacrifice. Inside the World Trade Center, one man who could have saved himself stayed until the end and at the side of his quadriplegic friend. A beloved priest died giving the last rites to a firefighter. Two office workers, finding a disabled stranger, carried her down sixty-eight floors to safety.

A group of men drove through the night from Dallas to Washington to bring skin grafts for burned victims. In these acts and many others, Americans showed a deep commitment to one another and in an abiding love for our country.

Today, we feel what Franklin Roosevelt called, "the warm courage of national unity." This is a unity of every faith and every background. This has joined together political parties and both houses of Congress. It is evident in services of prayer and candlelight vigils and American flags, which are displayed in pride and waved in defiance. Our unity is a kinship of grief and a steadfast resolve to prevail against our enemies. And this unity against terror is now extending across the world.

America is a nation full of good fortune, with so much to be grateful for, but we are not spared from suffering. In every generation, the world has produced enemies of human freedom. They have attacked America because we are freedom's home and defender, and the commitment of our fathers is now the calling of our time.

On this national day of prayer and remembrance, we ask Almighty God to watch over our nation and grant us patience and resolve in all that is to come. We pray that He will comfort and console those who now walk in sorrow. We thank Him for each life we now must mourn, and the promise of a life to come.

As we've been assured, neither death nor life nor angels nor principalities, nor powers nor things present nor things to come nor height nor depth can separate us from God's love.

May He bless the souls of the departed. May He comfort our own. And may He always guide our country.

God bless America.

Source: Free Republic, "Bush's Speech at the National Cathedral." Retrieved June 6, 2010, from http://www.freerepublic.com/focus/news/523290/posts.

CHAPTER 54

Kelo v. New London, 2005

In the case of *Susette Kelo, et al. v. City of New London, Connecticut, et al.* 545 U.S. 469 (2005), the U.S. Supreme Court once again addressed the right of a government agent, in this case a private development company, to use the legal process of eminent domain to take private property and use it for some public purpose. The U.S. Constitution used the phrase "for public use" in allowing the government eminent domain, and the original intent was to secure property for bridges, ports, or government structures for use by the public or the government itself. In this case, however, land was needed to entice a corporation to move into a city—land that would house its industrial facilities.

The case was argued on February 22, 2005, and the five-to-four decision was passed down on June 23, 2005. The Court held that since the development plan was broad and had been approved both by the city and state, it was taking the property for valid public purposes. The Court did not inquire into the reasonableness of the plan, which it considered outside the scope of the judiciary. In effect, it ruled that any property could be taken by government for any purpose as long as the governmental entity could show a plan for its use that might conceivably benefit the public. In this event, the corporation did not relocate to New London. The area is now open land, and the city has a much smaller tax base. The Court subtly shifted the public use clause to "public interest" (or, as another justice called it, "public good") potentially putting all private property at risk. If eminent domain was intended for the state to acquire needed land, why was the concept expanded to include transferring land from one private party to another? Freedom and private property rights have been firmly linked together since the founding of the United States. What about the protection of life, liberty, and property? Does the collective now always trump the individual?

Kelo v. New London

JUSTICE [JOHN P.] STEVENS DELIVERED THE OPINION OF THE Court.

In 2000, the City of New London approved a development plan that, in the words of the Supreme Court of Connecticut, was "projected to create in excess of one thousand jobs, to increase tax and other revenues, and to revitalize an economically distressed city, including its downtown and waterfront areas." In assembling the land needed for this project, the city's development agent has purchased property from willing sellers and proposes to use the power of eminent domain to acquire the remainder of the property from unwilling owners in exchange for just compensation. The question presented is whether the city's proposed disposition of this property qualifies as a "public use" within the meaning of the takings clause of the Fifth Amendment to the Constitution.

I

The City of New London (hereinafter City) sits at the junction of the Thames River and the Long Island Sound in southeastern Connecticut. Decades of economic decline led a state agency in 1990 to designate the City a "distressed municipality." . . .

These conditions prompted state and local officials to target New London, and particularly its Fort Trumbull area, for economic revitalization. To this end, respondent New London Development Corporation (NLDC), a private nonprofit entity established some years earlier to assist the City in planning economic development, was reactivated. In January 1998, the state authorized a $5.35 million bond issue to support the NLDC's planning activities and a $10 million bond issue toward the creation of a Fort Trumbull State Park. In February, the pharmaceutical company Pfizer Inc. announced that it would build a $300 million research facility on a site immediately adjacent to Fort Trumbull; . . . In May, the city council authorized the NLDC to formally submit its plans to the relevant state agencies for review. Upon obtaining state-level approval, the NLDC finalized an integrated development plan focused on ninety acres of the Fort Trumbull area.

. . . The development plan encompasses seven parcels. Parcel 1 is designated for a waterfront conference hotel at the center of a "small urban village" that will include restaurants and shopping. This parcel will also have marinas for both recreational and commercial uses. . . . Parcel 2 will be the site of approximately eighty new residences organized into an urban neighborhood. . . . Parcel 3, which is located immediately north of the Pfizer facility, will contain at least ninety thousand square feet of research and development office space. Parcel 4A is a 2.4 acre site that will be used either to support the adjacent state park, by providing parking or retail services for visitors, or to support the nearby marina. Parcel 4B will include a renovated marina, as well as the final stretch of the riverwalk. Parcels 5, 6, and 7 will provide land for office and retail space, parking, and water-dependent commercial uses. . . .

The city council approved the plan in January 2000, and designated the NLDC as its development agent in charge of implementation. The city council also authorized the NLDC to purchase property or to acquire property by exercising eminent domain in the City's name. The NLDC successfully negotiated the purchase of most of the real estate in the ninety acre area, but its negotiations with petitioners failed. As a consequence, in November 2000, the NLDC initiated the condemnation proceedings that gave rise to this case.

II

Petitioner Susette Kelo has lived in the Fort Trumbull area since 1997. She has made extensive improvements to her house, which she prizes for its water view. . . . In all, the nine petitioners own fifteen properties in Fort Trumbull—four in parcel 3 of the development plan and eleven in parcel 4A. . . . There is no allegation that any of these properties is blighted or otherwise in poor condition; rather, they were condemned only because they happen to be located in the development area.

In December 2000, petitioners brought this action in the New London Superior Court. They claimed, among other things, that the taking of their properties would violate the "public use" restriction in the Fifth Amendment. After a seven-day bench trial, the Superior Court granted a permanent restraining order prohibiting the taking of the properties located in parcel 4A (park or marina support). It, however, denied petitioners relief as to the properties located in parcel 3 (office space).

After the Superior Court ruled, both sides took appeals to the Supreme Court of Connecticut. That court held, over a dissent, that all of the City's proposed takings were valid. It began by upholding the lower court's determination that the takings were authorized by chapter 132, the state's municipal development statute. That statute expresses a legislative determination that the taking of land, even developed land, as part of an economic development project is a "public use" and in the "public interest." Next, relying on cases such as *Hawaii Housing Authority v. Midkiff*, and *Berman v. Parker*, the court held that such economic development qualified as a valid public use under both the federal and state constitutions. . . .

III

Two polar propositions are perfectly clear. On the one hand, it has long been accepted that the sovereign may not take the property of A for the sole purpose

of transferring it to another private party B, even though A is paid just compensation. On the other hand, it is equally clear that a state may transfer
property from one private party to another if future "use by the public" is the
purpose of the taking; the condemnation of land for a railroad with common-
carrier duties is a familiar example. Neither of these propositions, however,
determines the disposition of this case.

As for the first proposition, the City would no doubt be forbidden from
taking petitioners' land for the purpose of conferring a private benefit on a
particular private party. Nor would the City be allowed to take property under
the mere pretext of a public purpose, when its actual purpose was to bestow
a private benefit. The takings before us, however, would be executed pursuant
to a "carefully considered" development plan. The trial judge and all the members of the Supreme Court of Connecticut agreed that there was no evidence
of an illegitimate purpose in this case. Therefore, as was true of the statute
challenged in *Midkiff*, the City's development plan was not adopted "to benefit a particular class of identifiable individuals."

On the other hand, this is not a case in which the City is planning to open
the condemned land—at least not in its entirety—to use by the general public.
Nor will the private lessees of the land in any sense be required to operate like
common carriers, making their services available to all comers. But although
such a projected use would be sufficient to satisfy the public use requirement,
this Court long ago rejected any literal requirement that condemned property
be put into use for the general public. Indeed, while many state courts in the
mid-nineteenth century endorsed "use by the public" as the proper definition
of public use, that narrow view steadily eroded over time. Not only was the
"use by the public" test difficult to administer (e.g., what proportion of the
public need have access to the property? at what price?), but it proved to be
impractical given the diverse and always evolving needs of society. Accordingly, when this Court began applying the Fifth Amendment to the states at
the close of the nineteenth century, it embraced the broader and more natural
interpretation of public use as "public purpose." . . .

The disposition of this case therefore turns on the question whether the
City's development plan serves a "public purpose." Without exception, our
cases have defined that concept broadly, reflecting our longstanding policy of
deference to legislative judgments in this field.

In *Berman v. Parker* this Court upheld a redevelopment plan targeting a
blighted area of Washington, D. C., in which most of the housing for the area's
five thousand inhabitants was beyond repair. Under the plan, the area would
be condemned and part of it utilized for the construction of streets, schools,
and other public facilities. The remainder of the land would be leased or sold
to private parties for the purpose of redevelopment, including the construction
of low-cost housing.

The owner of a department store located in the area challenged the condemnation, pointing out that his store was not itself blighted and arguing that the creation of a "better balanced, more attractive community" was not a valid public use. Writing for a unanimous Court, Justice Douglas refused to evaluate this claim in isolation, deferring instead to the legislative and agency judgment that the area "must be planned as a whole" for the plan to be successful. The Court explained that "community redevelopment programs need not, by force of the Constitution, be on a piecemeal basis—lot by lot, building by building." The public use underlying the taking was unequivocally affirmed. . . .

In *Hawaii Housing Authority v. Midkiff*, the Court considered a Hawaii statute whereby fee title was taken from lessors and transferred to lessees (for just compensation) in order to reduce the concentration of land ownership. We unanimously upheld the statute and rejected the Ninth Circuit's view that it was "a naked attempt on the part of the state of Hawaii to take the property of A and transfer it to B solely for B's private use and benefit." Reaffirming *Berman's* deferential approach to legislative judgments in this field, we concluded that the state's purpose of eliminating the "social and economic evils of a land oligopoly" qualified as a valid public use. Our opinion also rejected the contention that the mere fact that the state immediately transferred the properties to private individuals upon condemnation somehow diminished the public character of the taking. "[I]t is only the taking's purpose, and not its mechanics," we explained, that matters in determining public use.

In that same term we decided another public use case that arose in a purely economic context. *In Ruckelshaus v. Monsanto, Co.*, the Court dealt with provisions of the Federal Insecticide, Fungicide, and Rodenticide Act under which the Environmental Protection Agency could consider the data (including trade secrets) submitted by a prior pesticide applicant in evaluating a subsequent application, so long as the second applicant paid just compensation for the data. We acknowledged that the "most direct beneficiaries" of these provisions were the subsequent applicants, but we nevertheless upheld the statute under *Berman* and *Midkiff*. We found sufficient Congress's belief that sparing applicants the cost of time-consuming research eliminated a significant barrier to entry in the pesticide market and thereby enhanced competition.

Viewed as a whole, our jurisprudence has recognized that the needs of society have varied between different parts of the nation, just as they have evolved over time in response to changed circumstances. Our earliest cases in particular embodied a strong theme of federalism, emphasizing the "great respect" that we owe to state legislatures and state courts in discerning local public needs. For more than a century, our public use jurisprudence has wisely eschewed rigid formulas and intrusive scrutiny in favor of affording legislatures broad latitude in determining what public needs justify the use of the takings power.

IV

Those who govern the City were not confronted with the need to remove blight in the Fort Trumbull area, but their determination that the area was sufficiently distressed to justify a program of economic rejuvenation is entitled to our deference. The City has carefully formulated an economic development plan that it believes will provide appreciable benefits to the community, including—but by no means limited to—new jobs and increased tax revenue. As with other exercises in urban planning and development, the City is endeavoring to coordinate a variety of commercial, residential, and recreational uses of land, with the hope that they will form a whole greater than the sum of its parts. To effectuate this plan, the City has invoked a state statute that specifically authorizes the use of eminent domain to promote economic development. Given the comprehensive character of the plan, the thorough deliberation that preceded its adoption, and the limited scope of our review, it is appropriate for us, as it was in *Berman*, to resolve the challenges of the individual owners, not on a piecemeal basis, but rather in light of the entire plan. Because that plan unquestionably serves a public purpose, the takings challenged here satisfy the public use requirement of the Fifth Amendment. . . .

Petitioners contend that using eminent domain for economic development impermissibly blurs the boundary between public and private takings. Again, our cases foreclose this objection. Quite simply, the government's pursuit of a public purpose will often benefit individual private parties. For example, in *Midkiff*, the forced transfer of property conferred a direct and significant benefit on those lessees who were previously unable to purchase their homes. In *Monsanto*, we recognized that the "most direct beneficiaries" of the data-sharing provisions were the subsequent pesticide applicants, but benefiting them in this way was necessary to promoting competition in the pesticide market. The owner of the department store in *Berman* objected to "taking from one businessman for the benefit of another businessman," referring to the fact that under the redevelopment plan land would be leased or sold to private developers for redevelopment. Our rejection of that contention has particular relevance to the instant case: "The public end may be as well or better served through an agency of private enterprise than through a department of government—or so the Congress might conclude. We cannot say that public ownership is the sole method of promoting the public purposes of community redevelopment projects." . . .

Alternatively, petitioners maintain that for takings of this kind we should require a "reasonable certainty" that the expected public benefits will actually accrue. Such a rule, however, would represent an even greater departure from our precedent. When the legislature's purpose is legitimate and its means are not irrational, our cases make clear that empirical debates over the wisdom of takings—no less than debates over the wisdom of other kinds of socio-economic legislation—are not to be carried out in the federal courts. . . .

Just as we decline to second-guess the City's considered judgments about the efficacy of its development plan, we also decline to second-guess the City's determinations as to what lands it needs to acquire in order to effectuate the project. It is not for the courts to oversee the choice of the boundary line nor to sit in review on the size of a particular project area. Once the question of the public purpose has been decided, the amount and character of land to be taken for the project and the need for a particular tract to complete the integrated plan rests in the discretion of the legislative branch.

In affirming the City's authority to take petitioners' properties, we do not minimize the hardship that condemnations may entail, notwithstanding the payment of just compensation. We emphasize that nothing in our opinion precludes any state from placing further restrictions on its exercise of the takings power. Indeed, many states already impose "public use" requirements that are stricter than the federal baseline. Some of these requirements have been established as a matter of state constitutional law, while others are expressed in state eminent domain statutes that carefully limit the grounds upon which takings may be exercised. As the submissions of the parties and their amici make clear, the necessity and wisdom of using eminent domain to promote economic development are certainly matters of legitimate public debate. This Court's authority, however, extends only to determining whether the City's proposed condemnations are for a "public use" within the meaning of the Fifth Amendment to the federal Constitution. Because over a century of our case law interpreting that provision dictates an affirmative answer to that question, we may not grant petitioners the relief that they seek.

The judgment of the Supreme Court of Connecticut is affirmed.

Source: Findlaw: For Legal Professionals, *Kelo et al. v. City of New London et al.* Retrieved May 22, 2010, from http://caselaw.lp.findlaw.com/scripts/getcase.pl?court= us&vol=000&invol=04-108.

CHAPTER 55

Barack Obama's "A New Beginning" Speech, 2009

In 2008 an almost unknown first-term Democrat senator from Illinois became president in an historic vote in which the first black man was elected to the office. As a half-African (his father was from Kenya) and half-white American, Barack Obama made an attractive candidate both racially and as a representative of the liberal Left. He enjoyed support from the highest quarters, including practically across-the-board endorsements from the nation's news and entertainment media. He spoke in a more moderate and intellectual style than Martin Luther King Jr. and proved to have broad appeal to liberal whites. His speeches were carefully crafted and rehearsed, and he used the slogans "hope" and "change," promising his supporters that they were close to "fundamentally transforming" the United States. His rhetoric was so powerful that it elevated his candidacy even though he often failed to address critical issues and had a record of voting "present" in Congress rather than taking a position on proposed legislation.

President Obama continued to dazzle with his speaking skills after he was elected, and the following speech reaching out to the Islamic world illustrates his multicultural appeal. Although he had promised to take the country "in a fundamentally new direction," that direction first became apparent to American voters in the words of his June 2009 speech at Cairo University, shocking or surprising many. Intended to disarm Muslims critical of American policy under Bush, and to charm the audience, the speech alienated many allies due to its extensive praise of Islam and citation of Muslim achievements in American society. His words were applauded by Islamic leaders, but within a year, according to polls, nearly 20 percent of the American electorate felt the president was actually a Muslim. Not since Jimmy Carter had an American president repudiated American exceptionalism so strongly. What did this speech mean for America? What was the reaction of Muslims around the world?

Speech at Cairo University, Egypt, June 4, 2009

THANK YOU VERY MUCH. GOOD AFTERNOON. I AM HONORED to be in the timeless city of Cairo, and to be hosted by two remarkable institutions. For over a thousand years, al-Azhar has stood as a beacon of Islamic learning; and for over a century, Cairo University has been a source of Egypt's advancement. And together, you represent the harmony between tradition and progress. I'm grateful for your hospitality, and the hospitality of the people of Egypt. And I'm also proud to carry with me the goodwill of the American people, and a greeting of peace from Muslim communities in my country: *Assalaamu alaykum.*

We meet at a time of great tension between the United States and Muslims around the world—tension rooted in historical forces that go beyond any current policy debate. The relationship between Islam and the West includes centuries of coexistence and cooperation, but also conflict and religious wars. More recently, tension has been fed by colonialism that denied rights and opportunities to many Muslims, and a cold war in which Muslim-majority countries were too often treated as proxies without regard to their own aspirations. Moreover, the sweeping change brought by modernity and globalization led many Muslims to view the West as hostile to the traditions of Islam.

Violent extremists have exploited these tensions in a small but potent minority of Muslims. The attacks of September 11, 2001, and the continued efforts of these extremists to engage in violence against civilians has led some in my country to view Islam as inevitably hostile not only to America and Western countries, but also to human rights. . . .

I've come here to Cairo to seek a new beginning between the United States and Muslims around the world, one based on mutual interest and mutual respect, and one based upon the truth that America and Islam are not exclusive and need not be in competition. Instead, they overlap, and share common principles—principles of justice and progress; tolerance and the dignity of all human beings.

. . . As the Holy Koran tells us, "Be conscious of God and speak always the truth." That is what I will try to do today—to speak the truth as best I can, humbled by the task before us, and firm in my belief that the interests we share as human beings are far more powerful than the forces that drive us apart.

Now part of this conviction is rooted in my own experience. I'm a Christian, but my father came from a Kenyan family that includes generations of Muslims. As a boy, I spent several years in Indonesia and heard the call of the *azaan* at the break of dawn and at the fall of dusk. As a young man, I worked in Chicago communities where many found dignity and peace in their Muslim faith.

As a student of history, I also know civilization's debt to Islam. It was Islam—at places like al-Azhar—that carried the light of learning through so many centuries, paving the way for Europe's Renaissance and Enlightenment. It was innovation in Muslim communities that developed the order of algebra; our magnetic compass and tools of navigation; our mastery of pens and printing; our understanding of how disease spreads and how it can be healed. Islamic culture has given us majestic arches and soaring spires; timeless poetry and cherished music; elegant calligraphy and places of peaceful contemplation. And throughout history, Islam has demonstrated through words and deeds the possibilities of religious tolerance and racial equality.

I also know that Islam has always been a part of America's story. The first nation to recognize my country was Morocco. In signing the Treaty of Tripoli in 1796, our second president, John Adams, wrote, "The United States has in itself no character of enmity against the laws, religion or tranquility of Muslims." And since our founding, American Muslims have enriched the United States. They have fought in our wars, they have served in our government, they have stood for civil rights, they have started businesses, they have taught at our universities, they've excelled in our sports arenas, they've won Nobel Prizes, built our tallest building, and lit the Olympic Torch. And when the first Muslim American was recently elected to Congress, he took the oath to defend our Constitution using the same Holy Koran that one of our Founding Fathers—Thomas Jefferson—kept in his personal library.

So I have known Islam on three continents before coming to the region where it was first revealed. That experience guides my conviction that partnership between America and Islam must be based on what Islam is, not what it isn't. And I consider it part of my responsibility as president of the United States to fight against negative stereotypes of Islam wherever they appear. . . .

Now, much has been made of the fact that an African American with the name Barack Hussein Obama could be elected president. But my personal story is not so unique. The dream of opportunity for all people has not come true for everyone in America, but its promise exists for all who come to our shores—and that includes nearly seven million American Muslims in our country today who, by the way, enjoy incomes and educational levels that are higher than the American average.

Moreover, freedom in America is indivisible from the freedom to practice one's religion. That is why there is a mosque in every state in our union, and over 1,200 mosques within our borders. That's why the United States government has gone to court to protect the right of women and girls to wear the *hijab* and to punish those who would deny it.

So let there be no doubt: Islam is a part of America. And I believe that America holds within her the truth that regardless of race, religion, or station in life, all of us share common aspirations—to live in peace and security; to get an education and to work with dignity; to love our families, our communities, and our God. These things we share. This is the hope of all humanity. . . .

Given our interdependence, any world order that elevates one nation or group of people over another will inevitably fail. So whatever we think of the past, we must not be prisoners to it. Our problems must be dealt with through partnership; our progress must be shared.

Now, that does not mean we should ignore sources of tension. Indeed, it suggests the opposite: We must face these tensions squarely. And so in that spirit, let me speak as clearly and as plainly as I can about some specific issues that I believe we must finally confront together.

The first issue that we have to confront is violent extremism in all of its forms.

In Ankara, I made clear that America is not—and never will be—at war with Islam. We will, however, relentlessly confront violent extremists who pose a grave threat to our security—because we reject the same thing that people of all faiths reject: the killing of innocent men, women, and children. . . .

. . . Indeed, none of us should tolerate these extremists. They have killed in many countries. They have killed people of different faiths—but more than any other, they have killed Muslims. Their actions are irreconcilable with the rights of human beings, the progress of nations, and with Islam. The Holy Koran teaches that whoever kills an innocent is as—it is as if he has killed all mankind. And the Holy Koran also says whoever saves a person, it is as if he has saved all mankind. The enduring faith of over a billion people is so much bigger than the narrow hatred of a few. Islam is not part of the problem in combating violent extremism—it is an important part of promoting peace.

Now, we also know that military power alone is not going to solve the problems in Afghanistan and Pakistan. That's why we plan to invest $1.5 billion each year over the next five years to partner with Pakistanis to build schools and hospitals, roads and businesses, and hundreds of millions to help those who've been displaced. That's why we are providing more than $2.8 billion to help Afghans develop their economy and deliver services that people depend on.

Let me also address the issue of Iraq. Unlike Afghanistan, Iraq was a war of choice that provoked strong differences in my country and around the world. Although I believe that the Iraqi people are ultimately better off without the tyranny of Saddam Hussein, I also believe that events in Iraq have reminded America of the need to use diplomacy and build international consensus to resolve our problems whenever possible. Indeed, we can recall the words of Thomas Jefferson, who said: "I hope that our wisdom will grow with our power, and teach us that the less we use our power the greater it will be."

Today, America has a dual responsibility: to help Iraq forge a better future—and to leave Iraq to Iraqis. And I have made it clear to the Iraqi people that we pursue no bases, and no claim on their territory or resources. Iraq's sovereignty is its own. And that's why I ordered the removal of our combat brigades by next August.

That is why we will honor our agreement with Iraq's democratically elected government to remove combat troops from Iraqi cities by July, and to remove all of our troops from Iraq by 2012. We will help Iraq train its security forces and develop its economy. But we will support a secure and united Iraq as a partner, and never as a patron.

And finally, just as America can never tolerate violence by extremists, we must never alter or forget our principles. Nine-eleven was an enormous trauma to our country. The fear and anger that it provoked was understandable, but in some cases, it led us to act contrary to our traditions and our ideals. We are taking concrete actions to change course. I have unequivocally prohibited the use of torture by the United States, and I have ordered the prison at Guantá-namo Bay closed by early next year.

So America will defend itself, respectful of the sovereignty of nations and the rule of law. And we will do so in partnership with Muslim communities which are also threatened. The sooner the extremists are isolated and unwelcome in Muslim communities, the sooner we will all be safer.

The second major source of tension that we need to discuss is the situation between Israelis, Palestinians, and the Arab world.

America's strong bonds with Israel are well known. This bond is unbreakable. It is based upon cultural and historical ties, and the recognition that the aspiration for a Jewish homeland is rooted in a tragic history that cannot be denied. . . .

On the other hand, it is also undeniable that the Palestinian people—Muslims and Christians—have suffered in pursuit of a homeland. For more than sixty years they've endured the pain of dislocation. Many wait in refugee camps in the West Bank, Gaza, and neighboring lands for a life of peace and security that they have never been able to lead. They endure the daily humiliations—large and small—that come with occupation. So let there be no doubt: The situation for the Palestinian people is intolerable. And America will not turn our backs on the legitimate Palestinian aspiration for dignity, opportunity, and a state of their own. . . .

Now is the time for Palestinians to focus on what they can build. The Palestinian Authority must develop its capacity to govern, with institutions that serve the needs of its people. Hamas does have support among some Palestinians, but they also have to recognize they have responsibilities. To play a role in fulfilling Palestinian aspirations, to unify the Palestinian people, Hamas must put an end to violence, recognize past agreements, recognize Israel's right to exist.

At the same time, Israelis must acknowledge that just as Israel's right to exist cannot be denied, neither can Palestine's. The United States does not accept the legitimacy of continued Israeli settlements. This construction violates previous agreements and undermines efforts to achieve peace. It is time for these settlements to stop.

And Israel must also live up to its obligation to ensure that Palestinians can live and work and develop their society. Just as it devastates Palestinian families, the continuing humanitarian crisis in Gaza does not serve Israel's security; neither does the continuing lack of opportunity in the West Bank. Progress in the daily lives of the Palestinian people must be a critical part of a road to peace, and Israel must take concrete steps to enable such progress. . . .

All of us have a responsibility to work for the day when the mothers of Israelis and Palestinians can see their children grow up without fear; when the Holy Land of the three great faiths is the place of peace that God intended it to be; when Jerusalem is a secure and lasting home for Jews and Christians and Muslims, and a place for all of the children of Abraham to mingle peacefully together as in the story of Isra, when Moses, Jesus, and Mohammed, peace be upon them, joined in prayer.

The third source of tension is our shared interest in the rights and responsibilities of nations on nuclear weapons.

This issue has been a source of tension between the United States and the Islamic Republic of Iran. . . . There will be many issues to discuss between our two countries, and we are willing to move forward without preconditions on the basis of mutual respect. . . . No single nation should pick and choose which nation holds nuclear weapons. And that's why I strongly reaffirmed America's commitment to seek a world in which no nations hold nuclear weapons. And any nation—including Iran—should have the right to access peaceful nuclear power if it complies with its responsibilities under the Nuclear Non-Proliferation Treaty. That commitment is at the core of the treaty, and it must be kept for all who fully abide by it. And I'm hopeful that all countries in the region can share in this goal.

The fourth issue that I will address is democracy.

I know there has been controversy about the promotion of democracy in recent years, and much of this controversy is connected to the war in Iraq. So let me be clear: No system of government can or should be imposed by one nation by any other. . . .

The fifth issue that we must address together is religious freedom.

Islam has a proud tradition of tolerance. We see it in the history of Andalusia and Córdoba during the Inquisition. I saw it firsthand as a child in Indonesia, where devout Christians worshiped freely in an overwhelmingly Muslim country. That is the spirit we need today. People in every country should be free to choose and live their faith based upon the persuasion of the mind and the heart and the soul. This tolerance is essential for religion to thrive, but it's being challenged in many different ways. . . .

Freedom of religion is central to the ability of peoples to live together. We must always examine the ways in which we protect it. For instance, in the United States, rules on charitable giving have made it harder for Muslims to fulfill their religious obligation. That's why I'm committed to working with American Muslims to ensure that they can fulfill *zakat*.

Likewise, it is important for Western countries to avoid impeding Muslim citizens from practicing religion as they see fit—for instance, by dictating what clothes a Muslim woman should wear. We can't disguise hostility towards any religion behind the pretence of liberalism.

In fact, faith should bring us together. And that's why we're forging service projects in America to bring together Christians, Muslims, and Jews. That's why we welcome efforts like Saudi Arabian king Abdullah's interfaith dialogue and Turkey's leadership in the Alliance of Civilizations. Around the world, we can turn dialogue into interfaith service, so bridges between peoples lead to action—whether it is combating malaria in Africa, or providing relief after a natural disaster.

The sixth issue that I want to address is women's rights.

I know—I know—and you can tell from this audience, that there is a healthy debate about this issue. I reject the view of some in the West that a woman who chooses to cover her hair is somehow less equal, but I do believe that a woman who is denied an education is denied equality. And it is no coincidence that countries where women are well educated are far more likely to be prosperous.

Now, let me be clear: Issues of women's equality are by no means simply an issue for Islam. In Turkey, Pakistan, Bangladesh, Indonesia, we've seen Muslim-majority countries elect a woman to lead. Meanwhile, the struggle for women's equality continues in many aspects of American life, and in countries around the world.

I am convinced that our daughters can contribute just as much to society as our sons. Our common prosperity will be advanced by allowing all humanity—men and women—to reach their full potential. I do not believe that women must make the same choices as men in order to be equal, and I respect those women who choose to live their lives in traditional roles. But it should be their choice. And that is why the United States will partner with any Muslim-majority country to support expanded literacy for girls, and to help young women pursue employment through microfinancing that helps people live their dreams.

Finally, I want to discuss economic development and opportunity.

I know that for many, the face of globalization is contradictory. The Internet and television can bring knowledge and information, but also offensive sexuality and mindless violence into the home. Trade can bring new wealth and opportunities, but also huge disruptions and change in communities. In all nations—including America—this change can bring fear. Fear that because of modernity we lose control over our economic choices, our politics, and most importantly our identities—those things we most cherish about our communities, our families, our traditions, and our faith.

But I also know that human progress cannot be denied. There need not be contradictions between development and tradition. Countries like Japan and South Korea grew their economies enormously while maintaining distinct cultures. The same is true for the astonishing progress within Muslim-majority countries from Kuala Lumpur to Dubai. In ancient times and in our times, Muslim communities have been at the forefront of innovation and education. . . .

On education, we will expand exchange programs, and increase scholarships, like the one that brought my father to America. At the same time, we will encourage more Americans to study in Muslim communities. And we will match promising Muslim students with internships in America; invest in online learning for teachers and children around the world; and create a new online network, so a young person in Kansas can communicate instantly with a young person in Cairo.

On economic development, we will create a new corps of business volunteers to partner with counterparts in Muslim-majority countries. And I will host a Summit on Entrepreneurship this year to identify how we can deepen ties between business leaders, foundations, and social entrepreneurs in the United States and Muslim communities around the world.

On science and technology, we will launch a new fund to support technological development in Muslim-majority countries, and to help transfer ideas to the marketplace so they can create more jobs. We'll open centers of scientific excellence in Africa, the Middle East, and Southeast Asia, and appoint new science envoys to collaborate on programs that develop new sources of energy, create green jobs, digitize records, clean water, grow new crops. Today I'm announcing a new global effort with the Organization of the Islamic Conference to eradicate polio. And we will also expand partnerships with Muslim communities to promote child and maternal health.

All these things must be done in partnership. Americans are ready to join with citizens and governments, community organizations, religious leaders, and businesses in Muslim communities around the world to help our people pursue a better life. . . .

We have the power to make the world we seek, but only if we have the courage to make a new beginning, keeping in mind what has been written.

The Holy Koran tells us: "O mankind! We have created you male and a female; and we have made you into nations and tribes so that you may know one another."

The Talmud tells us: "The whole of the Torah is for the purpose of promoting peace."

The Holy Bible tells us: "Blessed are the peacemakers, for they shall be called sons of God."

The people of the world can live together in peace. We know that is God's vision. Now that must be our work here on Earth.

Thank you. And may God's peace be upon you. Thank you very much.

Source: Retrieved August 29, 2010, from http://www.whitehouse.gov/the_press_office/Remarks-by-the-President-at-Cairo-University-6-04-09/.

INDEX